MOON

P9-DFY-220

GEORGIA

JIM MOREKIS

Columbus
FORT BENNING MILITARY RESERVATION
ALABAMA
Walter F George Reservoir
Chattahoochee River
Dothan
Perry
Dublin
Statesboro
Eastman
Vidalia
Americus
Plains
McRae
Savannah
FORT STEWART MILITARY RESERVATION
Cordele
Lake Blackshear
Dawson
Fitzgerald
Baxley
Pridgen
Jesup
Albany
Alma
Tifton
Sapelo Island
Colquitt
Moultrie
Waycross
St Simons Island
Brunswick
Jekyll Island
Homerville
Okefenokee Swamp
Bainbridge
Thomasville
Valdosta
Folkston
Okefenokee National Wildlife Refuge
Cumberland Island National Seashore
Lake Seminole
St. Marys
Fargo
TALLAHASSEE
Jacksonville
Apalachicola National Forest
Osceola National Forest
FLORIDA
St. Johns River
St. Marks National Wildlife Refuge
0
30 mi
0
30 km
© AVALON TRAVEL

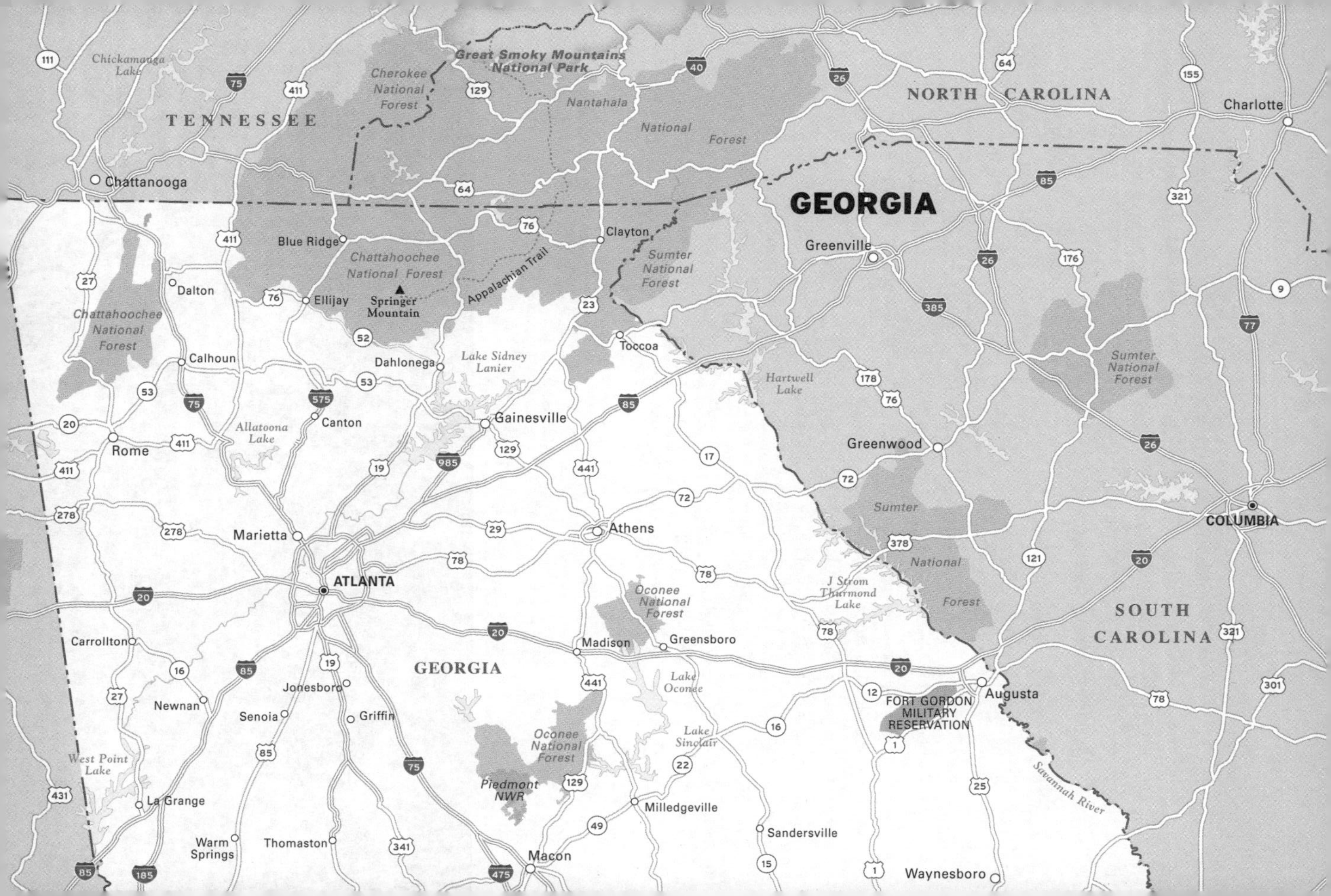

GEORGIA
TENNESSEE
NORTH CAROLINA
SOUTH CAROLINA
GEORGIA
Chattanooga
Chickamauga Lake
Great Smoky Mountains National Park
Cherokee National Forest
Nantahala National Forest
Chattahoochee National Forest
Springer Mountain
Appalachian Trail
Sumter National Forest
Blue Ridge
Clayton
Dalton
Ellijay
Calhoun
Dahlonega
Lake Sidney Lanier
Toccoa
Canton
Allatoona Lake
Gainesville
Rome
Marietta
ATLANTA
Athens
Hartwell Lake
Greenville
Greenwood
Charlotte
COLUMBIA
J Strom Thurmond Lake
Oconee National Forest
Madison
Greensboro
Lake Oconee
Lake Sinclair
Carrollton
Newnan
Senoia
Jonesboro
Griffin
West Point Lake
La Grange
Warm Springs
Thomaston
Macon
Piedmont NWR
Milledgeville
Sandersville
Waynesboro
Augusta
FORT GORDON MILITARY RESERVATION
Savannah River

Contents

DISCOVER

Georgia

Coca-Cola. *Gone with the Wind.* Martin Luther King Jr. Jimmy Carter. James Brown. Ted Turner. Jackie Robinson. The Allman Brothers. Ray Charles. Uncle Remus. Hank Aaron. R.E.M. How many states have offered as many iconic names to the world as Georgia?

The influence of Georgia goes far beyond its region. Its effect on the American experience has been profound but also difficult to qualify. A Deep South state with one of the nation's most cosmopolitan cities, a physically immense place with a tight-knit, small-town feel, Georgia defies easy labels. Georgia, it seems, is comfortable doing double duty as both the prototypical Southern state of Sherman-scarred legend and Scarlett O'Hara-derived myth, as well as one of America's engines of lasting change and innovation.

For example, you could make the case that the state's history of racial intolerance is more than balanced out by its role as epicenter of the American civil rights movement and birthplace of its key leader, Dr. King. One person might laugh at the derisive portrayal of North Georgia bumpkins in James Dickey's *Deliverance,* both in print and on film, but another could just as easily point to

Clockwise from top left: Amicalola Falls in North Georgia; Coca-Cola sign in Atlanta; paddling in the Okefenokee Swamp; Jimmy Carter Presidential Campaign Headquarters in Plains; Oakland Cemetery in Atlanta; the Cathedral of St. John the Baptist in Savannah.

the long list of truly world-changing global initiatives spawned in Georgia, such as Habitat for Humanity, the Ted Turner Foundation, or the Centers for Disease Control.

However, Georgia's main export to the world is its culture, specifically its folk culture, born from hard knocks and a deeply felt historical perspective. There are few corners of the planet that haven't been touched by the rhythms and melodies of the Peach State's musical titans, who often came from poverty and suffered from outright discrimination. There are few university students who haven't studied the works of Georgia's great writers and poets, most of whom struggled, successfully or not, with a host of personal demons and with the often-contradictory demands of regional and national identity. The common theme of Georgia arts, music, and letters is the conflict between the urge to transcend one's surroundings and the desire to celebrate one's roots.

It's still hard to say why so many big names have come out of this place. But they've no doubt left their mark, and no matter where they might travel to, Georgia has left its mark on them...as it likely will on you.

Clockwise from top left: Atlanta skyline; Providence Canyon; the birth home of Martin Luther King, Jr.; entrance to Wormsloe State Historic Site.

5 TOP EXPERIENCES

1 **Historic Savannah:** The nation's largest contiguous historic district is epitomized by nearly two dozen verdant squares, each with its own character (page 173).

2 Atlanta's New South: The still-growing economic engine of Georgia and indeed most of the southeastern U.S., "the city too busy to hate" defies stereotypes and offers cutting-edge cultural experiences (page 52).

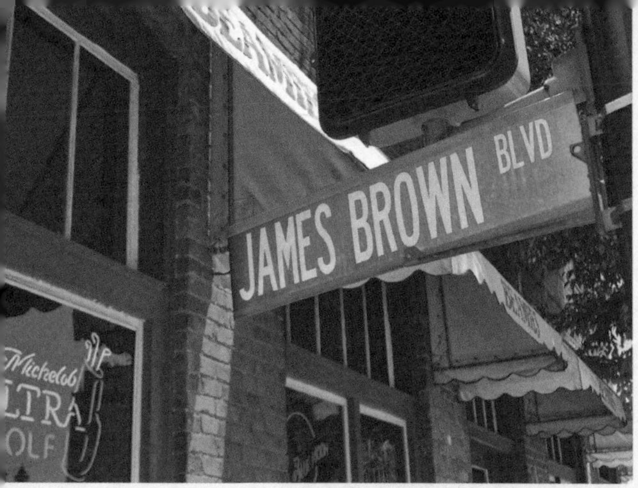

3 Musical Legacy: From legends like James Brown and the Allman Brothers to contemporary hip hop artists, Georgia is a musical powerhouse (page 17).

<<<

4 Southern Cookin': No trip to Georgia is complete without some traditional Southern comfort food (page 16)!

>>>

5 African American Heritage: This region has shaped the history of African Americans since before the nation's inception (page 21).

<<<

The Best of Georgia

The Peach State is physically immense, the largest east of the Mississippi River, so understandably it will take more than a few days to cover the highlights. A vehicle is required for this grand tour of Georgia, beginning in Atlanta and ending in Savannah on the coast.

Day 1

Your first day in **Atlanta** brings you up to Buckhead to visit the **Atlanta History Center,** with a tour of the ornate and unique **Swan House.** Do some shopping at **Lenox Square** and **Phipps Plaza.** For the afternoon head Downtown to the **Martin Luther King Jr. National Historic Site** and pay your respects to this great Georgian. Tonight if the **Braves** are in town go see a game at Turner Field.

Day 2

This morning head to **Centennial Olympic Park** and enjoy the **Georgia Aquarium** or perhaps some cheesy fun at the **World of Coca-Cola.** Head back to Midtown for lunch at **Empire State South** before visiting the **High Museum of Art** for the afternoon. After dinner and cocktails at **Einstein's,** take in a show at the historic **Fox Theatre.**

Day 3

Drive the short distance north of Atlanta to **Amicalola Falls State Park** and stay at the lodge there. Spend the early afternoon hiking in the area, especially around **Springer Mountain,** southern terminus of the **Appalachian Trail** (you'll have to come back to hike that when you have a few months!). If that's too strenuous, shoot over on Highway 52 to Dahlonega and learn about America's first gold rush at the **Dahlonega Gold Museum** on the square. Either way, tonight have brats and brews in the nearby Alpine village of **Helen.**

Day 4

Today head east and enjoy the view from the top of **Black Rock Mountain State Park** before stopping for a bite in charming **Clayton.** Spend the afternoon at nearby **Tallulah Gorge State Park.** Later head back to the lodge at Amicalola Falls.

Swan House

the National Prisoner of War Museum in Andersonville

Day 5

Take I-85 South through Atlanta to Highway 27 and down to little **Warm Springs** to visit **FDR's Little White House** and the nearby therapeutic pools where he swam. After lunch in cute **Pine Mountain,** head down to the wild folk-art compound of **Pasaquan** in Buena Vista before hitting **Americus** for the night, staying at the historic high-Victorian **Windsor Hotel.**

Day 6

Today you visit nearby **Plains,** birthplace and still home to former president **Jimmy Carter.** Visit his old high school, now a museum, and his boyhood farm. From there continue west on Highway 27 to **Providence Canyon,** a stunning and unique state natural area, before heading back to the Windsor Hotel.

Day 7

This morning head 12 miles northeast of Americus to **Andersonville** and the **National Prisoner of War Museum,** a stirring and affecting site encompassing Civil War history and beyond. From here you take back roads to I-75 again, this time north to **Macon,** hitting the ancient Indian mounds at **Ocmulgee National Monument** before getting to the best B&B in town, the **1842 Inn.**

Day 8

Enjoy your luxurious breakfast at 1842 Inn before touring the incredible **Hay House** nearby, one of the South's great house museums. For a change of pace after lunch, stop at the new **Allman Brothers Band Museum at the Big House.** At night, take the **Lights on Macon** free walking tour of the historic Intown neighborhood near the 1842 Inn.

Day 9

This morning head east on I-16 to **Savannah,** where you'll spend the day walking the moss-draped squares and perhaps touring the **Owens-Thomas House** before checking into a boutique hotel like the **Bohemian Hotel Savannah Riverfront** or a classic B&B like the **Eliza Thompson House.** Tonight, dine in style at **Elizabeth on 37th** and end with a nightcap at **Rocks on the Roof** at the Bohemian Hotel while watching the ships go up and down the river. Or, take one of the many **ghost tours** in town, if that's your thing.

Day 10

Get up early for the drive down to the **Jekyll Island Historic District** and the beachcombing on the nearby strand. After a late lunch at the **Jekyll Island Club,** drive a short ways down to **St. Simons Island** and spend the afternoon at historic **Fort Frederica National Monument** before dinner in the old **Village** and the drive back to Savannah.

Day 11

Have a morning stroll in green **Forsyth Park** in Savannah's Victorian district and lunch at world-famous **Mrs. Wilkes' Dining Room** (get in line early!) before heading back to downtown proper and the **Telfair Museums** on Telfair Square. Save time to visit the nearby **Ellis Square** and **City Market** area and do some shopping on bustling **Broughton Street.**

Day 12

This morning drive east to beautiful **Bonaventure Cemetery** on your way out to **Fort Pulaski National Monument** and the **Tybee Island Light Station** on Tybee Island for a day of beach-oriented fun. On the way back to downtown Savannah, grab fresh shrimp and oysters at **Desposito's.**

Southern Cookin'

Georgia is a big state with a big appetite. Here are some of the Southern culinary highlights to liven up your trip with the best it has to offer, from fried okra to fried catfish.

Atlanta

- Midtown Atlanta's favorite old-school **Mary Mac's Tea Room** brings Southern class to the traditional meat 'n' three. Don't forget the "pot likker" to dip your cornbread in (page 67)!
- **Bacchanalia,** Atlanta's premiere fine dining spot features a five-course prix fixe that rivals that of any other restaurant in the country, courtesy of the farm-to-table vision of owners Anne Quatrano and Clifford Harrison (page 72).

North Georgia

- Thank the building's owner, R.E.M.'s Michael Stipe, in part for the existence of Athens's go-to spot, **The Grit,** for unbelievably delicious, all-vegetarian cuisine in a friendly hipster/hippie atmosphere (page 115).

Middle and South Georgia

- Allman Brothers fans will know **H & H Restaurant** as the band's favorite hangout in Macon, but "Mama Louise" Hudson's place is also one of the best soul food diners anywhere (page 140).
- If barbecue's your thing, head straight to **The Whistlin' Pig Cafe** in Pine Mountain, a real local favorite that's also known far and wide for its pulled pork, absolutely out-of-this-world ribs, and excellent Brunswick stew (page 148).

Savannah

- Savannahians in the know will tell you that it's **Mrs. Wilkes' Dining Room** that delivers the best down-home cookin' in the city. Family-style dining and mouth-watering fried chicken are the big draws (page 214).
- For the absolute freshest local seafood, hit **Desposito's,** a humble cinder-block spot underneath a bridge in the fishing village of Thunderbolt, adjacent to Savannah (page 215).

Georgia's Musical Legacy

Get some insight into the backgrounds and experiences of the people who made Georgia a musical powerhouse.

ATLANTA

Eat at the **Flying Biscuit Cafe,** first opened by Emily Saliers of the Indigo Girls. Then it's over to Little Five Points and a rockabilly show at **The Star Community Bar.** Don't forget to pay your respects to the King at their shrine to Elvis! Hip-hop fans might prefer **Compound** in Downtown. Will you see Young Jeezy or Big Boi? Head over to Decatur for the legendary Monday open mic night at **Eddie's Attic** in Decatur, breeding ground of acts like John Mayer, the Indigo Girls, and yes, Justin Bieber.

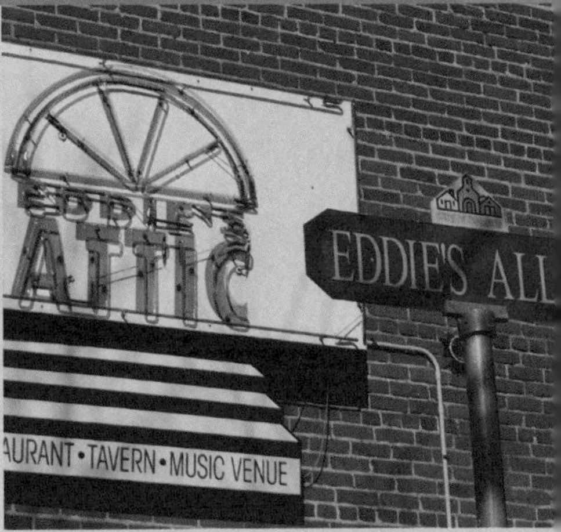

Eddie's Attic in Decatur

ATHENS

Take the local music walking tour downtown, with side trips to the rail trestle on the **R.E.M. album "Murmur"** and the remains of the church where they first rehearsed. Browse the vinyl at legendary **Wuxtry Records.** Have a sublime vegetarian lunch at **The Grit,** on a block restored in part by singer Michael Stipe. Carnivores can have a burger at **The Grill,** downstairs from the original location of the legendary **40 Watt Club.** Do a downtown bar crawl and take in a late show at the current location of the 40 Watt Club or the historic, restored **Georgia Theatre** around the corner.

AUGUSTA

Visit the **Augusta Museum of History** and its great exhibit on native son James Brown, the "Godfather of Soul." Get your picture taken with the **James Brown statue** on **Broad Street.** Enjoy a show at **The Soul Bar** on Broad Street, a longtime musician's hangout across the street from the **Imperial Theatre** where Brown often rehearsed his bands.

MACON

Tour the **Allman Brothers Band Museum at the Big House,** the band's former home and practice space. For lunch go for meat 'n' three at **H & H Restaurant,** where the band often dined. Pay your respects at the gravesites of Duane Allman and Berry Oakley at picturesque **Rose Hill Cemetery,** where you can also see the memorial to "Little Martha." Honor two of Macon's favorite native sons at the **Otis Redding Statue** at Gateway Park on the Ocmulgee River, and **Little Richard's boyhood home** in the **Pleasant Hill Historic District.**

- Get a taste of real Memphis-style barbecue at the excellent **Sandfly BBQ** (page 215).

The Golden Isles

- The Shellman Bluff area near Darien features several totally authentic fresh-catch waterfront seafood spots, but **Speed's Kitchen** is generally considered the best (page 244).
- Set within an Italian Villa-style cottage on the grounds of the historic, swank Jekyll Island Club, **Courtyard at Crane** features Mediterranean-meets-the South takes on crab cakes, lobster, and shrimp (page 234).

Civil War Sites

While Georgia wasn't the huge battleground that Virginia was in the Civil War, it has a sizable number of key sites in the war.

ATLANTA

- **Atlanta History Center:** This Buckhead site has an outstanding permanent Civil War exhibit.
- **Gainesville:** The home and final resting place of Robert E. Lee's second-in-command, James Longstreet, contains monuments to his life and times.
- **Kennesaw Mountain National Battlefield Park:** The opening stages of the Battle of Atlanta are documented outside of Marietta.
- **Stone Mountain:** The world's largest relief sculpture portrays Robert E. Lee, Jefferson Davis, and Stonewall Jackson.

NORTH GEORGIA

- **Chickamauga & Chattanooga National Military Park:** The last major Confederate victory is marked in this sprawling site and museum.
- **Tunnel Hill:** This entertaining site played a role in the "Great Locomotive Chase" intrigue.

PIEDMONT

- **Athens:** Its double-barrelled cannon was never used in combat but is now an entertaining photo opportunity.
- **Augusta:** A huge chimney marks the site of the old Confederate Powderworks, the largest gunpowder facility in the South.
- **Madison:** General William T. Sherman didn't burn this charming little town in part because of his friendship with a local Unionist senator.
- **Washington:** The nostalgic home of Confederate Secretary of State Robert Toombs is located in the first city named after George Washington.

Kennesaw Mountain National Battlefield Park

MIDDLE GEORGIA

- **Columbus:** At the National Civil War Naval Museum, find out everything you ever wanted to know about the Confederate Navy.
- **Milledgeville:** Union troops ransacked Georgia's statehouse, but it stands today as the Old Capitol Museum.

SAVANNAH

- **Fort Pulaski:** It was considered impregnable but fell to the first use of rifled cannon. Well-preserved and interpreted, the grounds are beautiful.
- **Green-Meldrim House:** Sherman's headquarters after his March to the Sea is now a grand church rectory open to public tours.

SOUTH GEORGIA

- **Andersonville:** Explore the notorious POW camp and visit the adjacent National Prisoner of War Museum.

Outdoor Adventure

For campers and green-minded adventurers, this hiking, rafting, paddling, and camping trip covers the most authentically unspoiled and scenic recreational offerings of the Peach State.

Day 1

Begin by setting up camp at amazing **Cloudland Canyon State Park** at the northwest tip of Georgia. Then head out for a day of **canyon floor hiking** and a guided **cave tour.** Consider joining the **Canyon Climbers Club.**

Day 2

This morning drive east to set up camp for a three-night stay at **Vogel State Park,** one of the first two state parks in Georgia. You'll hike just south of here today throughout the **Raven Cliffs Wilderness Area** and will cross portions of the great **Appalachian Trail.** Don't miss the falls!

Day 3

Drive up to **Brasstown Bald** to hike up to the tallest point in the state. If it's a clear day you can see the Atlanta skyline from the summit. This evening treat yourself to a fun, touristy night out in the recreated Alpine village of **Helen** before heading back to Vogel State Park.

Day 4

Get up early for a long day of **whitewater rafting** on the **Chattooga River** where Georgia meets the Carolinas and where the movie *Deliverance* was filmed. Tonight head into downtown **Clayton** for the flatbread pizza and craft beer at **Zeppelin's** before heading back to Vogel State Park.

Day 5

Break camp and head to **Tallulah Gorge State Park,** another Canyon Climbers Club location, where you'll get your free permit to hike across the bottom of the gorge floor. Tonight, head south to the college town of **Athens,** splurge on a hotel room, and enjoy some nightlife and live music.

Raven Cliffs Wilderness Area

Literary Roots

Georgia has an extremely rich and varied literary history, with stories of sin, redemption, human resilience, and folly as distinctive and gritty as the red Georgia soil itself. No matter how famous they got, most Georgia writers rarely strayed far from their roots. Here are some major sights associated with Georgia's writers.

Erskine Caldwell: Visit the Augusta Museum of History to learn more about the region chronicled in the novel *Tobacco Road.*

James Dickey: Raft the Chattooga River, where the film adaptation of his novel *Deliverance* was filmed.

Joel Chandler Harris: Visit the Uncle Remus author's home in Atlanta: The Wrens Nest. See his birthplace at the Uncle Remus Museum in Eatonton.

Carson McCullers: Visit the Carson McCullers Center for Writers and Musicians, her childhood home administered by Columbus State University.

Margaret Mitchell: In Atlanta, go to the Margaret Mitchell House and Museum to see where *Gone with the Wind* was written. The typewriter she used is at the Atlanta-Fulton Public Library.

Andalusia, the family farm of Flannery O'Connor in Milledgeville

Flannery O'Connor: See where she grew up at the Flannery O'Connor Childhood Home in Savannah. Visit Andalusia in Milledgeville, where she wrote most of her novels, and the nearby Flannery O'Connor Room at Georgia College and State University.

Eugenia Price: Visit her church, Christ Church, on St. Simons Island.

Alice Walker: Take the Alice Walker Driving Trail in her hometown of Eatonton.

Day 6

Today is a long drive to the coast. Tonight you camp at the **Hostel in the Forest** near Brunswick to prepare for your paddle down the Altamaha River tomorrow.

Day 7

Today you meet with the folks at **Altamaha Coastal Tours** for your pre-arranged custom **guided kayak trip** through the amazing **Altamaha River,** including old-growth cypress stands and maybe even a picnic on a sandbar.

Day 8

Break camp and head to the great **Okefenokee Swamp** for a day of **canoeing.** You'll set up at **Stephen Foster State Park** at the west entrance, where you'll rent a canoe for your blackwater fun. Tonight, head into **Folkston** for an excellent and affordable buffet dinner at **Okefenokee Restaurant.**

Days 9-10

Early this morning take the ferry to **Cumberland Island National Seashore** for an overnight camping stay. Spend today and part of tomorrow morning **hiking** through the maritime forest, **beachcombing,** checking out the **Dungeness ruins,** and looking for those famous wild horses before the ferry takes you back to shore.

African American Heritage

Georgia has played a critical role not only in the American civil rights movement but also in the history of African Americans since before the nation's inception.

Albany

- **Albany Civil Rights Institute:** Explores the Albany Movement of the early 1960s, a critical early phase of civil rights and of Martin Luther King Jr.'s legacy.

Atlanta

- **Atlanta University Center:** This influential collection of historically black colleges and universities—Spelman College, Morehouse College, and Clark Atlanta University—occupies a contiguous space near Downtown.
- **Martin Luther King Jr. National Historic Site:** The centerpiece of study of the civil rights movement's greatest hero, this site comprises his birth home, the King Center for Nonviolent Social Change, the tomb of Dr. King and his wife Coretta Scott King, the central Visitors Center, and Historic Ebenezer Baptist Church.
- **Sweet Auburn:** The MLK Jr. National Historic Site is within this district, marking the most influential traditionally black neighborhood in Atlanta.

Augusta

- **Augusta Museum of History:** The city museum has a permanent exhibit honoring native son James Brown, the "Godfather of Soul."
- **Lucy Craft Laney Museum of Black History:** The museum is set in a historically black neighborhood and is devoted to chronicling the black experience in Augusta.

Macon

- **Douglass Theatre:** This was a key stop on the old "Chitlin' Circuit" and is still in operation as a showcase of black culture.
- **Tubman African American Museum:** This museum is particularly focused on black arts and culture.

Plains

- **Jimmy Carter National Historic Site:** The president's early political career was largely based on fighting for social justice and equal rights. The museum at Plains High School, the 1976 campaign headquarters at the train depot, and his boyhood farm all examine aspects of this important facet of Carter's life and times.

Sapelo Island

- This Sea Island retains ancestral African American communities with direct links to General Sherman's "40 Acres and a Mule" order.

Savannah

- **First African Baptist Church:** The oldest black congregation in America worships in a historic building in downtown Savannah built by enslaved people.
- **Pin Point Heritage Museum:** This museum chronicles the oystering community where Supreme Court Justice Clarence Thomas grew up.
- **Ralph Mark Gilbert Civil Rights Museum:** Formerly a black-owned bank, this museum interprets Savannah's key role in civil rights in Georgia.

Planning Your Trip

Where to Go

Atlanta

There's always something to do in one of America's most dynamic cities, a burgeoning **multiethnic melting pot** that also has a friendly flavor of the Old South beneath the surface. For every snarled intersection, a delightfully bucolic neighborhood tantalizes with **cafés, shops,** and **green space.** Adventurous **restaurants** and quirky **nightlife** venues are Atlanta's specialties.

North Georgia

The Blue Ridge Mountains are the backdrop for this inspiring, scenic area full of **waterfalls, state parks,** and **outdoor adventures** for the whole family. The influence of the enormous **University of Georgia** in Athens pervades the rolling green **Piedmont** region.

Middle and South Georgia

From **Macon** to **Columbus,** the rhythmic heart of Georgia is the soulful cradle of the state's rich **musical tradition**—and where its **best barbecue** is located. The region's therapeutic value isn't only found in the legendary **Warm Springs** that gave solace to FDR. Farther south is the state's **agricultural cornucopia** and the **home of former president Jimmy Carter,** along with the mighty and mysterious **Okefenokee Swamp.**

the Arch at the University of Georgia in Athens

Savannah

Georgia's grand old city isn't just **full of history,** though that aspect remains very much worth exploring. Savannah has found new life as an **arts and culture mecca,** with as many or more things to do on any given day than cities two or three times its size. Come prepared for high tea or a rowdy party; either way, Savannah's got you covered.

The Golden Isles

History and salt-kissed air meet in the marshes of Georgia's chains of relatively undeveloped barrier islands. The feeling is timeless and tranquil. The Golden Isles are one of the country's **hidden vacation gems** and one of the most **unique ecosystems** in North America.

Savannah's historic waterfront

When to Go

First things first: Georgia gets very hot in the **summer.** For most parts of the state, August is the month you don't want to be here. An exception, however, would be North Georgia, where the mountain air keeps things a bit cooler.

Conversely, **winters** are mild throughout the state except in North Georgia, where many attractions, trails, and even some roads are closed due to ice and snow. Always check ahead.

Autumn leaf-watching season in North Georgia is extremely popular. While there are plenty of great state parks, they fill up well in advance. Because of the general dearth of lodging in the area, you should try to book well in advance for a fall trip to the mountains.

The **hurricane** threat on the coast is highest in August and September. Obviously there's no way to plan your trip in advance to avoid a hurricane, but that would be the time when trips, especially by plane, are most likely to be disrupted.

Savannah hotel rooms are difficult to get in the spring and fall, but especially difficult around St. Patrick's Day in the middle of March.

The Masters golf tournament in **Augusta** in April fills hotels, vacation rentals, and bed-and-breakfasts for many miles around throughout northeast Georgia and well into South Carolina.

autumn in Tallulah Gorge

Athens is much slower in the summer since most classes are not in session at the University of Georgia. However, during home football weekends in the fall, hotel rooms may be booked many months in advance.

Before You Go

Georgia is a very laidback state. Aside from some areas of Atlanta, such as Buckhead, dress is generally casual or casual-to-hip. Dress is more conservative in rural areas both north and south, but because of the often hot and sticky weather, even in those areas there's a lot of leeway.

Atlanta's **public transit system,** MARTA, is extensive and very reasonably priced. For anywhere outside of Atlanta a **car** is absolutely necessary.

Most people flying into Georgia do so through **Hartsfield-Jackson International Airport** in Atlanta, the busiest airport in the world. When there is a delay there, there's a delay pretty much everywhere. If you end up missing a flight, there are dozens of hotels in the vicinity with shuttle service to and from the airport.

North Georgia

Look for ★ to find recommended sights, activities, dining, and lodging.

Highlights

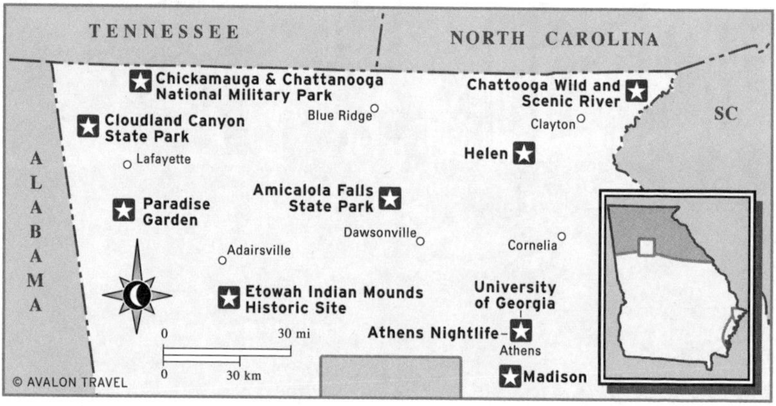

★ **Chattooga Wild and Scenic River:** Take a raft ride on the Carolina border down through *Deliverance* country (page 93).

★ **Helen:** A little cheesy and a lot of fun, this "Alpine village" re-creates *The Sound of Music* experience, but with beer (page 96).

★ **Amicalola Falls State Park:** View the tallest waterfall east of the Mississippi River, near where the Appalachian Trail begins (page 99).

★ **Etowah Indian Mounds Historic Site:** Climb to the top of an ancient Native American temple mound at this excellently preserved site and museum (page 105).

★ **Chickamauga & Chattanooga National Military Park:** Take in the huge battlefield where the Confederacy won its last major victory (page 106).

★ **Paradise Garden:** Immerse yourself in the eccentric, prolific vision of iconic folk artist Howard Finster (page 108).

★ **Cloudland Canyon State Park:** Dotted with caves, this fascinating geological feature offers jaw-dropping views and great hiking and spelunking (page 109).

★ **University of Georgia:** The nation's oldest chartered university is on a beautiful shaded campus full of historic buildings (page 110).

★ **Athens Nightlife:** The legacy of the B-52s and R.E.M. live on in this college town's robust live music scene (page 113).

★ **Madison:** One of the most charming and well-preserved old Southern towns is chock-full of eclectic and interesting architecture (page 117).

The southern tip of the Appalachian Mountain chain pushes into the northern portion of Georgia like a boot heel.

Though crisscrossed by gorges, rivers, creeks, and hollows, North Georgia is a distinctly accessible mountainous area, more logistically forgiving than many areas farther into the Blue Ridge, but with a similar culture of self-sufficiency.

The northeastern portion of Georgia between the great coastal plain to the south and the mountainous regions of the far north has been a hotbed of activity from the earliest days of the colony. Today, exurban Atlanta has encroached on its western edge.

PLANNING YOUR TIME

It's theoretically possible to barnstorm through North Georgia in a day or two by car, just seeing the highlights. The northeast section has more sights and more and better roads; that said, in the summer those two-lane roads, especially in the Helen area, can get pretty crowded with vacationers.

The Piedmont hosts the state's flagship (and oldest) university, in Athens. It can easily be experienced by car with a minimum of travel time. Using Athens as a base, you can take a fun day-trip circle route to Madison, Greensboro, Washington, and back.

Previous: the alpine village of Helen; a hiker enjoys the view from Brasstown Bald. **Above:** Tallulah Gorge.

North Georgia

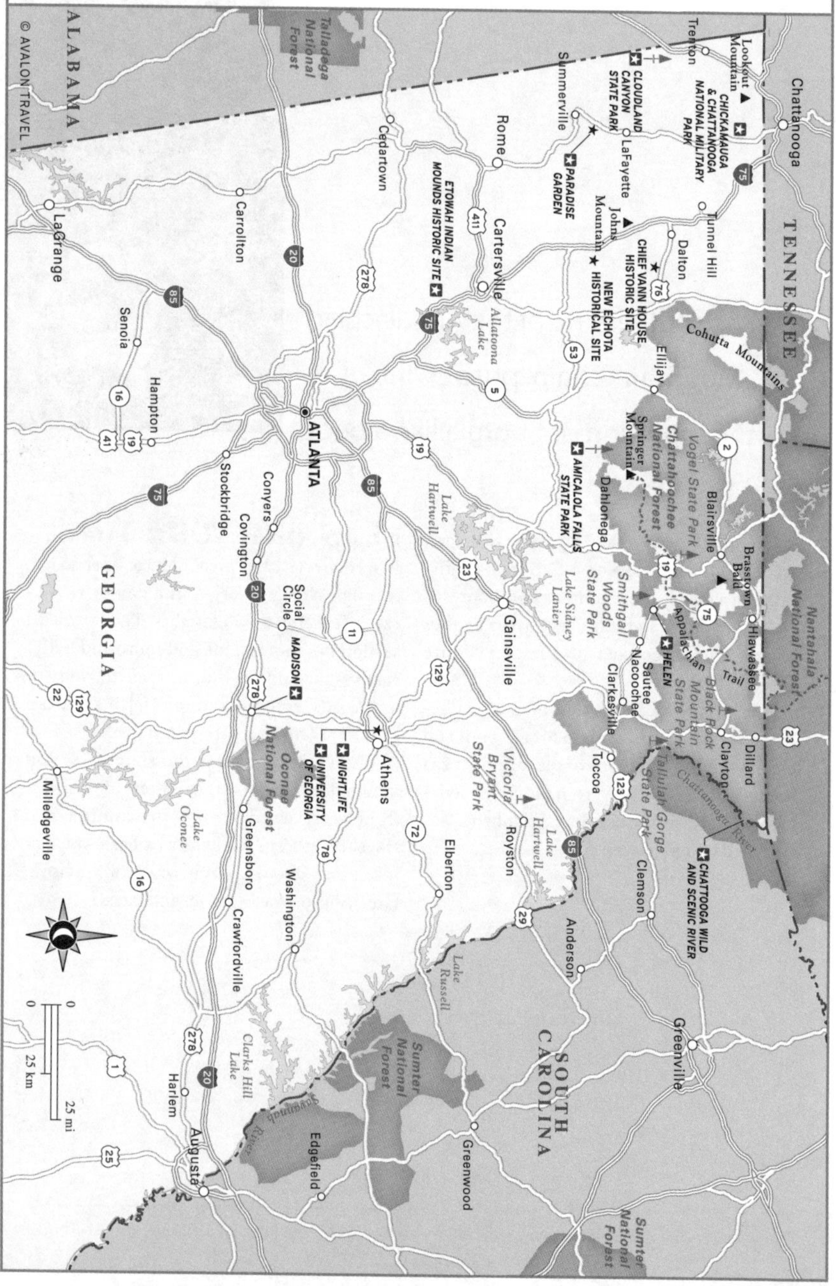

NORTH GEORGIA

Rabun County

In the northeast corner of the state on the border of the Carolinas, the Rabun County area (www.gamountains.com) is one of the most visited portions of North Georgia. It's where you'll find some of the state's most scenic vistas.

Rabun hit the global map in the 1890s, when the high Tallulah Falls Railway was constructed along the Tallulah Gorge, the deepest east of the Mississippi River. The railway brought vacationers to various Victorian-style mountain resorts, and the area served as the scenic location for several movies, including *The Great Locomotive Chase* and the Burt Reynolds film *Deliverance.*

CLAYTON

The Rabun County seat is Clayton (www.downtownclaytonga.org), a diverse little mountain town with rustic charm to spare but still a full slate of offerings for the more sophisticated traveler to this very conservative part of the country.

The **Rabun County Welcome Center** (232 U.S. 441, 706/782-4812, www.gamountains.com) is a good first stop. For a quick look at local history, go to the museum and research library at the **Rabun County Historical Society** (81 N. Church St., Mon. 10am-2pm, Wed. 12:30pm-4:30pm, Fri. 10am-2pm) near the county courthouse.

My favorite restaurant in this part of North Georgia is ★ **Zeppelin's** (88 Main St., 706/212-0101, www.zeppelinspastahouse.com, Mon.-Thurs. 11:30am-9pm, Fri.-Sat. 11am-10pm, Sun. 11am-9pm, $12). A menu of perfectly crispy flatbread pizzas (about $15 and big enough for two) is their main claim to fame, but their burgers are incredible as well, including a bison option.

Foxfire Museum & Heritage Center

For nearly 50 years, the *Foxfire* book and magazine series has chronicled and preserved the dwindling folkways of the southern Appalachians in North Georgia. The Foxfire organization funds and runs the **Foxfire Museum & Heritage Center** (Black Mountain Pkwy., 706/746-5828, www.foxfire.org, Mon.-Sat. 8:30am-4:30pm, $6 over age 10, $3 ages 7-10, free 6 and under) in Mountain City, a few minutes north of Clayton. This collection of vernacular log buildings just off U.S. 441 contains a wealth of authentic displays and equipment portraying the daily life of mountain people in this area. Each October in downtown Clayton is the **Foxfire Mountaineer Festival** (www.foxfire.org).

★ CHATTOOGA WILD AND SCENIC RIVER

If you've seen the 1972 film *Deliverance,* you've seen the Chattooga River (www.rivers.gov), the South's best white-water rafting locale (in the movie it bore the fictional name "Cahulawassee"). The Chattooga River forms part of the Georgia-South Carolina border. If you're white-water rafting, you'll likely be putting in farther upstream, but the easiest way to get to the Chattooga is to take U.S. 76 until you just cross the Chattooga River Bridge into South Carolina. On the Carolina side is a sizable parking area, unfortunately with subpar restroom facilities. You can park in Georgia if you'd like, but there's a $2 parking fee and fewer spaces.

Bull Sluice Falls is a popular thrill-seeking point for rafters and kayakers at the end of Section III of the river, with a 14-foot drop when the river is at full level (Bull Sluice also had a starring role in *Deliverance*). Bull Sluice is also a popular free place for area families to enjoy a dip in the cool water amid the roaring sounds of the sluice.

For recreational purposes the Chattooga is divided into four sections. Section I is primarily for anglers. Section II begins at Highway 28 and ends at Earl's Ford, where there's a 0.25-mile hike to reach the parking area. This is a great little seven-mile run for families, tubers, and novice rafters. The real action begins at Section III, a 14-mile run from Earl's Ford to the U.S. 76 bridge, with a 0.25-mile walk to put in. Beginning with Warwoman Rapid, you'll get a lot of Class II, III, and IV rapids, including the final Class IV-V rapid at Bull Sluice, which concludes Section III. In all, Section III will take 6-8 hours from beginning to end. The most challenging ride is Section IV, from the U.S. 76 bridge to the river's end at Lake Tugaloo.

For serious rafting, the starting points are upriver on the South Carolina side. The main professional rafting tour company on the river is **Nantahala Outdoor Center** (888/905-7238, www.noc.com, prices vary). Expect to pay at least $85 per person, more during the high season in the summer. While walk-ins are welcome, I recommend reserving your trip in advance. Another popular Chattooga rafting guide is **Wildwater Rafting** (800/451-9972, www.wildwaterrafting.com, prices vary).

The prime independent outfitter is **Chattooga Whitewater Outfitters** (14239 U.S. 76, Long Creek, 864/647-9083, www.

Chattooga Wild and Scenic River

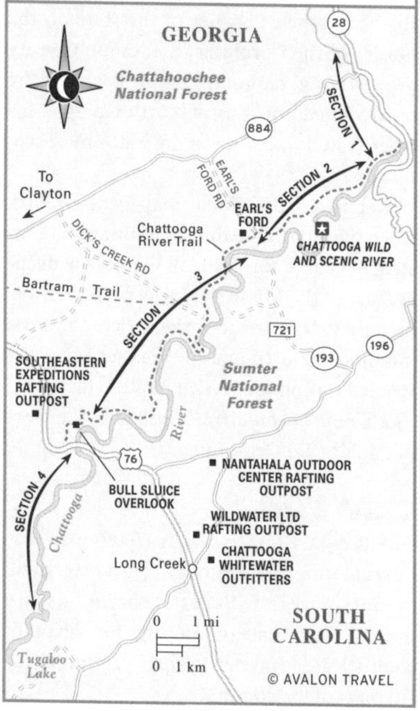

rafting on the Chattooga River

chattoogawhitewatershop.com). If you find yourself craving some carbs after a day of white-water rafting on the Chattooga, check out the pizza joint **Humble Pie** (14239 U.S. 76, Long Creek, 864/647-9083, www.chattoogawhitewatershop.com, Tues.-Sun. 3pm-10pm, $10), within and owned by Chattooga Whitewater Outfitters.

BLACK ROCK MOUNTAIN STATE PARK

The highest state park in Georgia and one of the most enjoyable, **Black Rock Mountain State Park** (3085 Black Rock Mountain Pkwy., 706/746-2141, www.gastateparks.org, Mar.-Nov. daily 7am-10pm, parking $5, campsites $25-28, walk-in campsites $15, cottages $125-145) attracts particularly large crowds during leaf-turning season in the fall. The visitors center at the summit of the mountain is a popular place for its relaxing views. Campers will find 44 tent and RV sites, 10 cottages, and a dozen walk-in campsites.

MOCCASIN CREEK STATE PARK

Moccasin Creek State Park (3655 Hwy. 197, 706/947-3194, www.gastateparks.org, Mar.-Nov. daily 7am-10pm, parking $5, campsites $25), nestled up against quiet, pretty Lake Burton, is focused on boating and fishing. Camping is a little snug here, with tent and RV gravel sites fairly close together. But it's a fine place for water recreation, with docks, a boat ramp, and a fishing pier open only to disabled people, seniors, and children.

Wildcat Creek

Just around the corner from Lake Burton is the access road to the hidden gem of **Wildcat Creek** (Forest Rd. 26, www.fs.usda.gov, campsites $10, first come, first served, no water) in Chattahoochee-Oconee National Forest. You'll find outstanding fishing in the creek stocked with rainbow trout. Lining Wildcat Creek are two primitive campgrounds run by the U.S. Forest Service. Hikers can access the Appalachian Trail from this route as well. A sturdy 4WD vehicle is strongly recommended.

TALLULAH GORGE STATE PARK

Tallulah Gorge State Park (338 Jane Hurt Yarn Dr., 706/754-7981, www.gastateparks.org, daily 8am-dusk, parking $5) has been one of the state's most visited parks since its

Moccasin Creek State Park

inception in the 1990s. It contains the eponymous and iconic Tallulah Falls as well as a vast area on either side of the deepest gorge (1,000 feet) in the eastern United States.

Your first stop is the **Jane Hurt Yarn Interpretive Center** (daily 8am-5pm), a combined visitors center and museum. This is where you get your free permit to hike to the floor of the gorge (only permit holders can go all the way to the bottom, and only 100 permits are given out each day; get here as early as you can).

For the less adventurous or those with less time, a simple walk along the north rim includes several viewing points. You may choose to go down the 531-step staircase and across a suspension walking bridge to the bottom of the gorge (you'll need a permit to actually walk onto the rocky bottom). Along the way you'll see the old iron towers used to stage Karl Wallenda's famous tightrope walk across the gorge in 1970. The most adventurous hikers can take the long trek from there to **Bridal Veil Falls,** where the only swimming in the park is allowed. At 600 feet, the second-tallest waterfall in the state is **Caledonia Cascade,** sometimes called Cascade Falls, near the beginning of Tallulah Gorge. You can see it from the hiking trail around the rim.

The trail system within the park is extensive. Lodging within the park includes 50 tent and RV sites and three backcountry shelters ($15).

Helen and Vicinity

The area around Helen is picturesque, easily accessible, and offers plenty of visitor amenities. No wonder, then, that it's an extremely popular summer and fall vacation spot, especially for day-trippers from metro Atlanta.

★ HELEN

For generations of Georgians, the word "Helen" has either meant a fun place to get away in the mountains, a hilariously cheesy living theme park, or a combination of both. Situated in a neat little valley at the headwaters of the Chattahoochee River, this once-decrepit former logging town was literally rebuilt from scratch in the late 1960s specifically to mimic a stereotypical German-Swiss mountain village. Local regulations require that every structure conform to a classic Alpine motif that will feel familiar to anyone who has seen *The Sound of Music.*

The highlight of the year is the annual **Oktoberfest** (706/878-1908, www.helenchamber.com, $8 Mon.-Fri., $9 Sat., free Sun.) centering on the town's Festhalle (1074 Edelweiss Strasse). Unlike many towns that hold similar events, Oktoberfest in Helen is no mere long weekend: It lasts from mid-September through the end of October. In true German style, the Festhalle is filled with rows of long tables for you to enjoy your beer and brats and listen to oompah music.

Sights

Charlemagne's Kingdom (8808 N. Main St., 706/878-2200, www.georgiamodelrailroad.com, Thurs.-Tues. 10am-5pm, $5) is the labor of love of a German couple who, over the course of the last two decades, have built an entirely self-contained little part of Germany traversed by an extensive model railroad, featuring over 400 feet of indoor track.

Directly adjacent to Helen is the more tasteful little community of Sautee Nacoochee. The **Folk Pottery Museum of Northeast Georgia** (283 Hwy. 255, 706/878-3300, www.folkpotterymuseum.com, Mon.-Sat. 10am-5pm, Sun. 1pm-5pm, $5 adults, $2 children) is within the Sautee Nacoochee Cultural Center.

Food and Accommodations

The oldest German restaurant in Helen, the iconic **Old Heidelberg** (8660 N. Main St., 706/878-3273, spring-fall daily 11:30am-9pm, $20) calls itself the "most photographed

windmill in Helen

building in Georgia." The menu has an entire page of schnitzel (about $20) and another for sausage dishes ($15). Conveniently across the street from the town's Festhalle, ★ **Bodensee** (64 Munich Strasse, 706/878-1026, www.bodenseerestaurant.com, spring-fall daily 11:30am-8pm, $15) serves a mean jaeger schnitzel along with all the other staples.

Quality chain lodging in Helen is scarce, but you can try the entirely Alpine-themed **Hampton Inn** (147 Unicoi St., 706/878-3310, www.hamptoninn.com, $100) or the **Country Inn & Suites** (877 Edelweiss Strasse, 706/878-9000, www.countryinns.com, $110-150) for a cut above the typical chain experience. For a romantic, and yes, German-themed getaway, head to **Black Forest Bed & Breakfast** (8902 N. Main St., 706/878-3995, www.black-forestvacationrentals.com, $135-250).

RAVEN CLIFF FALLS

Situated within the massive **Raven Cliffs Wilderness Area** (www.fs.usda.gov), itself a major trout-fishing and hiking mecca, Raven Cliff Falls on Dodd Creek is one of North Georgia's most popular cascades despite being a relatively strenuous five-mile round-trip hike. The falls, with a total drop of 400 feet, are present in several sections along the hike. There is walk-in camping, but it's not particularly recommended due to the crowds. To get here, take Highway 75 north from Helen about 1.5 miles and turn left onto Highway 356. From there go about 2.5 miles to the Richard B. Russell Scenic Highway, then turn right and go 3 miles to the well-marked trailhead and parking area.

SMITHGALL WOODS STATE PARK

With a focus on education, **Smithgall Woods State Park** (61 Tsalaki Tr., 706/878-3087, www.gastateparks.org, visitors center daily 8am-5pm, parking $5) is a delightful gem a bit north of Helen. The rustically attractive main visitors center contains displays on flora and fauna, with the highlight being the nearby raptor aviary, where rescued birds of prey live under care. There is no camping at Smithgall Woods per se, but there are five reservable and perhaps surprisingly upscale cottages ($150-500).

UNICOI STATE PARK

Unicoi State Park and Lodge (1788 Hwy. 356, 706/878-2201, www.gastateparks.org, parking $5, tents and RVs $29-35, walk-in campsites $25, cottages $80-100) offers something for everyone on a sprawling 1,000 acres within a few miles of Helen. There are nearly 100 camping spaces for tents and RVs and a couple dozen walk-in tent sites, a vast array of charming cottages in various multilevel clusters, and the associated 100-room lodge (800/573-9659, $75-100).

Anna Ruby Falls

Although it is within Unicoi State Park, **Anna Ruby Falls** (www.fs.usda.gov, daily 9am-6pm, entry gate closes 5pm, $3) is run by the U.S. Forest Service and requires a

Anna Ruby Falls

separate admission. However, it's worth the nominal fee, not only for the perfectly situated twin falls themselves—uniting to form Smith Creek at the bottom, which itself empties into Unicoi Lake and, much later, the Gulf of Mexico—but for the relaxing, scenic walk from the parking area and visitors center to the falls.

CLARKESVILLE

The seat of Habersham County, Clarkesville is primarily known for its tidy downtown shopping area and one of the premier B&B's in the state: ★ **Glen-Ella Springs Inn** (1789 Bear Gap Rd., 706/754-7295, www.glenella.com, $150-275). Set in a restored yet still rustic-feeling 1800s building on a scenic 12 acres, Glen-Ella's 16 guest rooms all boast covered porches with rocking chairs. The attached restaurant (daily 6pm-10pm, $25) is considered one of Georgia's best, and it's open to nonguests.

A few miles north of Clarkesville on Highway 197 is the venerable and charming pottery makers' collective **Mark of the Potter** (9982 Hwy. 197 N., 706/947-3440, www.markofthepotter.com, daily 10am-6pm), set within the restored Watts gristmill.

The Appalachian Trail

Following the lead of the country's first conservationist president, Theodore Roosevelt, the first stirrings of the concept of a national "super-trail" began making the rounds in the early 1920s. Work soon began on what was then called "America's Footpath."

By 1937 the entire Appalachian Trail was finished on both ends, from Georgia to Maine. However, almost immediately a hurricane did heavy damage to the path, and Skyline Drive was extended to the Blue Ridge Parkway in the 1940s, which destroyed a 120-mile-long section of the trail.

Renewed interest in the trail came in the postwar years. The designation of the Appalachian Trail, or "AT" as it's often known, as a National Scenic Trail in 1968 cemented its status as a national treasure under federal protection.

Amicalola Falls State Park

★ AMICALOLA FALLS STATE PARK

Home of the tallest cascade east of the Mississippi River, **Amicalola Falls State Park** (418 Amicalola Falls State Park Rd., 706/265-8888, www.gastateparks.org, daily 7am-10pm, visitors center daily 8:30am-5pm, parking $5) also happens to be a main gateway to the Appalachian Trail. It's an extremely popular park, especially during leaf-viewing season in the fall. The magnificent 730-foot falls are one of the "Seven Natural Wonders of Georgia" and are worth the crowds.

Lodging at Amicalola (www.galodges.com) includes the **Amicalola Falls Lodge** (from $150) near the top of the falls. You can also stay in one of 14 rustic cottages. However, the most distinctive lodging at Amicalola is the ★ **Len Foote Hike Inn** (www.hike-inn.com,

Appalachian Trail Through Georgia

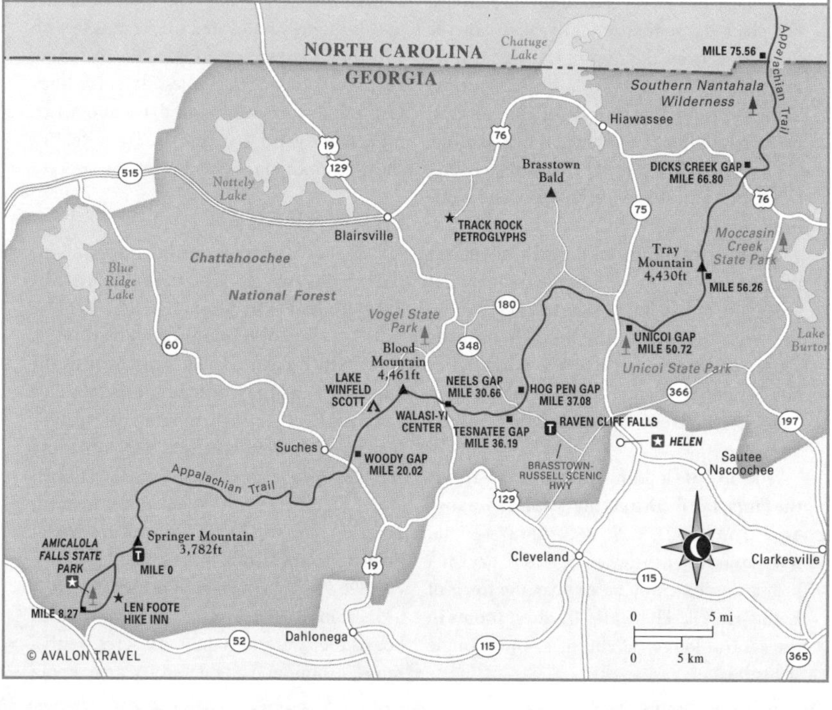

$100-140), an eco-friendly hiker's lodge that's a five-mile trek from the main park area. Run by a nonprofit, the inn has a staff that lives on-site. The 20 guest rooms are really only intended for sleeping, but the communal areas are charmingly appointed. From the Hike Inn, it is another mile to reach the AT.

There is a total of 12 miles of trails in the park, with the most popular and famous being the 8.5-mile **Southern Terminus Approach Trail** from the falls to Springer Mountain, the bottom tip of the AT.

Georgia's section of the AT (www.appalachiantrail.org) is 76 miles long, from Springer Mountain to Bly Gap and on into North Carolina. At its highest point in Georgia, Blood Mountain, the AT is 4,460 feet above sea level; its low spot is Dicks Creek Gap at 2,675 feet. White rectangular blazes mark the trail, and turns are marked with double blazes.

Brasstown Bald

At 4,784 feet, Georgia's highest point is the summit of **Brasstown Bald** (770/297-3000, www.fs.usda.gov, visitors center daily 10am-4pm, $3 pp). Deep in the Chattahoochee-Oconee National Forest and historic Cherokee country, the mountain is called Enotah by the Cherokee people. Unlike other mountains in the Blue Ridge called balds, Brasstown Bald is actually full of vegetation to the summit. On clear days, theoretically, you can see four states from the nostalgically charming and well-built observation deck: Georgia, Tennessee, and both Carolinas. You can even occasionally make out the Atlanta skyline. (The very top of the tower is for fire-spotting by the U.S. Forest Service, however, and is off-limits to visitors.)

Hike up from the parking area, about one mile round-trip, or wait for the frequent but seasonal shuttle buses ($3) to chug you up the winding path to the top. The visitors center underneath the observation tower has a number of interesting exhibits. Pack a lunch—the views from the picnic area are awesome.

The upscale lodging of note in the area is the fantastic ★ **Brasstown Valley Resort and Spa** (6321 U.S. 76, 706/379-9900, www.brasstownvalley.com, $200), set on a lush and scenic 500 acres near the town of Young Harris. There are 102 guest rooms in the central lodge, 32 cottages, and a single spa suite.

TRACK ROCK PETROGLYPHS

Track Rock Gap (Track Rock Gap Rd., 706/745-6928, www.fs.usda.gov, daily dawn-dusk, free), with its ancient Native American rock carvings, or petroglyphs, is the only such site on public land in Georgia. The soapstone rocks feature over 100 depictions of wildlife, animal tracks, symbols, and footprints. Get to this recently renovated site, complete with a historic marker, from Blairsville by taking U.S. 76 east about five miles. At Track Rock Gap Road, turn right and drive about two miles to the gap. Drive past the Track Rocks a short distance to the parking lot.

HIAWASSEE

Hiawassee (www.mountaintopga.com) is known for its **Georgia Mountain Fairgrounds** (1311 Music Hall Rd., 706/896-4191, www.georgiamountainfairgrounds.com), which hosts the **Georgia Mountain Fair** (July) and the **Georgia Mountain Fall Festival** (Oct.). The fairgrounds offer camping as well (706/896-4191, $21-34) with nearly 100 sites open year-round and nearly 200 open April-October, both paved and unpaved. For a more rustic brush with nature stay at **Enota Mountain Retreat** (1000 Hwy. 180, 706/896-7504, www.enota.com, tents $25, RVs $35, cabins $110-165) near Hiawassee, which boasts four waterfalls on its 60 acres. With a motel, cabins, and a tent and RV area, Enota combines a truly beautiful setting with no-frills, communal, pet-friendly living complete with attached 10-acre organic farm.

VOGEL STATE PARK

Vogel State Park (405 State Rt. 129, 706/745-2628, www.gastateparks.org, daily 7am-10pm, parking $5) is one of Georgia's oldest and most beloved. There's plenty of hiking with lots to see, including a peaceful 22-acre lake (no motorized watercraft allowed), complete with a little beachfront area, and the small but wonderful **Trahlyta Falls.** There's a 13-mile backcountry trail, and you can access the Appalachian Trail from the park as well. Perhaps the most unique aspect is the museum dedicated to the Civilian Conservation Corps (CCC), which constructed Vogel (along with many other Southern state parks) in the 1930s. This is also one of the better Georgia parks for camping, with roomy, woodsy sites.

Dahlonega

Epicenter of one of the first gold rushes in the United States, Dahlonega (www.dahlonega.org) still retains a fitting frontier vibe. Most everything in town revolves around either the town's literally golden history or the student life of North Georgia College and State University, the distinctive gold-leaf steeple of its administration building dominating the skyline. However, "purple gold" is making a big impact on the area these days in the form of a burgeoning wine region. The highlight of the Dahlonega calendar is the **Gold Rush Days** (www.dahlonegajaycees.com) festival every October, which features food, fun, and music in the square.

SIGHTS

Dahlonega Gold Museum State Historic Site

The **Dahlonega Gold Museum State**

Dahlonega's Gold Rush Days, held in October

Historic Site (1 Public Square, 706/864-2257, www.gastateparks.org, Mon.-Sat. 9am-5pm, Sun. 10am-5pm, $6 adults, $3.50 children) is in the old 1836 courthouse building, itself of great significance as the oldest surviving courthouse in Georgia. The museum commemorates and explains the phenomenon of the Georgia gold rush. Don't miss the excellent short film upstairs documenting the gold rush with oral history from Georgians who worked the mines, many still open well into the 20th century. The seats in the theater are the courthouse's original courtroom benches.

Crisson Gold Mine

The only remaining working gold mine in Georgia is the **Crisson Gold Mine** (2736 Morrison Moore Pkwy., 706/864-6363, www.crissongoldmine.com, daily 10am-6pm, cost varies). You can pan for gold or just shop for jewelry made from gold that is still mined on-site for the souvenir market. You can also opt to buy their ore by the bucket and take it home with you to see if you get lucky. Those who purchase six buckets of ore can use the mine's own tools for a really authentic experience. Tours are given of the old stamp mill on the grounds.

Consolidated Gold Mines

It's not a working mine anymore, but **Consolidated Gold Mines** (185 Consolidated Gold Mine Rd., 706/864-8473, daily 10am-5pm, $15 adults, $9 children) is the actual site of what was once one of the largest gold processing plants in the world, only open for about 10 years at the turn of the 20th century. Some of the old mine shafts, including the legendary "Glory Hole," have been excavated and restored for public tours, 200 feet underground, by knowledgeable guides.

a rock-crusher at Consolidated Gold Mines

WINERIES

The Dahlonega area has made quite a name for itself over the past 10-15 years or so as a regional wine center. The wine business is seasonal, however, so the wineries often take an extended hiatus from public visitation during the winter.

Wolf Mountain Vineyards (180 Wolf Mountain Tr., 706/867-9862, www.wolfmountainvineyards.com, tastings Thurs.-Sat. noon-5pm, Sun. 12:30pm-5pm, from $10) has rapidly established itself as Georgia's leading winemaker. **Frogtown Cellars** (700 Ridge Point Dr., 706/865-0687, www.frogtownwine.com, Mon.-Fri. noon-5pm, Sat. noon-6pm, Sun. 12:30pm-5pm, tastings from $15) has 42 acres on the outskirts of Dahlonega and a satellite tasting room in Helen (7601 S. Main St., daily). **Montaluce Estates** (946 Via Montaluce, 706/867-4060, www.montaluce.com, Tues.-Sat. 11am-5pm, Sun. noon-5pm, tastings from $16) boasts a state-of-the-art upscale facility. The first Dahlonega winery of the modern era is **Three Sisters Vineyards** (439 Vineyard Way, 706/865-9463, www.threesistersvineyards.com, Thurs.-Sat. 11am-5pm, Sun. 1pm-5pm, tastings $5-30). **Kaya Vineyards** (5400 Town Creek Rd., 706/219-3514, www.kayavineyards.com, Wed.-Sat. 11am-5pm, Sun. 12:30pm-5pm) offers several varietals, with tastings ranging $14-25.

FOOD AND ACCOMMODATIONS

The signature shepherd's pie at ★ **Shenanigan's Irish Pub** (87 N. Chestatee St., 706/482-0114, www.theshenaniganspub.com, Mon.-Thurs. 11am-10pm, Fri.-Sat. 11am-midnight, Sun. noon-7pm, $10) is just what the doctor ordered to warm you up from the inside on a brisk day in the foothills.

Mountain Laurel Creek Inn & Spa (202 Talmer Grizzle Rd., 706/867-8134, www.mountainlaurelcreek.com, rooms $150-200, cottage $220) offers six guest rooms and the freestanding Dancing Bear Cottage, all in a well-maintained scenic foothills setting. Children are not allowed.

Gold in Them Thar Hills

An accident of geology put one of the world's largest, most accessible, and purest veins of gold in North Georgia, a diagonal swath running northeast to southwest with its epicenter in Lumpkin County. Millions of years after being formed it would spur one of the first gold rushes in the United States.

Georgia gold is legendary for its extraordinary purity, in some places as high as 98 percent (most miners are happy with 80 percent). While the quality was certainly part of its allure, most of the draw was its easy abundance. Indeed, local legend has it that a hunter began the rush in 1828 by literally tripping over a huge nugget.

The earliest method was placer mining (pronounced "plasser"), which involves sorting through alluvial deposits by an open-pit technique or by the old familiar "panning for gold." However, within a few years the most easily accessible gold in North Georgia had been discovered. Mining techniques became much more invasive, including hydraulic mining—essentially erasing entire mountainsides with very powerful hoses—or the classic dynamite-in-the-shaft method. Above and below ground, the mines were everywhere, and the environmental devastation they caused can be seen to this day. The human devastation included the brutal removal of Native Americans and the Trail of Tears.

The sheer volume of gold extracted from these Appalachian foothills was so impressive that the U.S. Mint decided it would be more efficient to build a new branch in Dahlonega in 1838; it stayed open until the Civil War. You can see examples of the remarkably brilliant coins made at the Dahlonega Mint at the **Dahlonega Gold Museum State Historic Site** (1 Public Square, 706/864-2257, www.gastateparks.org, Mon.-Sat. 9am-5pm, Sun. 10am-5pm, $6 adults, $3.50 children) in the main square. Technically, Dahlonega wasn't the country's first gold rush town; that distinction belongs to nearby Auraria, which soon went extinct, with hardly a trace of the town remaining today.

As for the guy who first said, "There's gold in them thar hills," he was U.S. Mint chief assayer M. F. Stephenson, and what he really said was "There's millions in it." Ironically, he wasn't trying to kick off the Georgia gold rush; he was trying to convince prospectors to stay in Dahlonega instead of going to California, where another, and eventually much more famous, gold rush had just begun in 1849.

Cohutta Mountains

The central portion of North Georgia is dominated by the Cohutta Mountain range, which though technically not part of the Blue Ridge is for most purposes contiguous with it. The area is less populated than the Blue Ridge portion just to the east and almost completely dominated by the enormous Cohutta Wilderness Area.

ELLIJAY

For most of the year not much goes on in tiny, cute Ellijay, but it boasts one of Georgia's most popular annual festivals: the **Georgia Apple Festival** (www.georgiaapplefestival.org). Happening over two weekends each October, the Apple Festival celebrates the harvest of this area's chief crop—over 600,000 bushels a year. For a scenic look at the farms where the apples are grown, take a drive down "Apple Alley," Highway 52. Many farms are open in the autumn harvest season for tours, hayrides, and pick-your-own apples.

About 20 miles north of Ellijay is the popular and versatile **Fort Mountain State Park** (181 Fort Mountain Park Rd., 706/422-1932, www.gastateparks.org, parking $5, campsites $25-28, cottages $125-145), within the Chattahoochee National Forest and adjacent to the Cohutta Wilderness. The specialty here is 27 miles of mountain biking trails.

COHUTTA WILDERNESS AREA

The most heavily used in the region, the **Cohutta Wilderness Area** (706/695-6736, www.georgiawildlife.com, free) includes 36,000 acres in Georgia and another 1,000 acres in Tennessee. It has about 100 miles of hiking trails for various skill levels, running through some very beautiful and extremely interesting country. Anglers come from all over to fly-fish on the numerous rivers cutting through.

While camping without a permit is allowed anywhere in Cohutta except directly on trails, usage regulations severely limit campfires; consult the website or call ahead.

Cartersville to the Tennessee Border

Conveniently located roughly along I-75 from northwestern metro Atlanta up to the Tennessee border at Chattanooga are several areas of historical and educational significance. Here they are listed in geographical order northward from Atlanta.

CARTERSVILLE

Benefiting from its proximity to the Atlanta metro area, Cartersville is a fairly bustling old railroad town with an active town square and several notable attractions.

Booth Western Art Museum

North Georgia isn't where you'd expect to find a huge shiny museum dedicated to cowboy and Native American art, but you'll find that and more at the 120,000-square-foot limestone **Booth Western Art Museum** (501 Museum Dr., 770/387-1300, www.boothmuseum.org, Tues.-Wed. and Fri.-Sat. 10am-5pm, Thurs. 10am-8pm, Sun. 1pm-5pm, $10 adults, $8 students, free under age 12), which claims to be Georgia's biggest museum after the High in Atlanta. While the highlight for many is the permanent and succinctly named Cowboy Gallery, the entire multistory edifice does a good job of inclusivity, with artwork by and about Native Americans, African Americans, and women.

Tellus Science Museum

The **Tellus Science Museum** (100 Tellus Dr., 770/606-5700, www.tellusmuseum.org, daily 10am-5pm, $14 adults, $10 children, planetarium shows $3.50) focuses on astronomy and geology, with mineral and fossil exhibits galore. The building is constructed around a central observatory, open during monthly special events (check the website). The all-digital planetarium provides frequent shows at additional cost.

Rose Lawn House Museum

A short walk from the town square is **Rose Lawn House Museum** (224 W. Cherokee Ave., 770/387-5162, www.roselawnmuseum.com, Tues.-Fri. 10am-noon and 1pm-5pm, $5 adults, $2 children), former home of influential 19th-century evangelist Samuel Porter Jones. The museum features period furnishings and serves as a home for memorabilia of another famous Bartow County native, Rebecca Latimer Felton, the first woman to serve in the U.S. Senate.

Food

Tasty dining options downtown include **Appalachian Grill** (14 E. Church St., 770/607-5357, Mon.-Thurs. 11am-9pm, Fri. 11am-10pm, Sat. noon-10pm, $15), with its signature trout dishes and combo platters, and **Jefferson's** (28 W. Main St., 770/334-2069, www.jeffersonsrestaurant.com, Mon.-Wed. 11am-10pm, Thurs.-Sat. 11am-11pm, Sun. 11:30am-10pm, $10), known for its wings and oysters.

★ ETOWAH INDIAN MOUNDS HISTORIC SITE

The **Etowah Indian Mounds Historic Site** (813 Indian Mounds Rd., 770/387-3747, www.gastateparks.org, Wed.-Sat. 9am-5pm, $5), outside Cartersville, is the most intact mound-builder site in the Southeast. On this 54 acres was one of the most influential communities of the Mississippian culture from about AD 1000 to 1500. Its six masterfully constructed earthen mounds are in surprisingly good shape today, with full access to the top, providing a beautiful panorama of the surrounding area and the other mounds.

The small but well-curated visitors center has a nice museum with some stunning artifacts retrieved from the site. Bring a picnic lunch and enjoy the tranquil serenity of the shaded picnic area on the banks of the Etowah River directly beside the mound site.

the Etowah Indian Mounds Historic Site

NEW ECHOTA HISTORIC SITE

The beneficiary of a recent upgrade and renovation, **New Echota Historic Site** (1211 Chatsworth Hwy., 706/624-1321, www.gastateparks.org, Thurs.-Sat. 9am-5pm, $7 adults, $5.50 children) outside Calhoun has an especially bittersweet nature, serving both as capital of the Cherokee Nation from 1825 to 1838 and as the place where the Trail of Tears began. Today there are a dozen original and reconstructed period buildings. The visitors center plays a 17-minute film about the history of the site and hosts the Cherokee Research Library.

CHIEF VANN HOUSE HISTORIC SITE

A short drive east of Dalton is the **Chief Vann House Historic Site** (82 Hwy. 225 N., 706/695-2598, www.gastateparks.org, Thurs.-Sat. 9am-5pm, $6 adults, $3.50 children), the best-preserved extant house of the Cherokee Nation.

TUNNEL HILL

The chief attraction in this little mountain town is the **Historic Western & Atlantic Railroad Tunnel** (215 Clisby Austin Dr., 706/876-1571, www.tunnelhillheritagecenter.com, Mon.-Sat. 9am-5pm, $7 adults, $5 children), part of the first railroad through the Appalachians. For a few minutes in 1862 it hosted part of the Great Locomotive Chase. The tunnel can be toured at the top of each hour.

★ CHICKAMAUGA & CHATTANOOGA NATIONAL MILITARY PARK

Directly south of Fort Oglethorpe on Highway 1 (or off I-75's exit 350) is the **Chickamauga & Chattanooga National Military Park** (3370 LaFayette Rd., www.nps.gov, visitors center daily 8:30am-5pm, grounds daily dawn-dusk, free), preserving and interpreting the site of one of the last major Confederate victories of the Civil War. The focus is primarily on the savage fighting around Chickamauga in September 1863.

There's a small and well-done visitors center and museum with a 20-minute video explaining the rather complicated action of the battle. The main draw is the seven-mile walking tour over the battlefield, culminating in a trip up an observation tower to view the entire area. There are interpretive maps, or you can dial a number on your cell phone to listen to an audio tour (get the number from the rangers at the visitors center).

the Chickamauga & Chattanooga National Military Park

Ridge and Valley Country

The northwestern portion of Georgia is geologically and culturally somewhat different from the rest of North Georgia. It's often called the Ridge and Valley Country, an area to the west of the Cartersville-Great Smoky Fault and a clear differentiation from the Blue Ridge Mountains to the east. Rome is by far its biggest city.

ROME

Like the great Italian capital that is its namesake, Rome, Georgia, was built on seven hills. In front of **City Hall** (601 Broad St.) is a statue of Romulus and Remus nursing from a wolf, a nod to the creation story of the European city. A gift to the city from Italian dictator Benito Mussolini in 1929, the statue was taken down to prevent vandalism during World War II and returned in the 1950s. Today, Rome is a center of regional higher education, health care, and manufacturing. You might first want to check out the **Rome-Floyd County Visitors Center** (402 Civic Center Dr., 800/444-1834, www.romegeorgia.org).

Berry College

Rome's chief claim to fame is big and beautiful **Berry College** (2277 Martha Berry Hwy., 706/232-374, www.berry.edu), a liberal arts school on an expansive campus, the largest contiguous college campus in the world. Founder Martha Berry was the daughter of a wealthy area planter and was struck by the profound lack of educational opportunities for most young people in these hardscrabble foothills. She began an impromptu Sunday school at her home, which eventually expanded to a family log cabin, still on campus today. Much of the campus land is administered by the state as hunting and conservation areas; other parts are open to the public for walking and biking.

The highlight is **Oak Hill & The Martha Berry Museum** (24 Veterans Memorial Hwy., 706/368-6789, www.berry.edu, Mon.-Sat. 10am-5pm, tours every 30 minutes 10am-3:30pm, $5 adults, $3 children), Berry's Greek Revival home where you can learn much more about the school's history.

Clocktower Museum

Downtown Rome's most famous sight is the 1872 **Clocktower** (E. 2nd St., Mon.-Fri. 9am-3pm, free), a massive clock atop the 100-foot-tall former city water tower. There's a small museum inside, and visitors can climb to the top.

Chieftains Museum and Major Ridge Home

One of the key remaining sites along the Trail of Tears, the **Chieftains Museum** (501 Riverside Pkwy., 706/291-9494, www.chieftainsmuseum.org, Fri.-Sat. 1pm-5pm, $5 adults, $3 children) is within the home of Major Ridge, who gathered a band of Cherokee people to fight alongside colonists during the American Revolution. Out of gratitude, Andrew Jackson gave him the rank of major, which Ridge would adopt as his first name. However, by the 1830s, pressure on the Cherokee to give up their lands was so intense he felt compelled to sign the controversial Treaty of New Echota, which resulted in the Trail of Tears.

Food and Accommodations

A couple of good places to get a bite right downtown are **Harvest Moon Cafe** (234 Broad St., 706/292-0099, www.myharvestmooncafe.com, Mon. 11am-2:30pm, Tues.-Thurs. 11am-9pm, Fri.-Sat. 11am-10pm, $15), with good steaks, salmon, and catfish, and **Jefferson's** (340 Broad St., 706/378-0222, www.jeffersonsrestaurant.com, Mon.-Wed. 11am-10pm, Thurs.-Sat. 11am-11pm, Sun. 11:30am-10pm, $10), a regional chain famous for its wings and oysters.

The premier lodging in Rome is the ★ **Claremont House** (906 E. 2nd Ave.,

706/291-0900, www.theclaremonthouse.net, $150-170), set in an absolutely stunning high Victorian masterpiece of a building. There are four charming guest rooms with 14-foot ceilings and canopy beds.

NEAR ROME

★ Paradise Garden

You'd be forgiven for thinking that the late, great Georgia folk artist Howard Finster lived in Athens, Georgia, on the other side of the state. His collaborations on album-cover art for the iconic Athens band R.E.M. and later with the Talking Heads put Finster on the global map. He became known not only as one of the South's greatest and certainly hippest outsider artists but as a classic Southern showman-raconteur.

Finster's memory lives on in Athens, but the best place to view his fertile, almost feverish imagination in action is at **Paradise Garden** (200 N. Lewis St., 706/808-0800, www.paradisegardenfoundation.org, Wed.-Sat. 10am-4pm, Sun. 1pm-4pm, donation), his Summerville studio on a swampy four acres of land off a side street. Like the world's most eccentric theme park, Finster's drawing, painting, and craftwork cover just about every foot of available space on every structure. Here, you fully understand the provenance of the phrase, "one man's junk is another man's treasure." Each May the town park at Summerville hosts **Finster Fest,** an expansive celebration not only of Finster's work but that of regional folk artists from all around.

To get to the Garden, head north through Summerville on U.S. 27. Take a right on Rena Street, looking for the signs, and then make another right onto North Lewis Street. You can't miss it!

If you need a bite to eat while you're in Summerville, head straight for the delectable fried catfish at ★ **Jim's Family Restaurant** (6 Lyerly St., 706/857-2123, daily 8am-8pm, $10). Camp for the night at little **James H. "Sloppy" Floyd State Park** (2800 Sloppy Floyd Lake Rd., 706/857-0826, www.gastateparks.org, parking $5, campsites $25-28, cottages $135-145), one of Georgia's smaller yet still picturesque parks.

TAG CORNER

The extreme northwestern tip of Georgia, sometimes called "TAG corner," an acronym

Howard Finster's Paradise Garden

referring to its position astride the borders of Tennessee, Alabama, and Georgia, is yet another geological substratum. Part of the Cumberland Plateau, it's a flat-topped highland area, one of whose dominant features is limestone. Long story short, this means lots of caves.

Lookout Mountain

By far the main geological feature of the area is Lookout Mountain, part of the Cumberland Plateau. Most of the 84-mile-long mountain is in Tennessee, including the remnants of a key Civil War battlefield and the popular Raccoon Mountain and Ruby Falls caves.

The East Coast's premier hang gliding location is **Lookout Mountain Flight Park and Training Center** (7201 Scenic Hwy., 800/688-5637, www.hanglide.com, Thurs.-Tues. 9am-6pm). Under the tutelage of certified staff, hang gliding enthusiasts launch from 1,340-foot McCarty's Bluff into the wild blue yonder off Lookout Mountain.

★ Cloudland Canyon State Park

Lookout Mountain's most dramatic feature is the 1,000-foot canyon at Sitton's Gulch, renamed Cloudland Canyon in the 1930s during the park's construction by the Civilian Conservation Corps. **Cloudland Canyon State Park** (122 Cloudland Canyon Park Rd., 706/657-4050, www.gastateparks.org, daily 7am-10pm, parking $5, backcountry trails $3 pp, campsites $25-28) is quite simply one of the most striking of all Southern state parks. Its steep sandstone walls are the remnants of a 200-million-year-old shoreline. From the various lookout points along the West Rim Loop Trail skirting the edge of the main picnic area and parking lot along the canyon's edge, you can also see the entrances to some of the canyon's many limestone caves.

The rim trail is about five miles in length and gives you overlook opportunities into three canyon gorges. There is another five-mile network of backcountry trails, along which primitive camping is permitted, a particularly recommended option for those so inclined. You can hike to the bottom of the canyon via some steep but well-maintained and staircase-augmented trails. There are another 72 tent and RV sites divided between the east and west rims, and 16 cottages along the west rim, two of which are dog friendly.

Cloudland Canyon State Park

Athens

Home to the University of Georgia, Athens is a heady and often quirky mix of culture, partying, football, and progressive thought in an otherwise conservative area. What really makes Athens stand out, and clearly puts it head and shoulders above most college towns, is the fabled "Athens scene," a musical ethos that for the past 30 years has virtually defined, and in some cases directly authored, the sound of American indie rock and roll.

A forward-thinking state legislature in 1785 made a bold step to endow a "college or seminary of learning," essentially giving birth to the idea of state-supported higher education in the United States. The surrounding town, created in 1806, was to be called Athens to channel the spirit of the great artistic, literary, and scientific accomplishments of the ancient Greeks. Athens's most famous resident in the antebellum era was Henry W. Grady, who would go on to be a seminal editor of the *Atlanta Journal-Constitution* and founder of the University of Georgia school of journalism, which bears his name.

SIGHTS

Church-Waddel-Brumby House

The main Athens visitors center is within the restored **Church-Waddel-Brumby House** (280 E. Dougherty St., 706/353-1820, www.athenswelcomecenter.com, Mon.-Sat. 10am-5pm, Sun. noon-5pm, free), a circa-1820 house museum alleged to be the oldest residence in the city.

★ University of Georgia

As befitting its deep roots in the Deep South, the **University of Georgia** (www.uga.edu), "Georgia" or UGA in common parlance, boasts not only a devotion to tradition, but a large (over 600 acres) and scenic campus that is worth exploring whether you're affiliated with the university or not. You can take free student-guided tours leaving from the visitors center on South Campus or download a walking tour map (http://visit.uga.edu). Here's a quick look at the highlights:

Every visit to UGA should begin with the famous **Arch** at the old North Campus entrance on Broad Street. Old Bulldog etiquette demands that underclass students only walk around the Arch, not under it. As you walk through the Arch you'll see the Greek Revival **Hunter Holmes Academic Building**, actually two antebellum buildings combined in the early 20th century. In 2001 it was renamed to honor the first two African American students admitted to UGA: Hamilton Holmes and Charlayne Hunter-Gault (later a

University of Georgia

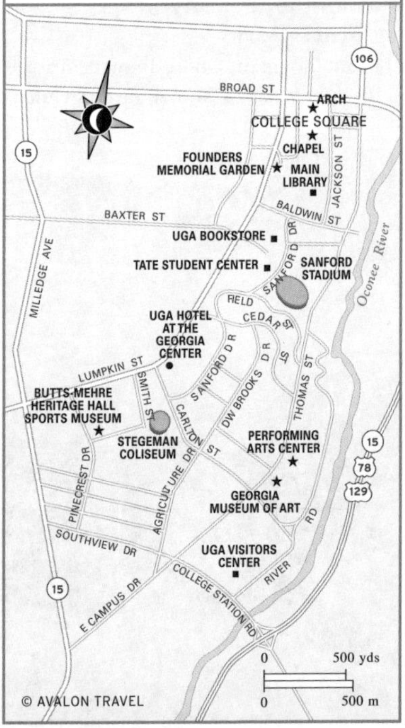

Athens

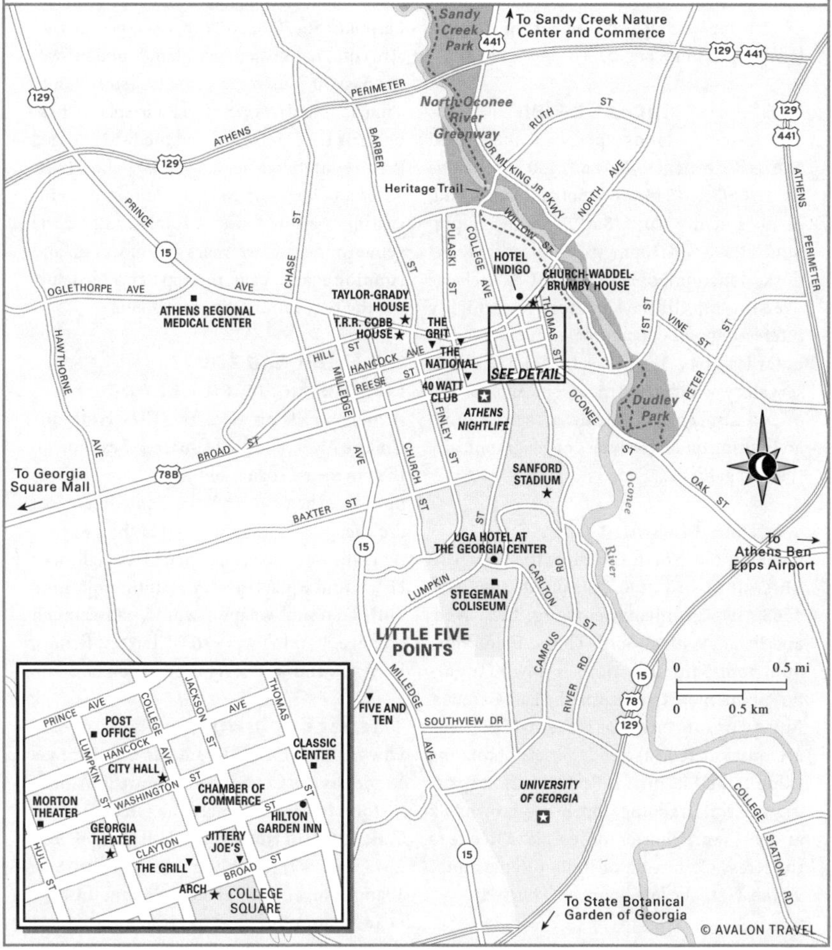

renowned broadcast journalist), who began classes in 1961.

Nearby is the 1832 **Chapel,** where students once attended services three days a week. These days, students take turns ringing the old chapel bell, now in a small tower nearby, until midnight after every Georgia football victory.

South of the Chapel and off to the right you'll run across verdant little **Herty Field,** where the Bulldogs played their first football game in 1892 (beating Mercer University 50-0) under the direction of coach Charles Herty, also a chemist of national repute. A parking lot actually occupied this rectangle from the 1940s to 1999, when the hallowed athletic ground was reclaimed as relaxing green space for casual enjoyment.

Continue down Sanford Drive to the impossible-to-miss, enormous **Sanford Stadium,** where the Bulldogs play home games "between the hedges" growing all along the sidelines.

At the extreme tip of South Campus at College Station Road is the **UGA Visitors Center** (Four Towers Building, 706/542-0842, http://visit.uga.edu), where the student-led campus tours begin.

State Botanical Garden

The tastefully landscaped and interpreted **State Botanical Garden** (2450 S. Milledge Ave., 706/542-1244, www.botgarden.uga.edu, visitors center Tues.-Sat. 9:30am-4:30pm, Sun. 11:30am-4:30pm, grounds daily 8am-dusk, donation), operated by UGA, eschews over-the-top displays of flora for a highly interesting and educational approach to the botanical arts. You enter through the conservatory, which has a nice tropical plant and orchid display. Just outside, arrayed around an inviting quad, is a series of geographically themed gardens.

Georgia Museum of Art

Once on old North Campus, the **Georgia Museum of Art** (90 Carlton St., 706/542-4662, www.georgiamuseum.org, Tues.-Wed. and Fri.-Sat. 10am-5pm, Thurs. 10am-9pm, Sun. 1pm-5pm, donation) is now in a purpose-built modern space on the East Campus. Run by the university, it is the state's official art museum. It hosts a wide variety of rotating exhibits, and its own collections are surprisingly eclectic, ranging from home-grown folk art by Howard Finster to Georgia O'Keeffe to the Kress Collection of Italian Renaissance works. Note the late hours on Thursday.

Butts-Mehre Heritage Hall Sports Museum

For fans of "the Dawgs," the **Butts-Mehre Heritage Hall Sports Museum** (1 Selig Circle, www.georgiadogs.com, Mon.-Fri. 8am-5pm, free) is a must-see. Football takes center stage, including the two Heisman Trophies won by UGA players Frank Sinkwich and Herschel Walker, and the national championship trophy won by the Dawgs in 1980 during Walker's tenure.

Georgia Theatre

With a foundation dating from 1889, the circa-1935 **Georgia Theatre** (215 N. Lumpkin St., 706/850-7670, www.georgiatheatre.com) has hosted many bands of note over the past 30-plus years since its restoration as a music venue in 1978. The Police played here on their first U.S. tour, and the B-52's forged their reputation after a legendary show here. After a bad fire in 2009, a community reinvestment effort led to a total repair of the venue, and only two years later it was up and running again. A fun rooftop bar, added during the renovation, is a great bonus.

City Hall and the Double-Barreled Cannon

Athens boasts an attractive **City Hall** (301 College Ave.). The double-barreled cannon on the northeast corner of the City Hall lot was built in Athens in 1862 as a Confederate "secret weapon." The idea was that the two cannonballs would be connected by an eight-foot chain, and when fired the resulting spinning antipersonnel weapon would cause much damage. It didn't work so well in test firings, however, and was never used in combat.

T. R. R. Cobb House

Lawyer and Confederate officer Thomas Reade Rootes Cobb is a key figure in Athens history, but interestingly the Greek Revival **T. R. R. Cobb House** (175 Hill St., 706/369-3513, www.trrcobbhouse.org, Tues.-Sat. 10am-4pm, $2) was at Stone Mountain Park near Atlanta for 20 years. It has since been returned to this site, about a block from the original location where it was first built in 1834. The ground floor is expertly restored to antebellum furnishings. The 2nd floor is more of a museum format.

Taylor-Grady House

Named for its two most notable owners, Confederate officer and Irish native Robert Taylor and *Atlanta Journal-Constitution* editor and UGA journalism school founder

Henry W. Grady, the **Taylor-Grady House** (634 Prince Ave., 706/549-8688, www.taylor-gradyhouse.com, Mon., Wed., and Fri. 9am-3pm, Tues. and Thurs. 9am-1pm, $3) was built in 1844 as a summer home for Taylor and his family. It's now a house museum.

ENTERTAINMENT AND EVENTS

★ Athens Nightlife

In a matter of great local pride, the University of Georgia is usually at or near the top of the annual lists of best party schools in the country. Indeed, urban legend maintains that Athens has the highest number of bars per capita in the United States.

First among equals, the legendary **40 Watt Club** (285 W. Washington St., 706/549-7871, www.40watt.com, open show nights only) has been at the forefront of the Athens music scene since 1978, when it was cofounded by Curtis Crowe, drummer with local legends Pylon (it's now owned by the ex-wife of R.E.M. guitarist Peter Buck). It's the CBGB of the South, but unlike that NYC club, it's still open for business, albeit in its fifth location.

Despite its swank name, **Manhattan Cafe** (337 N. Hull St., 706/369-9767, Mon.-Sat. 4pm-2am) is one of Athens's most humbly charming bars, a cross between a dive, a hipster bar, and a Prohibition-era speakeasy. The house cocktail is a refreshing blend of Maker's Mark and spicy Blenheim Ginger Ale. **Little Kings** (223 W. Hancock St., 706/369-3144, Mon.-Sat. 7pm-2am) is a go-to for high-profile indie acts; local legends Pylon chose it to kick off a reunion tour. If you're into concerts where even the band wears earplugs, **Caledonia Lounge** (256 W. Clayton St., 706/549-5577, www.caledonialounge.com, Mon.-Sat. 5pm-2am) is the place for you. Small and sweaty, **Go Bar** (195 Prince Ave., 706/546-5609, Mon.-Sat. 9pm-2am), next to the popular restaurant The Grit in a block restored and owned by R.E.M.'s Michael Stipe, is a popular spot to dance and enjoy live music.

Another great way to enjoy the local music scene is at **AthFest** (www.athfest.com). Happening every June in a blocked-off portion of downtown, this music festival features plenty of free live outdoor concerts,

the famous double-barreled cannon at City Hall

Rock-and-Roll Legacy

Athens is renowned for its contributions to rock and roll, spawning names such as R.E.M., the B-52's, Widespread Panic, and Pylon, among many others. An entertaining 1987 documentary chronicling the scene, *Athens, GA: Inside/Out,* is available on DVD. Here's a brief tour of venues that played a role in forming Athens's rock-and-roll legacy. Go to www.visitathensga.com for a full version courtesy of alt-weekly the *Flagpole*.

the trestle from R.E.M.'s *Murmur* album

- **40 Watt Club:** Named because its first incarnation was lit by a single lightbulb, Athens's most legendary club has hosted every major name in local rock history. It's had several locations, in this order: 2nd floor of 171 College Avenue (above The Grill); 2nd floor of 100 College Avenue (above Starbucks); 256 W. Clayton St.; 382 East Broad Street (now university offices), and 285 West Washington Street, where it is now.
- **Georgia Theatre:** 215 North Lumpkin Avenue. The century-old venue reopened after a 2009 fire; The Police played here on their first U.S. tour.
- ***Murmur* Railroad Trestle:** 270 South Poplar Street. The railroad trestle on the back cover of R.E.M.'s *Murmur* album was recently restored through a community effort. Park at the lot near Dudley Park around the corner.
- **140 East Washington Street:** This was once the Uptown Lounge, which in the 1980s hosted The Pixies, Jane's Addiction, R.E.M., and Black Flag. Now it's home to Copper Creek Brewing Co.
- **St. Mary's Steeple:** An Episcopal church was here until it was demolished in 1990, leaving only this steeple. R.E.M. rehearsed and played their first concert here, a birthday party for a friend in April 1980. It's now surrounded by condos but easily accessible from the street.
- **312 East Broad Street:** The "Frigidaire" building was built in the 1880s as the Athens Opera House. For 10 years beginning in 1997, Tasty World operated here and hosted acts such as The Shins and Kings of Leon.
- **260 North Jackson Street:** Now Jackson Street Books, it was record store Wax Jr. Facts in the early 1980s, managed by Pylon bassist Michael Lachowski, who now owns a local design firm.
- **Wuxtry Records:** 197 East Clayton Street. R.E.M.'s Peter Buck once worked here, among many other local musicians. It's been in business since 1975.

film screenings, arts and crafts displays, and product and food booths. The core experience, however, involves the ticketed bracelets ($17-20), which allow you to club-crawl.

SHOPPING

Before he became a rock star, R.E.M.'s Peter Buck once managed **Wuxtry Records** (197 E. Clayton St., 706/369-9428, www.wuxtry-records.com, Mon.-Fri. 10am-7pm, Sat. 11am-7pm, Sun. noon-6pm), and it remains one of the Southeast's best (and quirkiest) sources for vintage vinyl and hard-to-get recordings. Go upstairs to their even more eccentric cousin store **Bizarro Wuxtry Comics, Toys & Records** (197 E. Clayton St., 706/353-7938,

Mon.-Fri. 10am-7pm, Sat. 11am-7pm, Sun. noon-6pm), which has an extensive collection of alternative zines as well as shirts and offbeat items.

The best bookstore in town for the past 25 years has been **Jackson Street Books** (260 N. Jackson St., 706/546-0245, Mon.-Sat. 11am-6pm, Sun. noon-4pm), which deals in plenty of good-condition used and rare volumes.

SPORTS AND RECREATION

The premier overall outdoor activity in Athens is the **North Oconee River Greenway** (70 Sunset Dr., www.athensclarkecounty.com, daily dawn-dusk), a well-done project that has reclaimed much of the north bank of the Oconee, once the home of a thriving mill industry. Four miles of multilevel walking, jogging, and biking trails, including one along the river, meander through the peaceful wooded bank. Interpretive signage explains the rich heritage of the river's industry.

Needless to say, the premier spectator sport in Athens involves the **Georgia Bulldogs football team** (tickets from $55). They play in enormous Sanford Stadium on UGA's South Campus. The Dawgs are a huge deal around here, and for most big games, tickets are hard to come by, though there are often tickets for sale by enterprising individuals on game day. For less competitive games, check online. The home court of the Dawgs men's and women's **basketball teams** is venerable Stegeman Coliseum (100 Smith St.). The baseball-playing **Diamond Dawgs** play at Foley Field. The UGA **women's soccer team** consistently plays at the highest level of NCAA competition, and you can watch their games for free at their specially built soccer stadium. Ten-time national champs, the women's gymnastics team the **Gym Dogs** competes at Stegeman Coliseum (100 Smith St.). Go to georgiadogs.com to find out more information about any of these teams.

FOOD

Burgers and Barbecue

One of Athens's great food traditions, ★ **The Grill** (171 College Ave., 706/543-4770, www.thegrillathensga.com, daily 24 hours, breakfast daily midnight-noon, $7) is open 24-7 right on the town's most traveled block, so there's no excuse not to check it out. They serve traditional diner food amid 1950s retro decor. Upstairs is where the first incarnation of local music venue 40 Watt Club opened in the late 1970s.

Coffeehouses

An expanding local chain, ★ **Jittery Joe's** (www.jitteryjoes.com) has several locations around town, and all of them offer a delicious variety of expertly roasted beans. The flagship "tasting room" location (780 E. Broad St., 706/227-2161, Mon.-Fri. 7am-6pm, Sat.-Sun. 8am-6pm), just east of the main downtown area, is a nice getaway inside a rustic former warehouse. There's a smaller location farther into downtown (297 E. Broad St., 706/613-7449, Mon.-Fri. 6:30am-midnight, Sat.-Sun. 7:30am-midnight) and one south of downtown in the Five Points neighborhood (1230 S. Milledge Ave., 706/208-1979, Mon.-Fri. 6:30am-midnight, Sat.-Sun. 7:30am-midnight), along with several others around town.

Walker's Pub & Coffee (128 College Ave., 706/543-1433, www.walkerscoffee.com, Mon.-Sat. 7am-2am, Sun. 7am-9pm), ironically a couple of doors down from a Starbucks, is, as the name indicates, a hybrid spot: During the day, it's a lounge-worthy coffeehouse, with roomy wooden booths, and after about 10pm, it turns into a full-service bar.

Organic and Vegetarian

The kind of vegetarian and vegan place that even a carnivore could love, ★ **The Grit** (199 Prince Ave., 706/543-6592, www.thegrit.com, Mon.-Fri. 11am-10pm, Sat.-Sun. 10am-3pm and 5pm-10pm, $10) offers fresh, lovingly prepared, and extremely affordable meatless delicacies. Most are locally sourced, such as the grilled seitan steak, scintillating noodle bowls, and the signature must-try black bean chili.

A combination of natural food mecca and fine-dining date spot, ★ **The National** (232 W. Hancock St., 706/549-3450, www.thenationalrestaurant.com, Mon.-Thurs. 11am-3pm and 5pm-10pm, Fri.-Sat. 11am-3pm and 5pm-11pm, Sun. 5pm-10pm, $15-25) has perhaps the most tightly focused rotating menu in the city, all changing with the seasons. A recent visit featured pan-roasted North Carolina trout and a grilled hanger steak with marinated roasted peppers. There are always great veggie and vegan options. Or you could just content yourself with two or three starters, the "pizzettes" being particularly good choices. On Sunday-Tuesday nights they offer a dinner-and-a-movie deal with the Cine BarCafe theater next door.

Pizza

As the often-long line at both locations indicates, the most popular pizza place in town is **Transmetropolitan,** almost always just called "Transmet" (145 E. Clayton St., 706/613-8773, daily 11am-11pm, pizza $10). The vibe is combination college pizza joint, hipster bar, and sports bar. Any of the signature pizzas are great and affordable, with some adventurous options including, yes, the Hungry Sasquatch.

ACCOMMODATIONS

If you're coming to Athens on a graduation weekend or on one of the autumn Saturdays the Bulldogs play here, book your room well in advance or you'll be out of luck. Prices listed are for non-football nights; they double (or triple!) for football weekends.

Under $150

My favorite place to stay in Athens is the ★ **UGA Hotel at the Georgia Center** (1197 S. Lumpkin St., 800/884-1381, www.georgiacenter.uga.edu, $90-200). While constructed to serve as a lodging center for university-based conventions and for alumni, anyone can book a room. The location on campus is unbeatable and the 200 guest rooms and various public spaces are top-notch. Forget about staying here on a football weekend unless you've booked well in advance.

Athens has one B&B of note: **The Colonels** (3890 Barnett Shoals Rd., 706/559-9595, www.thecolonels.net, $115-200), a classic renovated seven-room antebellum farmhouse on historic Angel Oak Farm run by, yes, "Colonels" Marc and Beth. The breakfasts are magnificent. The location is about a 10-minute drive from downtown, but very convenient to the State Botanical Garden.

$150-300

The city's newest lodging, and Athens's first entry in the boutique category, is ★ **Hotel Indigo** (500 College Ave., 706/546-0430, www.hotelindigoathens.com, $145-235). Its swank decor, frequent generous receptions, LEED-certified green attitude, and downtown location make it a no-brainer.

INFORMATION AND SERVICES

Hospitals

The main hospital in town is **Athens Regional Medical Center** (1199 Prince Ave., 706/475-7000, www.athenshealth.org), with a Level II emergency room. Their **Regional FirstCare Clinic** (485 Hwy. 29 N.) offers walk-in service for nonemergencies.

Media

The newspaper of record in Athens is the ***Athens Banner-Herald*** (www.onlineathens.com). However, a more popular media outlet and certainly the one to consult for music and entertainment is the ***Flagpole*** (www.flagpole.com), the independent alt-weekly. Now weekly, ***The Red and Black*** (www.redandblack.com) is run by University of Georgia students, most of them in the journalism school. It is independent from the school administration, however.

The most unique radio station in town is the student-staffed and university-run **WUOG** (90.5 FM), which airs the usual eclectic and quirky blend of indie college rock, Americana, blues, and jazz.

GETTING THERE AND AROUND

Car

The main route to Athens from Atlanta is U.S. 78, the old "Atlanta Highway." It turns into Broad Street when you reach town. The main route into Athens from the south is U.S. 441, which runs into the Athens Perimeter (Hwy. 10), often called "the Loop" or the "Ten Loop," before you hit town.

Public Transit

The Athens city and county government runs a good bus system called simply **The Bus** (www.athenstransit.com, $1.60 per ride, free for UGA students). The Bus runs a UGA football shuttle ($5 round-trip, purchase ticket at airport) on home game Saturdays from Ben Epps Airport to the Arch on North Campus.

Madison and Vicinity

About 30 minutes south of Athens, this charming and well-kept little burg, named for founding father James Madison, routinely tops travel magazines' lists of best small town in the country and provides location sets for movies seeking Old South authenticity. Visitor traffic in Madison (www.madisonga.org) is steady, driven not only by the nostalgically picturesque town itself but also by an upscale real estate boom on nearby Lake Oconee.

Madison likes to market itself as "the town Sherman refused to burn." While technically true—Madison was the home of Unionist senator Joshua Hill, a friend of Sherman's brother—there are plenty of Georgia towns that Union troops spared from the torch. In any case, Madison is well worth a visit, not only to see its eclectic historic district but to enjoy its trim, pleasant vibe.

★ MADISON

The best way to enjoy Madison's sizable historic district is to pick up the official walking tour brochure at the **Madison Visitors**

Madison boasts beautiful antebellum architecture.

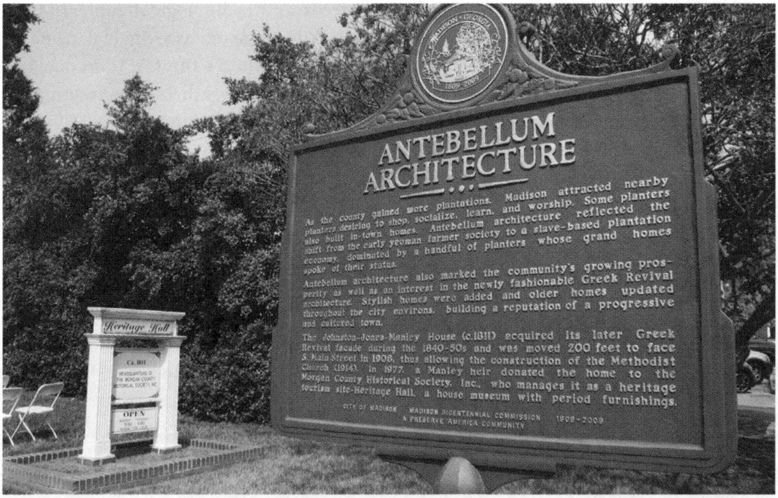

Center (115 E. Jefferson St., 706/342-4454, www.madisonga.org, Mon.-Fri. 9:30am-4pm, Sat. 10am-5pm, Sun. 1pm-4pm), itself inside the 1887 firehouse and original city hall.

Highlights include the magnificent 1811 Greek Revival **Heritage Hall** (277 S. Main St., 706/342-9627, www.friendsofheritage-hall.org, Mon.-Sat. 11am-4pm, Sun. 1:30pm-4:30pm, $7 adults, $3 children), now home of the Morgan County Historical Society and open for tours daily. Other homes of aesthetic and historical significance, now private residences, are the Queen Anne gingerbread-style **Hunter House** (580 S. Main St.) and the **Joshua Hill Home** (485 Old Post Rd.), home of the senator credited with saving Madison from General Sherman's fires. The **Rogers House and Rose Cottage** (179 E. Jefferson St., 706/343-1090, Mon.-Sat. 10am-4:30pm, Sun. 1:30pm-4:30pm, $5 adults, $3 children) are Madison's two house museums, side by side and adorably hard to resist from the outside. The former is a rarely seen Piedmont Plain cottage from the early 1800s, charmingly restored, and the latter is the restored home of Adeline Rose, who built the home after being emancipated from slavery.

The **Madison Museum of Art** (300 Hancock St., 706/485-4530, mmofa.org, call for hours, donation) has a small but intriguing collection of work by European and regional artists. The **Morgan County African American Museum** (154 Academy St., 706/342-9191, www.mcaam.org, Tues.-Sat. 10am-4pm, $5) is actually more of an arts and crafts co-op focusing on African American artists and culture. It features several small but well-curated collections in an adorable 1895 cottage.

Shopping

There are several good antiques stores near each other in the town center, making for a fine afternoon of browsing. Some highlights are three stores owned by the same folks and within shouting distance of each other: sprawling, fascinating **J&K Fleas An'Tiques** (184 S. Main St., 706/342-3009, www.j-and-k-enterprises.com, Mon.-Fri. 10:30am-5:30pm, Sat. 10:30am-6pm, Sun. 1pm-5:30pm), **J&K Antiques Etc.** (159 S. Main St., 706/752-0009, www.j-and-k-enterprises.com, Mon.-Sat. 10:30am-5:30pm), and the consignment shop **Just Out of the Kloset** (179 S. Main St., 706/752-1960, www.j-and-k-enterprises.com, Tues.-Sat. 10:30am-5:30pm).

Food and Accommodations

Madison's fine-dining spot is ★ **Town 220** (220 W. Washington St., 706/752-1445, www.town220.com, Tues.-Thurs. 11am-2:30pm and 5pm-9pm, Fri.-Sat. 11am-2:30pm and 5pm-10pm, $15-30), just behind the James Madison Inn, featuring chef Fransisco De La Torre's hip take on fusion-style cuisine. Your best bet for casual dining is **Madison Chop House Grille** (202 S. Main St., 706/342-9009, daily 7am-10am and 11:30am-9:30pm, $10-15), on the main drag, for killer burgers and fresh salads.

The small and plush boutique hotel **James Madison Inn** (260 W. Washington St., 706/342-7040, www.jamesmadisoninn.com, $190-220) is right off the big town park and offers full concierge service. The guest rooms are remarkably well appointed, both in terms of decor and technological compatibility. Book early; these rooms are in high demand. The ★ **Farmhouse Inn** (1051 Meadow Ln., 706/342-7933, www.thefarmhouseinn.com, rooms $100-170, farmhouse $400-500) offers a delightful getaway-style experience in a charmingly rustic (but not *too* rustic) farm setting on 100 green and glorious acres outside of town.

Information and Services

The **Madison Visitors Center** (115 E. Jefferson St., 706/342-4454, www.madisonga.org, Mon.-Fri. 9:30am-4pm, Sat. 10am-5pm, Sun. 1pm-4pm) is the place to go for brochures and information.

EAST ALONG I-20

Lake Oconee

The second-largest body of water in the state, Lake Oconee benefits from a gated-community boom and robust recreational tourism, including an internationally ranked Ritz-Carlton resort. Most residents live "behind the gates," as locals refer to the plethora of exclusive upscale communities. A good first stop for general visitor information is the **Lake Oconee Welcome Center** (5820 Lake Oconee Pkwy., Mon.-Fri. noon-8pm, Sat. 10am-5pm).

By far the premier property on Lake Oconee is the ★ **Ritz-Carlton Lodge, Reynolds Plantation** (1 Lake Oconee Tr., 706/467-0600, www.ritzcarlton.com, $260-450), one of the nation's top resorts. While more casual in approach than other properties in the brand, the level of attentiveness is everything you'd expect, with a nice retro feel to the buildings themselves. While technically closed to everyone but guests, you can generally get on the grounds if you are dining at one of the facilities. You can book an upscale golf package (starting around $300 per night) at **Reynolds Plantation** (800/800-5250, www.reynoldsplantation.com), which offers 99 holes of golf on five world-class public courses, including the Plantation Course and the Jack Nicklaus-designed Great Waters.

"I Will Make Georgia Howl"

Scorched-earth campaigns have been a part of war for centuries. But the first formal targeting of civilian infrastructure in modern times was **General William T. Sherman**'s infamous **"March to the Sea"** from Atlanta to Savannah during the Civil War. It took little more than a month, but by the time Sherman "gave" Savannah to President Abraham Lincoln as a Christmas present in December 1864, the March would enter Southern mythology as one of the war's most bitter memories, with Sherman himself regarded as satanic.

To keep the Confederates guessing, Sherman originally split his forces, 60,000 strong, into two wings deep in enemy territory with no supply lines—a daring, some said foolhardy, move that defied conventional military theory. The right wing headed toward Macon, while the left wing, farther north, headed to Augusta. Ironically, Sherman himself rode with a bodyguard unit made up entirely of Southerners, the Unionist 1st Alabama Cavalry Regiment.

Sherman's goal wasn't to starve Georgians into submission, but to break their will to resist and destroy confidence in the Confederate Army, to "make Georgia howl," as he told his boss, General Ulysses S. Grant. Sherman wanted his soldiers to feed on the move with local supplies. Foraging Union troops were called "bummers," and their behavior ranged from professional to atrocious. The destruction Sherman intended was for anything Confederates might use for military purposes: mills, manufacturing, bridges, and especially railroads, the tracks heated intensely and twisted into "Sherman's neckties."

So how much destruction did Sherman actually cause? If you travel today in the footsteps of his army, from Madison to Milledgeville, from Forsyth to Swainsboro, you'll see plenty of antebellum structures still standing, used as bed-and-breakfasts, law offices, and private homes. Contrary to reputation, the March's swath of destruction was actually quite narrow. (South Carolina, however, as the cradle of secession, would feel Northern vengeance intensely.)

Also contrary to opinion, Sherman never saw emancipating slaves as a chief goal. As crowds of freed slaves began following his army, Sherman just saw more mouths to feed: In his own orders, "Negroes who are able-bodied and can be of service to the several columns may be taken along, but each army commander will bear in mind that the question of supplies is a very important one and that his first duty is to see to them who bear arms."

Greensboro

Named for Revolutionary War hero Nathanael Greene, little Greensboro (www.visitlakeoconee.com) isn't as energetically marketed as Madison but offers much of the same friendly confidence. The highlight, as far as I'm concerned, is the historic 1807 **Old Gaol** (E. Greene St., 706/453-7592), the oldest jail still standing in Georgia. This sturdy, two-story little fortress has actual dungeons inside and includes an ominous hanging area with a trapdoor, complete with hangman's noose. You have to get the key from the nice folks around the corner at the **Greensboro Chamber of Commerce** (111 N. Main St., 706/453-7592, www.greeneccoc.org, Mon.-Sat. 10am-5pm) on the main drag.

Augusta

Yes, this is the home of the affluently aloof Augusta National Golf Club, which has refused to admit U.S. presidents on more than one occasion. But this is also where you'll find Tobacco Road, as in the actual Tobacco Road of Erskine Caldwell's eponymous novel about hardscrabble life in the Old South during the Great Depression. There it is, right there, on the outskirts of town when you come in on U.S. 25.

SIGHTS

Augusta Riverwalk

There are few better places to enjoy the natural vistas of the Savannah River than the **Augusta Riverwalk** (daily dawn-dusk, free), which stretches for about five city blocks, from 6th to 10th Streets.

In order to better negotiate the steepness of the bluff, the Riverwalk actually comprises two bricked walkways. Access the upper level by ramps at the ends of 10th Street, 8th Street Plaza, and 6th Street; get to the lower level via RiverWalk Marina (5th St.), 8th Street Plaza, the Jessye Norman Amphitheatre, and 10th Street Plaza (in front of the Marriott and where the Morris Museum of Art is located).

Morris Museum of Art

The **Morris Museum of Art** (1 10th St., 706/724-7501, http://themorris.org, Tues.-Sat. 10am-5pm, Sun. noon-5pm, $5 adults, $3 children) has quickly become one of the most important second-tier art museums in the South. The core of its all-Southern collections is the life's gatherings of Robert P. Coggins, whose collection was acquired by the nascent Morris board in the late 1980s.

Augusta Museum of History

Standouts among the well-curated exhibits at the **Augusta Museum of History** (560 Reynolds St., 706/722-8454, www.augustamuseum.org, Tues.-Sat. 10am-5pm, Sun. 1pm-5pm, $4 adults, $3 children) include the Civil War section, the exhibit of Savannah River Edgefield pottery, including works by the renowned Dave "The Slave" Drake, and an homage to Augusta's golf heritage.

James Brown Statue

It took a while, but a bronze commemoration of the Godfather of Soul in his hometown was erected in 2005 in the median of Broad Street between 8th and 9th Streets, within sight of the Imperial Theatre where Brown rehearsed and performed, and a block from the portion of 9th Street renamed James Brown Boulevard, where he shined shoes as a child.

The **James Brown Cam,** installed by the Augusta Arts Council, enables you to dial a number on your cell phone and have a picture taken for download later.

Laney-Walker Historic District

The city's old African American business district is commemorated today in the Laney-Walker Historic District north of

Augusta

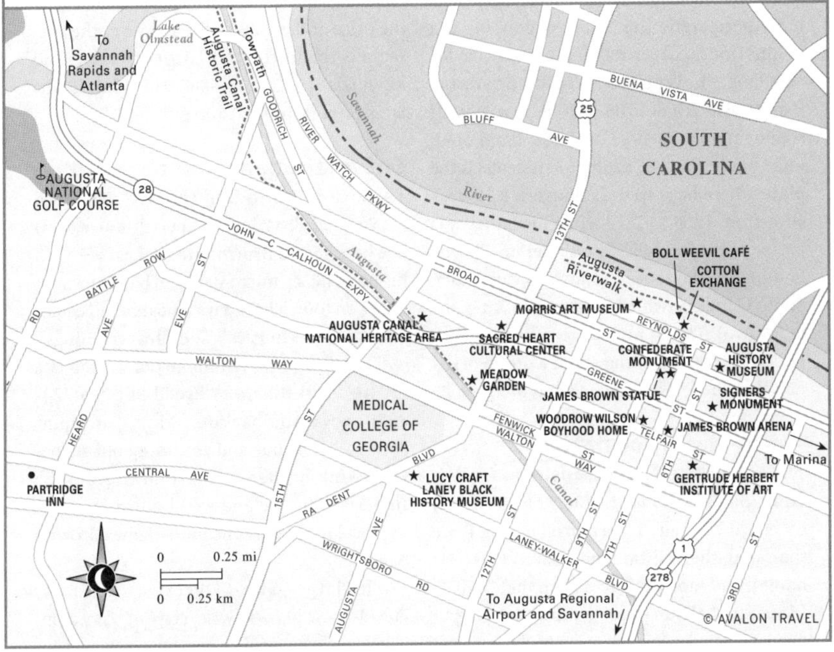

Laney-Walker Boulevard (formerly Gwinnett St.), bounded on the west by Phillips and Harrison Streets and on the east by 7th and Twiggs Streets (Twiggs St. was the boyhood neighborhood of James Brown).

The key attraction in Laney-Walker is the **Lucy Craft Laney Museum of Black History** (1116 Phillips St., 706/724-3546, www.lucycraftlaneymuseum.com, Tues.-Fri. 9am-5pm, Sat. 10am-4pm, $5 adults, $2 children). Ms. Laney herself, whose former home hosts the museum named for her, was one of the first black educators in the South.

Augusta Canal National Heritage Area

Fairly unique among American canals in that it wasn't built for commercial transportation but for hydromechanical power, the Augusta Canal is the South's only industrial canal in continuous use. The **Augusta Canal Interpretive Center** (1450 Greene St., 706/823-0440, www.augustacanal.com, Apr.-Nov. Mon.-Sat. 9:30am-5:30pm, Sun. 1pm-5:30pm, Dec.-Mar. Tues.-Sat. 9am-5:30pm, $6 adults, $4 children, free with $12.50-25 boat tour) at the well-restored Enterprise Mill building is the place to see related exhibits and artifacts and take boat tours on it.

The headgate area is best explored at **Savannah Rapids Park** (3300 Evans to Locks Rd., Martinez, 706/868-3349, www.columbiacountyga.gov, daily dawn-dusk, free) in the next county over. You can launch your own canoe or kayak from a low point along the bank at the launch dock at Petersburg Boat Dock at the headgate.

You can rent a canoe or kayak at **Broadway Tackle & Canoe Rentals** (1730 Broad St., 706/738-8848, www.broadwaytackle.com). The old towpath runs alongside this entire section and can be walked or biked. Get a free self-guided tour map at the Augusta Canal Interpretive Center.

Woodrow Wilson Boyhood Home

A native of Virginia, the future president led a peripatetic life before occupying the White House, never staying in one place for very long. The **Woodrow Wilson Boyhood Home** (419 7th St., 706/722-9828, www.wilsonboyhoodhome.org, Tues.-Sat. 10am-5pm, tours on the hour, $5 adults, $3 students) is the place where he stayed the longest, a 10-year stint from 1860 to 1870 while his father was pastor of the local First Presbyterian Church and before the family's move to Columbia, South Carolina (which boasts a Wilson home of its own). The 14 rooms are furnished with period pieces, including about a dozen originals that the Wilsons owned and used.

Tours and Information

The main city tour is the **Historic Trolley Tour** (560 Reynolds St., 706/724-4067, $12) on board the Lady Liberty trolley. You'll see the canal, the Wilson home, several historic homes, and more. It leaves from the Augusta Museum of History each Saturday at 1:30pm and is roughly two hours; they ask for 24-hour advance reservations. Admission to the Augusta Museum of History is included with the price of the tour. In the atrium of the museum is the **Augusta Visitors Center** (560 Reynolds St., 706/724-4067, Mon.-Sat. 10am-5pm, Sun. 1pm-5pm) and gift shop.

Entertainment and Nightlife

The circa-1918 **Imperial Theatre** (749 Broad St., 706/722-8341, www.imperialtheatre.com) is where James Brown often rehearsed with his notoriously micromanaged bands prior to going on tour. These days it hosts a full calendar of various musicals and film screenings.

The most hallowed nightspot in Augusta is **The Soul Bar** (984 Broad St., 706/724-8880, www.soulbar.com, Mon.-Sat. 4pm-3am), a cavernous and charming old-school rock-punk-hipster dive just down from the Imperial Theatre and well known for hosting local musicians, including James Brown's band.

The larger **Sky City** (1157 Broad St., 706/945-1270, www.skycityaugusta.com,

the Imperial Theatre in downtown Augusta

Mon.-Sat. 6pm-3am), down the road, is where to go for bigger-name touring acts such as Drive-By Truckers and Justin Townes Earle.

If only an Irish pub will do, head straight for **Tipsey McStumble's** (214 7th St., 706/955-8507, Mon.-Sat. 11:30am-3am), reportedly on the site of Augusta's first strip club. The current staff respects that spirit in that the women wear naughty Catholic schoolgirl outfits.

Festivals

Augusta's premier event is **The Masters** (www.themasters.com) golf tournament, which takes place each year on the first full weekend in April. While tickets to the actual weekend competition are notoriously difficult to come by, tickets to the qualifying rounds during the week are actually not so hard to score. Lucky members of the general public can score tickets to the Masters through a lottery system (apply at the website) nearly a full year ahead. Augusta's other event of note is the **Westobou Festival** (www.westoboufestival.com, ticket prices vary), which takes place the first week in October at various downtown venues and features a ton of regional and national performing and artistic talent.

SHOPPING

Head straight to **Artists Row** (www.artistsrowaugusta.com), a delightful consortium of galleries within restored Victorian storefronts, many complete with lofts and wrought-iron balconies, clustered in and around the 1000 block of Broad Street. One of Broad Street's most classically Augustan establishments is the kitschy antiques and bric-a-brac nostalgia market called **Merry's Trash & Treasures** (1236 Broad St., 706/722-3244, www.merrystrashandtreasures.com, Mon.-Fri. 9am-5:30pm, Sat. 9am-5pm). Forty years of history and 25,000 square feet of display space mean you can get a lot here among the various furniture and home goods offerings.

SPORTS AND RECREATION

Spectator Sports

The minor-league **Augusta GreenJackets** (www.milb.com), a single-A farm team of the San Francisco Giants, play at Lake Olmstead Stadium (78 Milledge Rd.). The great and infamous Ty Cobb, who was born near town, once played ball in Augusta.

Golf

If you're a member of **Augusta National Golf Club** (www.masters.com) or an invitee of a member, and hence eligible to play here, you already know who you are. Even to members, it's open for play only a few weeks out of the year. Area public courses include the renovated links-style **Augusta Municipal** (2023 Highland Ave., 706/731-9344, www.thepatchaugusta.com, greens fees $20), aka "the Patch," and a very good state park course over the Savannah River in South Carolina, **Hickory Knob State Resort Park** (1591 Resort Dr., McCormick, SC, 864/391-1764, www.hickoryknobresort.com, greens fees $30-35).

FOOD AND ACCOMMODATIONS

Most Augustans will tell you the best barbecue in town is at **Sconyer's** (2250 Sconyers Way, 706/790-5411, www.sconyersbar-b-que.com, Thurs.-Sat. 10am-10pm, $10). The hickory-smoked 'cue is delicious, with a tangy sauce a cut above the usual too-sweet variety you'll find in other parts of Georgia. You can get a beer here, not a given with most authentic barbecue joints in the Bible Belt. ★ **Boll Weevil Cafe & Sweetery** (10 9th St., 706/722-7772, http://thebollweevil.com, daily 11am-9pm, $20) is Augusta's nod to traditional, classic Southern cuisine. The best hushpuppies—those addictive fried cornmeal fritters renowned throughout the South—I've ever had were at **T's Restaurant** (3416 Mike Padgett Hwy., 706/798-4145, www.tsrestaurant.com,

Tues.-Thurs. 11am-9pm, Fri. 11am-10pm, Sat. 4:30pm-10pm, $10).

With few exceptions, the Augusta hotel scene is dominated by national chains. Keep in mind that during Masters week in early April, accommodations in Augusta and the surrounding area are not only extremely difficult to obtain at the last minute, they are extraordinarily expensive. Augusta's premier accommodations option is the ★ **Partridge Inn** (2110 Walton Way, 706/737-8888, www.partridgeinn.com, $130-150). This hotel and attached spa in a century-old building features 144 guest rooms. For maximum ease of access to the Riverwalk and downtown sights, go straight to the **Augusta Marriott at the Convention Center** (2 10th St., 706/722-8900, www.marriott.com, $150).

GETTING THERE AND AROUND

Augusta is very conveniently located near east-west I-20. A loop highway, I-520, circles the city. Keep in mind that just north of the Savannah River is North Augusta, South Carolina, part of the greater Augusta metro area.

The city is served by **Augusta Regional Airport** (AGS, 1501 Aviation Way, 706/798-3236, www.flyags.com), which hosts flights by Delta and American.

Greyhound (1128 Greene St., 706/722-6411, www.greyhound.com) offers bus service into and out of town. As for public transit, the city runs **Augusta Public Transit** (www.augustaga.gov, $1.25 per ride), with frequent bus routes around town.

OUTSIDE AUGUSTA

Harlem

Named after the famous neighborhood in New York City, Harlem was the birthplace in 1892 of Oliver Hardy, of the famed Laurel and Hardy comedy team. He wasn't here long, but Harlem really plays it up.

The main stop is the **Laurel & Hardy Museum** (250 N. Louisville St., 706/556-0401, www.harlemga.org, Tues.-Sat. 10am-4pm, free) on the main road, where the man's youth and life and times are celebrated in an exhibit and video. Old-timey cars and costumes abound the first weekend of each October as the entire town celebrates their native son's legacy at the **Oliver Hardy Festival** (http://harlemga.org), which brings as many as 30,000 people to this town that is normally home to fewer than 2,000 residents.

Washington

Founded in 1780, the first city in America named after George Washington (the nation's capital didn't bear his name until nearly 20 years later), stately Washington is also possibly the resting place of the legendary missing Confederate gold! In addition to the mythical lost treasure, the city figures large in Southern symbolism as onetime home of Alexander H. Stephens, vice president of the Confederacy, and as the place where Jefferson Davis convened the last meeting of his cabinet on May 5, 1865.

SIGHTS

Robert Toombs House

A hugely influential figure in U.S. and Georgia politics, Robert Toombs was a staunch Unionist for most of his political career (though also a slave-owning planter) who morphed into the state's most vocal advocate of secession. The **Robert Toombs House** (216 E. Robert Toombs Ave., 706/678-2226, www.gastateparks.org, Tues.-Sat. 9am-5pm, tours 10am-4pm, $5 adults, $3 children) brings his life, well, to life with guided tours of this antebellum Greek Revival mansion.

Washington Historical Museum

Run by the Washington-Wilkes Historical Foundation, the **Washington Historical Museum** (308 E. Robert Toombs Ave., 706/678-5001, www.historyofwilkes.org, Tues.-Sat. 10am-5pm, $3) is particularly interesting to Civil War buffs, chiefly because Wilkes County was so well connected at that time.

Tours

The delightful **"Miss Fanny"** (706/318-3128, http://missfanny.com, $20), whose real name is Elaine, gives very entertaining and informative tours that cover dozens of key homes and usually include a few invitations to come inside. And yes, you'll no doubt hear about the lost Confederate gold.

PRACTICALITIES

The well-restored 17-room **Fitzpatrick Hotel** (16 W. Square, 706/678-5900, www.thefitzpatrickhotel.com, $120-225) is oriented to weekend guests, so if you'd like to stay on a weekday, give them a call well ahead of time. The premier B&B in town is the circa-1828 **Washington Plantation Bed & Breakfast** (15 Lexington Ave., 877/405-9956, www.washingtonplantation.com, $160-230), known for its gourmet breakfasts and beautiful seven-acre grounds.

You don't have to look too hard for the best place to eat in town. The ★ **Washington Jockey Club** (5 E. Square, 706/678-1672, www.washingtonjockeyclub.com, Wed.-Thurs. 5pm-9:30pm, Fri.-Sat. 11am-2pm and 5pm-9:30pm, $10-30) is right on the courthouse square. Signature entrées are the pecan chicken and the shrimp and grits. There's also a full-service bar, pretty much the only watering hole in this sleepy town.

The **Washington-Wilkes Chamber of Commerce** (22 W. Square, 706/678-5111, www.washingtonwilkes.org, Mon.-Fri. 10am-4pm), right on the main courthouse square, is where to get brochures and other information.

Savannah River Lakes

The mighty Savannah River forms the border of Georgia and South Carolina, and since the 1950s the U.S. Army Corps of Engineers has controlled its flow. Dams make lakes, and millions come to frolic on three of them on the Savannah River each year; from north to south, they are Lake Hartwell, Lake Russell, and Clark's Hill-Lake Thurmond.

For a general overview, go to www.sas.usace.army.mil. Lakes Hartwell and Thurmond have **campgrounds** (877/444-6777, www.ReserveUSA.com) operated by the Corps. The general websites for reservations and info on Georgia and South Carolina state parks are www.gastateparks.org and www.discoversouthcarolina.com. Many recreation areas and campgrounds close in the off-season, after Labor Day, though most boat ramps stay open all year. Drought conditions can also affect water levels on Lakes Hartwell and Thurmond (Lake Russell is kept near full at all times). Check the Corps website for up-to-date info.

LAKE HARTWELL

Of the three lakes, northernmost Lake Hartwell (www.sas.usace.army.mil), named after Revolutionary War heroine Nancy Hart, has the most upscale feel and is focused more on private docks and private vacation rentals. For full information, stop by the **Hartwell Dam & Lake Office & Visitor Center** (5625 Anderson Hwy., Hartwell, 706/856-0300, year-round Mon.-Fri. 8am-4:30pm, summer

Sat.-Sun. 9am-5:30pm, fall-spring Sat.-Sun. 8am-4:30pm).

Optimized for serious anglers, **Tugaloo State Park** (1763 Tugaloo State Park Rd., 706/356-4362, www.gastateparks.org, office daily 8am-5pm, RV and tent sites $23-30, primitive campsites $15, cottages $135) has one of the biggest boat ramps in the area. There are over 100 RV and tent sites, 5 primitive campsites, and 20 cottages.

Hart Outdoor Recreation Area (330 Hart Park Rd., 706/213-2045, www.gastateparks.org, campsites $19-26, walk-in campsites $19) is a good base of operations for fishing, and also offers self-registration seasonal camping with nice views of the lake (62 sites), as well as 16 walk-in campsites. The boat ramp is open year-round.

Royston

Nestled near the South Carolina line, Royston's main contribution to history is as the hometown of baseball legend Ty Cobb, the "Georgia Peach," whose impressive and often controversial career is memorialized at the **Ty Cobb Museum** (461 Cook St., 706/245-1825, www.tycobbmuseum.org, Mon.-Fri. 9am-5pm, Sat. 10am-4pm, $5 adults, $3 children). The museum is actually inside the Ty Cobb Healthcare Center, a philanthropic legacy of Cobb himself, an astute investor who amassed a large personal fortune.

If you're in the area on a weekend, head straight to ★ **Vanna's Country Barbecue** (Hwy. 17 S., 706/246-0952, Fri.-Sat. 11am-9pm, Sun. 11am-3pm, $5) to get a bite in "beautiful downtown Vanna," a bit south of Royston. While the pulled pork is delectably soft and the Brunswick stew most excellent, I'd head straight for their legendary ribs.

Victoria Bryant State Park

Considered one of the best lesser-known state parks in Georgia, **Victoria Bryant State Park** (1105 Bryant Park Rd., 706/245-6270, www.gastateparks.org, parking $5, campsites $25-28) has a nice creek that runs through the camping area, with 27 tent and RV sites. The highlight is the selection of eight raised-platform tenting sites. The adjacent **Highland Walk Golf Course** (706/245-6770, http://georgiagolf.com, daily from 8am) offers 18 holes.

LAKE RUSSELL

Named after long-serving Georgia senator Richard B. Russell Jr., Lake Russell (www.sas.usace.army.mil) is the youngest of the three lakes. Because it was built after the Water Projects Act of 1974, private development on its shores is prohibited. For more information, stop by the **Russell Dam & Lake Office & Visitors Center** (4144 Russell Dam Dr., 706/213-3400, Mon.-Fri. 8am-4:30pm, Sat.-Sun. 8am-4pm).

Along Lake Russell is one of the gems in the Georgia state park system, **Richard B. Russell State Park** (2650 Russell State Park Rd., 706/213-2045, www.gastateparks.org, parking $5, tent and RV sites $25-28, cottages $130-140). It is home to the 18-hole **Arrowhead Pointe Golf Course** ($45-50) as well as a well-regarded disc golf course. There are only 28 RV and tent sites and no primitive sites, but there are 20 very nice lakefront cottages, two of which are dog-friendly ($40 per dog, maximum two).

CLARK'S HILL LAKE

Clark's Hill Lake is technically called Lake Strom Thurmond (www.sas.usace.army.mil); in 1988 Congress renamed it in honor of the controversial long-serving South Carolina politician. Georgia politicians refused to honor the change, and on Georgia maps it's still called Clark's Hill. It is the oldest of the three Army Corps of Engineers lakes on the Savannah River, and its 70,000 acres make it the largest such project east of the Mississippi. For more info, go across the border into South Carolina and visit the **Thurmond Lake Office & Visitors Center** (510 Clarks Hill

Hwy., Clarks Hill, SC, 864/333-1147, daily 8am-4:30pm).

A great way to enjoy the lake with the family is **Elijah Clark State Park** (2959 McCormick Hwy., 706/359-3458, www.gastateparks.org, parking $5, tent and RV sites $25, walk-in campsites $15, Pioneer campground $35, cottages $120). There are 165 RV and tent sites, 10 walk-in tent sites, the Pioneer campground, and 20 lakefront cottages, two of which are dog friendly ($40 per dog, maximum two).

Bass anglers should head straight to **Mistletoe State Park** (3725 Mistletoe Rd., 706/541-0321, www.gastateparks.org, parking $5, tent and RV sites $25, walk-in campsites $15, backcountry sites $10, cottages $140).

Elberton

The town of Elberton prides itself on being the "Granite Capital of the World." Fittingly, its chief attraction is made of granite as well, specifically the **Georgia Guidestones** (Guidestones Rd.) off Highway 77 north of town, known as "America's Stonehenge" because of the vague resemblance of the 19-foot-tall stones to the Druid monument. The Guidestones, erected in 1980, feature an assortment of New-Agey exhortations in 12 languages, including four ancient tongues.

Middle and South Georgia

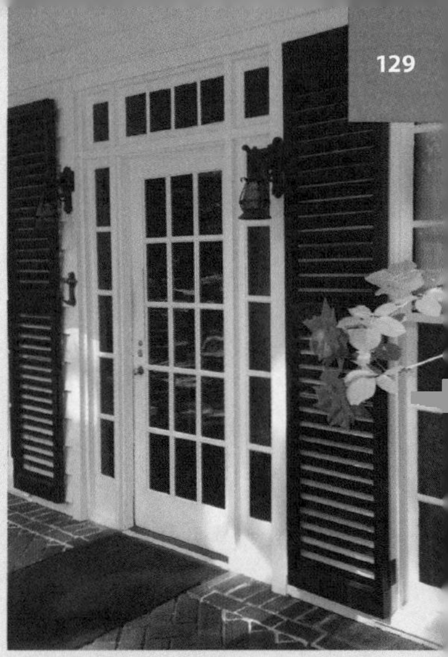

Middle Georgia is full of surprises. Besides being the home of the Allman Brothers and Otis Redding, Macon also has one of the most beautifully ornate cathedrals you'll see outside Europe. Columbus is where the inventor of Coca-Cola was born. President Franklin Roosevelt was inspired by the healing properties of Warm Springs to found the March of Dimes. The nation's first state park was at Indian Springs. And polite Milledgeville once housed the largest insane asylum on the planet.

South Georgia is the least populous part of the state and unquestionably the hottest during the summer. One might be tempted to ask, "Why go to South Georgia?" Where else can you find an entire town devoted almost entirely to celebrating the life and times of a president born there, as is the case with Plains and native son Jimmy Carter? Where else can you find a swamp the size of Delaware, filled with blackwater that is as clean as what comes out of your tap at home, as is the case with the Okefenokee? Where else can you walk in the footsteps of Civil War POWs and visit a stirring national museum devoted to the memory of American POWs from all wars, as you can at Andersonville?

PLANNING YOUR TIME

Basically, there are three routes of particular interest in South Georgia. The area occasionally called "Presidential Pathways" includes sites related to Jimmy Carter as well as the Andersonville POW camp and museum and the Kolomoki Mounds and Providence Canyon sights. Then there's the southern band along the Florida border, with Thomasville as the main stop; and finally, the huge Okefenokee Swamp, taking up virtually the entire southeastern corner of Georgia. The Okefenokee is something of a special case, as you can easily spend several days exploring it or simply confine it to a day trip.

Previous: an alligator in Okefenokee Swamp; the National Civil War Naval Museum in Columbus.
Above: FDR's Llittle White House.

Middle and South Georgia

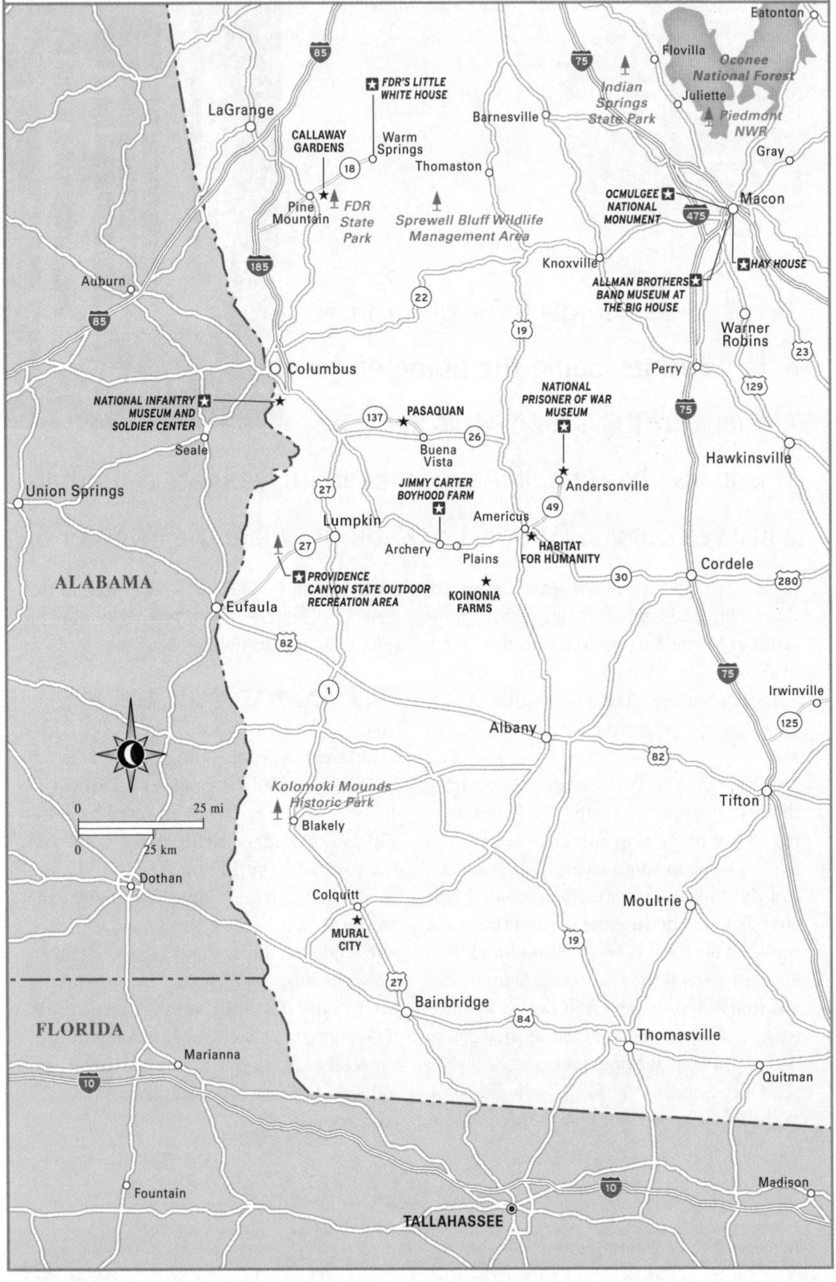

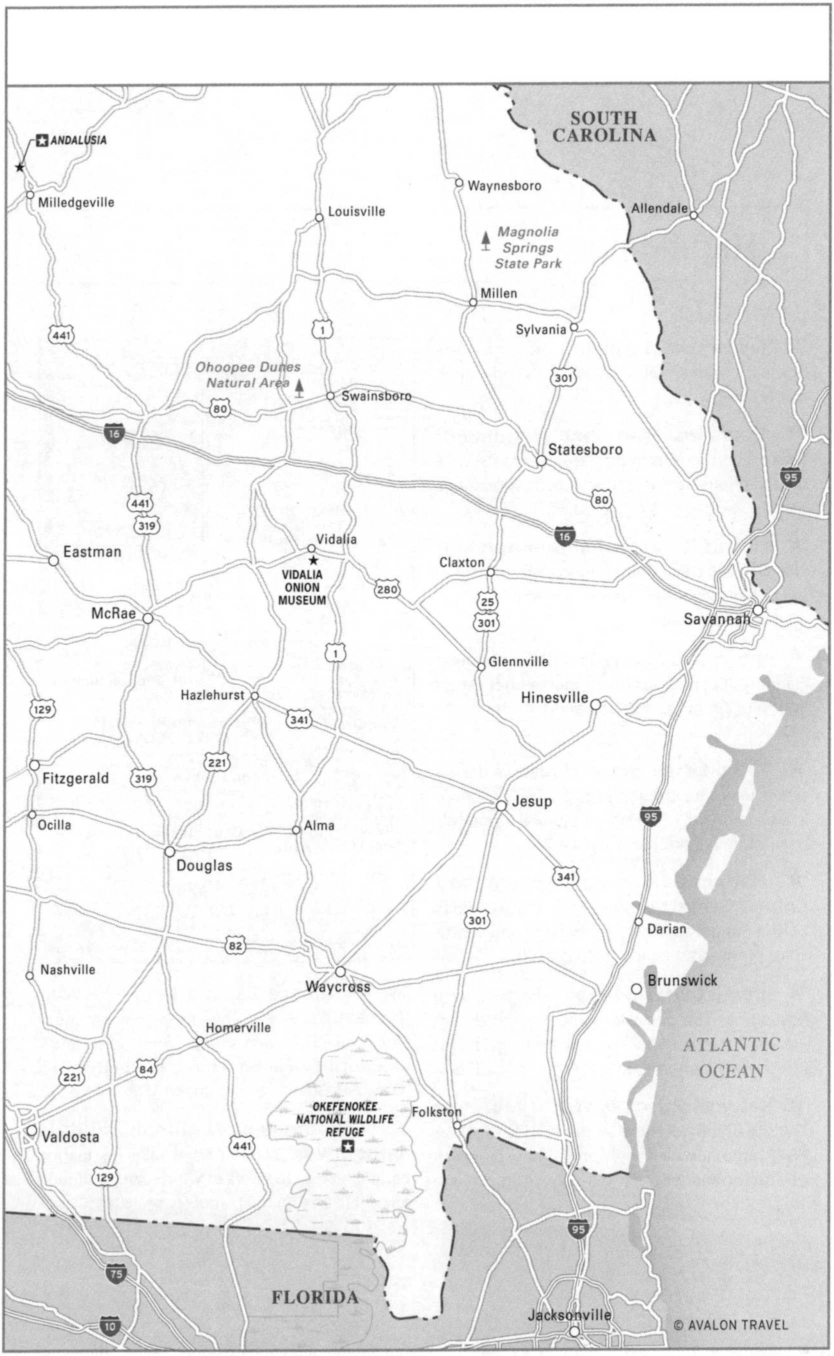
SOUTH CAROLINA
ANDALUSIA
Milledgeville
Louisville
Waynesboro
Magnolia Springs State Park
Allendale
Millen
Sylvania
Ohoopee Dunes Natural Area
Swainsboro
Statesboro
Eastman
Vidalia
VIDALIA ONION MUSEUM
Claxton
McRae
Savannah
Glennville
Hazlehurst
Hinesville
Fitzgerald
Jesup
Ocilla
Alma
Douglas
Darian
Nashville
Waycross
Brunswick
Homerville
ATLANTIC OCEAN
OKEFENOKEE NATIONAL WILDLIFE REFUGE
Folkston
Valdosta
FLORIDA
Jacksonville
441
1
80
16
301
95
319
280
25
129
341
221
82
84
75
10
© AVALON TRAVEL

Look for ★ to find recommended sights, activities, dining, and lodging.

Highlights

★ **Hay House:** One of the South's grandest house museums is also fascinatingly individualistic (page 133).

★ **Ocmulgee National Monument:** These enormous mounds are remnants of a once-glorious Native American civilization (page 135).

★ **Allman Brothers Band Museum at the Big House:** One of the country's favorite bands has a lovingly curated collection of unique memorabilia (page 137).

★ **Andalusia:** Visit the farm where the great Flannery O'Connor authored most of her classic Southern Gothic novels and short stories (page 142).

★ **FDR's Little White House:** A bittersweet look into the life of a pioneering figure is enriched with amazing memorabilia from his transformative presidency (page 146).

★ **National Infantry Museum and Soldier Center:** A stirring look at the exploits of the American fighting soldier comes with state-of-the-art technology (page 150).

★ **Jimmy Carter Boyhood Farm:** Take a nostalgic and insightful look into the Depression-era experiences of the Georgia-born president just outside his hometown of Plains (page 156).

★ **National Prisoner of War Museum:** The site of the notorious Andersonville Civil War POW camp hosts a deeply affecting exploration of cruelty and bravery during wartime (page 157).

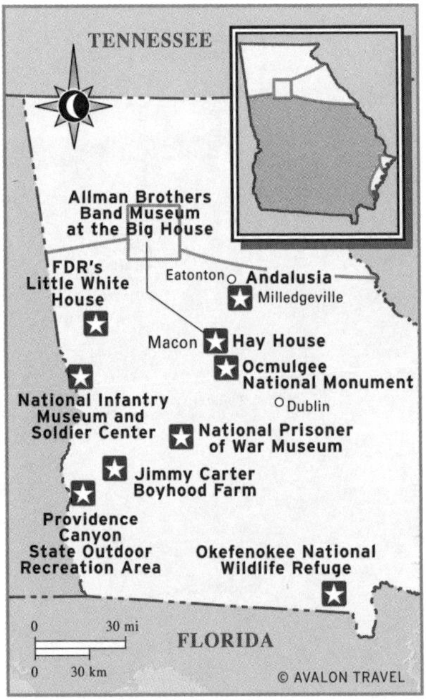

★ **Providence Canyon State Outdoor Recreation Area:** This geological feature of high white walls and a deep floor, surprisingly developed by human impact, has been called "Georgia's Grand Canyon" (page 158).

★ **Okefenokee National Wildlife Refuge:** Visit a vast and wholly fascinating natural feature the likes of which can't be found anywhere else on the planet (page 162).

Macon

It's fitting that Macon is pretty much dead center in the middle of Georgia, since in many ways it's the archetypal Georgia town: laid-back, churchified, heavy on fried food, built by the railroad, surrounded by seemingly endless farmland, and a center of cross-pollinating musical traditions.

SIGHTS

★ Hay House

Easily one of the most splendid and splendidly restored antebellum mansions in the South, the **Hay House** (934 Georgia Ave., 478/742-8155, www.georgiatrust.org, Sept.-Dec. and Mar.-June Tues.-Sat. 10am-4pm, Sun. 1pm-4pm, Jan.-Feb. and July-Aug. Tues.-Sat. 10am-4pm, last tour 3pm, $9 adults, $5 students) in the stately Intown neighborhood is worthy of a tour. Built in the Italian Renaissance Revival style and completed a scant five years before the outbreak of the Civil War, the Hay House was built by William Butler Johnston. It passed into the hands of insurance magnate Parks Lee Hay during the 1920s. The magnificent abode stayed in the Hay family until 1977, when it was given to the Georgia Trust for Historic Preservation.

St. Joseph Catholic Church

Oddly for this rigidly Baptist region, one of the most beautiful and ornate Roman Catholic churches pretty much anywhere is right in Macon's historic Intown neighborhood. **St. Joseph Catholic Church** (830 Poplar St., 478/745-1631, www.stjosephmacon.com, office Mon.-Fri. 9:30am-4:30pm) was completed at the turn of the 20th century, though it harks back to a much older tradition of grand European cathedrals. At the top of the church's left tower, as you face the sanctuary from Poplar Street, you'll see three huge bronze bells, named Jesus, Mary, and Joseph. You can hear them rung daily at 6am, noon, and 6pm.

Sidney Lanier Cottage

Just around the corner from St. Joseph, the **Sidney Lanier Cottage** (935 High St., 478/743-3851, Mon.-Sat. 10am-4pm, last tour 3:30pm, $5 adults, $3 children) is where that

the Hay House in downtown Macon

Macon

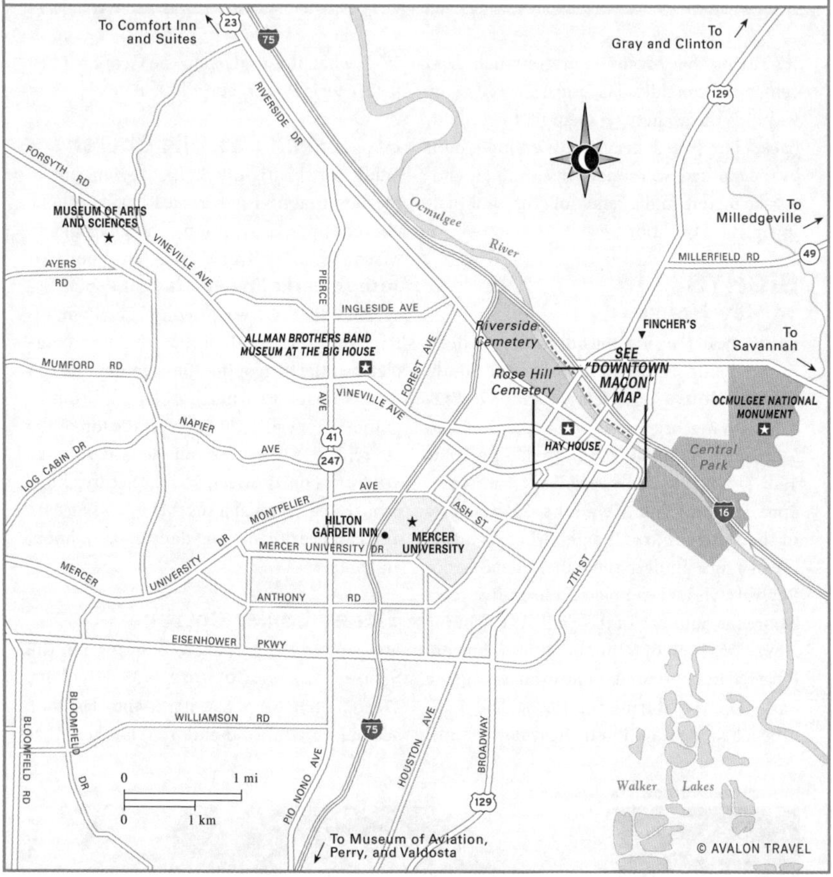

great man of letters was born in 1842; this was actually his grandparents' home at the time. While he didn't live in this house most of his life, he did spend much of his time in the Macon area.

Cannonball House

While General Sherman and his troops left Macon alone, an exchange of artillery fire led to some random shells hitting and embedding themselves into the antebellum **Cannonball House** (856 Mulberry St., 478/745-5982, www.cannonballhouse.org, Jan.-Feb. Mon.-Fri. 11am-last tour at 4:15pm, Sat. 10am-last tour at 4:15pm, Mar.-Dec. Mon.-Sat. 10am-last tour at 4:15pm, $8 adults, $6 students, free under age 4). Tours last 45 minutes and include the main house, with its furnishings and Civil War memorabilia, and the historically notable two-story brick kitchen building with servants quarters.

Grand Opera House

The 1,000-seat **Grand Opera House** (651

St. Joseph Catholic Church

Mulberry St., 478/301-5470, www.thegrandmacon.com, Mon.-Fri. 10am-5pm, showtimes vary), built in 1883, represents the height of Macon's opulent Victorian heyday. While Reconstruction and its aftermath were difficult throughout the South, Macon fared noticeably better than most Southern cities, and "the Grand" is proof.

Museum District

While not all offerings have worked out—the Georgia Music Hall of Fame was forced to close in 2011—Macon does boast its own fledgling museum district in a walkable, renovated section of downtown.

MUSEUM OF ARTS AND SCIENCES

Billing itself as Georgia's largest general-purpose museum, the **Museum of Arts and Sciences** (4182 Forsyth Rd., 478/477-3232, www.masmacon.org, Tues.-Sat. 10am-5pm, Sun. 1pm-5pm, $10 adults, $7 students, $5 ages 2-17) features a wide range of natural history exhibits and regionally oriented historical artifacts.

GEORGIA CHILDREN'S MUSEUM

Four floors of enriching, educational children's activities, some still under development, are the attraction in this handsome building in the heart of downtown, which also includes a decent café for the refreshment of the adults. Highlights of the **Georgia Children's Museum** (382 Cherry St., 478/755-9539, www.georgiachildrensmuseum.com, Tues.-Sat. 10am-5pm, $4) include a hands-on TV studio and an exhibit on the indigenous Creek people.

TUBMAN AFRICAN AMERICAN MUSEUM

Actually more of an art and art-history destination than strictly a historical museum, the **Tubman African American Museum** (340 Walnut St., 478/743-8544, www.tubmanmuseum.com, Tues.-Sat. 9am-5pm, $10 adults, $6 children) explores the African American experience and culture.

★ Ocmulgee National Monument

There are a couple of sites elsewhere with somewhat better-preserved Native American mounds, but none quite so extensive as the sprawling and entirely fascinating **Ocmulgee National Monument** (1207 Emery Hwy., 478/752-8257, www.nps.gov, daily 9am-5pm, free). To early white settlers of the region they were simply called the "Old Fields," but to the Mississippian people that lived here from about 900 to 1650, it was a bustling center of activity, from the enormous temple mound (from the top you can see most of downtown Macon) to the intimate and striking Earth Lodge, which, though completely restored, boasts the only original and unchanged lodge floor in North America.

Begin and end your visit at the charming art deco visitors center. Inside you'll find an extensive series of displays illustrating not

Downtown Macon

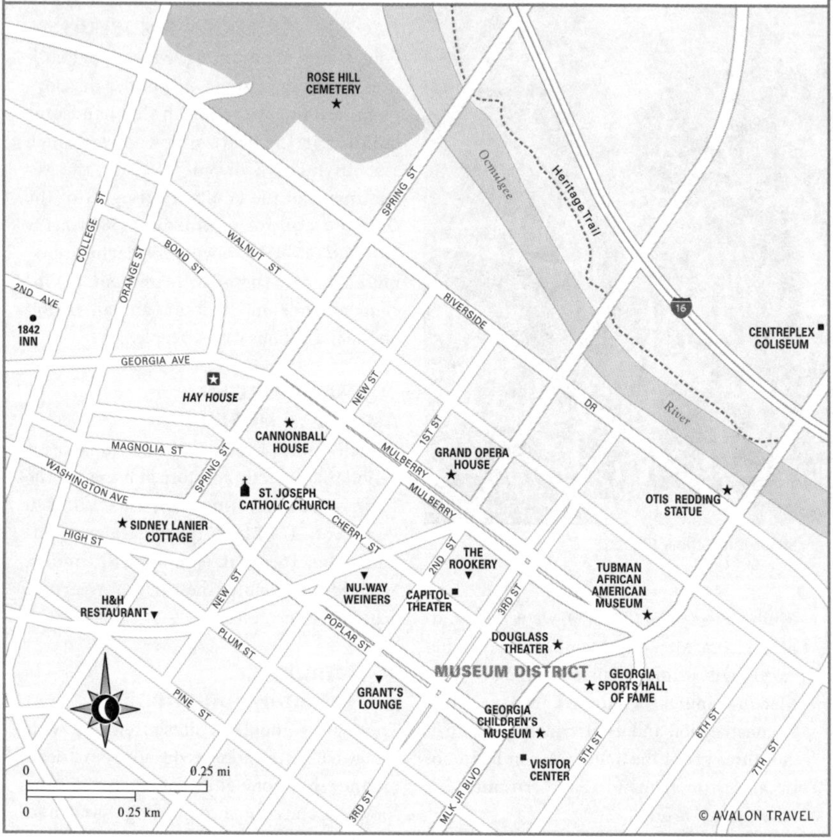

only artifacts from the area, but the scope of Native American life in the region covering at least 17,000 years. From the visitors center you take the trails through the actual mounds, which may not look like much more than grassy knolls until you fully digest the significance of this site, which some scholars say at its peak was more populous than modern-day Macon.

A major planned expansion of the grounds was announced in 2016; check the website for updates.

Otis Redding Statue

Just as you cross the bridge over the Ocmulgee River from downtown into east Macon, on your left you'll see Gateway Park and the beginning of the Ocmulgee Heritage Trail. The key landmark here, however, is the small but well-done memorial plaza to the late great Otis Redding, Macon native and beloved R&B-soul musician who influenced an entire generation before dying in a plane crash at the age of 26. A nice touch is the buried, vandalism-proof speakers surrounding the statue, which play a steady 24-hour diet of Redding songs.

Rose Hill Cemetery

One of two adjacent historic cemeteries along

Ocmulgee National Monument

Riverside Drive, **Rose Hill Cemetery** (1071 Riverside Dr., 478/751-9119, www.historicrosehillcemetery.org, daily dawn-dusk, free) is generally of more interest to visitors. This is where Duane Allman and Berry Oakley are buried side by side; they died in separate motorcycle accidents about a year and three blocks apart. A few feet away, in a separate plot across a walkway, is where Duane's brother Greg Allman was laid to rest after his death in 2017. Allman Brothers fans can also see the poignant graves of "Little Martha" Ellis and Elizabeth Reed, both of whom inspired band tunes.

Riverside Cemetery

While adjacent Rose Hill Cemetery tends to get more attention, **Riverside Cemetery** (1301 Riverside Dr., 478/742-5328, www.riversidecemetery.com, daily dawn-dusk, free) is much more walkable. Notable sites include the poignant Babyland (a late 19th-century plot where small children are buried) and the grave of Charles Reb Messenburg, who, at his request, was buried standing up.

★ Allman Brothers Band Museum at the Big House

If you're any kind of a fan of the Allman Brothers Band, or if the idea of vintage tube amps, beautiful guitars, well-used drums, handwritten set lists, and flamboyant 1970s outfits gets you excited, head straight to the wonderfully done **Allman Brothers Band Museum at the Big House** (2321 Vineville Ave., 478/741-5551, www.thebighousemuseum.com, Thurs.-Sun. 11am-6pm, $8 adults, $4 children). The rambling Tudor mansion, or "Big House," is a very short drive northwest of downtown. It's where the band lived as an extended community from 1970 to 1973, and where many of their iconic hits were written, and it has been beautifully and tastefully restored. In some cases the intent is to replicate rooms where the Allmans and friends hung out; others create light-filled and joyously celebratory display areas for the enormous volume of Allman-related memorabilia and vintage instruments.

Tours and Information

Easily the most distinctive tour in town is **Lights on Macon** (www.lightsonmacon.com), a free, self-guided, illuminated nighttime walking tour available every night of the year. A neighborhood of historic Intown Macon leaves its lights on every night so tourgoers can view at their leisure. Download the

Allman Brothers Tour

Though their family roots are actually in north Florida, perhaps no other musical name is so associated with Macon and middle Georgia as the Allman Brothers Band. Far ahead of their time musically in their sinuous and rhythmic blend of rock, blues, soul, and even country, they were also one of the first true multiracial bands.

Duane and Gregg Allman grew up as competing siblings, with Duane's fiery personality and virtuosic slide guitar work driving their early success. Touring with what would become a close-knit bunch of friends in various incarnations through the mid- to late 1960s, the whole bunch ended up in Macon as the Allman Brothers Band. With the 1969 release of their eponymous debut album, nothing in the rock world—or in Macon, for that matter—was ever the same.

The city is chock-full of Allman sites that have inspired pilgrimages for decades. The band had various residences, including **309 College Street** and **315 College Street,** which was on the cover of the band's first album. The most famous was the "Big House," a large Tudor rented by bassist Berry Oakley and his wife, Linda, and memorialized today in the **Allman Brothers Band Museum at the Big House** (2321 Vineville Ave., 478/741-5551, www.thebighouse-museum.com, Thurs.-Sun. 11am-6pm, $8 adults, $4 children).

Alas, the Allmans' heyday was short-lived. In October 1971 Duane perished in a motorcycle crash at **Hillcrest Avenue and Bartlett Street.** Barely a year later, Oakley died in another motorcycle crash at **Napier and Inverness Avenues.** Both were only 24. They are buried side by side at **Rose Hill Cemetery.** Greg Allman, who passed away in 2017, is laid to rest in a nearby plot a few feet away. At Rose Hill you can also see two gravesites that inspired Allman songs, "Little Martha" Ellis and Elizabeth Napier Reed. The Bond tomb at Rose Hill was on the back cover of the band's debut record.

Not all is gloom and doom, however. Down the road from the Big House you can have the best fried chicken and collard greens for miles around at **H & H Restaurant** (807 Forsyth St., 478/742-9810, www.mamalouise.com, Mon.-Sat. 6:30am-4pm, $12), where the band frequently ate and which features much Allmans memorabilia.

While in Macon, the band's label was **Capricorn Records** (535 D.T. Walton Sr. Way/Cotton Ave.), which, though now in other hands, still retains the old signage and exterior. The actual Capricorn studios were at **536 Martin Luther King Jr. Boulevard;** that exterior can be seen on the *Allman Brothers Band at Fillmore East* album.

the Allman Brothers Band Museum at the Big House

On the Chitlin Circuit

In the days of racial segregation, there was even a color line for music. Thus began the legendary "chitlin circuit" of African American entertainers playing to black audiences, with Macon as a key stop.

While an actual chitlin is an ingredient in Southern food, specifically fried pig intestine, or "chitterling," the chitlin circuit is best exemplified by four enormously influential Georgia artists: **Ray Charles, James Brown,** and two who grew up blocks apart in Macon's Pleasant Hill neighborhood, **Little Richard** and **Otis Redding.**

Richard "Little Richard" Penniman is considered in some circles the real father of rock and roll, emulated by white artists such as Elvis Presley and Jerry Lee Lewis. Little Richard wrote "Long Tall Sally" while working as a dishwasher at **Ann's Tic-Toc Room** (408 Broadway, now Martin Luther King Jr. Blvd.) about a waitress there. It's now a swank bar, but it's still the Tic-Toc Room, and a plaque outside explains the history of the building. A stone's throw away is the restored circa-1921 **Douglass Theatre** (355 Martin Luther King Jr. Blvd.), a major chitlin circuit venue that continues to host a full calendar of shows. Contrary to what many assume, the venue isn't named after early abolitionist Frederick Douglass but rather local black entrepreneur Charles Henry Douglass.

Otis Redding, though born in nearby Dawson, came of age in Macon. It's said that he won so many teen talent shows at the Douglass that he was eventually barred from competing. He sang at the Baptist church (850 Armory Dr.), where his father was pastor.

Redding nearly single-handedly brought chitlin circuit R&B to a white counterculture audience with his short but electrifying headlining appearance at the Monterey Pop Festival in 1967. Redding died in a plane crash only six months later, but his memory lives on at Macon's **Gateway Park,** where he is memorialized with a statue and plaza.

tour guide from the website or get the brochure at the **Downtown Macon Visitor Information Center** (450 Martin Luther King Jr. Blvd., 478/743-3401, www.maconga.org, Mon.-Fri. 9am-5pm, Sat. 10am-4pm). Begin your tour at one of two iconic Macon locations, the Hay House (934 Georgia Ave.) or 1842 Inn (353 College St.). Download a handy free daytime walking tour of downtown Macon at www.maconwalkingtours.com.

For another neat bit of Southern music history, have a cocktail at the **Tic-Toc Room** (408 Broadway, 478/744-0123, Mon.-Sat. 5pm-2am). It's more of a martini bar and swank café these days, but in the days before integration it was a key venue on the "chitlin circuit" of African American entertainment; James Brown, Little Richard, and Otis Redding all performed here. (Little Richard also worked here, and it's said he wrote "Long Tall Sally" about a coworker.)

ENTERTAINMENT AND EVENTS

Nightlife

The premier rock club in town and a key part of Georgia's music history is **Grant's Lounge** (576 Poplar St., 478/746-9191, www.grantslounge.com, Mon.-Sat. noon-2am), the "original home of Southern rock," which still hosts regular live music after over four decades of nourishing the budding careers of Southern names like Lynyrd Skynyrd, Tom Petty, and the Marshall Tucker Band.

Festivals

Without question Macon's premier event is the "pinkest party on earth," the **Cherry Blossom Festival** (www.cherryblossom.com, Mar.), which takes place in mid- to late March to take advantage of the annual blossoming of the city's estimated 300,000-plus Yoshino cherry trees, which are not indigenous but were imported from Japan. Events are varied, from a Bed Race to nightly concerts to, of course, the Cherry Blossom Parade, and take place at various venues, including Cherry

Street downtown, Central City Park (Willie Smokie Glover Dr.), Mercer University, and Wesleyan College. A free trolley takes festivalgoers from spot to spot. While some events and concerts are ticketed, the majority are free and open to the public.

Easily the most unique event in the area is the **Ocmulgee Indian Celebration** (www.nps.gov, Sept.), which takes place on the grounds of the National Park Service-operated Ocmulgee National Monument and celebrates the heritage and culture of the descendants of the Creek people, who built the enormous mound complex here.

FOOD

Because of Macon's central location near several interstate highways, pretty much every type of fast-food and chain restaurant you can think of has an outpost in town. Instead, here are some of the unique and recommended local and regional offerings.

American

With an active bar scene to go along with its well-received menu, ★ **The Rookery Restaurant & Bar** (543 Cherry St., 478/746-8658, www.rookerymacon.com, Mon. 11am-3pm, Tues.-Thurs. 11am-9:30pm, Fri.-Sat. 11am-10pm, Sun. 11:30am-9pm, $8-15) is a great all-purpose stop in the most happening area of Macon's restored downtown, with history back to 1976. Specialties include Betsy's Grilled Pimento Cheese, a Southern delicacy, and a range of great burgers, all half a pound and all named after famous Georgians, from the Allman Brothers (Swiss cheese and mushrooms) to Jerry Reed (pepper jack cheese and jalapeños) to Jimmy Carter (peanut butter and bacon).

Perhaps the most unique restaurant in Macon is **Nu-Way Weiners** (430 Cotton Ave., 478/743-1368, www.nu-wayweiners.com, Mon.-Fri. 6am-7pm, Sat. 7am-6pm, $2-4), which has grown to nine locations in its nearly 100-year history. At all of them you'll find the same inexpensive menu of hot dogs built around Nu-Way's "secret" chili topping.

Soul Food

Allman Brothers fans will know ★ **H & H Restaurant** (807 Forsyth St., 478/742-9810, www.mamalouise.com, Mon.-Sat. 6:30am-4pm, $12) as the band's favorite hangout in Macon, but "Mama Louise" Hudson's place is also one of the best soul food diners anywhere. It's very informal: When you're ready to leave, you come back behind the counter and pay the cook, who also runs the register. The menu is as simple as it has been for the last 50 years; you pick a meat (go with the fried chicken) and three veggies, such as perfect collard greens and their signature squash. The walls are covered with memorabilia of Southern rock, particularly the Allman Brothers, who were taken under Mama Louise's wing during their early days as starving artists.

ACCOMMODATIONS

Under $150

Due to its very central location at the confluence of three interstate highways (I-75, I-475, and I-16), Macon offers a vast range of budget chain accommodations that tend to group in large clusters.

The I-75 cluster is just north of downtown, about a five-minute drive. I'd recommend the **Comfort Inn & Suites** (3935 Arkwright Rd., 478/757-8688, www.comfortinn.com, $75-100) or the pet-friendly **Candlewood Suites** (3957 River Place Dr., 478/254-3531, www.ichotelsgroup.com, $75-100). The densest cluster is off I-475 on the western edge of Macon, with downtown about 10 minutes away. Try **Comfort Inn West** (4951 Eisenhower Pkwy., 478/788-5500, www.comfortinn.com, $75-100), with renovated guest rooms, or the pet-friendly **Sleep Inn West** (140 Plantation Inn Dr., 478/476-8111, www.sleepinn.com, $75-100).

A good budget choice a bit closer to downtown is the **Hilton Garden Inn** (1220

Stadium Dr., 478/741-5527, www.hilton.com, $130) adjacent to the tranquil Mercer University campus.

$150-300

The premier lodging in Macon is the ★ **1842 Inn** (353 College St., 478/741-1842, www.1842inn.com, $140-255), and I urge you to make every effort to secure a room if you're planning to visit the city. It's in a particularly striking Greek Revival building that was once the home of a mayor, with "opulent" a fair description of its interior. Ten of the inn's 19 guest rooms are in the main building, which boasts a classic wraparound veranda with 17 columns. There's a separate Victorian Cottage, which was actually moved onto this parcel of land in the 1980s and has nine guest rooms.

SOUTH OF MACON

Museum of Aviation

There's one very worthwhile reason to visit the town of Warner Robins, 14 miles south of Macon, and that's the excellent **Museum of Aviation** (Russell Pkwy., 478/926-6870, www.museumofaviation.org, daily 9am-5pm, free) on the massive Robins Air Force Base. Comprising several very large buildings with roughly outlined chronological themes, the core collection of the museum is its impressive array of many, many dozens of military aircraft from all eras of American aviation. Airplane buffs of all ages will go nuts seeing these beauties up close, from World War II classics like the P-51 Mustang to the host of Cold War and Vietnam War-era jets to the starkly elegant U-2 and SR-71 spy planes. A nice plus with the museum is that, despite being on a military installation, it's in an area where you don't have to go through the usual checkpoints for your driver's license and proof of car insurance.

INFORMATION AND SERVICES

The centrally located **Downtown Macon Visitor Information Center** (450 Martin Luther King Jr. Blvd., 478/743-3401, www.maconga.org, Mon.-Sat. 9am-5pm, Sat. 10am-4pm) is in the offices of the local convention and visitors bureau and is a must-stop. For those who prefer a visitors center off the interstate highway, go to the I-75 **Southbound Rest Area** (478/994-8181, info kiosk Mon.-Fri. 9am-5pm), a mile south of exit 181.

GETTING THERE AND AROUND

Macon is extraordinarily well served by the interstate highway system. I-75 passes through town north-south, and the western terminus of I-16 is here.

The small **Middle Georgia Regional Airport** (MCN, 1000 Terminal Dr., 478/788-3760, www.cityofmacon.net) hosts flights by Silver Airways to Atlanta and Orlando.

Macon is served by **Greyhound** (65 Spring St., 478/743-5411, www.greyhound.com). In town, the **Macon Transit Authority** (www.mta-mac.com, $1.25) runs buses and trolleys on various routes.

Milledgeville

Milledgeville may not get as much attention as some other cities in Georgia, but it's worth a visit and is actually vital to the state's history. It served as state capital during the antebellum era—Atlanta didn't get that title until after the Civil War—and so boasts more than its share of intriguing political shenanigans. Milledgeville's eccentric combination of lively social gatherings and Southern Gothic darkness meant that it was the perfect breeding ground for writer Flannery O'Connor's brand of darkly humorous symbolic fiction.

SIGHTS

Old Governor's Mansion

One of the preeminent examples of Greek Revival architecture in the country, the **Old Governor's Mansion** (120 S. Clark St., 478/445-4545, www.gcsu.edu, Tues.-Sat. 10am-4pm, Sun. 2pm-4pm, $10 adults, $2 children) was built in Georgia's antebellum heyday in the late 1830s. It hosted 10 Georgia governors and their families, until Atlanta became the state capital in 1868. It also briefly hosted General Sherman, who made it his headquarters during a portion of his March to the Sea. Tours begin at the top of each hour, and self-guided tours are not possible. There's a cute gift shop in a well-restored outbuilding to the mansion's rear.

Stetson-Sanford House

A great example of the local "Milledgeville federal" architectural style, the **Stetson-Sanford House** (601 W. Hancock St., 478/453-1803, www.oldcapitalmuseum.org, Thurs.-Sat., visit via Milledgeville Trolley Tours) was originally on North Wilkinson Street and hosted visiting dignitaries during Milledgeville's tenure as state capital. You can visit by taking a trolley tour; go to the Milledgeville Visitors Center (200 W. Hancock St.) to catch the trolley (Mon.-Fri. 10am, Sat. 2pm, $12 adults, $5 children).

★ Andalusia

On a 550-acre plot of wooded land north of the city center, **Andalusia** (U.S. 441, 4 miles northwest of Milledgeville, 478/454-4029, www.andalusiafarm.org, Mon.-Tues. and

Flannery O'Connor wrote her famous works at Andalusia.

Finding Flannery

Though born and raised in Savannah, Flannery O'Connor attended college in Milledgeville and did the bulk of her writing here. Her family had deep roots in the area and their imprint is felt all over town. Here are some related sites:

Her first home here is the **Cline-O'Connor-Florencourt House** (311 W. Greene St.), now a private residence, where she lived until her beloved father's early death from lupus (a hereditary disease that would later claim her life as well). As an aside, this handsome building briefly served as the governor's residence in the 1830s; indeed, it's a stone's throw from the grand Old Governor's Mansion.

Flannery and family faithfully attended **Sacred Heart Catholic Church** (110 N. Jefferson St.), which was actually built on land donated to the church by her great-grandmother. After her father died, Flannery became quite close with her mother, Regina Cline O'Connor, and the two often lunched at the tearoom and enjoyed peppermint chiffon pie in the **Stetson-Sanford House** (601 W. Hancock St., 478/453-1803, www.oldcapitalmuseum.org), now a house museum.

During World War II, Flannery attended Georgia State College for Women, now Georgia College & State University. Visit the **Flannery O'Connor Room** of the college museum to see vintage photos and personal items, including the manual typewriter on which those amazing novels and short stories were written.

The major stop is at **Andalusia** (U.S. 441, 4 miles northwest of Milledgeville, 478/454-4029, www.andalusiafarm.org, Mon.-Tues. and Thurs.-Sat. 10am-4pm, $5 donation), the ancestral Cline-O'Connor family dairy farm. After studying at the prestigious University of Iowa Writer's Workshop writing program and a brief stay at the Yaddo writer's retreat in New York, O'Connor was diagnosed, as she feared, with lupus. She returned to Milledgeville under the burden of the pessimistic prognosis to live out her days with her mother and write in the downstairs parlor, converted into a bedroom.

However, Flannery defied expectations and lived another 14 years at Andalusia before passing away at the age of 39. Visit her simple gravesite at **Memory Hill Cemetery** (Liberty St. and Franklin St., www.friendsofcems.org, daily 8am-5pm). Well-wishers often leave a single peacock feather at her tomb in memory of Flannery's well-known fondness for "the king of the birds."

Thurs.-Sat. 10am-4pm, $5 donation) is the name given to the dairy farm of the O'Connor family, where iconic Southern writer Flannery O'Connor lived most of her adult life. She wrote all her major works in a bedroom on the ground floor of the main house, actually a parlor converted so that the ailing Flannery, suffering from lupus, wouldn't have to climb the stairs (her crutches are right there by the bed).

Five rooms are open for viewing: Flannery's bedroom, the kitchen area, the dining room, a porch area with displays and a video, and an upstairs bedroom, plus there's a small reception area with a small but delightful selection of unique O'Connor-related items, some of them created by family members still in the area. Most of the furnishings are original, even the refrigerator.

The entrance to Andalusia isn't particularly obvious; heading north out of Milledgeville, pass the Wal-Mart on your left, then look for a Babcock furniture store on the right. The driveway entrance is directly across U.S. 441 on the left.

Central State Hospital

Fans of poignant abandoned sites will find themselves drawn to the evocative decay of the sprawling 1,700-acre Central State Hospital, one of the oldest in the United States and at one time the biggest. However, while you can drive around the buildings, you may not trespass within. You'll have to content yourself with a visit to the **Central State Hospital Museum** (620 Broad St., 478/445-4878, www.centralstatehospital.org, by appointment, free) in the old 1891 depot on the hospital campus, which chronicles the history of this darkly fascinating institution.

In 1837 the state legislature authorized a "State Lunatic, Idiot, and Epileptic Asylum," which admitted its first patient in 1842. By the time it was renamed again in 1967 as Central State Hospital, it was the largest mental hospital in the country. Shock therapy was common, as was outright neglect and abuse.

Today, the bulk of the 150 years' worth of buildings, some of them oddly ornate, are vacant and unused, except for the tortured ghosts that many swear walk the halls and stairwells each night.

Georgia College & State University Museums

Georgia's dedicated public liberal arts university, which has a variety of buildings all over downtown, offers a trio of small but solid museums, all free of charge. **Georgia College Museum** (221 N. Clark St., 478/445-4391, www.gcsu.edu, Mon.-Sat. 10am-4pm, free) is primarily known for its Flannery O'Connor Room, a repository of personal items specific to the Milledgeville-based author, including mementos from her time at the college. The highlight is the manual typewriter on which she typed most of her works. The **Natural History Museum and Planetarium** (Herty Hall, W. Montgomery St. and N. Wilkinson St., 478/445-2395, www.gscu.edu, Mon.-Fri. 8am-4pm, first Sat. of month 10am-4pm, free) features a region-leading collection of fossils and other paleontology-related artifacts as well as a state-of-the-art digital planetarium. The **Museum of Fine Arts** (102 S. Columbia St., 478/445-4572, www.gcsu.edu, by appointment, free) is housed in the beautiful restored 1935 Napier-Underwood House.

FOOD AND ACCOMMODATIONS

The "satellite location"—if that phrase can be used for such an old-school institution—of the original location in Gray, ★ **Old Clinton BBQ** (2645 N. Columbia St., 478/454-0084, www.oldclintonbbq.com, Mon.-Thurs. 10am-8pm, Fri.-Sat. 10am-9pm, Sun. 10am-4pm, $5) is considered one of Georgia's top-tier barbecue spots. Their sauce, atypical for Georgia, is of the tangier North Carolina variety. A full platter with the works is under $7, and a no-frills pulled-pork sandwich less than $3.

The premier accommodations in Milledgeville are at the ★ **Antebellum Inn** (200 N. Columbia St., 478/453-3993, www.antebelluminn.com, rooms $110-150, cottage $170), which has five guest rooms in the Greek Revival main house plus an adorable pool cottage with a full-size pool, quite a rarity for B&Bs in these parts. Standard hotels in the area aren't very impressive, but you might try the **Holiday Inn Express** (1839 N. Columbia St., 877/859-5095, www.hiexpress.com, $80-110).

NORTH OF MILLEDGEVILLE

Eatonton

A short drive from Milledgeville in Putnam County is the small, neat town of Eatonton (http://eatonton.com), whose main claim to fame is as the birthplace of writers Joel Chandler Harris and Alice Walker. Don't be deceived by the moribund main drag of U.S. 441 through town; Eatonton has some magnificent antebellum architecture one block west, on Madison Avenue.

The **Uncle Remus Museum** (214 Oak St., 706/485-6856, www.uncleremusmuseum.org, Mon.-Sat. 10am-5pm, Sun. 2pm-5pm, free) is right on the main drag on the site of the original homestead of Joseph Sidney Turner, the "Little Boy" in the classic folk tales told by Uncle Remus and chronicled by Joel Chandler Harris. The small but charming museum is within a log cabin, which actually comprises three slave cabins moved from a nearby location and intended to simulate Remus's cabin.

There isn't a museum about Alice Walker, but Eatonton markets the **Alice Walker Driving Trail** that includes her girlhood church, Wards Chapel AME Church. Get

the Uncle Remus Museum in Eatonton

the tour brochure at the **Eatonton-Putnam Chamber of Commerce** (305 N. Madison Ave., 706/485-7701, Mon.-Fri. 9am-5pm).

INFORMATION AND SERVICES

Pick up your brochures and tour info at the friendly **Milledgeville Visitors Center** (200 W. Hancock St., 478/452-4687, Mon.-Fri. 9am-5pm, Sat. 10am-4pm). While you're there, make sure you get the Milledgeville Historic Walking Tour brochure, a particularly well-done, user-friendly, and attractive little document. This is also where you can catch the **Guided Trolley Tour** (Mon.-Fri. 10am, Sat. 2pm, $12 adults, $5 children), including visits to the Old State Capitol and Lockerly Hall.

FDR Country

As you'll quickly notice from all the things named after him here, this entire area reflects the enormous impact of President Franklin D. Roosevelt (FDR). As governor of New York, FDR began visiting the town now called Warm Springs, eventually building his picturesque Little White House here, today a state historic site and museum. The expansive FDR State Park near Pine Mountain isn't only a mecca for area hikers, it also commemorates the president's legacy of community building and conservation, with some particularly well-preserved Depression-era Civilian Conservation Corps-built structures enjoyed by visitors to this day.

WARM SPRINGS

While Warm Springs owes its fame to FDR, the healing properties of its natural spring were well known to the indigenous Creek people. In the 18th and 19th centuries, the town, originally called Bullochville, was a familiar name to Southerners seeking relief from various ailments.

Franklin D. Roosevelt, at the time the governor of New York, began visiting the therapeutic springs in 1924, purchasing the historic Meriwether Inn and the 1,700 acres that the now-demolished building stood on. The 88°F water from sources deep within the surrounding hills (milder than the near-scalding water that some natural spas are known for) gave the town its more descriptive modern name. The gently warming, mineral-infused springs aided the management of Roosevelt's debilitation from polio.

★ FDR's Little White House

While Franklin D. Roosevelt began visiting Warm Springs in 1924, it wasn't until 1932—the year he was first elected president—that he had the charming six-room **Little White House** (401 Little White House Rd., 706/655-5870, www.gastateparks.org, daily 9am-4:45pm, $12 adults, $7 children) built from Georgia pine in a wooded area down the road from the town center. (The first building you'll see when walking toward the Little White House from the entrance building and museum is actually a servants quarters.)

While the president enjoyed all the amenities you'd expect, including a cook, a live-in secretary, servants, and constant U.S. Marine and Secret Service protection, the estate has a cozy and rustic feeling. Fascinating memorabilia are on hand, all arranged as they might have been during FDR's 16 visits here during his presidency.

While the Little White House itself is well worth seeing, the state of Georgia oversees the extensive **FDR Memorial Museum** on-site, contiguous with the entrance building and gift shop. Here you'll learn not only about FDR's political career but about his life and times in Warm Springs and how that community shaped some of his domestic policies.

Roosevelt Warm Springs Institute for Rehabilitation

Right around the corner from the Little White House on U.S. 27 is the **Roosevelt Warm Springs Institute for Rehabilitation** (6135 Roosevelt Hwy., 706/655-5670, www.rooseveltrehab.org, daily 9am-5pm, free), on the site of FDR's first land purchase in the Warm Springs area. It's a working hospital, not an attraction, but you can take a free self-guided tour of the grounds. Note the Roosevelt Warm Springs Institute is not the same as the FDR Historic Pools site. Both are on U.S. 27 and both have entrances on the same side of the road, which confuses a lot of visitors, but they are separate entities.

FDR Historic Pools and Springs

Just down the road from the Roosevelt Warm Springs Institute are the **FDR Historic Pools and Springs** (U.S. 27, 706/655-5870, www.

FDR's Little White House

gastateparks.org, daily 9am-4:45pm, $10, includes admission to the Little White House). At this simple, lovingly curated site, you can walk around the famous pools (usually empty) in which the president enjoyed the healing spring waters from beneath the nearby hills.

The pools are used occasionally, specifically on Labor Day each year, when they are open to the public. You have to sign up in advance, though, and swim time is limited to 90 minutes per person.

If you visit the Little White House, admission to the historic pools is included. Note the historic pools are not on the campus of the Roosevelt Warm Springs Institute, which is just down the road. Though both sites use the same spring water, they are unaffiliated and have completely separate entrances.

Food and Accommodations

The classic Warm Springs experience is a stay at the ★ **Warm Springs Hotel** (47 Broad St., 706/655-2114, www.hotelwarmspringsbb.org, $65-160) on the little main block. During the Roosevelt era, this circa-1907 inn hosted luminaries from all over the world who came to visit the president at the Little White House, including the king and queen of Spain. The guest rooms are cute and come in all sizes, hence the wide range of rates. The associated Tuscawilla Soda Shop downstairs is a great place for a cool drink or some tasty ice cream and fudge, in addition to being historic in its own right: FDR often snacked here.

For other dining, I strongly recommend heading north a few minutes to Pine Mountain, which offers a much better and wider variety of food options. However, if you simply must eat in Warm Springs, try **Mac's Barbecue** (5711 Spring St., 706/655-2472, daily 11am-8pm, $5), about one minute's walk from the Warm Springs Hotel.

PINE MOUNTAIN

The thoroughly charming little burg of Pine Mountain, while owing much of its current success to the nearby Callaway Gardens attraction, is worthy of a visit in and of itself. The main town area consists of a couple of well-restored blocks of shops and cafés, two very good barbecue spots, and the friendly little **visitors center** (101 Broad St., 706/663-4000, www.pinemountain.org, Mon.-Sat. 10am-5pm).

Callaway Gardens

It's a bit hard to describe **Callaway Gardens** (17800 U.S. 27, 800/225-5292, www.callawaygardens.com, daily 9am-5pm, $20 adults, $10 children) to those who don't know anything about it. Part nature preserve, part kids' theme park, part retiree playground, and part recreational dream, its 13,000 acres encompass all those pursuits as gracefully as could reasonably be expected.

Most visits start with a walk through the $12 million **Virginia Hand Callaway Discovery Center,** which features info kiosks and an orientation video in the big theater. A particular highlight at Callaway is the **Cecil B. Day Butterfly Center,** one of the largest butterfly observatories in North America. This LEED-certified building hosts at least 1,000 butterflies at any given time. The **John A. Sibley Horticultural Center** is a five-acre designed landscape featuring a hybrid garden-greenhouse-indoor waterfall area. Other offerings include a regular birds-of-prey show, a zip line, a beach, stocked fishing lakes, a nearly 10-mile bike trail, and miles of themed nature and garden walking trails. The annual Christmas lights show is always a huge hit.

Callaway Gardens' famous **Mountain View Golf Course** has hosted PGA events in the past and is a consistently high-rated course at the national level. The older course, **Lake View,** is less challenging but more scenic and quietly enjoyable.

Callaway Gardens' well-stocked lakes are known far and wide among anglers. **Mountain Creek Lake** is particularly known for its bass fishing; you can rent a boat or even go on a guided fishing trip. **Robin Lake** at Callaway Gardens bills itself as the world's largest artificial white-sand beach, stretching for a mile around the huge lake.

FDR State Park

It's fitting that **Franklin D. Roosevelt State Park** (2970 Hwy. 190, 706/663-4858, www.gastateparks.org, daily 7am-10pm, parking $5) would bear the president's name, since the circa-1935 park was one of the first built under the auspices of his now-legendary Civilian Conservation Corps (CCC). Of course, it had a head start; Roosevelt owned most of the land that the park now sits on.

Georgia's largest state park, the centerpiece is the 23-mile **Pine Mountain Trail.** The historic main building and ranger station offers numerous trail maps; you'll need one if you plan on doing any serious hiking. Pay a visit to **Dowdell's Knob,** the highest point in the park, where the president enjoyed picnics. Several of the cottages in the park are original CCC-era constructions. Take a dip in the historic **Liberty Bell Swimming Pool,** also a CCC project and a very enjoyable pool fed by natural springs.

Food

I recommend dining in town rather than at the Callaway Gardens facilities if you can. If barbecue's your thing, head straight to ★ **The Whistlin' Pig Cafe** (572 S. Main Ave., 706/663-4647, Mon.-Sat. 10:30am-3pm, $7), a real local favorite that's also known far and wide for its pulled pork, absolutely out-of-this-world ribs, and excellent Brunswick stew. Don't confuse it with **Three Lil Pigs** (146 S. Main Ave., 706/307-7109, daily 11am-7pm, $7, cash only), which is not far away on the same side of the road and also has a local following. Stick with the pig that whistles.

If you must eat at Callaway Gardens, the best bet is the **Country Kitchen** (17800 U.S. 27, 800/225-5292, www.callawaygardens.com, Sun.-Thurs. 8am-8pm, Fri.-Sat. 8am-9pm, $12), inside the Country Store, with offerings a cut above the usual meat-and-three Southern fare at diners like this all over Georgia.

Accommodations

UNDER $150

A surprisingly good stay for a low rate can be found at the **Days Inn & Suites** (368 S. Main Ave., 706/663-2121, www.daysinn.com, under $100) in Pine Mountain near Callaway Gardens. A nice B&B experience is in the heart of Pine Mountain proper at the charming **Chipley Murrah House** (207 W. Harris St., 706/663-9801, www.chipleymurrah.com, $95-150), with four guest rooms in the main house and three cottages.

Franklin D. Roosevelt State Park is one of Georgia's oldest.

$150-300

Callaway Gardens (17800 U.S. 27, 800/225-5292, www.callawaygardens.com) offers a variety of lodging, mostly geared for family getaways and often offering packages that include park admission. For larger families and groups, cottage and villa stays are available from about $300 per night. The 150-room ★ **Lodge at Callaway Gardens** (4500 Southern Pine Dr., 706/489-3300, www.callawaygardens.com, from $220), actually a Marriott property, is the choice for swank upscale lodging, complete with a large beautiful pool area and the on-site Spa Prunifolia. Packages that include park admission are available.

CAMPING

If camping or cabin life is your thing, choose among the 22 cottages and 140 tent and RV campsites offered at historic **FDR State Park** (2970 Hwy. 190, 706/663-4858, www.gastateparks.org, parking $5, primitive campsites $9 pp, tent and RV sites $25, cottages $100-135, 5-night minimum). Many of the tent and RV sites are on scenic Lake Delanor, which also has canoe rental. There are 16 primitive campsites as well along the Pine Mountain Trail.

INFORMATION AND SERVICES

The **Pine Mountain Visitors Center** (101 Broad St., 706/663-4000, www.pinemountain.org) provides a range of information for the entire area. The tiny **Warm Springs Welcome Center** (1 Broad St., 706/655-3322, hours vary) is in a restored train depot.

Oconee Regional Medical Center (821 N. Cobb St., Milledgeville, 478/454-3505, www.oconeeregional.com) provides a full range of emergency care.

GETTING THERE AND AROUND

U.S. 27 is the main route into and out of Warm Springs. The Pine Mountain area and all other FDR-related sites are along Highway 190.

Columbus

Unlike some of the more visually monotonous rural areas of Georgia, the state's western edge is scenically inviting and has a gently rolling landscape. Billing itself as the last city founded in the original 13 colonies and site of the last engagement of the Civil War, Columbus has retained a robust presence into the 21st century, due in no small part to its very close association with the massive U.S. Army installation at Fort Benning.

In recent years, downtown revitalization and the long, scenic Riverwalk on the Chattahoochee River have sparked visitor interest. To the world at large, however, Columbus is best known as the hometown of several key figures in Southern arts and commerce: author Carson McCullers *(The Heart Is a Lonely Hunter),* "Mother of the Blues" Ma Rainey, Coca-Cola inventor John Pemberton, and longtime Coca-Cola president and philanthropist extraordinaire Robert Woodruff.

SIGHTS

National Civil War Naval Museum

It surprises many people to hear that the **National Civil War Naval Museum** (1002 Victory Dr., 706/327-9798, www.portcolumbus.org, Sun.-Mon. 12:30pm-4:30pm, Tues.-Sat. 10am-4:30pm, $7.50 adults, $6 children) is located far away from the nearest ocean, but any Civil War buff will tell you that naval warfare during that conflict was mostly of a riverine nature, not out on the deep blue sea. That said, all maritime phases of the war are well represented here, from coastal to blue water.

Both the Civil War Naval Museum and the National Infantry Museum at Fort Benning are located off Victory Parkway, a short drive

Columbus

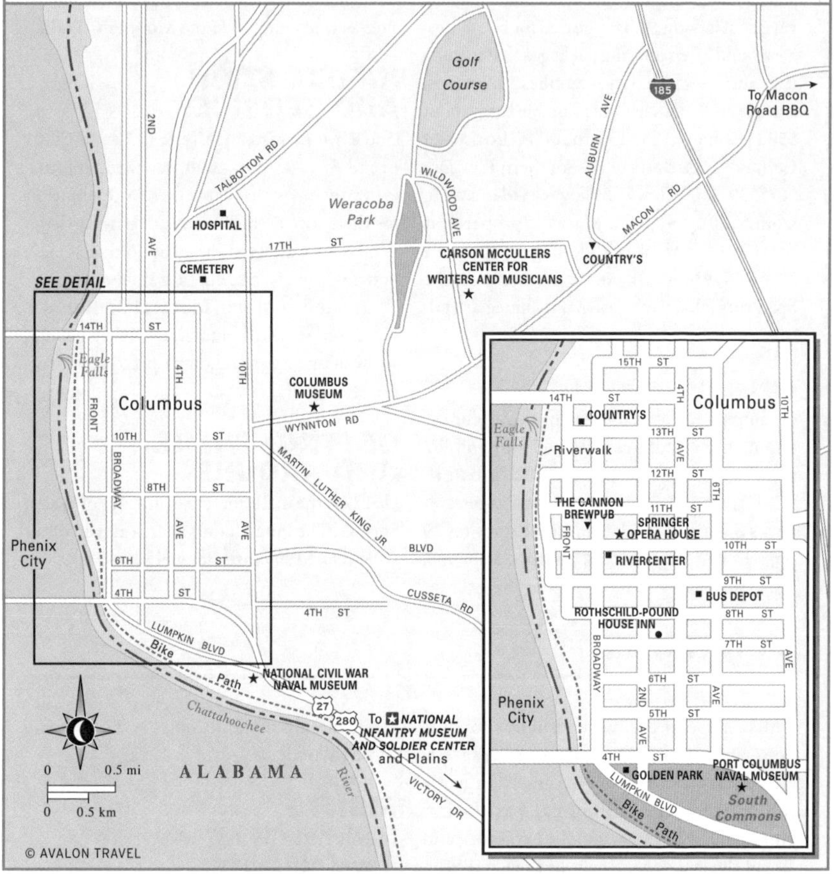

from each other, so one can easily make an afternoon of visiting the pair.

★ National Infantry Museum and Soldier Center

The **National Infantry Museum and Soldier Center** (1775 Legacy Way, 706/685-5800, www.nationalinfantrymuseum.org, Tues.-Sat. 9am-5pm, Sun. 11am-5pm, $5 donation) is a well-funded and well-designed extended love letter to the soldiers, paratroopers, and Rangers of the U.S. Army Infantry, a large portion of whom received their training at Fort Benning, where the museum resides.

The grand entrance, featuring a giant statue of a World War II-era squad leader exhorting his men to attack, sets the tone. From there you enter a series of stimulating multimedia vignettes highlighting notable small-unit infantry actions from the Revolutionary War through the Vietnam War. From there, the bulk of the museum comprises separate galleries, each dealing with a specific period of U.S. Army history. The galleries are well assembled and informative, featuring a range of uniforms, armaments, memorabilia, and instructional multimedia about individual campaigns and engagements through the present day. The Ranger Hall of Honor memorializes 200 individual U.S. Army Rangers of note.

An affiliated IMAX theater shows thematic movies in the IMAX format, in addition to special seasonal films. Check the website for showtimes and ticket prices.

Uptown Columbus

Most cities would call this "downtown," but in Columbus it's Uptown (www.uptowncolumbusga.com). It's a National Historic District and the center of Columbus social and nightlife. The bulk of the activity centers on Broadway, which has a grassy median with a fountain.

Just a couple of blocks off Broadway is the renowned **Springer Opera House** (103 10th St., 706/324-5714, www.springeroperahouse.org), a handsome, cast iron, balcony-bedecked late 19th-century venue of 700 seats that has hosted luminaries such as Oscar Wilde, Will Rogers, Tom Thumb, Franklin D. Roosevelt, and Garrison Keilor (see the "Walk of Stars" on the sidewalk in front of the building). Built in 1871, the Springer was declared the official state theater of Georgia in the 1970s by then-governor Jimmy Carter. It continues to host a regular schedule of performances by its in-house theater company.

Columbus Museum

The **Columbus Museum** (1251 Wynnton Rd., 706/748-2562, www.columbusmuseum.com, Tues.-Wed. and Fri.-Sat. 10am-5pm, Thurs. 10am-8pm, Sun. 1pm-5pm, free) is among the best-curated museums I've seen in a medium-small city, with the not-trivial added benefit of having free admission every day. The space itself is bright, inviting, clean, and contemporary in feel, but without the sense of lonely emptiness that many such modern museums tend to evoke. The permanent collection boasts an excellent variety of stimulating American impressionists, and the 3rd floor hosts rotating exhibits of national and international value and interest. There's a standing exhibit on Columbus history as well, with a particular focus on the Native American presence.

RECREATION

Most recreation in Columbus centers on the **Chattahoochee River.** The most obvious choice is a walk or ride along the **Chattahoochee River Trail,** which extends

the Springer Opera House

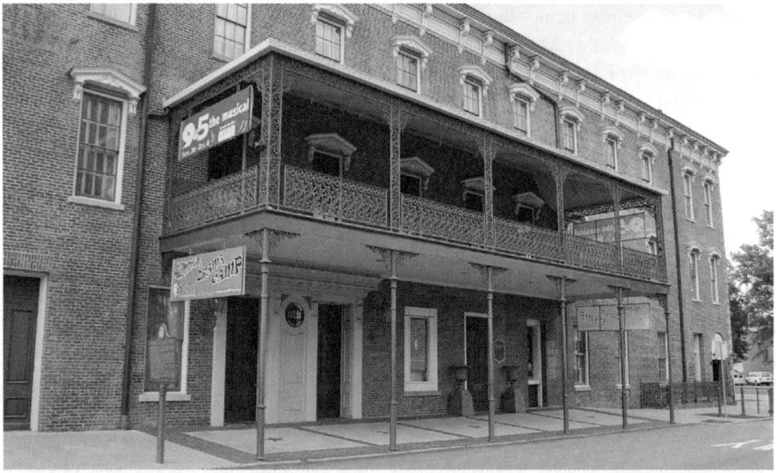

Rebels at Sea

Though the Union blockaded the Southern coast almost immediately with war's outbreak, that didn't stop the Confederacy from embarking on a crash course to build its own navy. At its peak, the Confederate Navy counted only about 5,000 personnel—outnumbered literally 10 to 1 by the U.S. Navy in both vessels and sailors. However, what the rebels lacked in numbers they made up for in innovation and bravery.

Confederate subs made the first submarine attacks in history. The rebel raider CSS *Alabama* sank U.S. ships as far away as the coast of France. A particularly feared Southern innovation—as represented by the CSS *Virginia* or "Merrimac" in its epic fight with the USS *Monitor*—was the ironclad, a regular wooden warship stripped to its berth deck and topped with an impenetrable iron superstructure. By war's end a menagerie of bizarre-looking contraptions was the norm in both fleets. As awkward as some vessels were—many were simply too underpowered to drag around that extra metal—they were the forerunners of the sophisticated warships to come.

The best place to find out more is at the **National Civil War Naval Museum** (1002 Victory Dr., 706/327-9798, www.portcolumbus.org, Sun.-Mon. 12:30pm-4:30pm, Tues.-Sat. 10am-4:30pm, $7.50 adults, $6 children) in Columbus. You'll leave not only with a certain admiration for the ragtag but plucky Confederate Navy, but also with an appreciation of the profound paradigm shift in naval technology, which echoes in the present day.

roughly 15 miles from Uptown Columbus all the way to Fort Benning, concluding at Oxbow Meadows. The trail includes the Riverwalk section adjacent to the popular Uptown area of restaurants and nightlife.

By far the biggest news in Columbus outdoors life is **Whitewater Express** (1000 Bay Ave., 706/321-4720, www.columbusgawhitewater.com, daily 9am-6pm, raft trips $33-49), more popularly known as "River City Rush." Two antiquated earthen dams near the falls on the river have been demolished to reveal a magnificent 2.5-mile white-water run that goes from Class I all the way to Class IV. The city, which bills the white-water project as the longest urban white-water course in the world, hopes it will spur ecotourism development.

FOOD

Every imaginable chain restaurant is available in the Columbus area. Otherwise, your best bet is to stick with pub food, which seems to set the standard here.

American

Known for its lively bar scene, ★ **The Cannon Brewpub** (1041 Broadway, 706/653-2337, www.thecannonbrewpub.com, Mon.-Thurs. 11am-10pm, Fri.-Sun. 11am-11pm, $15) is a linchpin of Uptown nightlife. All of the burgers are excellent, and you can get them with the Cannon's signature sweet potato "sunspots." Of course, you have your selection of handcrafted beers brewed on-site. Try the sampler flight of beers if you can't quite decide.

Barbecue

There are two major purveyors of Columbus 'cue, and each has its fan base. The best-known and the one with the longest tradition is ★ **Country's** (3137 Mercury Dr., 706/563-7604, www.countrysbarbecue.com, Sun.-Thurs. 11am-10pm, Fri.-Sat. 11am-11pm, $8-12), which has a well-rounded menu featuring equally good pulled pork, grilled chicken, ribs, and brisket. Seasonal favorites are always welcomed by regular patrons. Tuesday night is all-you-can-eat barbecue chicken, and Friday and Saturday nights bring live bluegrass to the original location. There is also an Uptown location (1329 Broadway), a little closer to the action.

Some aficionados will tell you that the humble **Pepper's** (4620 Warm Springs Rd., 706/569-0051, Mon.-Tues. and Sat.

10:30am-2:30pm, Wed.-Fri. 10:30am-8pm, $7) is at least as good, with a leaner cut of meat, and offers a particularly tasty take on that Georgia side dish known as Brunswick stew.

ACCOMMODATIONS

The vast military presence in Columbus means there is plenty of inexpensive lodging. While quality can vary, generally speaking you can book a brand-name hotel for well under what you'd pay in other markets.

Under $150

The pet-friendly ★ **Staybridge Suites Columbus** (1678 Whittlesley Rd., 706/507-7700, www.sbscolumbus.com, $100) is close to I-185 and has a nice kitchen in each suite, and there is a hot breakfast each morning included in the rates. The **Hampton Inn Columbus** (7390 Bear Ln., 706/256-2222, www.hamptoninn.com, $100) is also off I-185 and is one of the least expensive Hampton Inns you'll find, with the guarantee of quality typical of the chain. There are no hidden charges here, and the Wi-Fi and parking really are included in the rates.

$150-300

The ★ **Rothschild-Pound House Inn** (201 7th St., 706/322-4075, www.thepoundhouseinn.com, $185-365) is the premier B&B in Columbus, set in an ornately appointed Second Empire-style home. There are four sumptuous suites in the main house, with another six spread out in three cottages that are part of the whole enterprise.

INFORMATION AND SERVICES

The spacious and well-done **Columbus Visitors Center** (900 Front Ave., 706/322-1613, www.visitcolumbusga.com, Mon.-Fri. 8:30am-5:30pm, Sat. 10am-2pm) is conveniently located. For emergencies go to **The Medical Center** of the Columbus Regional Healthcare System (710 Center St., 706/571-1000, www.columbusregional.com). The newspaper of record is the ***Ledger-Enquirer*** (www.ledger-enquirer.com).

GETTING THERE AND AROUND

Car

Columbus is on the Georgia-Alabama border, and several highways lead directly to and from both states over the Chattahoochee River. A major interstate highway doesn't pass through, but a spur of I-75 called I-185 takes you directly to Columbus. When driving in Columbus, keep in mind that Fort Benning in effect surrounds the city on the Georgia side. While highways going through that military facility are open to the public, traffic laws tend to be more strictly enforced.

Air

Columbus Metropolitan Airport (CSG, 3250 W. Britt David Rd., 706/324-2449, www.flycolumbusga.com) has flights to Atlanta on Delta.

Bus

Columbus is served by **Greyhound** (818 Veterans Pkwy., 706/322-7391, www.greyhound.com). There's a good public transportation service, **METRA** (www.columbusga.org, $1.30), with extensive routes throughout the city. It runs a charming trolley service through the Uptown-downtown-historic areas.

OUTSIDE COLUMBUS

Pasaquan

On the outskirts of Buena Vista about 20 miles outside Columbus is a unique place, the folk-art compound of **Pasaquan** (238 Eddie Martin Rd., 229/649-9444, www.pasaquan.blogspot.com, Apr.-Nov. first Sat. of the month 10am-4pm, $5). The sprawling collection of almost psychedelic pagoda-like temples, statues, and masonry walls, all of them brightly painted, is the product of the late visionary artist Eddie Owens Martin, known as "Saint EOM." Sadly, Martin committed suicide in 1986.

Note the very limited hours, although for a $100 donation you can make an appointment for a private visit. To get here from the Buena Vista town square, drive north 1.5 miles on Highway 41, then veer left onto Highway 137. Go about 4.5 miles and take a right on Eddie Martin Road. Pasaquan is 0.5 mile north.

Jimmy Carter Country

With the notable exception of Providence Canyon, the deeply rural farm country around Americus isn't very scenically stimulating, but it contains some of the nation's most important and interesting history.

Many come just to see tiny Plains, population under 700, birthplace of the 39th U.S. president, Jimmy Carter. The former president and his wife, Rosalynn, still live on the main road in the only house they've ever owned, and Carter himself still teaches Sunday school (open to the public) many times a year at his church on the outskirts of town.

Every American should visit the National Prisoner of War Museum, at the site of the notorious Andersonville POW camp. The Civil War site is grimly fascinating, and the adjacent museum is deeply moving in its portrayal of the plight and ingenuity of U.S. prisoners of war throughout history.

AMERICUS

Americus is the best base of operations from which to explore Carter Country, and this cute town perched on a little hill offers a few things of its own worth seeing as well. Because it's home to Georgia Southwestern University and is the international headquarters of Habitat for Humanity, Americus is a little more resistant to the ups and downs of the economy than many comparatively hard-hit rural towns.

Habitat for Humanity Global Village and Discovery Center

Its administrative offices are in Atlanta, but the global operations center for Habitat for Humanity and the associated **Global Village and Discovery Center** (721 W. Church St., 229/410-7937, www.habitat.org, Mon.-Fri. 9am-5pm, Sat. 10am-2pm, $4 adults, $3 children) is in its hometown of Americus. The centerpiece of the experience is seeing replicas of typical third world housing, along with tours of 15 of the special low-cost sustainable buildings that Habitat for Humanity seeks to build in those areas, each design customized for the particular area's climate and terrain.

Koinonia Farms

Before founding Habitat for Humanity, Millard and Linda Fuller met at **Koinonia Farms** (1324 Hwy. 49, 877/738-1741, www.koinoniapartners.org, Mon.-Sat. 9am-5pm, Sun. 1pm-5pm, free). This 70-year-old agricultural and ministerial institution was established by two couples, Clarence and Florence Jordan and Martin and Mabel England, specifically to embody what they saw as the ideals of early Christianity. By growing and providing food and spreading fellowship, they aimed to overcome the then-ingrained racism and economic disparity endemic to the South Georgia region and to be an example to other "intentional communities."

Today, visitors are always welcome at this working farm, especially at the weekday noon community lunches. The emphasis is on *working*, however, and Koinonia is mainly a place where people come to volunteer their labor on the farm or their trade skills, or even their musicianship, in exchange for a stay at the attached RV and lodging area, where people can stay for up to two weeks (longer during harvest time). Koinonia goods can be purchased on-site or at shops around the Americus and Plains area.

Georgia Rural Telephone Museum

About 20 minutes south of Americus in a restored cotton warehouse in tiny Leslie is one of the quirkiest and most fun little museums around, the **Georgia Rural Telephone Museum** (135 N. Bailey Ave., 229/874-4786, www.grtm.org, Mon.-Fri. 9am-3:30pm, nominal fee). We're not just talking rotary phones here; we're talking the old-timey phone exchanges with live operators who manually connected your call.

Food and Accommodations

Your best bet for lodging in Americus is the historic ★ **Windsor Hotel** (125 Lamar St., 229/924-1555, www.windsor-americus.com, $200), itself a landmark worth visiting. Now a Best Western property, it's a stirring image of Victoriana with its imposing turrets and broad balcony. Book in advance, as the Windsor often hosts dignitaries in the area to visit Carter and Habitat for Humanity.

Another recommended lodging option is the well-run, clean, and recently upgraded **Jameson Inn** (1605 E. Lamar St., 229/924-2726, www.jamesoninns.com, $100), several blocks away, which offers a free full breakfast.

The Windsor also happens to be your best bet for food and adult beverages in this corner of the Bible Belt. The Windsor has two excellent dining options: the sit-down, farm-to-table **Rosemary & Thyme** (125 Lamar St., 229/924-1555, www.windsor-americus.com, Mon.-Fri. 6:30am-9:30am and 5pm-9pm, Sat. 6:30am-10am and 5pm-9pm, Sun. 6:30am-10am, $20) and the upstairs ★ **Floyd's Pub** (125 Lamar St., 229/924-1555, www.windsor-americus.com, Mon.-Sat. from 5pm, $15), named after a longtime bellman. My favorite meal in Americus consists of sitting down at the bar at Floyd's and ordering the sublime gyro wrap; any of their sandwiches are excellent.

PLAINS

Plains (www.plainsgeorgia.com) itself is little more than a single block of businesses and a few houses and churches. For most intents and purposes, the entire town is the Jimmy Carter National Historic Site and can be enjoyed within a single day. It's surrounded by intensively cultivated farmland, which includes the exceptionally well-interpreted Jimmy Carter Boyhood Farm. All the Carter-oriented sites are free of charge.

As you'd expect from the place where a peanut farmer became president, the big

Main Street, Plains

annual event is the **Plains Peanut Festival** (www.plainsgeorgia.com), happening each September, which almost always features appearances by Jimmy and Rosalynn Carter.

Jimmy Carter National Historic Site

Start your visit at the Victorian-era **Plains Depot Museum and Presidential Campaign Headquarters** (Main St., 229/824-4104, www.nps.gov, daily 9am-4:30pm, free) on Main Street next to the block of shops comprising Plains's "downtown." Not just the train depot and oldest building in the area, it was where Jimmy Carter symbolically based his presidential campaign and is a must-stop for any political junkie. The interior of the depot (warning: no air-conditioning) features much memorabilia about Carter's insurgent run in the post-Watergate years, shocking not only the Democratic Party establishment but the entire globe, which marveled at a peanut farmer becoming leader of the free world.

Technically, the **Plains High School Visitors Center and Museum** (300 N. Bond St., 229/824-4104, www.nps.gov, daily 9am-5pm, free), housed in the old Plains High School, is the premier Carter-oriented site in Plains, but for those expecting an in-depth interpretation of his legacy and influential post-presidential activity, it might be underwhelming (for that, go to the Carter Center in Atlanta). But certainly, it's neat to walk around in the same school where both the future president and his future wife, Rosalynn, attended classes, and the museum does a good job in explaining the social and political circumstances of the times in which Carter grew up and his motivations for running for office after a successful career in the U.S. Navy submarine service.

Maranatha Baptist Church (148 Hwy. 45 N., 229/824-7896, www.mbcplains.com) isn't nearly the largest church in Plains (that distinction goes to Plains Baptist, which Jimmy and Rosalynn left decades ago in protest of its now-repudiated policy of refusing African American congregants). But it's where the Carters still attend church each Sunday. Dozens of times a year Carter himself gives an hour-long Sunday school lesson right before the regular 11am service. You can stay for the service or just attend the lesson; all you have to do is show up about 8am or 9am, get checked out quickly by the Secret Service, take a seat at a pew, listen to an orientation, and enjoy.

You won't be able to tour the **Carter Family Compound** on the town's main road, but you'll spot it instantly by the tall fence and the Secret Service checkpoint at the entrance. The simple 1961 ranch home is on 4.5 acres of land and is the only home Carter and his wife have ever owned. There's a video tour at the museum in the old Plains High School.

★ Jimmy Carter Boyhood Farm

It's not in Plains proper—it's actually in even smaller Archery—but the impeccably maintained **Jimmy Carter Boyhood Farm** (Old Plains Hwy., 229/824-4104, www.nps.gov, daily 10am-5pm, free) a few miles out of town, is a must-see, not only to get a better perspective on Carter's boyhood but for a charming and educational slice-of-life of rural and agricultural Americana gone by.

While the centerpiece is the well-restored one-story farmhouse where Earl and Lillian Carter raised the future president and his siblings during the Depression era, there's plenty more to see, including lovingly tended native-plant gardens, the old Carter general store, domestic animals, and the restored home of the Clarks, an African American family who were often employed by the Carters and who provided a window on the real need for social justice in the Jim Crow-era South.

The farm itself is expertly maintained by the National Park Service, but keep in mind that there's no air-conditioning on-site, just as when the Carters lived here. There are restrooms and a water fountain at the entrance by the parking lot, and a park ranger is always around if you have any questions. Stay

the restored home of the Carters at the Jimmy Carter Boyhood Farm

hydrated and use sunscreen. Walking tours of the farm are led on Saturday and Sunday at 11:30am and 3:30pm.

Get there by taking U.S. 280 west out of Plains for 0.5 mile, then bearing left on Old Plains Highway for 1.5 miles. The farm is on the right side of the road. The family burial ground in Lebanon Cemetery is along the same road; Carter's parents and brother and sister are interred here.

SAM Shortline

The railroads are still very active in this part of Georgia, and the tracks through Plains host the tourist-oriented passenger shuttle **SAM Shortline** (877/427-2457, www.samshortline.com). These 1949 vintage cars are a fun way to get around from the Boyhood Farm with stops in Plains, Americus, and Leslie (site of the Georgia Rural Telephone Museum). Check the website for schedules and fares.

★ NATIONAL PRISONER OF WAR MUSEUM

First off, don't be confused: The **National Prisoner of War Museum** (760 POW Rd., 229/924-0343, www.nps.gov, museum daily 9am-5pm, grounds and cemetery daily 8am-5pm, free), about 12 miles north of Americus, is also where you'll find Camp Sumter, the infamous Civil War prison camp, now called Andersonville Prison, as well as Andersonville National Cemetery. The multiple nature of the site is deliberate and entirely appropriate.

The museum not only describes the history, atmosphere, and ensuing controversy of the Andersonville POW camp (called Camp Sumter at the time) through exhibits and an excellent short film, it also delves into the poignant human chronicle of American prisoners of war from all conflicts, from the Revolution to the world wars, the Korean War, the Vietnam War, and the Iraq War. Young children might find some of the exhibits disturbing, but I consider the museum a must-visit for any American high schooler or older.

Behind the air-conditioned and fully appointed museum is the entrance to the **Andersonville Prison,** formerly known as **Camp Sumter,** demarcated by a memorial wall and sculpture. You're greeted by an expanse of open space, split by a still-existing creek. At one point nearly 40,000 Union POWs were confined here, completely exposed to the elements, using the creek as both

the National Prisoner of War Museum

a toilet and for drinking water. The site was picked clean of artifacts decades ago, but the National Park Service has done a great job of maintaining replicas of the 18-foot stockade wall and associated "deadline," as well as facsimiles of the "she-bangs," or makeshift tents, of the otherwise sun-blasted prisoners. There are a series of ornate monuments erected by various Northern states to memorialize their citizens' sacrifices while in captivity.

You can drive a small loop road around the entire Andersonville camp, but unless the afternoon sun is just too intense, I recommend walking the site to get the full impact of what actually went on here 150 years ago. Adjacent to Camp Sumter is **Andersonville National Cemetery,** which contains graves of POWs and Civil War veterans and was established specifically to keep the lessons of Andersonville in public memory.

Food

Really good food is hard to find in this area, but one notable exception is ★ **Yoder's Deitsch Haus** (5252 Hwy. 26, 478/472-2024, Tues. and Thurs.-Sat. 11:30am-2pm and 5pm-8:30pm, Wed. 11:30am-2pm, $8) near the otherwise bereft town of Montezuma a few miles from Andersonville. Yoder's menu—cooked and served by local Mennonites, part of a sizable contingent in the surrounding area—draws people from miles around. The delectable, hearty Southern-meets-German cuisine is served in a clean, open, community-style buffet atmosphere. Save room for the amazing pies and other desserts, which are signature items. The only drinks are iced tea, coffee, and water. Dress conservatively.

POINTS WEST

★ Providence Canyon State Outdoor Recreation Area

While at first glance it looks like a cluster of little canyons parachuted in from out west, the truth about **Providence Canyon State Outdoor Recreation Area** (8930 Canyon Rd., 229/838-6870, www.gastateparks.org, mid-Sept.-mid-Apr. daily 7am-6pm, mid-Apr.-mid-Sept. daily 7am-9pm, $5, backcountry campsites $9), aka "Georgia's Grand Canyon," is a bit more complicated. Though it doesn't look that way when you wander among these steep white walls dotted with trees and patrolled overhead by circling hawks, the canyons are actually products of human activity. Poor farming practices in the early 1800s in

Ambiguity and Andersonville

The very word *Andersonville* is synonymous with harsh cruelty to captives, one reason the National Prisoner of War Museum was established a stone's throw from the notorious Confederate camp. From February 1864 to May 1865, 45,000 Union prisoners lived on this bare 26-acre plot, with no roof or shelter of any kind to shield them from the blistering South Georgia sun, nor from the winter cold. Nearly 13,000 died.

Within Andersonville's 20-foot stockade walls was a grotesque city all its own, with its own rules and rulers. Food was thrown into the compound to be fought over, sold, and resold by prisoners. The only drinking water was a fetid creek running through the middle of the camp, with the downstream portion the camp's only latrine. The world's first war crimes trial came out of the Andersonville experience, as camp commandant Colonel Henry Wirz was hanged for his role after the war in a court-martial presided over by Union general Lew Wallace, who would later write *Ben-Hur*.

As horrible as Andersonville was, however, the only reason the camp existed at all was because of a decision by Union general Ulysses S. Grant to stop the practice of POW exchanges, previously the norm throughout the war. The concept was simple: Regular agreements were made to trade roughly equal numbers of prisoners, thus relieving the burden on both sides of feeding and caring for them. But the sudden halt in exchanges and the deterioration of Southern military and civilian standards meant that Confederates suddenly found themselves responsible for thousands of prisoners, but with dwindling supplies and people to devote to them. Colonel Wirz sent a petition north asking that POW exchanges be reinstated; it was denied. By late 1864 the Confederacy even offered to release all prisoners if the Union would provide transportation; it refused.

So, as awful as it was, Andersonville represented a deeply flawed and imperfect response to a nearly impossible situation, a situation mirrored by similarly horrific POW camps in the North such as Camp Elmira, New York. Southerners were far from immune to the degrading effect of the prisoners' plight. Many Andersonville prison guards themselves broke down under the strain and guilt.

this soft-soil area led to topsoil erosion followed by dramatic washouts, carving the deep gulches that now form a picturesque attraction.

There are plenty of opportunities to drive or walk around the rim and look down into the fingers of Providence Canyon, but the best way to enjoy the 16 separate canyons that form the park is to take the short, pleasant hike onto the canyon floor. (It's strictly forbidden to climb the fragile walls once you're down here.) You might consider joining the **Canyon Climbers Club** (www.gastateparks.org, $10), which coordinates activity in Providence Canyon and two other Georgia parks with similar topography, Tallulah Gorge and Cloudland Canyon. Backpackers can camp on the seven-mile backcountry trail.

There is a **visitors center** (Sept. 1-Nov. 30 and Mar. 1-May 31 Sat.-Sun. 8am-5pm) where you can find restrooms and park-related information.

INFORMATION AND SERVICES

The **Plains Welcome Center** (1763 U.S. 280 W., 229/824-7477) is a short way outside the tiny town, and as of this writing was facing budget issues. The best bet for information in Plains is at the **Plains High School Visitors Center and Museum** (300 N. Bond St., 229/824-4104, www.nps.gov, daily 9am-5pm, free), also the main portal for exploring all Jimmy Carter-related sights.

If you pass through Americus, check out the **Americus Welcome Center** (123 W. Lamar St., 229/928-6059, www.visitamericusga.com) on the 1st floor of the town's municipal building.

GETTING THERE AND AROUND

This part of South Georgia is very well served by roads and is fairly easy to get around by car. Americus, the best base of operations, is easily accessible from I-75 south of Atlanta. U.S. 280/27 heads due west out of Americus and takes you right through Plains, and on to Westville and Providence Canyon. To get to Andersonville, head north out of Americus on Highway 49.

A unique way to get around Carter County is by the **SAM Shortline** (877/427-2457, www.samshortline.com), a light passenger rail running a route from Plains to Cordele and points between. Check the website for frequently changing schedules and fares.

Southwest Georgia

Agriculture is the name of the game down here in this sparsely populated area, with peanuts, pecans, and cotton, including the state's dedicated agricultural college. Though largely free of fighting during the Civil War, this is where the Confederacy ended for good with the capture of Confederate president Jefferson Davis. The city of Albany played a key role in national civil rights, chiefly with the groundbreaking Albany Movement, orchestrated in part by Martin Luther King Jr. The main natural attraction is the scenic and intriguing Flint River.

ALBANY

South Georgia's largest city, Albany (www.visitalbanyga.com) owes its history to the scenic Flint River, one of the South's great waterways. The Flint's bounty sparked the city's founding as a trade center, named after the capital of New York State, in case anyone didn't get the hint. Although the former Food Network icon moved her operations to Savannah long ago, Paula Deen is actually an Albany native—and by the way, locals like Paula pronounce it "all-BEN-ee," not "ALL-buh-ny." It ain't in New York, y'all!

Learn about the area's human and natural history at the **Thronateeska Heritage Center** (100 W. Roosevelt Ave., 229/432-6955, www.heritagecenter.org, Thurs.-Sat. 10am-4pm, free), named for the ancient Native American word for the area. There's a Museum of History, a Science Discovery Center, and a good model train layout within its cavernous interior—the main building is the repurposed 1913 rail depot—but for many the highlight is the **Wetherbee**

How Do You Say Pecan?

PEA-can or pe-CON? The debate continues in South Georgia, where the meadows are dotted with picturesque pecan orchards and roadside stands sell bushels of the freshly harvested nut each autumn. What's the right way to pronounce *pecan*? Old-timers insist it ain't French, and the emphasis should be on the first syllable: PEA-can. More recent arrivals—perhaps enamored of the nut's newly acquired foodie cachet as a key part of reinvented Southern cuisine—say it's the more refined pe-CON. The Georgia Department of Agriculture has actually come up with a Solomonic answer to the debate. The official pronunciation of *pecan* for state agricultural purposes is with the emphasis on the first syllable: PEA-can. However, the Agriculture Department also says the original pronunciation of the word, derived from an ancient Native American tongue, was almost certainly pe-CON. So you're not nuts. You can say it any way you like.

Planetarium (showtimes vary, $3) in the adjacent building, which holds various themed shows on the night sky.

Albany's chief claim to fame to the world at large is as the boyhood home of the great Ray Charles, one of the first performers to move traditional gospel into the realm of popular R&B. He is commemorated in the neat **Ray Charles Plaza** (Front St.) on the Flint Riverwalk. The elaborate memorial features Charles at a rotating baby grand piano. He "plays" music through a discreet sound system, and each evening there is a light and fountain show. The audience sits in the round on huge piano keys.

The centerpiece of a recent public-private effort to revitalize downtown Albany is the **Flint RiverQuarium** (117 Pine Ave., 229/639-2650, www.flintriverquarium.com, Tues.-Sat. 10am-5pm, Sun. 1pm-5pm, $9 adults, $6.50 children), a 175,000-gallon, 22-foot-deep aquarium on the river—one of the few such open-air facilities you'll find—exploring the area's interesting riverine ecosystem.

Albany's key role in the national struggle for civil rights is documented at the **Albany Civil Rights Institute** (326 Whitney Ave., 229/432-1698, www.albanycivilrightsinstitute.org, Tues.-Sat. 10am-4pm, $6 adults, $5 students), a new facility next to the historic 1906 Mt. Zion Baptist Church, where Martin Luther King Jr. made speeches during the push to integrate Albany public facilities in the early 1960s. The entire history of the Albany Movement is chronicled in fascinating detail. The second Saturday of the month you can hear a performance by the Freedom Singers, a group with roots going back to 1962.

The **Albany Museum of Art** (311 Meadowlark Dr., 229/439-8300, www.albanymuseum.com, Tues.-Sat. 10am-5pm, $4 adults, $2 children) has a solid collection of European and American art, but it's chiefly known for the Davis collection of sub-Saharan African art, one of the largest in the country. The museum hosts a performance series by the Albany Symphony Orchestra.

WEST OF ALBANY

Kolomoki Mounds Historic Park

One of the best-preserved pre-Columbian mound-builder sites in the United States, **Kolomoki Mounds Historic Park** (205 Indian Mounds Rd., 229/724-2150, www.gastateparks.org, daily 7am-10pm, parking $5, campsites $25-27) is also Georgia's oldest, its sprawling complex inhabited from AD 350 to 750, nearly 1,000 years older than the Etowah Mounds up in Cartersville.

You'll see the mounds on the drive in, but you'll first want to go to the end of the road to the visitors center, which incorporates a theater and boardwalk within a partially excavated mound, opened in the less enlightened era of the 1930s. The film explores the history of the site and the culture of the Woodland people who built it, part of a thriving network of similar compounds across the Southeast.

The real highlight is a trip up the stairs to the top of the enormous great temple mound, the tallest in Georgia at 57 feet. It feels much higher than that because of its dominant view overlooking a broad plain featuring two smaller burial mounds and several even smaller ceremonial mounds. Because this is a relatively isolated area, there are times you can have the entire top of the mound to yourself—quite a powerful experience.

Kolomoki offers 27 tent and RV sites. There are a couple of small lakes to boat and fish on, a boat ramp, and a swimming beach. Hikers will find a lake trail and a forest trail with a total of five miles of paths.

Colquitt, "Mural City"

With not even 2,000 residents and tucked away deep into some of Georgia's most productive farmland, Colquitt (www.colquitt-georgia.com) wouldn't seem to merit much attention from visitors. But over the last decade the tiny town has been rejuvenated through cultural tourism.

The most obvious aspect is the nearly 20 large-scale murals throughout the downtown area, seemingly on every flat surface. Initiated with the Millennium Mural Project and representing various aspects of regional life and history, the murals are of extremely high artistic quality and are a photographer's dream.

The other component of Colquitt's vibrant cultural scene for its small size is **Swamp Gravy** (229/758-5450, www.swampgravy.com, $27), Georgia's "official folk-life play" performed at the historic **Cotton Hall** (158 E. Main St.), a renovated cotton warehouse turned into a 300-seat venue, which also hosts other productions throughout the year. *Swamp Gravy* is a humorous musical performed by a huge volunteer cast. A new edition premieres each October, portraying segments of local life, history, and culture, and is reprised each March.

The Okefenokee Swamp

Scientists often refer to Okefenokee as an "analogue," an accurate representation of a totally different epoch in the earth's history. In this case it's the Carboniferous Period, about 350 million years ago, when the living plants were lush and green and the dead plants simmered in a slow-decaying peat that would one day end up as the oil that powers our civilization.

But for the casual visitor, Okefenokee might also be simply a wonderful place to get almost completely away from human influence and witness firsthand some of the country's most interesting wildlife in its natural habitat. Despite the enormous wildfires of the spring of 2007 and the summer of 2011—some of the largest the Southeast has seen in half a century, so large they were visible from space—the swamp has bounced back, for the most part, and is once again hosting visitors who wish to experience its timeless beauty.

★ OKEFENOKEE NATIONAL WILDLIFE REFUGE

It's nearly the size of Rhode Island and just a short drive off I-95, but the massive and endlessly fascinating **Okefenokee National Wildlife Refuge** (912/496-7836, www.fws.gov/okefenokee, Mar.-Oct. daily dawn-7:30pm, Nov.-Feb. daily dawn-5:30pm, $5 per vehicle) is one of the lesser-visited national public lands. Is it that very name "swamp" that keeps people away, with its connotations of fetid misery and lurking danger? Or simply its location, out of sight and out of mind in South Georgia?

In any case, while it long ago entered the collective subconscious as a metaphor for the most untamed, darkly dangerous aspects of the American South—as well as the place where Pogo the Possum lived—the Okefenokee remains one of the most intriguing natural areas on the planet.

The Okefenokee Swamp was created by an accident of geology. About 250,000 years ago, the Atlantic Ocean washed ashore about 70 miles farther inland from where it does today. Over time, a massive barrier island formed off this primeval Georgia coastline, running from what is now Jesup, Georgia, south to Starke, Florida. When the ocean level dropped during the Pleistocene Era, this sandy island became a topographical feature known today as the Trail Ridge, its height effectively creating a basin to its west. Approximately 90 percent of the Okefenokee's water comes from rainfall into that basin, which drains slowly via the Suwannee and St. Marys Rivers.

Native Americans used the swamp as a hunting ground and gave us its current name, which means "Land of the Trembling Earth," a reference to the floating peat islands, called "houses," that dominate the landscape.

It's a common mistake to call the Okefenokee "pristine," because like much of the heavily timbered and farmed southeastern coast, it is anything but. The swamp's ancient cypress stands and primordial longleaf

The Okefenokee Swamp

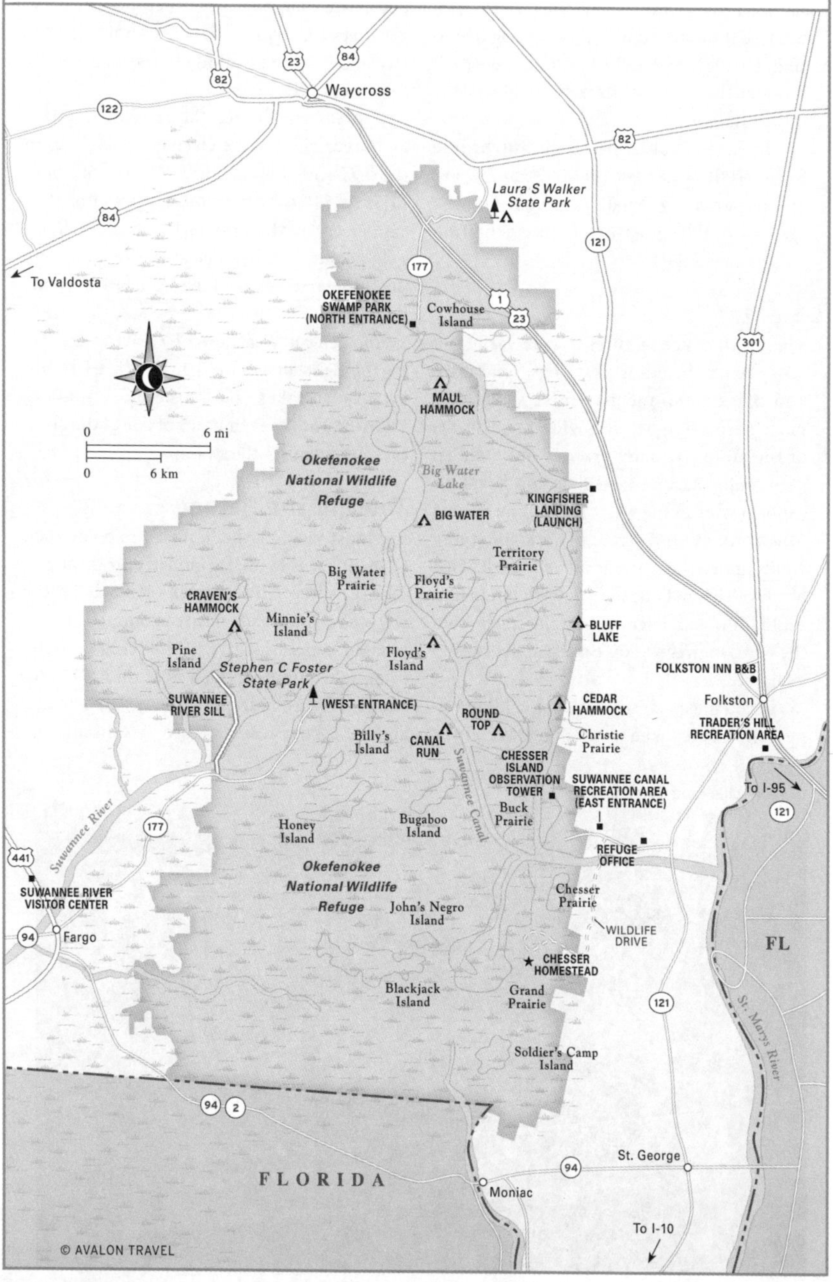
Waycross
23
84
82
122
82
84
Laura S Walker State Park
121
177
To Valdosta
OKEFENOKEE SWAMP PARK (NORTH ENTRANCE)
Cowhouse Island
1
23
301
MAUL HAMMOCK
0
6 mi
0
6 km
Okefenokee National Wildlife Refuge
Big Water Lake
KINGFISHER LANDING (LAUNCH)
BIG WATER
Territory Prairie
Big Water Prairie
Floyd's Prairie
CRAVEN'S HAMMOCK
Minnie's Island
BLUFF LAKE
Floyd's Island
Pine Island
Stephen C Foster State Park
(WEST ENTRANCE)
FOLKSTON INN B&B
Folkston
SUWANNEE RIVER SILL
CEDAR HAMMOCK
ROUND TOP
TRADER'S HILL RECREATION AREA
Billy's Island
CANAL RUN
Christie Prairie
CHESSER ISLAND OBSERVATION TOWER
SUWANNEE CANAL RECREATION AREA (EAST ENTRANCE)
To I-95
Suwannee Canal
Buck Prairie
121
Suwannee River
177
Honey Island
Bugaboo Island
REFUGE OFFICE
441
Okefenokee National Wildlife Refuge
SUWANNEE RIVER VISITOR CENTER
Chesser Prairie
John's Negro Island
WILDLIFE DRIVE
FL
94
Fargo
CHESSER HOMESTEAD
Blackjack Island
Grand Prairie
121
St. Marys River
Soldier's Camp Island
94
2
St. George
94
FLORIDA
Moniac
To I-10
© AVALON TRAVEL

pine forests were heavily harvested in the early 20th century. About 200 miles of old railbed through the swamp remain as a silent testament to the scope of that logging operation. In 1937, President Franklin Roosevelt brought the area within the federal wildlife refuge system.

The state has also opened the **Suwannee River Visitor Center** (912/637-5274, www.gastateparks.org, Wed.-Sun. 9am-5pm), a "green" building featuring an orientation video and exhibits.

Sights

The Okefenokee features a wide variety of ecosystems, including peat bogs, sand hills, and black gum and bay forests. Perhaps most surprising are the wide-open vistas of the swamp's many prairies or extended grasslands, 22 in all. And as you kayak or canoe on one of the water trails or on the old **Suwannee Canal** (a relic of the logging era), you'll notice the water is all very dark. This blackwater is not due to dirt or silt but to natural tannic acid released into the water from the decaying vegetation that gave the swamp its name.

As you'd expect in a national wildlife refuge, the Okefenokee hosts a huge variety of animal life—more than 400 species of vertebrates, including over 200 varieties of birds and more than 60 types of reptiles. Birders get a special treat in late November-early December when sandhill cranes come south to winter in the swamp.

A great way to see the sandhill cranes and other birds of the Okefenokee is to hike the 0.75-mile boardwalk out to the 50-foot **Chesser Island Observation Tower** on the eastern end of the swamp. This boardwalk is a by-product of the huge 2011 fire; you can see the charred piers of the old boardwalk as you stroll.

You can get to the tower by driving or biking the eight-mile round-trip **Wildlife Drive,** which also takes you by the old **Chesser Homestead,** the remnants of one of the oldest settlements in the swamp.

Touring the Refuge

For most visitors, the best way to enjoy the Okefenokee is to book a guided tour through **Okefenokee Adventures** (866/843-7926, www.okefenokeeadventures.com), the designated concessionaire of the refuge. They offer a 90-minute guided boat tour ($18.50 adults, $11.25 children) that leaves each hour, and a 2.5-hour reservation-only sunset tour

the ever-changing Okefenokee Swamp

($25 adults, $17 children) that takes you to see the gorgeous sunset over Chesser Prairie. Extended or custom tours, including multiday wilderness excursions, are also available. They also rent bikes, canoes, and camping gear, and even run a decent little café where you can either sit down and have a meal or take it to go out on the trail.

Privately owned canoes and boats with motors under 10 hp may put in with no launch fee, but you must sign in and out. No ATVs are allowed on the refuge, and bicycles are allowed only on designated bike trails. Keep in mind that some hunting goes on in the refuge at designated times. Pets must be leashed at all times.

Camping

If fire and water levels permit, it's possible to stay the night in the swamp, canoeing to one of the primitive camping "islands" in the middle of the refuge. You need to make reservations up to two months in advance, however, by calling **U.S. Fish and Wildlife** (912/496-3331, Mon.-Fri. 7am-10am). A nonrefundable fee of $10 per person (which also covers your entrance fee) must be received 16 days before you arrive (mailing address: Okefenokee National Wildlife Refuge, Route 2, Box 3330, Folkston, GA 31537). Campfires are allowed only at Canal Run and Floyds Island. A camp stove is required for cooking at all other shelters. (Keep in mind that in times of extreme drought or fire threat, boat trips may not be allowed. Always check the website for the latest announcements.)

At **Stephen Foster State Park** (17515 Hwy. 177, 912/637-5274, fall-winter daily 7am-7pm, spring-summer daily 6:30am-8:30pm), aka the **West Entrance,** near Fargo, Georgia, there are 66 tent sites ($24) and nine cottages ($100). This part of the Okefenokee is widely considered the best way to get that "true swamp" experience.

Transportation and Services

For anyone using this guide as a travel resource, the best way to access the Okefenokee—and the one I recommend—is the **East Entrance** (912/496-7836, www.fws.gov/okefenokee, Mar.-Oct. daily dawn-7:30pm, Nov.-Feb. daily dawn-5:30pm, $5 per vehicle), otherwise known as the **Suwannee Canal Recreation Area.** This is the main U.S. Fish and Wildlife Service entrance and the most convenient way to hike, rent boating and camping gear, and observe nature. The **Richard S. Bolt Visitor Center** (912/496-7836) has some cool nature exhibits and a surround-sound orientation video. Get to the East Entrance by taking I-95 exit 3 for Kingsland onto Highway 40 west. Go through Kingsland and into Folkston until Highway 40 dead-ends. Take a right, and then an immediate left onto Main Street. At the third light, make a left onto Okefenokee Drive (Hwy. 121) south.

Families with kids may want to hit the **North Entrance** at the privately run **Okefenokee Swamp Park** (U.S. 1, 912/283-0583, www.okeswamp.com, daily 9am-5:30pm, $12 adults, $11 ages 3-11) near Waycross, Georgia. (Fans of the old *Pogo* will recall Waycross from the comic strip, and yes, there's a real "Fort Mudge" nearby.) Here you will find a more touristy vibe, with a reconstructed pioneer village, a serpentarium, and animals in captivity. From here you can take various guided tours for an additional fee.

There's camping at the nearby but unaffiliated **Laura S. Walker State Park** (5653 Laura Walker Rd., 800/864-7275, www.gastateparks.org). Be aware the state park is not in the swamp and isn't very swampy, but it does have a nice man-made lake where you can rent canoes. Get to the North Entrance by taking I-95 exit 29 and going west on U.S. 82 about 45 miles to Highway 177 (Laura Walker Rd.). Go south through Laura S. Walker State Park; the Swamp Park is several miles farther.

If you really want that cypress-festooned, classic swamp look, take the long way around the Okefenokee to **Stephen Foster State Park** (17515 Hwy. 177, 912/637-5274, fall-winter daily 7am-7pm, spring-summer daily 6:30am-8:30pm), aka the **West Entrance,** near Fargo, Georgia. Guided tours are available. Get to Stephen Foster State Park by taking I-95 exit 3 and following the signs to Folkston. Get on Highway 121 south to St. George, and then go west on Highway 94.

FOLKSTON

The chief attraction in Folkston and its main claim to fame is the viewing depot for the **Folkston Funnel** (912/496-2536, www.folkston.com), a veritable train-watcher's paradise. This is the spot where the big CSX double-track rail line—following the top of the ancient Trail Ridge—hosts 60 or more trains a day. They say 90 percent of all freight trains to and from Florida use this track.

Railroad buffs from all over the South congregate here, anticipating the next train by listening to their scanners. The first Saturday each April brings buffs together for the all-day Folkston RailWatch.

The old Atlantic Coast Line depot across the track from the viewing platform has been converted into the very interesting **Folkston Railroad Transportation Museum** (3795 Main St., 912/496-2536, www.charltoncountyga.us, Mon.-Fri. 9am-5pm, Sat. 10am-3pm, free), with lots of history, maps, and technical stuff for the hard-core rail buff and novice alike.

Food

To fuel up in Folkston for your trek in the swamp, go no further than the friendly ★ **Okefenokee Restaurant** (1507 Third St., 912/496-3263, daily 11am-8pm, $10-20), across from the handsome county courthouse. Their huge buffet is a steal at under $10; come on Friday nights for a massive seafood buffet (mostly fried) for under $20 per person. In any case don't miss the fried catfish, featured at both buffets. It's some of the best I've had anywhere in the South.

Accommodations

For a bit of luxury in town, right outside the refuge's East Entrance is the excellent ★ **Inn at Folkston Bed and Breakfast** (509 W. Main St., 888/509-6246, www.innatfolkston.com, $120-170). There is nothing like coming back to its cozy Victorian charms after a long day out in the swamp. The four-room inn boasts an absolutely outstanding breakfast, an extensive reading library, and a whirlpool tub.

Savannah

Highlights

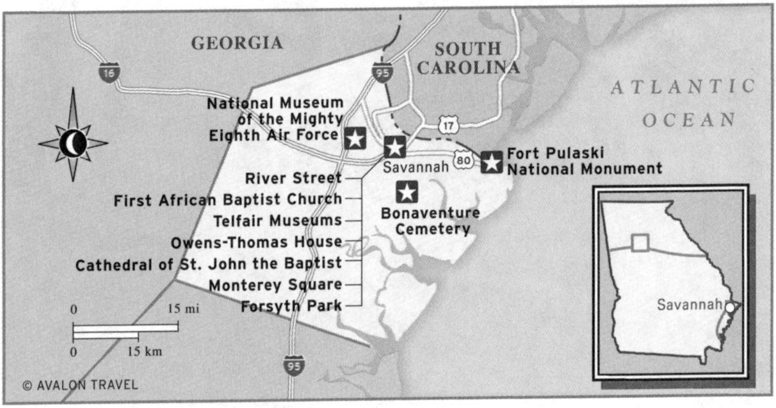

★ **River Street:** Despite River Street's tourist tackiness, there's nothing like strolling the cobblestones amid the old cotton warehouses, enjoying the cool breeze off the river, and watching the huge ships on their way to the bustling port (page 175).

★ **First African Baptist Church:** The oldest black congregation in the United States still meets in this historic sanctuary, a key stop on the Underground Railroad (page 177).

★ **Telfair Museums:** Old school meets new school in this museum complex that comprises the traditional **Telfair Academy of Arts and Sciences** (page 182) and the ultramodern **Jepson Center for the Arts** (page 182).

★ **Owens-Thomas House:** Savannah's single greatest historic home is one of the country's best examples of Regency architecture and a fine example of state-of-the-art historical preservation (page 183).

★ **Cathedral of St. John the Baptist:** This soaring Gothic Revival edifice is complemented by its ornate interior and its matchless location on verdant Lafayette Square, stomping ground of the young Flannery O'Connor (page 186).

★ **Monterey Square:** Savannah's quintessential square has some of the best examples of local architecture and world-class ironwork all around its periphery (page 188).

★ **Forsyth Park:** This verdant expanse ringed by old live oaks is the true center of downtown life; it's Savannah's backyard (page 192).

★ **Bonaventure Cemetery:** This historic burial ground is the final resting place for some of Savannah's favorite citizens, including the great Johnny Mercer (page 195).

★ **Fort Pulaski National Monument:** This well-run site, built with the help of a young Robert E. Lee, is not only historically significant, its beautiful setting makes it a great place for the entire family (page 197).

★ **National Museum of the Mighty Eighth Air Force:** This museum tells the story of the U.S. Eighth Air Force, who executed American bombing missions over Nazi Germany, and includes restored WWII and Cold War-era aircraft (page 200).

In an increasingly homogenized society, Savannah is one of the last places where eccentricity is celebrated and even encouraged. This outspoken, often stubborn determination to make one's own way in the world is personified by the old Georgia joke about Savannah being the capital of "the state of Chatham," a reference to the county in which it resides. In typical contrarian fashion, Savannahians take this nickname as a compliment.

Savannah was built as a series of rectangular "wards," each constructed around a central square. As the city grew, each square took on its own characteristics, depending on who lived on the square and how they made their livelihood. Sounds simple—and it is. That's why its effectiveness has lasted so long.

It is this individuality that is so well documented in John Berendt's *Midnight in the Garden of Good and Evil.* The squares of Savannah's downtown—since 1965 a National Landmark Historic District—are also responsible for the city's walkability, another defining characteristic. Just as cars entering a square must yield to traffic already within, pedestrians are obliged to slow down and interact with the surrounding environment, both constructed and natural. You become participant and audience simultaneously, a feat made easier by the local penchant for easy conversation.

This spirit of independence extends to Savannah's growing hipster culture, helped along by the steady expansion of the Savannah College of Art and Design (SCAD), which boasts much of downtown Savannah as its campus.

Savannah is also known for being able to show you a rowdy good time, and not only during its massive, world-famous St. Patrick's Day celebration. Savannahians will use any excuse for a party, exemplified by the city's very liberal open-container law—adults can walk with alcoholic beverages around downtown—which adds to the generally merry atmosphere.

Previous: the Cathedral of St. John the Baptist; Bonaventure Cemetery. **Above:** a cannon at Fort Pulaski National Monument.

HISTORY

To understand the inferiority complex that Savannah occasionally feels with regards to Charleston, you have to remember that from day one Savannah was intended to play second fiddle to its older, richer neighbor to the north. By the early 1700s, the land south of Charleston had become a staging area for attacks on the settlement by the Spanish and Native Americans. So in 1732, King George II granted a charter to the Trustees of Georgia, a proprietary venture that was the brainchild of a 36-year-old general and member of parliament, General James Edward Oglethorpe. Though the mission was to found a colony to buffer Charleston from the Spanish, Oglethorpe had a far more sweeping vision in mind.

On February 12, 1733, the *Anne* landed with 114 passengers along the high bluff on the south bank of the Savannah River. Oglethorpe laid out his settlement in a deceptively simple plan that is still studied the world over as a model of nearly perfect urban design. He bonded with Tomochichi, the local Creek Indian chief, and the colony prospered. Ever the idealist, Oglethorpe had a plan for the new "classless society" in Savannah that prohibited slavery, rum, and—wait for it—lawyers! But as the settlers enviously eyed the dominance of Charleston's slave-based rice economy, the Trustees bowed to public pressure and relaxed restrictions on slavery and rum.

By 1753, the crown reclaimed the charter, making Georgia England's 13th American colony. Though part of the new United States in 1776, Savannah was captured by British forces in 1778, who held the city against a combined assault a year later. After the Revolution, Savannah became the first capital of Georgia, a role it had until 1786.

Despite hurricanes and yellow fever epidemics, Savannah's heyday was the antebellum period from 1800 to 1860, when for a time it outstripped Charleston as a center of commerce. Savannah's population boomed after an influx of European immigrants, chief among them Irish workers coming to lay track on the new Central of Georgia line.

Blockaded for most of the Civil War, Savannah didn't see much action other than the fall of Fort Pulaski in April 1862, when a Union force successfully laid siege using rifled artillery, a revolutionary technology that instantly rendered the world's masonry forts obsolete. War came to Savannah's doorstep when General William T. Sherman's March to the Sea concluded with his capture of the town in December 1864. On December 22, Sherman sent a now-legendary telegram to President Lincoln bearing these words: "I beg to present you as a Christmas gift, the City of Savannah with 150 heavy guns and plenty of ammunition and also about 25,000 bales of cotton."

After a lengthy Reconstruction period, Savannah began reaching out to the outside world. From 1908 to 1911 it was a national center of road racing. In the Roaring '20s, native son Johnny Mercer rose to prominence, and the great Flannery O'Connor was born in downtown Savannah. World War II provided an economic lift, but the city was still known as the "pretty woman with a dirty face," as Britain's Lady Astor famously described it in 1946.

Almost in answer to Astor's quip, city leaders in the 1950s began a misguided program to retrofit the city's infrastructure for the automobile era. Savannah's preservation movement had its seed in the fight by seven Savannah women to save the Davenport House and other buildings from demolition.

Savannah played a pioneering, though largely unsung, role in the civil rights movement. Ralph Mark Gilbert, pastor of the historic First African Baptist Church, launched one of the first black voter registration drives in the South. Gilbert's efforts were kept alive in the 1950s and 1960s by the beloved W. W. Law, a letter carrier who was head of the local chapter of the NAACP for many years.

The opening of the Savannah College of Art and Design in 1979 ushered another important chapter in Savannah's renaissance, which is ongoing to this day.

Greater Savannah

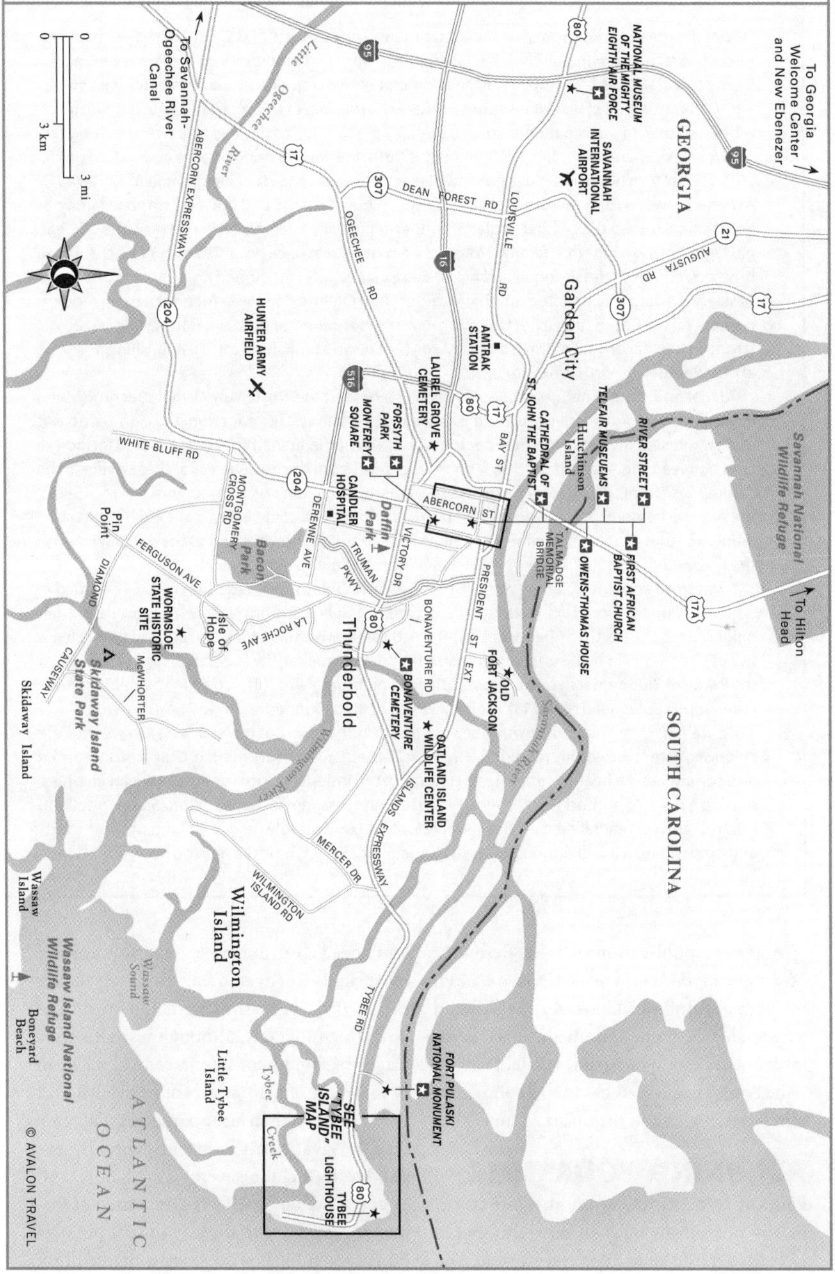
To Georgia Welcome Center and New Ebenezer
GEORGIA
SOUTH CAROLINA
Savannah National Wildlife Refuge
To Hilton Head
NATIONAL MUSEUM OF THE MIGHTY EIGHTH AIR FORCE
SAVANNAH INTERNATIONAL AIRPORT
Garden City
AUGUSTA RD
DEAN FOREST RD
LOUISVILLE RD
OGEECHEE RD
AMTRAK STATION
LAUREL GROVE CEMETERY
ST. JOHN THE BAPTIST CATHEDRAL OF
TELFAIR MUSEUMS
RIVER STREET
Hutchinson Island
FIRST AFRICAN BAPTIST CHURCH
OWENS-THOMAS HOUSE
TALMADGE MEMORIAL BRIDGE
BAY ST
ABERCORN ST
FORSYTH PARK
MONTEREY SQUARE
CANDLER HOSPITAL
Daffin Park
VICTORY DR
TRUMAN PKWY
DERENNE AVE
HUNTER ARMY AIRFIELD
WHITE BLUFF RD
MONTGOMERY CROSS RD
Bacon Park
FERGUSON AVE
Pin Point
DIAMOND CAUSEWAY
Isle of Hope
LA ROCHE AVE
WORMSLOE STATE HISTORIC SITE
Skidaway Island State Park
McWHORTER
Skidaway Island
Thunderbolt
BONAVENTURE RD
BONAVENTURE CEMETERY
PRESIDENT ST EXT
OLD FORT JACKSON
OATLAND ISLAND WILDLIFE CENTER
Savannah River
Wilmington River
ISLANDS EXPRESSWAY
MERCER DR
WILMINGTON ISLAND RD
Wilmington Island
Wassaw Island
Wassaw Sound
Wassaw Island National Wildlife Refuge
Boneyard Beach
Little Tybee Island
Tybee Creek
TYBEE RD
FORT PULASKI NATIONAL MONUMENT
SEE "TYBEE ISLAND" MAP
TYBEE LIGHTHOUSE
ATLANTIC OCEAN
To Savannah-Ogeechee River Canal
ABERCORN EXPRESSWAY
Little Ogeechee River
0 3 mi
0 3 km
© AVALON TRAVEL

A Visionary Aristocrat

One of the greatest products of the Enlightenment, **James Edward Oglethorpe** was a study in contrasts, embodying all the vitality, contradiction, and ambiguity of that turbulent age. A stern moralist yet an avowed liberal, an aristocrat with a populist streak, an abolitionist and an anti-Catholic, a man of war who sought peace—the founder of Georgia would put his own inimitable stamp on the new nation to follow, a legacy personified to this day in the city he designed.

After making a name for himself fighting the Turks, the young London native and Oxford graduate would return home only to serve a two-year prison sentence for killing a man in a brawl. The experience was a formative one for Oglethorpe, scion of a large and upwardly mobile family, as he was now forced to see how England's underbelly really lived. Upon his release, the 25-year-old Oglethorpe ran for the "family" House of Commons seat once occupied by his father and two brothers, and won. He distinguished himself as a campaigner for human rights and an opponent of slavery. Another jail-related epiphany came when Oglethorpe saw a friend die of smallpox in debtors prison. More than ever, Oglethorpe was determined to right what he saw as a colossal wrong in the draconian English justice system. His crusade took the form of establishing a sanctuary for debtors in North America.

To that end, he and his friend Lord Perceval established the Trustees, a 21-member group who lobbied King George for permission to establish such a colony. The grant from the king—who was more interested in containing the Spanish than in any humanitarian concerns—would include all land between the Altamaha and Savannah Rivers and from the headwaters of these rivers to the "south seas." Ironically, there were no debtors among Savannah's original colonists. Nonetheless, the new settlement was indeed a reflection of its founder's core values, banning rum as a bad influence (though beer and wine were allowed), prohibiting slavery, and eschewing lawyers on the theory that a gentleman should always be able to defend himself.

Nearing 40 and distracted by war with the Spanish, Oglethorpe's agenda gradually eroded in the face of opposition from settlers, who craved not only the more hedonistic lifestyle of their neighbors to the north in Charleston but the economic advantage that city enjoyed through the use of slave labor. In nearly the same hour as his greatest military victory, crushing the Spanish at the Battle of Bloody Marsh on St. Simons Island, Oglethorpe also suffered an ignominious defeat: being replaced as head of the 13th colony, which he had founded.

He went back to England, never to see the New World again. But his heart was always with the colonists. After successfully fending off a political attack and a court-martial, Oglethorpe married and commenced a healthy retirement. He supported independence for the American colonies, making a point to enthusiastically receive the new ambassador from the United States, one John Adams. The old general died on June 30, 1785, at age 88. Fittingly for this lifelong philanthropist and humanitarian, his childhood home in Godalming, Surrey, is now a nursing home.

After the publication of John Berendt's *Midnight in the Garden of Good and Evil* in 1994, nothing would ever be the same in Savannah. Old-money families cringed as idiosyncrasies and hypocrisies were laid bare in "The Book." Local merchants and politicians, however, delighted in the influx of tourists.

PLANNING YOUR TIME

Plan on **two nights** at an absolute minimum—not only to enjoy all the sights, but to fully soak in the local color and attitude. You don't need a car to have a great time and see most sights worth enjoying. A strong walker can easily traverse the length and breadth of downtown in a day, although less energetic travelers should consider a central location or make use of the free downtown shuttle.

Much more than just a parade, St. Patrick's Day in Savannah—an event generally expanded to include several days before and after the holiday itself—is also a time of immense crowds, with the city's usual population of about 150,000 doubling with the influx of partying visitors. Be aware that lodging on and around March 17 fills up well in advance.

ORIENTATION

The downtown area is bounded on the east by East Broad Street and on the west by Martin Luther King Jr. Boulevard (formerly West Broad St.). Technically, Gwinnett Street is the southern boundary of the National Historic Landmark District, though in practice locals extend the boundary several blocks southward.

Sights

It's best to introduce yourself to the sights of Savannah by traveling from the river southward. It's no small task to navigate the nation's largest contiguous historic district, but when in doubt it's best to follow James Oglethorpe's original plan of using the five "monumental" squares on Bull Street (Johnson, Wright, Chippewa, Madison, and Monterey) as focal points.

TOP EXPERIENCE

TOURS

Fair warning: Although local tour guides technically must pass a competency test demonstrating their knowledge of Savannah history, facts sometimes get thrown out the window in favor of whatever sounds good at the time. Keep in mind that not everything you hear from a tour guide may be true.

Trolley Tours

The vehicles of choice for the bulk of the masses visiting Savannah, trolleys allow you to sit back and enjoy the views in reasonable comfort. As in other cities, the guides provide commentary while attempting, with various degrees of success, to navigate the cramped downtown traffic environment. The main trolley companies in town are **Old Savannah Tours** (912/234-8128, www.oldsavannahtours.com, basic on-off tour $27 adults, $12 children), **Old Town Trolley Tours** (800/213-2474, www.trolleytours.com, basic on-off tour $27.99 adults, $10 children), and **Oglethorpe Trolley Tours** (912/233-8380, www.oglethorpetours.com, basic on-off tour $22.50 adults, $10 children). All embark from the Savannah Visitors Center on Martin Luther King Jr. Boulevard about every 20-30 minutes on the same schedule, daily 9am-4:30pm.

Frankly there's not much difference between them, as they all offer a very similar range of services for similar prices, with most offering pickup at your downtown hotel. While the common "on-off privileges" allow trolley riders to disembark for a while and pick up another of the same company's trolleys at marked stops, be aware there's no guarantee the next trolley—or the one after that—will have enough room to take you on board.

Horse and Carriage Tours

Ah, yes—what could be more romantic and more traditional than enjoying downtown Savannah the way it was originally intended to be traveled, by horse-drawn carriage? This is one of the most fun ways to see the city, for couples as well as for those with horse-enamored children. There are three main purveyors of equine tourism in town: **Carriage Tours of Savannah** (912/236-6756, www.carriagetoursofsavannah.com), **Historic Savannah Carriage Tours** (888/837-1011, www.savannahcarriage.com), and **Plantation Carriage Company** (912/201-0001, http://plantationcarriagecompany.com). The length of the basic tour and the price are about the same for all—45-60 minutes, about $25 adults and $15 children. All offer specialty tours as well, from ghost tours to evening romantic rides with champagne. Embarkation points vary;

check company websites for pickup points. Some will pick you up at your hotel.

Specialty Tours

The premium tour option is **Old City Walks** (E. Jones Ln., 912/358-0700, www.oldcitywalks.com, $48), explorations of well-known and of little-known Savannah attractions, guided by longtime local expert Phil Sellers. These aren't budget tours, but they are the state of the art locally. There are several tours and many times; Sellers also offers privately scheduled tours.

Consistently one of the highest-quality tours in town, **Savannah Taste Experience** (meets on River Street outside the Bohemian Hotel, 912/221-4439, www.savannahtasteexperience.com, $49 adults, $37 children) takes you on several foodie stops to taste, sip, and learn about Savannah's culinary scene. The basic tour is "First Squares," which focuses on spots within easy walking distance of the waterfront.

Longtime tour guide and raconteur Greg Proffit and his staff offer fun walking "pub crawls" through **Savannah Tours by Foot** (527 E. Gordon St., 912/238-3843, www.savannahtours.com, $10-18 adults), wherein the point is to meet your guide at some local tavern, ramble around, learn a little bit, and imbibe a lot, though not necessarily in that order. The adult tour is the "Creepy Crawl" ($25), whereas the tour suitable for kids and Girl Scouts is the "Creepy Stroll" ($16 adults, $10 children). You may not want to believe everything you hear, but you're sure to have a lot of fun. The tours book up early, so make arrangements in advance.

Storyteller and author Ted Eldridge leads **A Walk Through Savannah Tours** (meeting point at various locations in the historic district, 912/921-4455, www.awalkthroughsavannah.bravehost.com, $15 adults, $5 ages 6-12, free under age 6) and offers all kinds of specialty walking tours, such as a garden tour, a ghost tour, a historic churches tour, and, of course, a *Midnight in the Garden of Good and Evil* tour.

To learn about Savannah's history of filmmaking and to enjoy the best of local cuisine, try a **Savannah Movie Tour** (meets at Savannah Visitors Center, 301 MLK Jr. Blvd., 912/234-3440, www.savannahmovietours.com, $25 adults, $15 children), which takes you to various film locations in town. The company also offers the Foody Tour ($48) featuring local eateries.

Ghost Tours

The copious ghost tours can be fun for the casual visitor who wants entertainment rather than actual history. Students of the paranormal are likely to be disappointed by the cartoonish, Halloween aspect of some of the tours.

A standout in the ghost field is **Hearse Ghost Tours** (various pickup locations, 912/695-1578, www.hearseghosttours.com, $15), a unique company that also operates tours in New Orleans and St. Augustine, Florida. Up to eight guests at a time ride around in the open top of a converted hearse—painted all-black, of course—and get a 90-minute, suitably over-the-top narration from the driver-guide. It's still pretty cheesy, but a hip kind of cheesy.

For those who take their paranormal activity *very* seriously, there's Shannon Scott's **Sixth Sense Savannah Ghost Tour** (meets at Clary's Cafe, 404 Abercorn St., 866/666-3323, www.sixthsensesavannah.com, $20, midnight tour $38.50), an uncensored, straightforward look at Savannah's poltergeist population.

Biking Tours

To see downtown Savannah by bicycle—quite a refreshing experience—try **Savannah Bike Tours** (41 Habersham St., 912/704-4043, www.savannahbiketours.com, $15 adults, $10 under age 12) for a two-hour trip through 19 squares and Forsyth Park with your "rolling concierge." Pedaling around the squares and stopping to explore certain sights is a unique pleasure. Tours leave daily at 9:30am,

12:30pm, and 4pm. Rent bikes from them or ride your own.

For a unique tour experience, take a seat on the **Savannah Slow Ride** (various meeting points, 912/414-5634, www.savannahslowride.com, $25), a sort of combination bar, bicycle, and carriage ride. You get on with a group and everyone helps pedal around the squares on about a two-hour ride at five miles per hour or less. You can even bring your to-go cup with you. Pickup points depend on the tour; call for details.

WATERFRONT

★ River Street

It's much tamer than it was 30 years ago—when muscle cars cruised its cobblestones and a volatile mix of local teenagers, sailors on shore leave, and soldiers on liberty made things less than family-friendly after dark—but River Street still has more than enough edginess to keep things interesting. Families are safe and welcome here, but energetic pub crawling remains a favorite pastime for locals and visitors alike.

If you have a car, park it somewhere else and walk. The cobblestones—actually old ballast stones from some of the innumerable ships that docked here over the years—are tough on the suspension, and much of River Street is dedicated to pedestrian traffic anyway.

THE WAVING GIRL

At the east end of River Street is the statue of Florence Martus, aka ***The Waving Girl,*** set in the emerald-green expanse of little Morrell Park. Beginning in 1887 at the age of 19, Martus—who actually lived several miles downriver on Elba Island—took to greeting every passing ship with a wave of a handkerchief by day and a lantern at night, without fail for the next 40 years. Ship captains returned the greeting with a salute of their own on the ship's whistle, and word spread all over the world of the beguiling woman who waited on the balcony of that lonely house. Martus became such an enduring symbol of the personality and spirit of Savannah that a U.S. Liberty ship was named for her in 1943.

WORLD WAR II MEMORIAL

Near the foot of the Bohemian Hotel Savannah Riverfront on River Street is a 21st-century addition to Savannah's public monuments. Installed in 2010, the **World War II Memorial**—fairly modernist by local standards—features a copper-and-bronze globe torn in half to represent the European and Pacific theaters of the war. The more than 500 local people who gave their lives in that conflict are memorialized by name.

Bay Street

Because so few downtown streets can accommodate 18-wheelers, Bay Street unfortunately has become the default route for industrial traffic in the area on its way to and from the industrial west side of town. In front of the Hyatt Regency Savannah is a concrete bench marking the spot on which Oglethorpe pitched his first tent.

Dominating Bay Street is **City Hall** (2 E. Bay St.), with its gold-leaf dome. The 1907 building was designed by acclaimed architect Hyman Witcover and erected on the site of Savannah's first town hall. Directly adjacent to City Hall on the east is a small canopy sheltering two cannons, which together compose the oldest monument in Savannah. These are the **Chatham Artillery Guns,** presented to the local militia group of the same name by President George Washington during his one and only visit to town in 1791.

Behind the Chatham Artillery Guns is the ornate **Savannah Cotton Exchange** (100 E. Bay St.), built in 1886 to facilitate the city's huge cotton export business. The fanciful lion figure in front—sometimes mistakenly referred to as a griffin—represents Mark the Evangelist. However, it isn't original—the first lion was destroyed in 2009 in a bizarre traffic accident.

Downtown Savannah

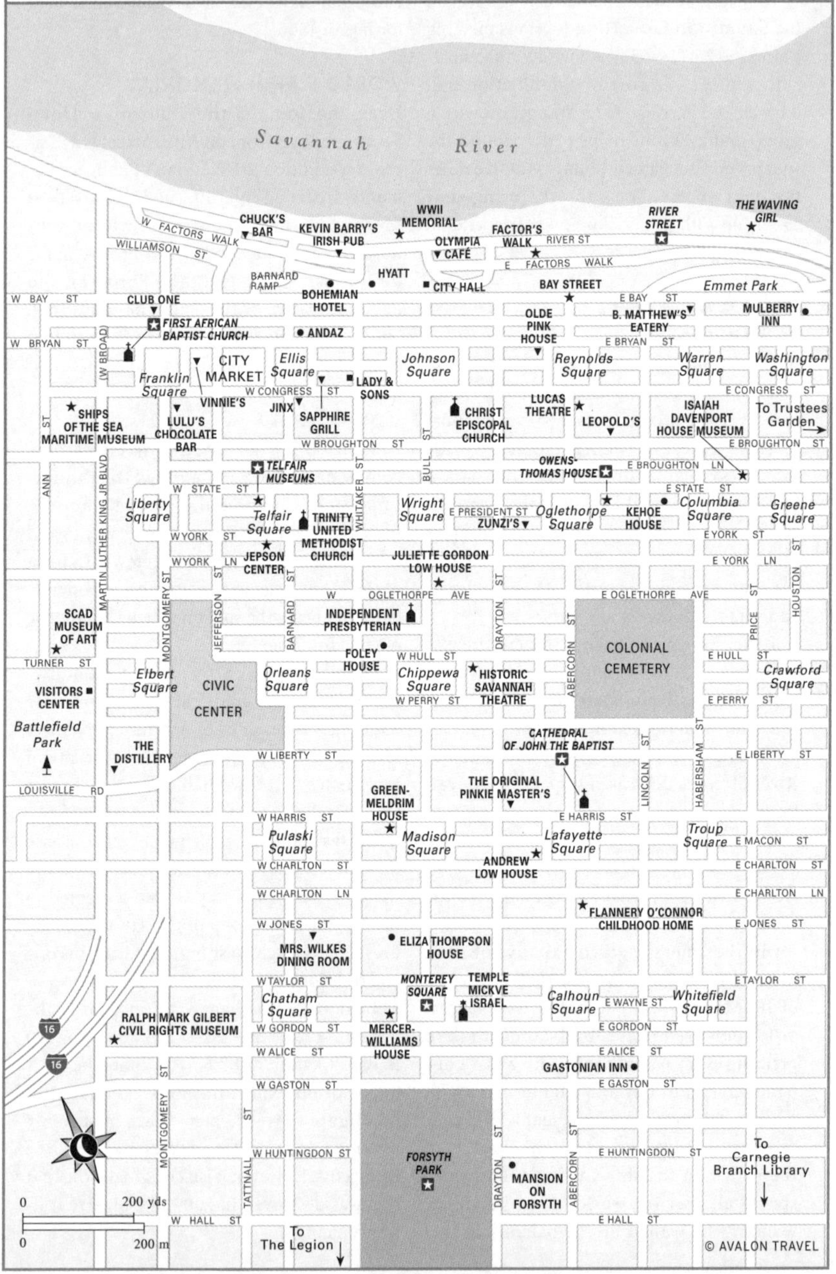
Savannah River
W FACTORS WALK
WILLIAMSON ST
CHUCK'S BAR
KEVIN BARRY'S IRISH PUB
WWII MEMORIAL
OLYMPIA CAFÉ
FACTOR'S WALK
RIVER ST
RIVER STREET
THE WAVING GIRL
E FACTORS WALK
BARNARD RAMP
BOHEMIAN HOTEL
HYATT
CITY HALL
BAY STREET
Emmet Park
W BAY ST
E BAY ST
CLUB ONE
FIRST AFRICAN BAPTIST CHURCH
ANDAZ
OLDE PINK HOUSE
B. MATTHEW'S EATERY
MULBERRY INN
W BRYAN ST
E BRYAN ST
(W BROAD)
Franklin Square
CITY MARKET
Ellis Square
Johnson Square
Reynolds Square
Warren Square
Washington Square
LADY & SONS
W CONGRESS ST
E CONGRESS ST
VINNIE'S
JINX
SAPPHIRE GRILL
CHRIST EPISCOPAL CHURCH
LUCAS THEATRE
LEOPOLD'S
ISAIAH DAVENPORT HOUSE MUSEUM
To Trustees Garden
SHIPS OF THE SEA MARITIME MUSEUM
LULU'S CHOCOLATE BAR
W BROUGHTON ST
E BROUGHTON ST
E BROUGHTON LN
TELFAIR MUSEUMS
OWENS-THOMAS HOUSE
W STATE ST
E STATE ST
ANN ST
MARTIN LUTHER KING JR BLVD
WHITAKER ST
BULL ST
Liberty Square
Telfair Square
TRINITY UNITED METHODIST CHURCH
Wright Square
E PRESIDENT ST
ZUNZI'S
Oglethorpe Square
KEHOE HOUSE
Columbia Square
Greene Square
W YORK ST
E YORK ST
W YORK LN
E YORK LN
JEPSON CENTER
JULIETTE GORDON LOW HOUSE
W OGLETHORPE AVE
E OGLETHORPE AVE
MONTGOMERY ST
JEFFERSON ST
BARNARD ST
DRAYTON ST
ABERCORN ST
PRICE ST
HOUSTON ST
SCAD MUSEUM OF ART
INDEPENDENT PRESBYTERIAN
COLONIAL CEMETERY
FOLEY HOUSE
W HULL ST
E HULL ST
TURNER ST
Elbert Square
CIVIC CENTER
Orleans Square
Chippewa Square
HISTORIC SAVANNAH THEATRE
Crawford Square
VISITORS CENTER
W PERRY ST
E PERRY ST
Battlefield Park
THE DISTILLERY
CATHEDRAL OF JOHN THE BAPTIST
LINCOLN ST
HABERSHAM ST
W LIBERTY ST
E LIBERTY ST
LOUISVILLE RD
GREEN-MELDRIM HOUSE
THE ORIGINAL PINKIE MASTER'S
W HARRIS ST
E HARRIS ST
Pulaski Square
Madison Square
Lafayette Square
Troup Square
E MACON ST
ANDREW LOW HOUSE
W CHARLTON ST
E CHARLTON ST
W CHARLTON LN
E CHARLTON LN
FLANNERY O'CONNOR CHILDHOOD HOME
W JONES ST
E JONES ST
MRS. WILKES DINING ROOM
ELIZA THOMPSON HOUSE
W TAYLOR ST
E TAYLOR ST
MONTEREY SQUARE
TEMPLE MICKVE ISRAEL
Chatham Square
Calhoun Square
E WAYNE ST
Whitefield Square
RALPH MARK GILBERT CIVIL RIGHTS MUSEUM
16
W GORDON ST
E GORDON ST
MERCER-WILLIAMS HOUSE
W ALICE ST
E ALICE ST
GASTONIAN INN
W GASTON ST
E GASTON ST
TATTNALL ST
W HUNTINGDON ST
E HUNTINGDON ST
FORSYTH PARK
MANSION ON FORSYTH
To Carnegie Branch Library
0
200 yds
200 m
W HALL ST
E HALL ST
To The Legion
© AVALON TRAVEL

the First African Baptist Church

CITY MARKET
Ellis Square

Ellis Square's history as Savannah's main open-air marketplace goes back to 1755, when there was a single City Market building in the square itself. The fourth City Market was built in 1872, an ornate Romanesque affair with a 50-foot roofline. In 1954, the city decided to build a parking garage in the square. So the magnificent City Market building—and Ellis Square—simply ceased to exist.

Several large warehouses surrounding City Market survived. Now a hub of tourism, City Market encompasses working art studios, hip bars, cute cafés, live music in the east end of the courtyard, cutting-edge art galleries, gift shops, and restaurants.

The eyesore that was the Ellis Square parking garage is gone, and the square has been rebuilt as a pedestrian hangout, complete with a fountain, all atop a huge underground parking garage. Be sure to check out the smallish bronze of native Savannahian and Oscar-winning lyricist Johnny Mercer on the square's western edge.

Franklin Square

Until recently, Franklin Square was, like Ellis Square, a victim of "progress," this time in the form of a highway going right through the middle of it. But as part of the city's effort to reclaim its history, Franklin Square was returned to its original state in the mid-1980s. The **Haitian Monument** in the center of the square commemorates the sacrifice and service of "Les Chasseurs Volontaires de Saint-Domingue," the 750 Haitian volunteers who fought for American independence and lost many of their number during the unsuccessful attempt to wrest Savannah back from the British in 1779.

★ FIRST AFRICAN BAPTIST CHURCH

The premier historical attraction on Franklin Square is the **First African Baptist Church** (23 Montgomery St., 912/233-2244, http://firstafricanbc.com, tours Tues.-Sat. 11am and 2pm, Sun. 1pm, $7 adults, $6 students/seniors), the oldest black congregation in North America, dating from 1777. The church also hosted the first African American Sunday school, begun in 1826. The church's founding pastor, George Liele, was the first black Baptist in Georgia and perhaps the first black missionary in the country. The present building dates from 1859 and was built almost entirely by members of the congregation themselves, some of whom redirected savings intended to purchase their freedom toward the building of the church. A key staging area for the Underground Railroad, First African Baptist still bears the scars of that turbulent time. In the floor of the fellowship hall—where many civil rights meetings were held, because it was safer for white citizens to go there instead of black activists going outside the church—you'll see breathing holes, drilled for use by escaped slaves hiding in a cramped crawlspace.

In the Footsteps of Bartram

The West has its stirring tale of Lewis and Clark, but the Southeast has its own fascinating—if somewhat less dramatic—tale of discovery, in the odyssey of William Bartram. In March 1773, the 33-year-old Bartram—son of royal botanist John Bartram and definitely a chip off the old block—arrived in Savannah to begin what would become a four-year journey through eight colonies. As Lewis and Clark would do in the following century, Bartram not only exhaustively documented his encounters with nature and with Native Americans, he also made discoveries whose impact has stayed with us to this day.

William Bartram

Young "Willie," born near Philadelphia in 1739, had a talent for drawing and for plants. A failure at business, Bartram was happy to settle on a traveling lifestyle that mixed both his loves. After accompanying his father on several early trips, Bartram set out on his own at the request of an old friend of his father's in England, Dr. John Fothergill, who paid Bartram 50 pounds per year plus expenses to send back specimens and drawings.

Though Bartram's quest would eventually move farther inland and encompass much of the modern American South, most of its first year was spent in coastal Georgia. After arriving in Savannah he moved southward, roughly paralleling modern U.S. 17, to the now-dead town of Sunbury, through Midway, and on to Darien, where he stayed at the plantation of Lachlan McIntosh on the great Altamaha River, which inspired Bartram to pen some of his most beautiful writing. Bartram also journeyed to Sapelo Island, Brunswick, St. Marys, and even into the great Okefenokee Swamp. Using Savannah and Charleston as bases, Bartram mostly traveled alone, either by horse, by boat, or on foot. Word of his trip preceded him, and he was usually greeted warmly by local traders and Indian chiefs (except for one encounter with a hostile Native American near the St. Marys River). In many places, he was the first European seen since De Soto and the Spanish. His epic journey ended in late 1776, when Bartram gazed on his beloved Altamaha for the last time. Heading north and crossing the Savannah River south of Ebenezer, he proceeded to Charleston and from there to his hometown of Philadelphia—where he would remain for the rest of his days.

At its publication, his 1791 chronicle, *Travels Through North and South Carolina, Georgia, East and West Florida,* was hailed as "the most astounding verbal artifact of the early republic." In that unassuming yet timeless work, Bartram cemented his reputation as the country's first native-born naturalist and practically invented the modern travelogue. Thanks to the establishment of the William Bartram Trail in 1976, you can walk in his footsteps—or close to them, anyway, since historians are not sure of his route. The trail uses a rather liberal interpretation, including memorials, trails, and gardens, but many specific "heritage sites" in coastal Georgia have their own markers, as follows:

- River and Barnard Streets in Savannah to mark the beginning of Bartram's trek
- LeConte-Woodmanston Plantation in Liberty County (Barrington Ferry Rd. south of Sandy Run Rd. near Riceboro)
- 1.5 miles south of the South Newport River off U.S. 17
- St. Simon's Island on Frederica Road near the Fort Frederica entrance
- Off Highway 275 at Old Ebenezer Cemetery in Effingham County

Among the indigenous species Bartram was the first to record are the Fraser magnolia, gopher tortoise, Florida sandhill crane, flame azalea, and oakleaf hydrangea.

HISTORIC DISTRICT NORTH

Johnson Square

Due east of City Market, Johnson Square, Oglethorpe's very first square, is named for Robert Johnson, governor of South Carolina at the time of Georgia's founding. The roomy, shaded square, ringed with major bank branches and insurance firms, is dominated by the **Nathanael Greene Monument** in honor of George Washington's second-in-command, who was granted nearby Mulberry Grove plantation for his efforts. In typically maddening Savannah fashion, there is a separate square named for Greene, which has no monument to him at all.

Reynolds Square

Walk directly east of Johnson Square to find yourself at Reynolds Square, named for John Reynolds, the first (and exceedingly unpopular) royal governor of Georgia. First called "Lower New Square," Reynolds Square originally served as site of the filature, or cocoon storage warehouse, during the fledgling colony's ill-fated flirtation with the silk industry (a federal building now occupies the site). As with Johnson Square, the monument in Reynolds Square has nothing to do with its namesake, but is instead a likeness of John Wesley dedicated in 1969 near the spot believed to have been his home.

OLDE PINK HOUSE

A Reynolds Square landmark, the **Olde Pink House** (23 Abercorn St.) is not only one of Savannah's most romantic restaurants but quite a historic site as well. It's the oldest Savannah mansion from the 18th century still standing as well as the first place in Savannah where the Declaration of Independence was read aloud. The Georgian mansion was built in 1771 for rice planter James Habersham Jr., one of America's richest men at the time and a member of the notorious "Liberty Boys" who plotted revolution. The building's pink exterior was a matter of serendipity, resulting from its core redbrick seeping through the formerly white stucco outer covering.

LUCAS THEATRE FOR THE ARTS

Built in 1921 as part of Arthur Lucas's regional chain of movie houses, the **Lucas Theatre for the Arts** (32 Abercorn St., 912/525-5040, www.lucastheatre.com) also featured a stage for road shows. In 1976, the Lucas closed after a screening of *The Exorcist*. When the building faced demolition in 1986, a group of citizens created a nonprofit to save it. Despite numerous starts and stops, the 14-year campaign finally paid off in a grand reopening in 2000, an event helped immeasurably by timely donations from *Midnight* star Kevin Spacey and the cast and crew of the locally shot *Forrest Gump*. The theater's schedule stays pretty busy, so it should be easy to check out a show while you're in town.

Columbia Square

Named for the mythical patroness of America, Columbia Square features at its center not an expected portrait of that female warrior figure but the original fountain from Noble Jones's Wormsloe Plantation, placed there in 1970.

ISAIAH DAVENPORT HOUSE MUSEUM

Columbia Square is primarily known as the home of the **Isaiah Davenport House Museum** (324 E. State St., 912/236-8097, www.davenporthousemuseum.org, Mon.-Sat. 10am-4pm, Sun. 1pm-4pm, $9 adults, $5 children). The house museum is a delightful stop in and of itself because of its elegant simplicity, sweeping double staircase, and near-perfect representation of the Federalist style. But the Davenport House occupies an exalted place in Savannah history as well, because the fight to save it began the preservation movement in the city. In 1955 the Davenport House, then a tenement, was to be demolished for a parking lot. But Emma Adler and six other Savannah women, angered by the recent destruction of Ellis Square, refused to let it go down quietly. Together they formed the Historic Savannah Foundation in order to raise the $22,500 needed to purchase the Davenport House.

Warren and Washington Squares

Warren Square and its neighbor Washington Square formed the first extension of Oglethorpe's original four squares, and they boast some of the oldest houses in the historic district. Both squares are lovely little garden spots, ideal for a picnic in the shade. Two houses near Washington Square were restored by the late Jim Williams of *Midnight* fame: the **Hampton Lillibridge House** (507 E. St. Julian St.), which once hosted an Episcopal exorcism, and the **Charles Oddingsells House** (510 E. St. Julian St.).

Greene Square

Named for Revolutionary War hero Nathanael Greene, but bearing no monument to him whatsoever, Greene Square is of particular importance to local African American history. At the corner of Houston (pronounced "HOUSE-ton") and East State Streets is the 1810 **Cunningham House,** built for Henry Cunningham, former slave and founding pastor of the **Second African Baptist Church** (124 Houston St., 912/233-6163, www.secondafrican.org), on the west side of the square, in which General Sherman made his famous promise of "40 acres and a mule." In 1818, the residence at 542 East State Street was constructed for free blacks Charlotte and William Wall. The property at 513 East York Street was built for Catherine DeVeaux, part of a prominent African American family.

Old Fort

One of the lesser-known aspects of Savannah history is this well-trod neighborhood at the east end of Bay Street, once the site of groundbreaking experiments and piratical intrigue, and then a diverse melting pot of Savannah citizenry.

EMMET PARK

Just north of Reynolds Square on the north side of Bay Street you'll come to **Emmet Park** (E. Bay St. west of E. Broad St.), first a Native American burial ground and then known as "the Strand" or "Irish Green" because of its proximity to the Irish slums of the Old Fort. In 1902 the park was named for Robert Emmet, an Irish patriot of the early 1800s, who was executed by the British for treason. Within it is the eight-foot **Celtic Cross,** erected in 1983 and carved of Irish limestone. The Celtic Cross is at the center of a key ceremony for local Irish Catholics during the week prior to St. Patrick's Day.

TRUSTEES' GARDEN

At the east end of Bay Street where it meets East Broad Street rises a bluff behind a masonry wall—at 40 feet off the river, still the highest point in Chatham County. This is **Trustees' Garden** (10 E. Broad St., 912/443-3277, http://trusteesgarden.com), the nation's first experimental garden. Trustees' Garden became the site of Fort Wayne, named after General "Mad Anthony" Wayne of Revolutionary War fame, who retired to a plantation near Savannah. The Fort Wayne area—still called the "Old Fort" neighborhood by old-timers—fell from grace and became associated with the "lowest elements" of Savannah society, which in the 19th and early 20th centuries were Irish and African Americans. It also became known for its illegal activity and as the haunt of sea salts such as the ones who frequented what is now the delightfully schlocky **Pirates' House** restaurant. That building began life in 1753 as a seamen's inn and was later chronicled by Robert Louis Stevenson in *Treasure Island* as a rogue's gallery of pirates and nautical ne'er-do-wells.

Find the **Herb House** on East Broad Street, the older-looking clapboard structure next to the Pirates' House entrance. You're looking at what is considered the single oldest building in Georgia and one of the oldest in the United States. Constructed in 1734, it was originally the home of Trustees' Garden's chief gardener.

A Southern St. Paddy's Day

Savannah hosts the second-largest St. Patrick's Day celebration in the world, second only to New York City's. With its fine spring weather and walkability—not to mention its liberal rules allowing you to carry an adult beverage on the street—Savannah is tailor-made for a boisterous outdoor celebration.

Ironically, given St. Patrick's Day's current close association with the Catholic faith, the first parade in Savannah was organized by Irish Protestants. Thirteen members of the local Hibernian Society—the country's oldest Irish society—took part in a private procession to Independent Presbyterian Church in 1813. The first public procession was in 1824, when the Hibernians invited all local Irishmen to parade through the streets. The first recognizably modern parade, with bands and a "grand marshal," happened in 1870.

Organized by a "committee" of about 700 local Irish residents, today's three-hour procession includes marchers from all the local Irish organizations, in addition to marching bands and floats representing many local groups. The assembled clans wear kelly-green blazers, brandishing their walking canes and to-go cups, some pushing future committee members in strollers.

Broughton Street

Downtown's main shopping district for most of the 20th century was Broughton Street. Postwar suburbs and white flight brought neglect to the area by the 1960s, and many thought Broughton was gone for good. But with the downtown renaissance brought about largely by the Savannah College of Art and Design (SCAD), Broughton was able not only to get back on its feet, but also to thrive as a commercial center once again.

JEN LIBRARY

The Savannah College of Art and Design's **Jen Library** (201 E. Broughton St.) is a state-of-the-art facility set in the circa-1890 Levy and Maas Brothers department stores.

TRUSTEES THEATER

Around the corner from the Lucas Theatre on Reynolds Square is the art moderne **Trustees Theater** (216 E. Broughton St., 912/525-5051, www.trusteestheater.com), a Savannah College of Art and Design (SCAD) operation that seats 1,200 and hosts concerts, film screenings, and the school's much-anticipated spring fashion show. It began life in the postwar boom of 1946 as the Weis Theatre, another one of those ornate Southern movie houses that took full commercial advantage of being the only buildings at the time to have air-conditioning. But by the end of the 1970s it had followed the fate of Broughton Street, lying dormant and neglected until its purchase and renovation by SCAD in 1989.

Wright Square

The big monument in Wright Square, Oglethorpe's second square, has nothing to do with James Wright, royal governor of Georgia before the Revolution, for whom it's named. Instead the monument honors William Gordon, former mayor and founder of the Central of Georgia Railway. But more importantly, Wright Square is the final resting place for the great Yamacraw chief Tomochichi, buried in 1737 in an elaborate state funeral at James Oglethorpe's insistence. A huge boulder of North Georgia granite honoring the chief was placed in a corner of the square in 1899. However, Tomochichi is not buried under the boulder but rather somewhere underneath the Gordon monument.

Telfair Square

Telfair Square was named for Mary Telfair, last heir of a family that was one of the most important in Savannah history. Mary bequeathed the family mansion to the Georgia Historical Society upon her death in 1875 to serve as a museum. Originally called St. James Square after a similar square in London, Telfair was the last of Oglethorpe's original four squares.

Telfair Square hosts two of the three buildings operated by **Telfair Museums,** an umbrella organization that relies on a combination of private and public funding and has driven much of the arts agenda in Savannah for the last 125 years. The third building operated by Telfair Museums is the Owens-Thomas House on Oglethorpe Square.

Get a triple-site pass to the Jepson Center, the Telfair Academy, and the Owens-Thomas House for $20 per person.

★ JEPSON CENTER FOR THE ARTS

The proudest addition to the Telfair Museums group is the striking, 64,000-square-foot **Jepson Center for the Arts** (207 W. York Ln., 912/790-8800, www.telfair.org, Sun.-Mon. noon-5pm, Tues.-Sat. 10am-5pm, $12 adults, $5 students), whose ultramodern exterior sits catty-corner from the Telfair Academy of Arts and Sciences. Promoting a massive, daringly designed new facility devoted to nothing but modern art was a hard sell in this traditional town, especially when renowned architect Moshe Safdie insisted on building a glassed-in flyover across a lane between two buildings. After a few delays in construction, the Jepson opened its doors in 2006 and has since wowed locals and visitors alike with its cutting-edge traveling exhibits and rotating assortment of late 20th-century and 21st-century modern art. If you get hungry, you can enjoy lunch in the expansive atrium café, and, of course, there's a nice gift shop.

Each late January-early February the Jepson Center hosts most events of the unique Pulse Art + Technology Festival, a celebration of the intersection of cutting-edge technology and performing and visual arts.

★ TELFAIR ACADEMY OF ARTS AND SCIENCES

The oldest public art museum in the South, the **Telfair Academy of Arts and Sciences** (121 Barnard St., 912/790-8800, www.telfair.org, Sun.-Mon. noon-5pm, Tues.-Sat. 10am-5pm, $12 adults, $5 students) was built in 1821 by the great William Jay for Alexander Telfair, scion of that famous Georgia family. The five statues in front are of Phidias, Raphael,

the Jepson Center for the Arts

Rubens, Michelangelo, and Rembrandt. As well as displaying Sylvia Judson Shaw's now-famous *Bird Girl* sculpture, which originally stood in Bonaventure Cemetery (actually the third of four casts by the sculptor), the Telfair Academy features an outstanding collection of primarily 18th- and 20th-century works, most notably the largest public collection of visual art by Khalil Gibran. Major paintings include works by Childe Hassam, Frederick Frieseke, Gari Melchers, and the massive *Black Prince of Crécy* by Julian Story.

TRINITY UNITED METHODIST CHURCH

Directly between the Telfair and the Jepson stands **Trinity United Methodist Church** (225 W. President St., 912/233-4766, www.trinitychurch1848.org, sanctuary daily 9am-5pm, services Sun. 8:45am and 11am), Savannah's first Methodist church. Built in 1848 on the site of the Telfair family garden, its masonry walls are of famous "Savannah Gray" bricks—a lighter, more porous, and elegant variety—under stucco. Virgin longleaf pine was used for most of the interior, fully restored in 1969. Call ahead for a tour.

Oglethorpe Square

Don't look for a monument to Georgia's founder in the square named for him. His monument is in Chippewa Square. Originally called "Upper New Square," Oglethorpe Square was created in 1742.

JULIETTE GORDON LOW BIRTHPLACE

Around the corner from Wright Square at Oglethorpe and Bull is the **Juliette Gordon Low Birthplace** (10 E. Oglethorpe Ave., 912/233-4501, www.juliettegordonlowbirthplace.org, Mar.-Oct. Mon.-Sat. 10am-4pm, $15 adults, $12 children, $10 Girl Scouts), declared the city's very first National Historic Landmark in 1965, and fresh off a significant restoration effort. The founder of the Girl Scouts of the USA lived here from her birth in 1860 until her marriage. The house was completed in 1821 for Mayor James Moore Wayne, future Supreme Court justice, but the current furnishings, many original, are intended to reflect the home during the 1880s.

Also called the Girl Scout National Center, the Low birthplace is probably Savannah's most festive historic site because of the heavy traffic of Girl Scout troops from across the United States. They flock here year-round to take part in programs and learn more about their organization's founder, whose family sold the house to the Girl Scouts in 1953. You don't have to be affiliated with the Girl Scouts to tour the home. Tours are given every 15 minutes, and tickets are available at the Oglethorpe Avenue entrance.

★ OWENS-THOMAS HOUSE

The square's main claim to fame, the **Owens-Thomas House** (124 Abercorn St., 912/233-9743, www.telfair.org, Sun.-Mon. noon-5pm, Tues.-Sat. 10am-5pm, last tour 4:30pm, $20 adults, $15 students, ticket includes Jepson Center and Telfair Academy), lies on the northeast corner. Widely known as the finest example of Regency architecture in the United States, the Owens-Thomas House was designed by brilliant young English architect William Jay. One of the first professionally trained architects in the United States, Jay was only 24 when he designed the home for cotton merchant or "factor" Richard Richardson, who lost the house in the depression of 1820 (all that remains of Richardson's tenure are three marble-top tables). The house's current name is derived from Savannah mayor George Owens, who bought the house in 1830.

Perhaps most interestingly, a complex plumbing system features rain-fed cisterns, flushing toilets, sinks, bathtubs, and a shower. When built, the Owens-Thomas House in fact had the first indoor plumbing in Savannah. On the south facade is a beautiful cast-iron veranda from which Revolutionary War hero Marquis de Lafayette addressed a crowd of starstruck Savannahians during his visit in 1825. The associated slave quarters are in a surprisingly intact state, including the original

Scout's Honor

Known as "Daisy" to family and friends, **Juliette Magill Kinzie Gordon** was born to be a pioneer. Her father's family took part in the original settlement of Georgia, and her mother's kin were among the founders of Chicago. Mostly known as the founder of the **Girl Scouts of the USA,** Daisy was also an artist, adventurer, and healer. Born and raised in the house on Oglethorpe Avenue in Savannah known to Girl Scouts across the nation as simply "the Birthplace," she was an animal lover with an early penchant for theater, drawing, and poetry.

In 1911 while in England, Daisy met Robert Baden-Powell, founder of the Boy Scouts and Girl Guides in Britain. Struck by the simplicity and usefulness of his project, she carried the seeds of a similar idea back with her to the United States. "I've got something for the girls of Savannah, and all of America, and all the world, and we're going to start it tonight," were her famous words in a phone call to a cousin after meeting Baden-Powell. So on March 12, 1912, Daisy gathered 18 girls to register the first troop of American Girl Guides, later the Girl Scouts of the USA.

Juliette "Daisy" Gordon Low died of breast cancer in her bed in the Andrew Low House on January 17, 1927. She was buried in Laurel Grove Cemetery. Girl Scout troops from all over the United States visit her birthplace, the Andrew Low House, and her gravesite to this day, often leaving flowers and small personal objects near her tombstone as tokens of respect and gratitude.

"haint blue" paint. The carriage house, where all tours begin, is now the home's gift shop.

The Owens-Thomas House is owned and operated by the Telfair Museums. Get a combination pass to all Telfair sites—the Jepson Center for the Arts, the Telfair Academy of Arts and Sciences, and the Owens-Thomas House—for $20 per person.

Martin Luther King Jr. Boulevard

SHIPS OF THE SEA MARITIME MUSEUM

One of Savannah's more unique museums is the quirky **Ships of the Sea Maritime Museum** (41 MLK Jr. Blvd., 912/232-1511, http://shipsofthesea.org, Tues.-Sun. 10am-5pm, $9 adults, $7 students). The stunning Greek Revival building in which it resides is known as the Scarbrough House because it was initially built in 1819 by the great William Jay for local shipping merchant William Scarbrough, co-owner of the SS *Savannah,* the first steamship to cross the Atlantic. After the Scarbroughs sold the property, it became the West Broad School for African Americans from Reconstruction through integration.

Inside, children, maritime buffs, and crafts connoisseurs can find intricate and detailed scale models of various historic vessels, such as Oglethorpe's *Anne,* the SS *Savannah,* and the NS *Savannah,* the world's first nuclear-powered surface vessel. There's even a model of the *Titanic.*

HISTORIC DISTRICT SOUTH

Chippewa Square

Named for a battle in the War of 1812, Chippewa Square has a large monument not to the battle, natch, but to James Oglethorpe, clad in full soldier's regalia. Notice the general is still facing south, toward the Spanish.

Yes, the bench on the square's north side is in the same location as the one Tom Hanks occupied in *Forrest Gump,* but it's not the same bench that hosted the two-time Oscar winner's backside—that one was donated by Paramount Pictures to be displayed in the Savannah History Museum on MLK Jr. Boulevard.

COLONIAL CEMETERY

Just north of Chippewa Square is Oglethorpe Avenue, originally called South Broad and the southern boundary of the original colony. At Oglethorpe and Abercorn Streets is **Colonial Cemetery** (Oglethorpe St. and Abercorn

St., www.savannahga.gov, daily 8am-dusk, free), first active in 1750. You'd be forgiven for assuming it's the "DAR" cemetery; the Daughters of the American Revolution contributed the ornate iron entranceway in 1913, thoughtfully dedicating it to themselves instead of the cemetery itself.

This is the final resting ground of many of Savannah's yellow fever victims. Famous people buried here include Button Gwinnett, one of Georgia's three signers of the Declaration of Independence. The man who reluctantly killed Gwinnett in a duel, General Lachlan McIntosh, is also buried here. The original burial vault of Nathanael Greene is in the cemetery, although the Revolutionary War hero's remains were moved to Johnson Square over a century ago.

HISTORIC SAVANNAH THEATRE

At the square's northeast corner is the **Historic Savannah Theatre** (222 Bull St., 912/233-7764, www.savannahtheatre.com), which claims to be the oldest continuously operating theater in the United States. Designed by William Jay, it opened in 1818 with a production of *The Soldier's Daughter.* In the glory days of gaslight theater in the 1800s, some of the nation's best actors, including Edwin Booth, brother to Lincoln's assassin, regularly trod the boards of its stage. Due to a fire in 1948, little remains of Jay's original design except a small section of exterior wall. The building is currently home to a semiprofessional revue company specializing in oldies shows.

INDEPENDENT PRESBYTERIAN CHURCH

Built in 1818, possibly by William Jay—scholars are unsure of the scope of his involvement—**Independent Presbyterian Church** (207 Bull St., 912/236-3346, www.ipcsav.org, services Sun. 11am, Wed. noon) is called the "mother of Georgia Presbyterianism." A fire destroyed most of Independent Presbyterian's original structure in 1889, but the subsequent rebuilding was a very faithful rendering of the original design, based on London's St. Martin-in-the-Fields. The church's steeple made a cameo appearance in *Forrest Gump* as a white feather floated by. In 1885 Woodrow Wilson married local parishioner Ellen Louise Axson in the manse to the rear of the church. Call ahead for a tour.

Madison Square

Named for the nation's fourth president, Madison Square memorializes a local hero who gave his life for his city during the American Revolution. Irish immigrant Sergeant William Jasper, hero of the Battle of Fort Moultrie in Charleston three years earlier, was killed leading the American charge during the 1779 Siege of Savannah, when an allied army failed to retake the city from the British. The monument in the square honors Jasper, but he isn't buried here.

GREEN-MELDRIM HOUSE

Given the house's beauty and history, visitors will be forgiven for not immediately realizing that the **Green-Meldrim House** (1 W. Macon St., 912/232-1251, www.stjohnssav.org, tours every 30 minutes Tues. and Thurs.-Fri. 10am-4pm, Sat. 10am-1pm, $8 adults, $5 students and children) is also the rectory of the adjacent St. John's Episcopal Church, which acquired it in 1892. This is the place where Sherman formulated his ill-fated "40 acres and a mule" Field Order No. 15, giving most of the Sea Islands of Georgia and South Carolina to freed blacks. A tasteful example of Gothic Revival architecture, this 1850 design by John Norris features a beautiful external gallery of filigree ironwork.

Lafayette Square

One of Savannah's favorite squares, especially on St. Patrick's Day, verdant Lafayette Square boasts a number of important sights and attractions.

ANDREW LOW HOUSE MUSEUM

A major landmark on Lafayette Square is the **Andrew Low House Museum** (329

Abercorn St., 912/233-6854, www.andrewlowhouse.com, Mon.-Sat. 10am-4pm, Sun. noon-4pm, $10 adults, $8 children), once the home of Juliette "Daisy" Gordon Low, the founder of the Girl Scouts of the USA, who was married to cotton heir William "Billow" Low, Andrew Low's son. Despite their happy-go-lucky nicknames, the union of Daisy and Billow was a notably unhappy one. Still, divorce was out of the question, so the couple lived separate lives until William's death in 1905. The one good thing that came out of the marriage was the germ for the idea for the Girl Scouts, which Juliette got from England's "Girl Guides" while living there with her husband, Savannah being the couple's winter residence. Designed by the great New York architect John Norris, the Low House is a magnificent example of the Italianate style. Author William Makepeace Thackeray ate in the dining room, now sporting full French porcelain service, and slept in an upstairs room; he also wrote at the desk by the bed. Also on the 2nd floor you'll see the room where Robert E. Lee stayed during his visit and the bed where Juliette Gordon Low died.

★ CATHEDRAL OF ST. JOHN THE BAPTIST

Spiritual home to Savannah's Irish community and the oldest Catholic church in Georgia, the **Cathedral of St. John the Baptist** (222. E. Harris St., 912/233-4709, www.savannahcathedral.org, daily 9am-noon and 12:30pm-5pm, mass Sun. 8am, 10am, 11:30am, Mon.-Sat. noon, Latin mass Sun. 1pm) was initially known as Our Lady of Perpetual Help. It's the place to be for mass the morning of March 17 at 8am, as the clans gather in their green jackets and white dresses to take a sip of communion wine before moving on to harder stuff in honor of St. Patrick.

Despite its overt Celtic character today, the parish was originally founded by French émigrés from Haiti who arrived after the successful overthrow of the colonial government by a slave uprising on the island in the late 1700s. The first sanctuary on the site was built in 1873. In a distressingly common event back then in Savannah, fire swept through the edifice in 1898, leaving only two spires and the external walls. The cathedral was completely rebuilt within a year and a half. In the years since, many renovations have been

the Cathedral of St. John the Baptist

The Story of "Jingle Bells"

Boston and Savannah vie over bragging rights as to where the classic Christmas song "Jingle Bells" was written. The song's composer, James L. Pierpont, led a life at times as carefree as the song itself. Born in Boston, Pierpont ventured from his wife and young children in 1849 to follow the gold rush to San Francisco. When his brother John was named minister of the new Unitarian congregation in Savannah in 1853, Pierpont followed him, becoming music director and organist, again leaving behind his wife and children in Boston. During this time Pierpont became a prolific composer of secular tunes, including polkas, ballads, and minstrel songs.

In August 1857, a Boston-based publisher, Oliver Ditson and Co., published Pierpont's song "One Horse Open Sleigh." Two years later it was rereleased with the current title, "Jingle Bells." At neither time, however, was the song a popular hit. It took action by his son Juriah in 1880 to renew the copyright to what would become one of the most famous songs of all time.

In Massachusetts, they swear Pierpont wrote the song while at the home of one Mrs. Otis Waterman. In Georgia, scholars assure us a homesick Pierpont wrote the tune during a winter at a house at Oglethorpe and Whitaker Streets, long since demolished. The Savannah contingent's ace in the hole is the fact that "Jingle Bells" was first performed in public at a Thanksgiving program at the local Unitarian Universalist Church in 1857. And despite persistent claims in Massachusetts that he wrote the song there in 1850, Southern scholars point out that Pierpont was actually in California in 1850.

undertaken. The most recent, from 1998 to 2000, involved the intricate removal, cleaning, and re-leading of more than 50 of the cathedral's stained-glass windows, a roof replacement, and an interior makeover.

FLANNERY O'CONNOR CHILDHOOD HOME

On a corner of Lafayette Square stands the rather Spartan facade of the **Flannery O'Connor Childhood Home** (207 E. Charlton St., 912/233-6014, www.flanneryoconnorhome.org, Fri.-Wed. 1pm-4pm, $6 adults, $5 students, free under age 15). The Savannah-born novelist lived in this three-story townhome from her birth in 1925 until 1938 and attended church at the cathedral across the square. Once a fairly nondescript attraction for so favorite a native daughter, a recent round of renovations has returned the two main floors to the state Flannery would have known, including an extensive library.

HAMILTON-TURNER INN

Across from the O'Connor house is the **Hamilton-Turner Inn** (330 Abercorn St., 912/233-1833, www.hamilton-turnerinn.com). Now a privately owned bed-and-breakfast, this 1873 Second Empire mansion is best known for the showmanship of its over-the-top Victorian appointments and its role in *Midnight in the Garden of Good and Evil* as the home of Joe Odom's girlfriend, "Mandy Nichols" (real name Nancy Hillis). In 1883 it was reportedly the first house in Savannah to have electricity.

Troup Square

Low-key Troup Square boasts the most modern-looking monument downtown, the **Armillary Sphere.** Essentially an elaborate sundial, the sphere is a series of astrologically themed rings with an arrow that marks the time by shadow. It is supported by six tortoises.

BEACH INSTITUTE

Just east of Troup Square, near the intersection of Harris and Price Streets, is the **Beach Institute** (502 E. Harris St., 912/234-8000, Tues.-Sun. noon-5pm, $4). Built as a school by the Freedmen's Bureau soon after the Civil War, it was named after its prime benefactor, Alfred Beach, editor of *Scientific American.*

It served as an African American school through 1919. Restored by SCAD and given back to the city to serve as a museum, the Beach Institute houses the permanent Ulysses Davis collection and a rotating calendar of art events with a connection to black history.

JONES STREET

There aren't a lot of individual attractions on Jones Street, the east-west avenue between Taylor and Charlton Streets just north of Monterey Square. Rather, it's the small-scale, throwback feel of the place and its tasteful, dignified homes, including the former home of **Joe Odom** (16 E. Jones St.), that are the attraction. The **Eliza Thompson House** (5 W. Jones St.), now a bed-and-breakfast, was the first home on Jones Street.

UNITARIAN UNIVERSALIST CHURCH OF SAVANNAH

Troup Square is the home of the historic **Unitarian Universalist Church of Savannah** (313 E. Harris St., 912/234-0980, www.jinglebellschurch.org, service Sun. 11am). This original home of Savannah's Unitarians, who sold the church when the Civil War came, was recently reacquired by the congregation. It is where James L. Pierpont first performed his immortal tune "Jingle Bells." When he did so, however, the church was actually on Oglethorpe Square. The entire building was moved to Troup Square in the mid-1800s.

★ Monterey Square

Originally named "Monterrey Square" to commemorate the local Irish Jasper Greens' participation in a victorious Mexican-American War battle in 1846, the spelling morphed into its current version somewhere along the way. But Monterey Square remains one of the most visually beautiful and serene spots in all of Savannah. At the center of the square is a monument not to the victory for which it is named but to Count Casimir Pulaski, killed while attempting to retake the city from the British, and whose remains supposedly lie under the 55-foot monument. Fans of ironwork will enjoy the ornate masterpieces in wrought iron featured at many houses on the periphery of the square.

Amazing ironwork surrounds Monterey Square.

MERCER-WILLIAMS HOUSE MUSEUM

Many visitors come to see the **Mercer-Williams House Museum** (429 Bull St., 912/236-6352, www.mercerhouse.com, Mon.-Sat. 10:30am-4pm, Sun. noon-4pm, $12.50 adults, $8 students). While locals never begrudge the business Savannah has enjoyed since the publishing of "The Book," *Midnight in the Garden of Good and Evil,* it's a shame that this grand John Norris building is now primarily known as a crime scene involving late antiques dealer Jim Williams and his lover. Therefore it might come as no surprise that if you take a tour of the home, you might hear less about "The Book" than you may have expected. Now proudly owned by Jim Williams's sister Dorothy Kingery, an established academic in her own right, the Mercer-Williams House deliberately concentrates on the early

the Mercer-Williams House Museum

history of the home and Jim Williams's prodigious talent as a collector and conservator of fine art and antiques. That said, Dr. Kingery's mama didn't raise no fool, as we say down here. The house was known to generations of Savannahians as simply the Mercer House until *Midnight in the Garden of Good and Evil* took off, at which time the eponymous nod to the late Mr. Williams was added.

The house was built for General Hugh W. Mercer, Johnny Mercer's great-grandfather, in 1860. Just so you know, and despite what any tour guide might tell you, the great Johnny Mercer himself never lived in the house. Tours of the home's four main rooms begin in the carriage house to the rear of the mansion. They're worth it for art aficionados even though the upstairs, Dr. Kingery's residence, is off-limits. Be forewarned that if you're coming just to see things about the book or movie, you might be disappointed.

TEMPLE MICKVE ISRAEL

Directly across Monterey Square from the Mercer House is Temple Mickve Israel (20 E. Gordon St., 912/233-1547, www.mickveisrael.org, Mon.-Fri. 10am-1pm and 2pm-4pm, closed Jewish holidays, $4 suggested donation), a notable structure for many reasons: It's Georgia's first synagogue; it's the only Gothic synagogue in the country; and it's the third-oldest Jewish congregation in North America (following those in New York and Newport, Rhode Island). Notable congregants have included Dr. Samuel Nunes Ribeiro, who helped stop an epidemic in 1733, and his descendant

Temple Mickve Israel

Raphael Moses, considered the father of the peach industry in the Peach State.

Mickve Israel offers 30- to 45-minute tours of the sanctuary and museum. No reservations are necessary for tours.

Calhoun Square

The last of the 24 squares in Savannah's original grid, Calhoun Square is also the only square with all its original buildings intact.

MASSIE HERITAGE CENTER

Dominating the south side of Calhoun Square is Savannah's first public elementary school and the spiritual home of Savannah educators, the **Massie Heritage Center** (207 E. Gordon St., 912/201-5070, www.massieschool.com, Mon.-Sat. 10am-4pm, Sun. noon-4pm, $8 adults, $5 youth). In 1841, Peter Massie, a Scots planter with a populist streak, endowed the school to give poor children as good an education as the children of rich families (like Massie's own) received. After the Civil War, the "Massie School," as it's known locally, was designated as the area's African American public school. Classes ceased in 1974, and it now operates as a living-history museum, centering on the period-appointed one-room "heritage classroom" but with several other exhibit spaces of note.

A million-dollar renovation in 2012 added an interactive model of Oglethorpe's urban design and several interesting exhibits on aspects of Savannah architecture and history. In all, Massie provides possibly the best one-stop tour for an all-encompassing look at Savannah history and culture. You can either do a self-guided tour or take the very informative guided tour at 11am or 2pm for the same admission price.

WESLEY MONUMENTAL UNITED METHODIST CHURCH

The **Wesley Monumental United Methodist Church** (429 Abercorn St., 912/232-0191, www.wesleymonumental.org, sanctuary daily 9am-5pm, services Sun. 8:45am and 11am), named not only for movement founder John Wesley but also for his musical younger brother Charles, is home to Savannah's first Methodist parish. Built in 1875 on the model of Queen's Kirk in Amsterdam and the fourth incarnation of the parish home, this is another great example of Savannah's Gothic churches.

Martin Luther King Jr. Boulevard

BATTLEFIELD PARK

Right off MLK Jr. Boulevard is **Battlefield Park** (corner of MLK Jr. Blvd. and Louisville Rd., dawn-dusk, free), aka the Spring Hill Redoubt, a reconstruction of the British fortifications at the Siege of Savannah with an interpretive site. Note that the redoubt is not at the actual location of the original fort; that lies underneath the nearby Sons of the Revolution marker. Eight hundred granite markers signify the battle's casualties, most of whom were buried in mass graves soon afterward. Sadly, most of the remains of these brave men were simply bulldozed up and discarded without ceremony during later construction projects.

GEORGIA STATE RAILROAD MUSEUM

The **Georgia State Railroad Museum** (601 W. Harris St., 912/651-6823, www.chsgeorgia.org, daily 9am-5pm, $10 adults, $6 students), aka "The Roundhouse," is an ongoing homage to the deep and strangely underreported influence of the railroad industry on Savannah. Constructed in 1830 for the brand-new Central of Georgia line, the Roundhouse's design was cutting-edge for the time, the first building to put all the railroad's key facilities in one place. Spared by Sherman, the site saw its heyday after the Civil War. The highlight of the Roundhouse is the thing in the middle that gave the structure its name, a huge central turntable for positioning rolling stock for repair and maintenance. Frequent demonstrations occur with an actual steam locomotive firing up and taking a spin on the turntable.

Family Fun in Savannah

Savannah is more than historic mansions and to-go-cup pub crawls. There's plenty for tykes to see and do. Here are a few spots:

- **Ellis Square:** This square's modernist renovation includes a large wading fountain—a great spot to cool off when it gets hot.
- **Georgia State Railroad Museum:** Climb aboard these big machines, which feature frequent train rides along a short length of track complete with old-fashioned steam whistle. As a bonus, located within the Railroad Museum complex is the small but growing **Savannah Children's Museum.**
- **Jepson Center for the Arts:** In addition to being that rarity—a shiny new modernist building in this very historic old city—there is a neat children's section inside this arts center, the **Artzeum.**
- **Massie School Heritage Center:** This restored historic schoolhouse was the first school for emancipated African Americans in Savannah, and indeed was a public school in the 1970s. Not only is this a charming slice of nostalgia, but a recent upgrade and renovation also possibly makes it the single best stop for an all-around Savannah history lesson.
- **Oatland Island Educational Center:** To view wildlife up close and personal, head a few minutes east of town to this facility, which houses cougars and an entire wolf pack, in addition to many other animals along its winding marsh-side nature trail.
- **Fort Pulaski National Monument:** Kids can climb on the parapets, earthworks, and cannons, and burn off calories on the great nature trail nearby. Along the way they'll no doubt learn a few things as well.

SAVANNAH CHILDREN'S MUSEUM

Next to the Railroad Museum is the **Savannah Children's Museum** (655 Louisville Rd., 912/651-6823, www.savannahchildrensmuseum.org, Tues.-Sat. 10am-4pm, Sun. 11am-4pm, $7.50), open since 2012. The children's museum is a work in progress that currently has an outdoor "Exploration Station" and a pending larger facility.

RALPH MARK GILBERT CIVIL RIGHTS MUSEUM

One of the former black-owned bank buildings on MLK Jr. Boulevard is now home to the **Ralph Mark Gilbert Civil Rights Museum** (460 MLK Jr. Blvd., 912/231-8900, Tues.-Sat. 10am-4pm, $10). Named for a pastor of the First African Baptist Church and a key early civil rights organizer, the building was also the local NAACP headquarters for a time. Three floors of exhibits here include photos and interactive displays, the highlight for historians being a fiber-optic map of nearly 100 significant civil rights sites.

SAVANNAH HISTORY MUSEUM

The **Savannah History Museum** (303 MLK Jr. Blvd., 912/651-6825, www.chsgeorgia.org, daily 9am-5:30pm, $7 adults, $4 children) is the first stop for many a visitor to town because it's in the same restored Central of Georgia passenger shed as the visitors center. It contains many interesting exhibits on local history, concentrating mostly on colonial times. Toward the rear of the museum is a room for rotating exhibits, as well as one of Johnny Mercer's four Oscars, and, of course, the historic "Forrest Gump bench" that Tom Hanks sat on during his scenes in Chippewa Square.

SCAD MUSEUM OF ART

In 2011, the **Savannah College of Art and Design Museum of Art** (601 Turner Blvd.,

912/525-5220, www.scadmoa.org, Tues.-Wed. and Fri.-Sat. 10am-5pm, Thurs. 10am-8pm, Sun. noon-5pm, $10 adults, $5 students) expanded this handsome building into an old railroad facility immediately behind it, more than doubling its exhibition space and adding the impressive Walter O. Evans Collection of African American Art. The SCAD Museum of Art now hosts a rotating series of exhibits, from standard painting to video installations, many of them commissioned by the school itself.

VICTORIAN DISTRICT

CARNEGIE BRANCH LIBRARY

The **Carnegie Branch Library** (537 E. Henry St., 912/652-3600, www.liveoakpl.org, Mon. 10am-8pm, Tues.-Thurs. 10am-6pm, Fri. 2pm-6pm, Sat. 10am-6pm) is the only example of prairie architecture in town, designed by Savannah architect Julian de Bruyn Kops and built, as the name implies, with funding from tycoon-philanthropist Andrew Carnegie in 1914. But more importantly, the Carnegie Library was for decades the only public library for African Americans in Savannah. One of its patrons was a young Clarence Thomas, who would of course grow up to be a U.S. Supreme Court justice.

★ FORSYTH PARK

A favorite with locals and visitors alike, the vast, lush expanse of **Forsyth Park** (bordered by Drayton St., Gaston St., Whitaker St., and Park Ave., 912/351-3850, daily 8am-dusk) is a center of local life, abuzz with activity and events year-round. The park owes its existence to William B. Hodgson, who donated its core 10 acres to the city for use as a park. Deeply influenced by the then-trendy design of green-space areas in France, Forsyth Park's landscape design by William Bischoff dates to 1851.

SOFO DISTRICT

LAUREL GROVE CEMETERY

Its natural vista isn't as alluring as Bonaventure Cemetery's, but **Laurel Grove Cemetery** (802 W. Anderson St. and 2101 Kollock St., daily 8am-5pm, free) boasts its own exquisitely carved memorials and a distinctly Victorian type of surreal beauty that not even Bonaventure can match. In keeping with the racial apartheid of Savannah's early days, there are actually two cemeteries: **Laurel Grove North** (802 W. Anderson St.) for whites, and **Laurel Grove South** (2101 Kollock St.) for blacks. Both are well worth visiting.

By far the most high-profile plot in the

Laurel Grove Cemetery

A Walking Tour of Forsyth Park

As you approach the park, don't miss the ornate ironwork on the west side of Bull Street marking the **Armstrong House,** designed by Henrik Wallin. Featured in the 1962 film *Cape Fear* as well as 1997's *Midnight in the Garden of Good and Evil,* this Italianate mansion was once home to Armstrong Junior College before its move to the city's south side. Directly across Bull Street is another site of *Midnight* fame, the **Oglethorpe Club,** one of the many brick and terra-cotta designs by local architect Alfred Eichberg.

Forsyth Fountain

It's easy to miss, but as you enter the park's north side, you encounter the **Marine Memorial,** erected in 1947 to honor the 24 Chatham County Marines killed in World War II. Subsequently, the names of Marines killed in Korea and Vietnam were added. Look west at the corner of Whitaker and Gaston Streets; that's **Hodgson Hall,** home of the Georgia Historical Society. This 1876 building was commissioned by Margaret Telfair to honor her late husband, William Hodgson.

Looking east at the corner of Drayton and Gaston Streets, you'll see the old **Poor House and Hospital,** in use until 1854, when it was converted to serve as the headquarters for the Medical College of Georgia. During the Civil War, General Sherman used the hospital to treat Federal soldiers. From 1930 to 1980 the building was the site of Candler Hospital. Behind the old hospital's cast-iron fence is Savannah's most famous tree, the 300-year-old **Candler Oak.** During Sherman's occupation, wounded Confederate prisoners were treated within a barricade around the oak. The tree is in the National Register of Historic Trees and was the maiden preservation project of the Savannah Tree Foundation, which secured the country's first-ever conservation easement on a single tree.

Walking south into the park proper, you can't miss the world-famous **Forsyth Fountain,** an iconic Savannah sight. Cast in iron on a French model, the fountain was dedicated in 1858. Two other versions of this fountain exist—one in Poughkeepsie, New York, and the other in, of all places, the central plaza in Cusco, Peru.

Continuing south, you'll encounter two low buildings in the center of the park. The one on the east side is the so-called "Dummy Fort," circa 1909, formerly a training ground for local militia. Now it's the **Forsyth Park Café** (daily 7am-dusk). To the west is the charming **Fragrant Garden for the Blind.** One of those precious little Savannah gems that is too often overlooked, the Fragrant Garden was initially sponsored by the local Garden Club and based on others of its type throughout the United States.

The tall monument dominating Forsyth Park's central mall is the **Confederate Memorial.** Dedicated in 1875, it wasn't finished until several years later. A New York sculptor carved the Confederate soldier atop the monument.

My favorite Forsyth Park landmark is at the extreme southern end. It's the Memorial to Georgia Veterans of the Spanish-American War, more commonly known as ***The Hiker*** because of the subject's casual demeanor and confident stride. Savannah was a major staging area for the 1898 conflict, and many troops were bivouacked in the park. Sculpted in 1902 by Alice Ruggles Kitson, more than 50 replicas of *The Hiker* were made and put up all over the United States.

North Cemetery is that of Juliette Gordon Low, founder of the Girl Scouts of the USA. Other historically significant sites there include the graves of 8th Air Force founder Frank O. Hunter, Central of Georgia Railway founder William Gordon, and "Jingle Bells" composer James Pierpont.

Laurel Grove South features the graves of Savannah's early black Baptist ministers, such as Andrew Bryan and Andrew Cox Marshall. Some of the most evocative gravesites are those of African Americans who obtained their freedom and built prosperous lives for themselves and their families.

SOUTHSIDE

WORMSLOE STATE HISTORIC SITE

The one-of-a-kind **Wormsloe State Historic Site** (7601 Skidaway Rd., 912/353-3023, www.gastateparks.org/info/wormsloe, Tues.-Sun. 9am-5pm, $10 adults, $4.50 children) was first settled by Noble Jones, who landed with Oglethorpe on the *Anne* and fought beside him in the War of Jenkins' Ear. One of the great renaissance men of history, this soldier was also an accomplished carpenter, surveyor, forester, botanist, and physician. The house, dating from 1828, and 65.5 acres of land are still owned by his family, and no, you can't visit them.

The stunning entrance canopy of 400 live oaks, Spanish moss dripping down the entire length, is one of those iconic images of Savannah that will stay with you forever. A small interpretive museum, a one-mile nature walk, and occasional living-history demonstrations make this a great site for the entire family. Walk all the way to the Jones Narrows to see the ruins of the site's original 1739 fortification, one of the oldest and finest examples of tabby construction in the United States.

Pin Point

Off Whitefield Avenue (Diamond Causeway) on the route to Skidaway Island is tiny Pin Point, a predominantly African American township better known as the boyhood home of Supreme Court justice Clarence Thomas. Pin Point traces its roots to a community of former slaves on Ossabaw Island. Displaced by a hurricane, they settled at this idyllic site overlooking the Moon River, itself a former plantation.

Pin Point on the Moon River

On Ossabaw Island, former slaves had settled into freedom as subsistence farmers after the Civil War. But when a massive hurricane devastated the island in 1893, many moved to the mainland, south of Savannah along what would later be known as Moon River, to a place called Pin Point. While many continued farming, plenty gained employment at local factories, where crabs and oysters were packed and sold. The largest and longest-lived of those factories was A. S. Varn & Son, which employed nearly 100 Pin Point residents—about half of the adult population.

Because so many local people worked at the same place, Pin Point developed a strong community bond, one that was instrumental in forging the life and career of future Supreme Court justice Clarence Thomas, who was born at Pin Point in 1948. Until he was seven, Thomas lived in a tiny house there with his parents, one without plumbing and insulated with newspapers. After a house fire, Thomas moved to Savannah with his grandparents.

While times have certainly changed here—paved roads finally came in the 1970s, and most of the old shotgun shacks have been replaced with mobile homes—Pin Point remains a small, close-knit community of about 300 people, with most property still owned by descendants of the freedmen who bought it after Reconstruction. The Varn factory remained the economic heart of Pin Point until it shut down in 1985. Today, the old factory forms the heart of an ambitious new project, the **Pin Point Heritage Museum** (www.pinpointheritagemuseum.com), which conveys the spirit and history of that community, including its most famous native son, through a series of exhibits and demonstrations.

PIN POINT HERITAGE MUSEUM

Many Pin Point residents made their living by shucking oysters at the Varn Oyster Company, the central shed of which still remains and forms the basis of the **Pin Point Heritage Museum** (9924 Pin Point Ave., http://chs-georgia.org/PHM, Thurs.-Sat. 9am-5pm, $8 adults, $4 children), opened in 2012. The museum tells the story of the Pin Point community through exhibits, a film, and demonstrations of some of the maritime activities at the Varn Oyster Company through the decades, such as crabbing, canning, shucking, and shrimp-net making.

Skidaway Island

Skidaway Island is notable for two beautiful and educational nature-oriented sites.

SKIDAWAY ISLAND STATE PARK

A site of interest to visitors is **Skidaway Island State Park** (52 Diamond Causeway, 912/598-2300, www.gastateparks.org/info/skidaway, daily 7am-10pm, parking $5). You can camp here ($25-28), but the awesome nature trails leading out to the marsh—featuring an ancient Native American shell midden and an old whiskey still—are worth a trip just on their own, especially when combined with the Marine Educational Center and Aquarium. To get here, take Victory Drive (U.S. 80) until you get to Waters Avenue and continue south as it turns into Whitefield Avenue and then the Diamond Causeway. The park is on your left after the drawbridge. An alternative route from downtown is to take the Truman Parkway all the way to its dead end at Whitefield Avenue; then take a left on Whitefield and continue as it turns into Diamond Causeway where it enters Skidaway.

UNIVERSITY OF GEORGIA MARINE EDUCATIONAL CENTER AND AQUARIUM

The **University of Georgia Marine Educational Center and Aquarium** (30 Ocean Science Circle, 912/598-3474, www.marex.uga.edu, Mon.-Fri. 9am-4pm, Sat. 10am-5pm, $6 adults, $3 children, cash only) shares a picturesque 700-acre campus on the scenic Skidaway River with the research-oriented **Skidaway Institute of Oceanography,** also University of Georgia (UGA) affiliated. It hosts scientists and grad students from around the nation, often for trips on its research vessel, the RV *Sea Dawg*. The main attraction of the Marine Center is the small but well-done and recently upgraded aquarium featuring 14 tanks with 200 live animals.

EASTSIDE

★ BONAVENTURE CEMETERY

On the banks of the Wilmington River just east of town lies one of Savannah's most distinctive sights, **Bonaventure Cemetery** (330 Bonaventure Rd., 912/651-6843, daily 8am-5pm, free). While its pedigree as Savannah's premier public cemetery goes back 100 years, it was used as a burial ground as early as 1794. In the years since, this achingly poignant vista of live oaks and azaleas has been the final resting place of such local and national luminaries as Johnny Mercer, Conrad Aiken, and, of course, the Trosdal plot, former home of the famous *Bird Girl* statue (the original is now in the Telfair Academy of Arts and Sciences). Fittingly, the late, great Jack Leigh, who took the *Bird Girl* photo for the cover of *Midnight in the Garden of Good and Evil,* is interred here as well.

If you're doing a self-guided tour, go by the small visitors center at the entrance and pick up one of the free guides to the cemetery, assembled by the Bonaventure Historical Society. By all means, do the tourist thing and pay your respects at Johnny Mercer's final resting place, and go visit beautiful little "Gracie" in Section E, Lot 99.

OATLAND ISLAND WILDLIFE CENTER

The closest thing to a zoo in Savannah is the vast, multipurpose **Oatland Island Wildlife Center** (711 Sandtown Rd., 912/898-3980,

Johnny Mercer's Black Magic

The great Johnny Mercer is not only without a doubt Savannah's most noteworthy progeny, he is also one of the greatest lyricists music has ever known. Born in 1909, he grew up in southside Savannah on a small river then called the Back River but since renamed Moon River in honor of his best-known song.

Armed with an innate talent for rhythm and a curious ear for dialogue—both qualities honed by his frequent boyhood contact with Savannah African American culture and musicians during the Jazz Age—Mercer wrote what is arguably his greatest song, "Moon River," in 1961. The song, debuted by Audrey Hepburn in the film *Breakfast at Tiffany's,* won an Academy Award for Best Original Song. In addition to "Moon River," Mercer won three other Oscars, for "On the Atchison, Topeka and the Santa Fe" (1946), "In the Cool, Cool, Cool of the Evening" (1951), and "Days of Wine and Roses" (1962).

Today you can pay your respects to Mercer in three places: his boyhood home (509 E. Gwinnett St., look for the historical marker in front of this private residence); the bronze sculpture of Mercer in the revitalized Ellis Square near City Market; and at his gravesite in beautiful Bonaventure Cemetery. And regardless of what anyone tells you, neither Johnny Mercer nor any member of his family ever lived in the Mercer-Williams House on Monterey Square, of *Midnight in the Garden of Good and Evil* fame. Although it was built for his great-grandfather, the home was sold to someone else before it was completed.

www.oatlandisland.org, daily 10am-5pm, $5 adults, $3 children). Set on a former Centers for Disease Control site, it has undergone an extensive environmental cleanup and is now owned by the local school system, although supported purely by donations. Families by the hundreds come here for a number of special Saturdays throughout the year, including an old-fashioned cane grinding in November and a day of sheep shearing in April.

The main attractions here are the critters, located at various points along a meandering two-mile nature trail through the woods and along the marsh. All animals at Oatland are there because they're somehow unable to return to the wild. Highlights include a tight-knit pack of eastern wolves, a pair of bison, cougars (once indigenous to the region), some really cute foxes, and an extensive raptor aviary. Kids will love the petting zoo of farm animals, some of which are free to roam the grounds at will.

OLD FORT JACKSON

The oldest standing brick fort in Georgia, **Old Fort Jackson** (Fort Jackson Rd., 912/232-3945, http://chsgeorgia.org, daily 9am-5pm, $7 adults, $4 children), named for Georgia governor James Jackson (1798-1801), is also one of eight remaining examples of the so-called Second System of American forts built prior to the War of 1812. Operated by the non-profit Coastal Heritage Society, Fort Jackson is in an excellent state of preservation and provides loads of information for history buffs as well as for kids. Most visitors especially love the daily cannon firings during the summer. If you're really lucky, you'll be around when Fort Jackson fires a salute to passing military vessels on the river—the only historic fort in the United States that does so.

To get to Fort Jackson, take the President Street Extension (Islands Expressway) east out of downtown. The entrance is several miles down on the left.

TYBEE ISLAND

Its name means "salt" in the old Euchee tongue, indicative of the island's chief export in those days. Eighteen miles and about a half-hour drive from Savannah, in truth Tybee is part and parcel of the city's social and cultural fabric. Many of the island's 3,000 full-time residents, known for their boozy bonhomie and quirky personal style, commute to work in the city.

Tybee Island

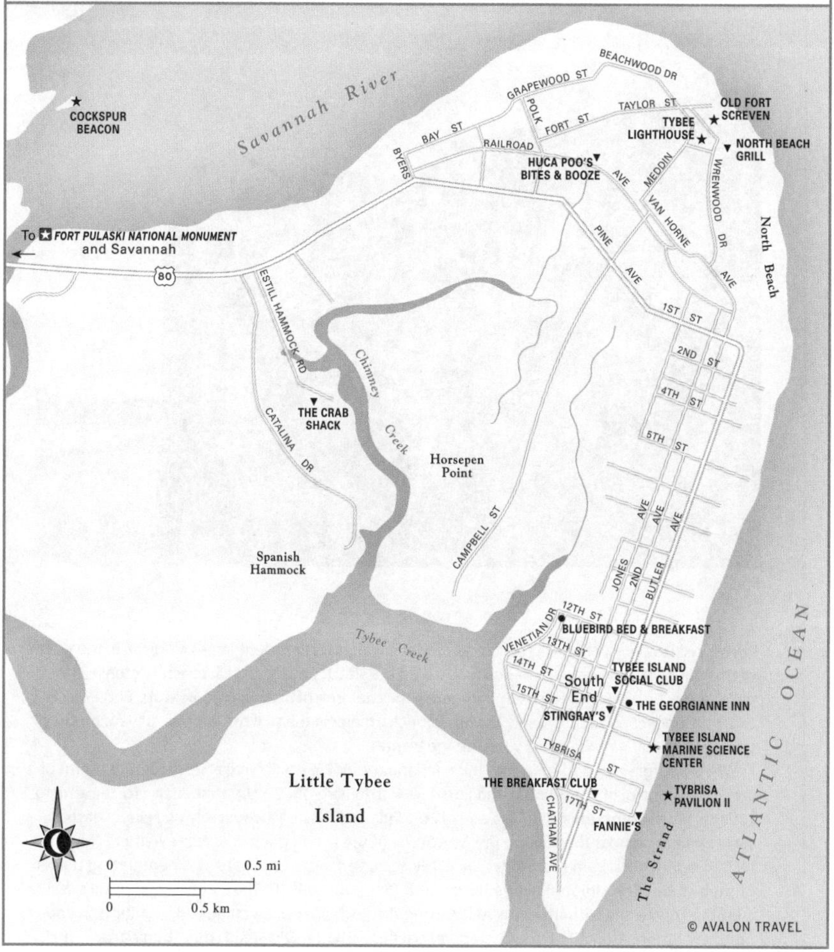

The entire island has become a focal point of Georgia's booming film industry. The 2017 reboot of *Baywatch* with Dwayne "the Rock" Johnson was filmed on Tybee's beach, as was the Miley Cyrus film *The Last Song*.

★ FORT PULASKI NATIONAL MONUMENT

There's one must-see before you get to Tybee Island proper. On Cockspur Island you'll find **Fort Pulaski National Monument** (U.S. 80 E., 912/786-5787, www.nps.gov/fopu, daily 9am-5pm, $7, free under age 16), a delight for any history buff. The pleasure starts when you cross the drawbridge over the moat and see a cannon pointed at you from a narrow gun port. Enter the inside of the fort and take in just how big it is—Union occupiers regularly played baseball on the huge, grassy parade ground. Take a walk around the perimeter, underneath the ramparts. This is where the soldiers lived and worked, and you'll

The Siege of Fort Pulaski

Fort Pulaski

Fort Pulaski's construction was part of a broader initiative by President James Madison in the wake of the War of 1812, which dramatically revealed the shortcomings of U.S. coastal defense. Based on state-of-the-art European design forged in the cauldron of the Napoleonic Wars, Fort Pulaski's thick masonry construction used 25 million bricks, many of them of the famous "Savannah Gray" variety handmade at the nearby Hermitage Plantation.

When Georgia seceded from the Union in January 1861, a small force of Confederates immediately took control of Fort Pulaski and Fort Jackson. In early 1862 a Union sea-land force came to covertly lay the groundwork for a siege of Fort Pulaski. The siege would rely on several batteries secretly set up across the Savannah River. Some of the Union guns utilized new rifled-chamber technology, which dramatically increased the accuracy, muzzle velocity, and penetrating power of their shells. The Union barrage began at 8:15am on April 10, 1862, and Fort Pulaski's walls crumbled under the withering fire. At least one shell struck a powder magazine, igniting an enormous explosion. After 30 hours, Confederate general Charles Olmstead surrendered the fortress.

It was not only Fort Pulaski that was rendered obsolete—it was the whole concept of masonry fortification. From that point forward, military forts would rely on earthwork rather than brick. The section of earthwork you see as you enter Fort Pulaski, the "demilune," was added after the Civil War.

see re-creations of officers' quarters, meeting areas, sick rooms, and prisoners' bunks among the cannons, where Confederate prisoners of war were held after the fort's surrender. Cannon firings happen most Saturdays.

TYBEE ISLAND MARINE SCIENCE CENTER

At the foot of the Tybrisa Pavilion is the little **Tybee Island Marine Science Center** (1510 Strand Ave., 912/786-5917, www.tybeemarinescience.org, daily 10am-5pm, $4 adults, $3 children), with nine aquariums and a touch tank featuring native species. Here is the nerve center for the Tybee Island Sea Turtle Project, an ongoing effort to document and preserve the local comings and goings of the island's most beloved inhabitant and unofficial mascot, the endangered sea turtle.

TYBEE ISLAND LIGHT STATION AND MUSEUM

At North Campbell Avenue is the entrance to the less-populated, more historically significant north end of Tybee Island, once almost entirely taken up by Fort Screven, a coastal defense fortification of the early 1900s. Rebuilt several times in its history, the **Tybee Island Light Station** (30 Meddin Ave., 912/786-5801, www.tybeelighthouse.org, Wed.-Mon. 9am-5:30pm, last ticket sold 4:30pm, $9 adults, $7 children) traces its construction to the first year of the colony, based on a design by the multitalented Noble Jones. At its completion in 1736, it was the tallest structure in the United States. One of a handful of working 18th-century lighthouses today, the facility has been restored to its 1916-1964 incarnation, featuring a nine-foot-tall first-order Fresnel lens installed in 1867.

All the outbuildings on the lighthouse grounds are original, including the residence of the lighthouse keeper, also the oldest building on the island. If you've got the legs and the lungs, definitely take all 178 steps up to the top of the lighthouse for a stunning view of Tybee, the Atlantic, and Hilton Head Island.

Tybee Island Light Station

The Tybee Bomb

On a dark night in 1958 at the height of the Cold War, a USAF B-47 Stratojet bomber made a simulated nuclear bombing run over southeast Georgia. A Charleston-based F-86 fighter on a mock intercept came too close, clipping the bomber's wing. Before bringing down the wounded B-47 at Savannah's Hunter Airfield, Commander Howard Richardson decided to jettison his lethal cargo: a 7,000-pound Mark 15 hydrogen bomb, serial number 47782. Richardson, who won the Distinguished Flying Cross for his efforts that night, jettisoned the bomb over water. What no one knows is exactly where. And thus began the legend of "the Tybee Bomb." Speculation ran wild, with some locals fearing a nuclear explosion, radioactive contamination, or even that a team of scuba-diving terrorists would secretly retrieve the weapon.

Commander Richardson, now retired, says the bomb wasn't armed when he jettisoned it. Environmentalists say that doesn't matter, because the enriched uranium the Air Force admits was in the bomb is toxic whether or not there's the risk of a nuclear detonation. People who work in the fishing industry on Tybee say the fact that the bomb also had 400 pounds of high explosive "nuclear trigger" is reason enough to get it out of the waterways.

The Air Force has made several attempts to locate the weapon. In 2000 it sent a team to Savannah to find the bomb, concluding it was buried somewhere off the coast in 5-15 feet of mud. In 2005, in another attempt to find the weapon, it sent another team of experts down to look one last time. Their verdict: The bomb's still lost.

All around the area of the north end around the lighthouse complex you'll see low-lying concrete bunkers. These are remains of Fort Screven's coastal defense batteries, and many are in private hands. Battery Garland is open to tours, and also houses the **Tybee Island Museum,** a charming, almost whimsical little collection of exhibits from various eras of local history.

One entrance fee gives you admission to the lighthouse, the lighthouse museum, and the Tybee Island Museum.

TYBEE POST THEATER

The new pride of the north end is the **Tybee Post Theater** (10 Van Horne Ave., 912/472-4790, www.tybeeposttheater.org, prices vary), a fully restored performing arts venue that was once, as the name implies, the theater for the Fort Screven military facility. The small but cozy 200-seat space now offers a range of programming from live music to live theatre to film screenings, the latter its original purpose when built in 1930. Indeed, the theater was one of the first in Georgia to host the new "talkie" films.

Pooler

★ NATIONAL MUSEUM OF THE MIGHTY EIGHTH AIR FORCE

Military and aviation buffs should not miss the **National Museum of the Mighty Eighth Air Force** (175 Bourne Ave., Pooler, 912/748-8888, www.mightyeighth.org, daily 9am-5pm, $10 adults, $6 children and active-duty military) in Pooler, Georgia, right off I-95. The 8th Air Force was born at Hunter Field in Savannah as the 8th Bomber Command in 1942, becoming the 8th Air Force in 1944; it is now based in Louisiana.

A moving testament to the men and machines that conducted those strategic bombing campaigns over Europe in World War II, the museum also features later 8th Air Force history such as the Korean War, the Linebacker II bombing campaigns over North Vietnam, and the Persian Gulf. Inside you'll find airplanes like the P-51 Mustang and the German ME-109. The centerpiece, however, is the restored B-17 bomber *City of Savannah,* the newest jewel of the collection, acquired from the National Air and Space Museum in Washington DC.

Entertainment and Events

NIGHTLIFE

Savannah is a hard-drinking town, and not just on St. Patrick's Day. The ability to legally walk downtown streets with beer, wine, or a cocktail in hand definitely contributes to the overall joie de vivre. Bars close in Savannah at 3am, a full hour later than in Charleston. A citywide indoor smoking ban is in effect and you may not smoke cigarettes in any bar in Savannah.

Bars and Pubs

One of Savannah's favorite and most raucous historic taverns is possibly the River Street bar most visited by actual locals. The **Bayou Café** (4 N. Abercorn Ramp, 912/233-6411, daily 11am-3am), overlooking River Street but situated on one of the cobblestone "ramps" going down from Bay Street to the waterfront, offers a convivial dive-bar-type atmosphere and a solid Cajun-style pub food menu. The main floor is the traditional tavern, where the best local blues musicians play frequent gigs. The 2nd floor is more of a game room and general younger folks' party area.

For over 65 years, perhaps Savannah's most beloved dive bar/watering hole has been **The Original Pinkie Master's** (318 Drayton St., 912/999-7106, www.theoriginalsavannah.com, Mon.-Thurs. 3pm-3am, Fri.-Sat. noon-3am). For decades this has been a gathering place for local politicos; according to local lore, this is where then-governor Jimmy Carter announced his run for presidency (even though he's a teetotaler). A recent change of ownership has managed that rarest of accomplishments: They've lovingly retained the kitschy dive bar motif, complete with historic memorabilia, while expanding the drink menu and making things a bit more palatable for the general public.

The main landmark on the west end of River Street is the famous (or infamous, depending on which side of "the Troubles" you're on) **Kevin Barry's Irish Pub** (117 W. River St., 912/233-9626, www.kevinbarrys.com, daily 11am-3am), one of Savannah's most beloved establishments. KB's is open seven days a week, with evenings seeing performances by a number of Irish troubadours, all veterans of the East Coast trad circuit.

Without question, the place in Savannah that comes closest to replicating an actual, authentic Irish pub environment is tiny, cozy **O'Connell's** (42 Drayton St., 912/231-2298, daily 3pm-3am), where they know how to pour a Guinness, feature Magners cider on tap, and the house specialty is the "pickleback"—a shot of Jameson's followed by a shot of, yes, pickle brine. In classic Emerald Isle tradition, most seating is bench-style, to encourage conversation.

Uncharacteristically, Savannah now sports several good hotel bars, and one of the best is **Rocks on the Roof** (102 W. Bay St., 912/721-3800, Fri.-Sat. 11am-1am, Sun.-Thurs. 11am-midnight), atop the Bohemian Hotel Savannah Riverfront on the waterfront. In good weather the exterior walls are opened up to reveal a large wraparound seating area with stunning views of downtown on one side and of the Savannah River on the other.

No, Lincoln Street in Savannah isn't named for Abraham Lincoln. But dark, fun little **Abe's on Lincoln Street** (17 Lincoln St., 912/349-0525, http://abesonlincoln.com, Mon.-Sat. 4pm-3am) is the oldest bar in town, with a very eclectic clientele.

On Whitaker Street is a hip hangout with an excellent menu, **Circa 1875** (48 Whitaker St., 912/443-1875, www.circa1875.com, Mon.-Thurs. 6pm-10pm, Fri.-Sat. 6pm-11pm), where the burgers are as good as the martinis. The vintage vibe takes you back to the days of the Parisian salons.

Yes, **The Distillery** (416 W. Liberty St., 912/236-1772, www.distillerysavannah.com, Mon.-Sat. 11am-close, Sun. noon-close) is located in a former distillery. As such, the atmosphere isn't exactly dark and romantic—it's sort of one big open room—but the excellent location at the corner of MLK Jr. Boulevard and Liberty Street, the long vintage bar, and the great selection of beers on tap combine to make this a happening spot. The fish-and-chips are also great.

Gamers and geeks alike will enjoy video and board game action—as well as the food and drink—at **The Chromatic Dragon** (514 MLK Jr. Blvd., 912/289-0350, www.chromaticdragon.com, Thurs.-Sat. 11am-2am, Sun.-Wed. 11am-11pm). While you can get a meal and a brew here, the focus is on the gaming, so much so that you are asked "analog or digital?" as you walk in; in other words, board games or video consoles, the latter mainly Xbox360 and PS3. They offer a vast array of both, or you can bring your own.

Moon River Brewing Company (21 W. Bay St., 912/447-0943, www.moonriverbrewing.com, Mon.-Thurs. 11am-11pm, Fri.-Sat. 11am-midnight, Sun. 11am-10pm) is directly across from the Hyatt Regency Savannah and offers half a dozen handcrafted beers in a rambling old space that housed Savannah's premier hotel back in antebellum days. The particular highlight these days, however, is the dog-friendly enclosed beer garden on the busy corner of Bay and Whitaker.

In the City Market area, your best bet is **The Rail Pub** (405 W. Congress St., 912/238-1311, www.therailpub.com, Mon.-Sat. 3pm-3am), one of Savannah's oldest and most beloved taverns. This two-story spot is a great place to get a pint or a shot or do karaoke in a boisterous but still cozy and friendly environment.

Craft Breweries

Savannah is finally catching up to the craft brewery trend, and **Southbound Brewing Company**'s (107 E. Lathrop Ave., 912/335-7716, http://southboundbrewingco.com, tours 5:30pm Wed.-Fri., 2pm Sat., $15) tasting events are getting rave reviews. Tours include 36 ounces of beer served on-site and your choice of a 22-ounce bomber, a 32-ounce growler fill, a six-pack, or a pint glass. The tastings attract a large crowd, so don't dillydally. Southbound's offerings include a rotating series of special-event beers and the occasional rock concert. As is the case with many up-and-coming breweries, the large, restored warehouse space isn't in the most scenic neighborhood.

Savannah's other key craft brewery is **Service Brewing** (574 Indian St., http://servicebrewing.com, tours 5:30pm-7:30pm Thurs.-Fri., 2pm-4pm Sat., $12 pp), so named because its founders are former military; they donate a portion of all profits to veterans service organizations. Basic tastings include either a 36-ounce flight of 6 ounces per pour or three 12-ounce pours. Service is a wee bit

The To-Go Cup Tradition

Arguably the single most civilized trait of Savannah, and certainly one of the things that most sets it apart, is the glorious old tradition of the "to-go cup." True to its history of hard partying and general open-mindedness, Savannah, like New Orleans, legally allows you to walk the streets downtown with an open container of your favorite adult beverage. Of course, you have to be 21 or over, and the cup must be Styrofoam or plastic, never glass or metal, and no more than 16 ounces. While there are boundaries to where to-go cups are legal, in practice this includes almost all areas of the historic district frequented by visitors. The quick and easy rule of thumb is to keep your to-go cups north of Jones Street.

Every downtown watering hole has stacks of cups at the bar for patrons to use. You can either ask the bartender for a to-go cup—aka a "go cup"—or just reach out and grab one yourself. Don't be shy; it's the Savannah way.

closer to downtown than is Southbound, and within walking distance of the River Street/City Market area.

Live Music and Karaoke

Savannah's undisputed karaoke champion is **McDonough's** (21 E. McDonough St., 912/233-6136, www.mcdonoughsofsavannah.com, Mon.-Sat. 8pm-3am, Sun. 8pm-2am), an advantage compounded by the fact that a lot more goes on here than karaoke. The kitchen at McDonough's is quite capable, and many locals swear you can get the best burger in town here. Despite the sports bar atmosphere, the emphasis is on the karaoke, which ramps up every night at 9:30pm.

Despite its high-volume offerings, **The Jinx** (127 W. Congress St., 912/236-2281, www.thejinx.net, Mon.-Sat. 4pm-3am) is a friendly watering hole and the closest thing Savannah has to a full-on music club, with a very active calendar of rock and metal shows. Shows start late here, never before 11pm and often later than that. If you're here for the music and have sensitive ears, bring earplugs. The beer offerings are good, but this is the kind of place where many regular patrons opt for tallboy PBRs.

LGBTQ-Friendly

Any examination of LGBTQ nightlife in Savannah must, of course, begin with **Club One Jefferson** (1 Jefferson St., 912/232-0200, www.clubone-online.com, Mon.-Sat. 5pm-3am, Sun. 5pm-2am) of *Midnight in the Garden of Good and Evil* fame, with its famous drag shows, including the notorious Lady Chablis, upstairs in the cabaret, and its rockin' 1,000-square-foot dance floor downstairs. Cabaret showtimes are Thursday-Saturday 10:30pm and 12:30am, Sunday 10:30pm, and Monday 11:30pm. Call for Lady Chablis's showtimes.

A friendly, kitschy little tavern at the far west end of River Street near the Jefferson Street ramp, **Chuck's Bar** (301 W. River St., 912/232-1005, Mon.-Wed. 8pm-3am, Thurs.-Sat. 7pm-3am) is a great place to relax and see some interesting local characters. Karaoke at Chuck's is especially a hoot, and they keep the Christmas lights up all year.

PERFORMING ARTS

Theater

The semipro troupe at the **Historic Savannah Theatre** (222 Bull St., 912/233-7764, www.savannahtheatre.com) performs a busy rotating schedule of oldies revues (a typical title: *Return to the '50s*), but they make up for their lack of originality with the tightness and energy of their talented young cast of regulars.

Music

The **Savannah Philharmonic** (box office 216 E. Broughton St., 912/525-5050, www.savannahphilharmonic.org, Mon.-Fri 10am-5pm) is a professional symphony orchestra that performs concertos and sonatas at various venues around town and is always worth checking out.

Cinema

The ornate, beautifully restored **Lucas Theatre for the Arts** (32 Abercorn St., 912/525-5040, www.lucastheatre.com, most screenings under $10) downtown is a classic Southern movie house. The Savannah Film Society and Savannah College of Art and Design host screenings there throughout the year. Check the website for schedules.

FESTIVALS AND EVENTS

Savannah's calendar fairly bursts with festivals, many outdoors. Dates shift from year to year, so it's best to consult the listed websites for details.

January

Floats and bands take part in the **Martin Luther King Jr. Day Parade** downtown to commemorate the civil rights leader and Georgia native. The bulk of the route is on historic MLK Jr. Boulevard, formerly West Broad Street.

Straddling January and February is the weeklong **PULSE Art + Technology Festival** (www.telfair.org), an adventurous event that brings video artists and offbeat electronic performance art into the modern Jepson Center for the Arts.

February

Definitely not to be confused with St. Patrick's Day, the **Savannah Irish Festival** (912/232-3448, www.savannahirish.org) focuses on Celtic music.

Hosted by the historically black Savannah State University at various venues around town, the monthlong **Black Heritage Festival** (912/691-6847) is tied into Black History Month and boasts name entertainers like the Alvin Ailey Dance Theatre (performing free!). This event also usually features plenty of historical lectures devoted to the very interesting and rich history of African Americans in Savannah.

Also in February is the quickly growing **Savannah Book Festival** (www.savannahbookfestival.org), modeled after a similar event in Washington DC and featuring many national and regional authors at various venues downtown.

March

One of Savannah's unique festivals is the multiday indie rock festival **Savannah Stopover** (www.savannahstopover.com) in early or mid-March. The idea is simple: Book bands that are already driving down to Austin, Texas, for the following week's South By Southwest so they can "stop over" and play at various venues in downtown Savannah. Get it?

More than just a day, the citywide **St. Patrick's Day** (www.savannahsaintpatricksday.com) celebration generally lasts at least half a week and temporarily triples the population. The nearly three-hour parade—second biggest in the United States—always begins at 10am on St. Patrick's Day (unless that falls on a Sunday, in which case it's generally on the previous Saturday) and includes an interesting mix of marching bands, wacky floats, and sauntering local Irishmen in kelly-green jackets. The appeal comes not only from the festive atmosphere and generally beautiful spring weather, but also from Savannah's unique law allowing partiers to walk the streets with a cup filled with the adult beverage of their choice.

The three-week **Savannah Music Festival** (912/234-3378, www.savannahmusic

Savannah's St. Patrick's Day Parade is the nation's second-largest.

festival.org) is held at various historic venues around town and begins right after St. Patrick's Day. Past festivals have featured Wynton Marsalis, Dianne Reeves, and the Avett Brothers.

April

Short for "North of Gaston Street," the **NOGS Tour of Hidden Gardens** (912/961-4805, www.gcofsavnogstour.org, $30) is available two days in April and focuses on a selection of Savannah's amazing private gardens chosen for excellence of design, historical interest, and beauty.

Everyone loves the annual free **Sidewalk Arts Festival** (912/525-5865, www.scad.edu) presented by the Savannah College of Art and Design in Forsyth Park. Contestants claim a rectangular section of sidewalk on which to display their chalk art talent. There's a noncontest section with chalk provided.

May

The SCAD-sponsored **Sand Arts Festival** (www.scad.edu) on Tybee Island's North Beach centers on a competition of sand castle design, sand sculpture, sand relief, and wind sculpture. You might be amazed at the level of artistry lavished on the sometimes-wondrous creations, only for them to wash away with the tide.

If you don't want to get wet, don't show up at the **Tybee Beach Bum Parade,** an uproarious event held the weekend prior to Memorial Day weekend. With a distinctly boozy overtone, this unique 20-year-old event features homemade floats filled with partiers who squirt the assembled crowds with various water pistols. The crowds, of course, pack their own heat and squirt back.

September

The second-largest LGBTQ event in Georgia (only Atlanta's version is larger), the **Savannah Pride Festival** (www.savannahpride.org, various venues, free) happens every September. Crowds get pretty big for this festive, fun event, which usually features lots of dance acts and political booths.

Over Labor Day weekend you can check out the **Savannah Craft Brew Festival** (International Trade & Convention Center, 1 International Dr., www.savannahcraftbrewfest.com, $50). This daylong tasting event features a healthy range of breweries from around the nation, not only from Georgia's own burgeoning craft brew industry.

October

The Savannah Philharmonic Orchestra plays a free **Picnic In The Park** concert in Forsyth Park that draws thousands of noshers. Arrive early to check out the ostentatious, whimsical picnic displays, which compete for prizes. Then set out your blanket, pop open a bottle of wine, and enjoy the sweet sounds.

The combined aroma of beer, sauerkraut, and sausage that you smell coming from the waterfront is the annual **Oktoberfest on the River** (www.riverstreetsavannah.com), which has evolved to be Savannah's second-largest celebration (behind only St. Patrick's Day). Live entertainment of varying quality is featured, though the attraction, of course, is the aforementioned beer and German food. A highlight is Saturday morning's "Weiner Dog Races" involving, you guessed it, competing dachshunds.

It's a fairly new festival, but the **Tybee Island Pirate Festival** (http://tybeepiratefest.com) is a fun and typically rollicking Tybee event in October featuring, well, everybody dressing up like pirates, saying "Arr" a lot, eating, drinking, and listening to cover bands. It may not sound like much, and it's really not, but it's typically very well attended.

Sponsored by St. Paul's Greek Orthodox Church, the popular **Savannah Greek Festival** (www.stpaulsgreekorthodox.org) features food, music, and Greek souvenirs. The weekend event is held across the street from the church at the parish center—in the gym, to be exact, right on the basketball court. Despite the pedestrian location, the food is authentic and delicious, and the atmosphere convivial and friendly.

Hosted by the Savannah College of Art and Design, the weeklong **Savannah Film Festival** (www.scad.edu) beginning in late October is rapidly growing not only in size but in prestige as well. Lots of older, more established Hollywood names appear as honored guests for the evening events, while buzzworthy up-and-coming actors, directors, producers, writers, and animators give excellent workshops during the day.

One of Savannah's most unique events is late October's **"Shalom Y'all" Jewish Food Festival** (912/233-1547, www.mickveisrael.org), held in Forsyth Park and sponsored by the historic Temple Mickve Israel. Latkes, matzo, and other nibbles are all featured along with entertainment.

Shopping

Downtown Savannah's main shopping district is **Broughton Street.** There are many vibrant local shops as well as national chain stores on the avenue.

A bit south of downtown proper, but still a short drive away, is the **Starland District**. This up-and-coming mixed-use area is home to a growing variety of more hipster-oriented shops.

Focusing on upscale art and home goods, the small but chic and friendly **Downtown Design District** runs three blocks on Whitaker Street, a short walk from Forsyth Park.

WATERFRONT

Antiques

One of the coolest antiques shops in town is **Jere's Antiques** (9 N. Jefferson St., 912/236-2815, www.jeresantiques.com, Mon.-Sat. 9:30am-5pm). It's in a huge historic warehouse on Factor's Walk and has a concentration on fine European pieces.

Gourmet Treats

Cater to your sweet tooth—and buy some goodies to bring back with you—at **River Street Sweets** (13 E. River St., 912/234-4608, www.riverstreetsweets.com, daily 9am-11pm), where you can witness Southern delicacies like pralines being made as you shop. And of course, there are free samples.

HISTORIC DISTRICT NORTH

Art Supply

A great art town needs a great art supply store, and in Savannah that would be **Blick Art Materials** (318 E. Broughton St., 912/234-0456, www.dickblick.com, Mon.-Fri. 8am-8pm, Sat. 10am-7pm, Sun. 11am-6pm), which has all the equipment and tools for the serious artist—priced to be affordable for students. But casual shoppers will enjoy it as well for its collection of offbeat gift items.

Clothes and Fashion

Perhaps Broughton Street's most beloved old shop is **Globe Shoe Co.** (17 E. Broughton St., 912/232-8161, Mon.-Sat. 10am-6pm), a Savannah institution and a real throwback to a time of personalized retail service. They have no website and no Facebook page—they're all about simple one-to-one service, like in the old days.

Inhabiting a well-restored upstairs space, **Civvie's New and Recycled Clothing** (14 E. Broughton St., 912/236-1551, Mon.-Sat. 11am-7pm, Sun. 11am-5pm) is perhaps Savannah's most well-regarded vintage store, with a variety of retro clothes and shoes and a strong local following. They also have a nifty section of campy, kitschy gift items.

Now at what's considered Savannah's prime downtown corner, at Bull and Broughton, is

A City of Art

There are more art galleries per capita in Savannah than in New York City—one gallery for every 2,191 residents, to be exact. Savannah College of Art and Design (SCAD) galleries are in abundance all over town, displaying the handiwork of students, faculty, alumni, and important regional and national artists. Savannah's arts scene also shines a spotlight on theatre, classical music, and cool movie houses.

For art lovers, the no-brainer package experience for the visitor is the combo of the **Telfair Academy of Arts and Sciences** (121 Barnard St., 912/790-8800, www.telfair.org) and the **Jepson Center for the Arts** (207 W. York St., 912/790-8800, www.telfair.org). These two arms of the Telfair Museums run the gamut of art, from old-school portraiture to cutting-edge contemporary art.

SCAD galleries (912/525-5225, www.scad.edu) are abundant. Outposts with consistently impressive exhibits are the **Gutstein Gallery** (201 E. Broughton St.) and **Pinnacle Gallery** (320 E. Liberty St.). The college also runs its own museum, the **SCAD Museum of Art** (227 MLK Jr. Blvd., 912/525-7191, www.scad.edu), which recently doubled in size to accommodate a new wing devoted to the Walter O. Evans Collection of African American Art.

The small and avant-garde **ArtRise Savannah** (2427 DeSoto Ave., 912/335-8204, www.artrisesavannah.org) helps coordinate "Art March" gallery crawls in the SoFo (South of Forsyth) district the first Friday of the month. **Non-Fiction Gallery** (1522 Bull St., 912/662-5152), also in SoFo, exhibits work by many of Savannah's up-and-coming talents. Nearby is **Sulfur Studios** (2301 Bull St., sulfurstudios.org), which not only hosts rotating exhibits, but also coordinates many community forums and events of a cutting-edge nature.

Overlooking Ellis Square downtown is well-regarded **Kobo Gallery** (33 Barnard St., 912/201-0304, www.kobogallery.com), a local artist co-op featuring some of Savannah's best contemporary artists who frequently put on group shows. One of the featured artists is always on duty, so stopping in can be a very informative experience.

There are several good galleries in the beach town of Tybee Island as well, chief among them **Dragonfly Studio** (1204 Hwy 80, 912/786-4431, www.dragonflystudioarts.com), which hosts work by the very best coastal artists in a cute little roadside shack.

century-old family-owned **Levy Jewelers** (2 E. Broughton St., 912/233-1163, Mon.-Sat. 10am-9pm, Sun. noon-6pm). They have a complete showcase of necklaces, watches, and rings from two dozen internationally recognized designers.

Gourmet Treats

One of the more unique Savannah retail shops is the **Savannah Bee Company** (104 W. Broughton St., 912/233-7873, www.savannahbee.com, Mon.-Sat. 10am-7pm, Sun. 11am-5pm), which carries an extensive line of honey and honey-based merchandise, from foot lotion to lip balm. All the honey comes from area hives owned by company founder and owner Ted Dennard. The flagship Broughton location provides plenty of sampling opportunities at the little café area and even boasts a small theater space for instructional films. There is also a location on **River Street** (1 W. River St., 912/234-7088, Mon.-Sat. 10am-7pm, Sun. 11am-8pm) on the ground floor of the Hyatt Regency hotel.

Chocolate lovers need to head straight to **Chocolat by Adam Turoni** (323 W. Broughton St., 912/335-2914, www.chocolatat.com, daily 11am-6pm), a tiny space with a big taste. Adam's handcrafted, high-quality chocolates are miniature works of art—and delicious ones at that. Be prepared to be overwhelmed.

Home Goods

While Savannah is an Anglophile's dream, Francophiles will enjoy **The Paris Market**

& Brocante (36 W. Broughton St., 912/232-1500, www.theparismarket.com, Mon.-Sat. 10am-6pm, Sun. 11am-4pm), set on a beautifully restored corner of Broughton Street. Home and garden goods, bed and bath accoutrements, and a great selection of antique and vintage items combine for a rather opulent shopping experience. Plus there's an old-school Euro café inside, where you can enjoy a coffee, tea, or hot chocolate.

Those looking for home decorating ideas with inspiration from both global and Southern aesthetics, traditional as well as sleekly modern, should check out **24e Furnishings at Broughton** (24 E. Broughton St., 912/233-2274, www.twentyfoure.com, Mon.-Thurs. 10am-6pm, Fri.-Sat. 10am-7pm, Sun. noon-5pm), located in an excellently restored 1921 storefront. Be sure to check out the expansive 2nd-floor showroom.

HISTORIC DISTRICT SOUTH

Antiques

Possibly the most beloved antiques store in town is **Alex Raskin Antiques** (441 Bull St., 912/232-8205, www.alexraskinantiques.com, Mon.-Sat. 10am-5pm) in Monterey Square, catty-corner from the Mercer-Williams House Museum, set in the historic Hardee Mansion. A visit is worth it just to explore the home. But the goods Alex lovingly curates are among the best and most tasteful in the region.

Small Pleasures (412 Whitaker St., 912/234-0277, Mon.-Sat. 10:30am-5pm) is one of Savannah's hidden gems. They deal in a tasteful range of vintage and estate jewelry, in a suitably small but delightfully appointed space in the Downtown Design District.

Books and Music

Specializing in "gently used" books in good condition, **The Book Lady** (6 E. Liberty St., 912/233-3628, Mon.-Sat. 10am-5:30pm) on Liberty Street features many rare first editions. Enjoy a gourmet coffee while you browse the stacks.

The fact that **E. Shaver Bookseller** (326 Bull St., 912/234-7257, Mon.-Sat. 9am-6pm) is one of the few locally owned independent bookstores left in town should not diminish the fact that it is also one of the best bookstores in town. The friendly, well-read staff can help you around the rambling old interior of their ground-level store and its generous stock of regionally themed books.

The beautiful Monterey Square location and a mention in *Midnight in the Garden of Good and Evil* combine to make **V&J Duncan** (12 E. Taylor St., 912/232-0338, www.vjduncan.com, Mon.-Sat. 10:30am-4:30pm) a Savannah "must-shop." Owner John Duncan and his wife, Virginia ("Ginger" to friends), have collected an impressive array of prints, books, and maps over the past quarter century, and are themselves a treasure trove of information.

Clothes

Custard Boutique (414 Whitaker St., 912/232-4733, Mon.-Sat. 10:30am-6pm, Sun. noon-5pm) in the Downtown Design District has a cute, cutting-edge selection of women's clothes in a range of styles and is easily the match of any other women's clothing store in town.

Gifts and Souvenirs

Set in a stunningly restored multilevel Victorian within a block of Forsyth Park, the globally conscious **Folklorico** (440 Bull St., 912/232-9300, Mon.-Sat. 10am-5pm, Sun. 1pm-5pm) brings in a fascinating and diverse collection of sustainably made jewelry, gifts, and home goods from around the world, focusing on Central and South America and Asia.

In this town so enamored of all things Irish, a great little locally owned shop is **Saints and Shamrocks** (309 Bull St., 912/233-8858, www.saintsandshamrocks.org, Mon.-Sat. 9:30am-5:30pm, Sun. 11am-4pm), across the intersection from the Book Lady. Pick up your St. Patrick's-themed gear and gifts to celebrate Savannah's highest holiday along with high-quality Irish imports.

Not only a valuable outlet for SCAD students and faculty to sell their artistic wares, **shopSCAD** (340 Bull St., 912/525-5180, www.shopscadonline.com, Mon.-Wed. 9am-5:30pm, Thurs.-Fri. 9am-8pm, Sat. 10am-8pm, Sun. noon-5pm) is also one of Savannah's most unique boutiques. You never really know what you'll find, but whatever it is, it will be one-of-a-kind. The jewelry in particular is always cutting edge and showcases good craftsmanship. The designer T-shirts are a hoot too.

Sports and Recreation

Savannah offers copious outdoor options that take full advantage of the city's temperate climate and the natural beauty of its marshy environment next to the Atlantic Ocean.

WATER TOURS

The heavy industrial buildup on the Savannah River means that the main river tours, all departing from the docks in front of the Hyatt Regency Savannah, tend to be disappointing in their unrelenting views of cranes, docks, storage tanks, and smokestacks. Still, for those into that kind of thing, narrated trips up and down the river on the *Georgia Queen* and the *Savannah River Queen* are offered by **Savannah Riverboat Cruises** (9 E. River St., 800/786-6404, www.savannahriverboat.com, starts at $22.95 adults, $13.95 ages 4-12). You can opt for just sightseeing, or add a dinner cruise.

If you've just *got* to get out on the river for a short time, by far the best bargain is to take one of the four little water ferries of **Savannah Belles** (River St. at City Hall and Waving Girl Landing, www.catchacat.org, daily 7:30am-10:30pm, free), named after famous women in Savannah history, which shuttle passengers from River Street to Hutchinson Island and back every 15-20 minutes. Pick one up on River Street in front of City Hall or at the Waving Girl Landing a few blocks east.

one of the Savannah Belles ferries

KAYAKING AND CANOEING

Maybe the single best kayak or canoe adventure in Savannah is the run across the Back River from Tybee to **Little Tybee Island,** an undeveloped state heritage site that is actually twice as big as Tybee, albeit mostly marsh. To get here, take Butler Avenue all the way to 18th Street and take a right, then another quick right onto Chatham Avenue. The parking lot for the landing is a short way up Chatham Avenue on your left. Warning: Do not attempt to swim to Little Tybee, no matter how strong a swimmer you think you are.

Lazaretto Creek, on the western edge of Tybee Island, is a great place to explore Tybee and environs. From here you can meander several miles through the marsh, or go the other way and head into a channel of the Savannah River. Put in at the Lazaretto Creek landing, at the foot of the Lazaretto Creek bridge on the south side of U.S. 80 on the way to Tybee Island. You can also put in at the nearby **Tybee Marina** (4 Old Tybee Rd., 912/786-5554, www.tybeeislandmarina.com), also on Lazaretto Creek.

One of the great overall natural experiences in the area is the massive **Savannah National Wildlife Refuge** (694 Beech Hill Ln., Hardeeville, SC, 843/784-2468, www.fws.gov/refuge/savannah, daily dawn-dusk, free). This 30,000-acre reserve—half in Georgia, half in South Carolina—is on the Atlantic flyway, so you'll be able to see birdlife in abundance, in addition to alligators and manatees. Earthen dikes crisscrossing the refuge are vestigial remnants of paddy fields from plantation days.

You can kayak on your own, but many opt to take guided tours offered by **Wilderness Southeast** (912/897-5108, www.wildernesssoutheast.org, two-hour trips from $37.50 for two people), **Sea Kayak Georgia** (888/529-2542, www.seakayakgeorgia.com, $55 pp), and **Swamp Girls Kayak Tours** (843/784-2249, www.swampgirls.com, $45). To get to the refuge, take U.S. 17 north over the big Talmadge Bridge, over the Savannah River into South Carolina. Turn left on Highway 170 south and look for the entrance to Laurel Hill Wildlife Drive on the left.

HIKING

A relic of the pre-railroad days, the **Savannah-Ogeechee River Canal** (681 Ft. Argyle Rd., 912/748-8068, www.savannahogeecheecanal.com, daily 9am-5pm, $2 adults, $1 students) is a 17-mile barge route joining the two rivers. Finished in 1830, it saw three decades of prosperous trade in cotton, rice, bricks, guano, naval stores, and food crops before the coming of the railroads finished it off. You can walk some of its length today near the Ogeechee River terminus, admiring the impressive engineering of its multiple locks used to stabilize the water level.

To get here, get on I-95 south, take exit 94, and go west on Fort Argyle Road (Hwy. 204). The canal is a little over two miles from the exit.

BIKING

Many locals like to load up their bikes and go to **Fort Pulaski National Monument** (912/786-5787, www.nps.gov, daily 9am-5pm, $7 pp, free under age 16). From the grounds you can ride all over scenic and historic Cockspur Island.

Outside of town, much biking activity centers on Tybee Island, with the six-mile **McQueen's Island Trail** (U.S. 80 near Fort Pulaski National Monument) being a popular and simple ride. The trail started as a rail route for the Central of Georgia Railway and was converted to a multiuse trail in the 1990s.

GOLF

The **Club at Savannah Harbor** (2 Resort Dr., 912/201-2007, www.theclubatsavannahharbor.com, greens fees $135, $70 for twilight) is across the Savannah River on Hutchinson Island, adjacent to the Westin Savannah Harbor Resort. Home to the Liberty Mutual Legends of Golf Tournament each spring, the club's tee times are 7:30am-3pm.

FISHING

A highly regarded local fishing charter is Tybee-based **Amick's Deep Sea Fishing** (1 Old Hwy. 80, Tybee Island, 912/897-6759, www.amicksdeepseafishing.com, from $120 pp). Captain Steve Amick and crew run offshore charters daily. Go east on U.S. 80 and turn right just past the Lazaretto Creek Bridge.

BIRD-WATCHING

An excellent birding spot on the **Colonial Coast Birding Trail** (http://georgiawildlife.dnr.state.ga.us) is Tybee Island's **North Beach area** (Savannah River to 1st St., Tybee Island, parking $5 per day, meters available). You'll see a wide variety of shorebirds and gulls, as well as piping plovers, northern gannets, and purple sandpipers (winter).

SPECTATOR SPORTS

For sports action that's hard-hitting and comes with a certain hipster kitsch quotient, check out the bruising bouts of the women of the **Savannah Derby Devils** (Savannah Civic Center, 301 W. Oglethorpe Ave., 912/651-6556, www.savannahderby.com), who bring the roller derby thunder against other regional teams. They skate downtown at the Savannah Civic Center.

The newest hit on the Savannah sports scene is the college summer league team **The Savannah Bananas** (1401 E. Victory Dr., 912/712-2482, thesavannahbananas.com). This very popular local summer pasttime happens at historic Grayson Stadium, where greats such as Babe Ruth and Jackie Robinson played back in the day. This isn't NCAA ball—these young players use real wooden bats and play for the love of the game while they're out of class for the summer. Single game tickets start at $9. Most games sell out, so get your tickets early.

Food

Savannah is a fun food town, with a selection of cuisine concocted by a cast of executive chefs who despite their many personal idiosyncrasies tend to go with what works rather than experiment for the sake of experimentation.

For the freshest seafood, consider a trip to Tybee Island or Thunderbolt (which is on the way to Tybee).

WATERFRONT

Classic Southern

The bustling, friendly interior of **Treylor Park** (115 E. Bay St., 912/495-5557, www.treylorpark.com, Mon.-Fri. noon-1am, Sat. 10am-2am, Sun. 10am-1am, $10-15) plays up the shabby-chic undertone of Savannah life, with tasty gourmet takes on downmarket Southern classics like the chicken biscuit, pot pie, and sloppy joe. Don't miss their signature starter dish, the PB&J Wings. A particularly tasteful cocktail menu and a well-curated craft beer list round out the experience.

Very few restaurants on River Street rise above tourist schlock, but a standout is **Vic's on the River** (16 E. River St., 912/721-1000, www.vicsontheriver.com, Sun.-Thurs. 11am-10pm, Fri.-Sat. 11am-11pm, $25-35). With dishes like wild Georgia shrimp, stone-ground grits, and blue crab cakes with a three-pepper relish, Vic's combines a romantic old Savannah atmosphere with an adventurous take on Lowcountry cuisine. Note the entrance to the dining room is not on River Street but on the Bay Street level on Upper Factor's Walk.

Breakfast

★ **B. Matthew's Eatery** (325 E. Bay St., 912/233-1319, www.bmatthewseatery.com, Mon.-Thurs. 8am-9pm, Fri.-Sat. 8am-10pm, Sun. 9am-3pm, $10-15) serves what is widely considered the best breakfast in the entire Savannah historic district. The omelets—most under $10—are uniformly wonderful, and the sausage and bacon are excellent and not greasy. There are healthier selections as well, and you can actually get a decent bowl of oatmeal—but I suggest something more decadent. Sunday brunch is incredible.

CITY MARKET

Classic Southern

Every year, thousands of visitors come to Savannah to wait for hours for a chance to sample some of local celebrity Paula Deen's "home" cooking at **The Lady & Sons** (102 W. Congress St., 912/233-2600, www.ladyandsons.com, Mon.-Sat. 11am-3pm and 5pm-close, Sun. 11am-5pm, $15-20). There's actually a fairly typical Southern buffet with some decent fried chicken, collard greens, and mac and cheese. For the privilege, you must begin waiting in line as early as 9:30am for lunch and as early as 3:30pm for dinner in order to be assigned a dining time.

Coffee, Tea, and Sweets

Combine a hip bar with outrageously tasty dessert items and you get ★ **Lulu's Chocolate Bar** (42 MLK Jr. Blvd., 912/238-2012, www.luluschocolatebar.net, Sun.-Thurs. noon-midnight, Fri.-Sat. 2pm-2am,). While the whole family is welcome before 10pm to enjoy chocolate-chip cheesecake and the like, after that it's 21-and-over. The late crowd is younger and trendier and comes mostly for the unique specialty martinis like the pineapple upside-down martini. The prices are quite reasonable at this fun place.

Italian

One would never call Savannah a great pizza town, but the best pizza here is **Vinnie VanGoGo's** (317 W. Bryan St., 912/233-6394, www.vinnievangogos.com, Mon.-Thurs. 4pm-11:30pm, Fri. 4pm-1am, Sat. noon-1am, Sun. noon-11:30pm, $10-15, cash only), at the west end of City Market on Franklin Square. Their pizza is a thin-crust Neapolitan style—although the menu claims it to be New York style—with a delightful tangy sauce and fresh cheese. Individual slices are huge, so don't feel obliged to order a whole pie. The waiting list for a table can get pretty long.

HISTORIC DISTRICT NORTH

Classic Southern

Savannah's most dramatic restaurant success story is ★ **The Grey** (109 MLK Jr. Blvd., 912/662-5999, www.thegreyrestaurant.com, Sun. and Tues.-Thurs. 5:30pm-10pm, Fri.-Sat. 5:30pm-11pm, supper every third Sunday of the month, $25-35), located in a stunningly restored former bus depot. It has taken the national foodie world by storm with its take on beloved regional vernacular and soul food cuisine classics like seafood boudin, veal sweetbreads, roasted yardbird, fisherman's stew, and more, depending on seasonal whim and sourcing availabilities. A James Beard Award finalist in 2015, the Grey features the talents of standout executive chef Mashama Bailey, who grew up in Savannah and has a close eye for what makes the South tick food-wise. At the entrance is the "Diner Bar," a smaller offset bar area offering a punchy bar food menu strong on sandwiches.

The best lunch on Broughton Street is at **Kayak Kafe** (1 E. Broughton St., 912/233-6044, www.eatkayak.com, Mon.-Thurs. 11am-10pm, Fri.-Sat. 11am-11pm, Sun. 11am-5pm, $10-15), where you can get a killer fresh salad or a fish taco to refresh your energy level during a busy day of shopping or sightseeing. Vegetarians, vegans, and those on a gluten-free diet will be especially pleased by the available options. As one of the very few Broughton Street places with outdoor sidewalk tables, this is also a great people-watching spot.

Olde Pink House (23 Abercorn St., 912/232-4286, Sun.-Thurs. 5:30pm-10:30pm, Fri.-Sat. 5:30pm-11pm, $20-30) is known for its savvy (and often sassy) service and the uniquely regional flair it adds to traditional dishes, with liberal doses of pecans, Vidalia onions, shrimp, and crab. The she-crab soup

To Market, To Market

Savannah's first and still premier health-food market, **Brighter Day Natural Foods** (1102 Bull St., 912/236-4703, www.brighterdayfoods.com, Mon.-Sat. 9am-7pm, Sun. noon-5:30pm) has been the labor of love of Janie and Peter Brodhead for 30 years, all of them in the same location at the southern tip of Forsyth Park. Boasting organic groceries, regional produce, a sandwich and smoothie bar with a takeout window, and an extensive vitamin, supplement, and herb section, Brighter Day is an oasis in Savannah's sea of chain supermarkets.

Opened in 2013, **Whole Foods Market** (1815 E. Victory Dr., www.wholefoodsmarket.com, daily 8am-9pm) offers the chain's usual assortment of organic produce, with a very good fresh meat and seafood selection.

Fairly new but already thriving, the **Forsyth Park Farmers Market** (www.forsythfarmersmarket.org, Sat. 9am-1pm) happens in the south end of scenic and wooded Forsyth Park. You'll find very fresh fruit and produce from a variety of fun and friendly regional farmers. If you have access to a real kitchen while you're in town, you might be glad to know there's usually a very good selection of organic, sustainably grown meat and poultry products as well—not always a given at farmers markets.

If you need some good-quality groceries downtown—especially after hours—try **Parker's Market** (222 E. Drayton St., 912/231-1001, daily 24 hours). In addition to a pretty wide array of gourmet-style grab 'n' go victuals inside, there are gas pumps outside to fuel your vehicle.

There's one 24-hour full-service supermarket in downtown Savannah: **Kroger** (311 E. Gwinnett St., 912/231-2260, daily 24 hours).

and lamb chops in particular are crowd-pleasers, and the scored crispy flounder stacks up to similar versions of this dish at several other spots in town. Reservations are recommended.

Coffee, Tea, and Sweets

The best coffee on Broughton is at **The Coffee Fox** (102 W. Broughton St., 912/401-0399, www.thecoffeefox.com, Mon.-Sat. 7am-11pm, Sun. 8am-4pm), a locally owned joint that expertly treads the fine line between hipster hangout and accessible hot spot. The freshly baked goodies are nearly as good as the freshly brewed java, which includes cold-brew and pour-over offerings.

He helped produce *Mission Impossible III* and other movies, but Savannah native Stratton Leopold's other claim to fame is running the 100-year-old family business at ★ **Leopold's Ice Cream** (212 E. Broughton St., 912/234-4442, www.leopoldsicecream.com, Sun.-Thurs. 11am-10pm, Fri.-Sat. 11am-11pm). Leopold's also offers soup and sandwiches to go with its delicious family ice cream recipe and sweet treats. Memorabilia from Stratton's various movies is all around the shop, which stays open after every evening performance at the Lucas Theatre around the corner. You can occasionally find Stratton himself behind the counter doling out scoops.

Mexican

The best Mexican spot downtown is **Tequila's Town** (109 Whitaker St., 912/236-3222, www.tequilastown.com, Mon.-Thurs. 11am-10pm, Fri.-Sat. 11am-11pm, Sun. noon-10pm, $15-25), a relatively new place that fills an oft-noted void in the Savannah foodie scene. The menu is comprehensive and authentic, a clear step above the usual gringo-oriented fat-fest. Highlights include the chilies rellenos and the seafood, not to mention the guacamole prepared tableside.

South African

Look for the long lunchtime line outside the tiny storefront that is **Zunzi's** (108 E. York St., 912/443-9555, http://zunzis.com, Mon.-Sat. 11am-6pm, $10). This takeout joint is one of

Savannah's favorite lunch spots, the labor of love of South African expatriates Gabby and Johnny DeBeer, who've gotten a lot of national attention for their robust, rich dishes like the exquisite South African-style sausage.

HISTORIC DISTRICT SOUTH

Classic Southern

A very popular spot with locals and tourists alike, the **Crystal Beer Parlor** (301 W. Jones St., 912/349-1000, www.crystalbeerparlor.com, daily 11am-10pm, $15-20) offers one of the best burgers downtown. With a history going back to the 1930s, this has been a friendly family tradition for generations of Savannahians. The lively bar area has a very wide range of craft brews, and there are plenty of snug booths to sit in and enjoy the solid American menu.

The rise of Paula Deen and her Lady & Sons restaurant has only made local epicures even more exuberant in their praise for ★ **Mrs. Wilkes' Dining Room** (107 W. Jones St., 912/232-5997, www.mrswilkes.com, Mon.-Fri. 11am-2pm, $25), Savannah's original comfort-food mecca. The delightful Sema Wilkes herself has passed on, but nothing has changed—not the communal dining room, the cheerful service, the care taken with takeout customers, nor, most of all, the food, which is a succulent mélange of the South's greatest hits, including the best fried chicken in town, snap beans, black-eyed peas, and collard greens. Be prepared for a long wait, however; lines begin forming early in the morning.

SOFO DISTRICT

New Southern

Before there was Paula Deen, there was Elizabeth Terry, Savannah's first high-profile chef and founder of ★ **Elizabeth on 37th** (105 E. 37th St., 912/236-5547, daily 6pm-10pm, $30-40), Savannah's most elegant restaurant. Executive chef Kelly Yambor uses eclectic, seasonally shifting ingredients that blend the South with the south of France. Reservations are recommended.

Burgers

The cozy **Green Truck Neighborhood Pub** (2430 Habersham St., 912/234-5885, http://greentruckpub.com, Tues.-Sat. 11am-11pm, $15) earns rave reviews with its delicious regionally sourced meat and produce offered at reasonable prices. (The large selection of craft beers on tap is a big draw too.) The marquee item is the signature five-ounce grass-fed burger. It's a small room that often has a big line, and they don't take reservations, so be prepared.

Coffee, Tea, and Sweets

Primarily known for its sublime sweet treats, James Beard Award-nominated **Back in the Day Bakery** (2403 Bull St., 912/495-9292, www.backinthedaybakery.com, Tues.-Fri. 9am-5pm, Sat. 8am-3pm) also offers a small but delightfully tasty (and tasteful) range of lunch soups, salads, and sandwiches (11am-2pm). Lunch highlights include the baguette with camembert, roasted red peppers, and lettuce, as well as the caprese, the classic tomato, mozzarella, and basil trifecta on a perfect ciabatta. But whatever you do, save room for dessert, which runs the full sugar spectrum: red velvet cupcakes, lemon bars, macaroons, carrot cake, and many others.

Foxy Loxy (1919 Bull St., 912/401-0543, www.foxyloxycafe.com, Mon.-Sat. 7am-11pm) is a classic coffeehouse set within a cozy multistory Victorian on Bull Street. Pluses include the authentic Tex-Mex menu, wine and beer offerings, and freshly baked sweet treats.

The coffee at **The Sentient Bean** (13 E. Park Ave., 912/232-4447, www.sentientbean.com, daily 7:30am-10pm) is all fair trade and organic, and the all-vegetarian fare is a major upgrade above the usual coffeehouse offerings. But "the Bean" is more than a coffeehouse—it's a community. Probably the best indie film venue in town, the Bean regularly hosts screenings of cutting-edge left-of-center documentary and kitsch films, as well as rotating art exhibits.

EASTSIDE

Classic Southern

Located just across the Wilmington River from the fishing village of Thunderbolt, **Desposito's** (187 Old Tybee Rd., 912/897-9963, www.despositosseafood.com, Tues.-Fri. 5pm-10pm, Sat. noon-10pm, $20) is a big hit with locals and visitors alike, although it's not in all the guidebooks. The focus here is on crab, shrimp, and oysters, and lots of them, all caught wild in local waters and served humbly on tables covered with newspapers.

Barbecue

If you're out this way visiting Wormsloe or Skidaway Island State Park, or if you're just crazy about good barbecue, make a point to hit little ★ **Sandfly BBQ** (8413 Ferguson Ave. 912/356-5463, www.sandflybbq.com, Mon.-Sat. 11am-8pm, $10), unique in the area for its dedication to real Memphis-style barbecue. Anything is great—this is the best brisket in the area—but for the best overall experience try the Hog Wild platter.

TYBEE ISLAND

Breakfast and Brunch

Considered the best breakfast in the Savannah area for 30 years and counting, **The Breakfast Club** (1500 Butler Ave., 912/786-5984, http://tybeeisland.com/breakfast-club, daily 6:30am-1pm, $15), with its brisk diner atmosphere and hearty Polish sausage-filled omelets, is like a little bit of Chicago in the South. Lines start early for a chance to enjoy such house specialties as Helen's Solidarity, the Athena Omelet, and the Chicago Bear Burger.

Casual Dining

Set in a large former fishing camp overlooking Chimney Creek, **The Crab Shack** (40 Estill Hammock Rd., 912/786-9857, www.thecrabshack.com, Mon.-Thurs. 11:30am-10pm, Fri.-Sun. 11:30am-11pm, $20) is a favorite local seafood place and something of an attraction in itself. Don't expect gourmet fare or quiet seaside dining; the emphasis is on mounds of fresh, tasty seafood, heavy on the raw-bar action. Getting there is a little tricky: Take U.S. 80 to Tybee, cross the bridge over Lazaretto Creek, and begin looking for Estill Hammock Road to Chimney Creek on the right. Take Estill Hammock Road and veer right. After that, it's hard to miss.

One of Tybee's more cherished restaurants is on the north end in the shadow of the Tybee Light Station. Like a little slice of Jamaica near the dunes, the laid-back **North Beach Grill** (33 Meddin Ave., 912/786-4442, daily 11:30am-10pm, $15) deals in tasty Caribbean fare, such as its signature jerk chicken, fish sandwiches, and, of course, delicious fried plantains, all overseen by chef-owner "Big George" Spriggs. Frequent live music adds to the island vibe.

For a leisurely and tasty dinner, try **Tybee Island Social Club** (1311 Butler Ave., 912/472-4044, http://tybeeislandsocialclub.com, Tues. 5pm-9:30pm, Wed.-Fri. noon-9:30pm, Sat.-Sun. 11:30am-10pm, $20). Their menu is somewhat unusual for this seafood-heavy island: It's primarily an assortment of gourmet-ish tacos, including fish, duck, and lime- and tequila-marinated steak, all under $10 each. The beer and wine list is accomplished, and the live entertainment is usually very good—which is fortunate, since the service here is on the slow side.

Accommodations

The good news for visitors is that there are now many comparatively new hotels of note directly in the downtown area within walking distance of most sites. Some of them are the more widely recognized chains, and others represent more boutique companies and provide a commensurately higher level of service. The less-good news, especially for locals, is that the ominously rising skyline the newer, bigger hotels represent is a change from the friendly small-scale historical footprint Savannah is known for in the first place.

WATERFRONT

$150-300

The ★ **Bohemian Hotel Savannah Riverfront** (102 W. Bay St., 912/721-3800, www.bohemianhotelsavannah.com, $225-350) is gaining a reputation as one of Savannah's premier hotels, both for the casual visitor as well as visiting celebrities. Located between busy River Street and bustling City Market, this isn't the place for peace and quiet, but its combination of boutique-style retro-hip decor and happening rooftop bar scene makes it a great place to go for a fun stay that's as much Manhattan as Savannah. Valet parking is available, which you will come to appreciate.

It's not exactly brand-new—it occupies the space formerly occupied by the well-regarded Mulberry Inn—but ★ **The Brice** (601 E. Bay St., 912/238-1200, www.thebricehotel.com, $175-225) features a complete boutique-style upgrade to this historic building, which formerly housed Savannah's first Coca-Cola bottling plant, on the eastern edge of the historic district. With great service and 145 rooms, most complete with a modernized four-poster bed, the Brice also features **Pacci Italian Kitchen + Bar** (breakfast daily 7am-10:30am, brunch Sat.-Sun. 8am-3pm, dinner Sun.-Thurs. 5pm-10pm, Fri.-Sat. 5pm-10:30pm, $15-25), one of the better hotel restaurant/bar combos in town.

For years critics have called it an insult to architecture and to history. The modernist **Hyatt Regency Savannah** (2 E. Bay St., 912/238-1234, www.savannah.hyatt.com, $200-250) is more than three decades old, but a competent renovation means that the Hyatt—a sort of exercise in cubism straddling an entire block of River Street—has avoided the neglect of many older chain properties downtown. Three sides of the hotel offer views of the bustling Savannah waterfront, with its massive ships coming in from all over the world.

If you require a swank pool, look no further than the **Westin Savannah Harbor Golf Resort and Spa** (1 Resort Dr., 912/201-2000, www.westinsavannah.com, $250-500), which has a beautiful resort-style pool across the Savannah River from downtown and overlooking the old city. Accessing the hotel—located on a cross-channel island—is a bit of a process, but one made easier by charming river ferries that run regularly and free of charge. The attached golf course is a good one, and packages are available.

CITY MARKET

$150-300

Providing a suitably modernist decor to go with its somewhat atypical architecture for Savannah, the ★ **Andaz Savannah** (14 Barnard St., 912/233-2116, www.savannah.andaz.hyatt.com, $250-350) overlooks restored Ellis Square and abuts City Market with its shopping, restaurants, and nightlife. A boutique offering from Hyatt, the Andaz's guest rooms and suites feature top-of-the-line linens, extra-large and well-equipped baths, in-room snack bars, and technological features such as MP3 docking stations, free Wi-Fi, and, of course, the ubiquitous flat-screen TV. Customer service is a particular strong suit. Just off the lobby is a very hip lounge-wine bar that attracts locals as well as hotel guests. Keep in mind things can get a little noisy in this area at night on weekends.

HISTORIC DISTRICT NORTH

Under $150

Famous for its host of resident ghosts—which many employees do swear aren't just tourist tales—**17hundred90 Inn** (307 E. President St., 912/236-7122, www.17hundred90.com, $140) offers 14 cozy rooms within a historic building that dates from, yep, 1790. The addition of several nearby guesthouses, booked through the inn, has expanded the footprint of this great old Savannah name. The great plus here—other than the ghost stories, of course—is the excellent on-site restaurant and bar, popular with both locals and tourists alike.

$150-300

Once a bordello, the 1838 mansion that is home to the 16-room **Ballastone Inn** (14 E. Oglethorpe Ave., 912/236-1484, www.ballastone.com, $250-400) is one of Savannah's favorite inns. Highlights include an afternoon tea service and one of the better full breakfasts in town. Note that some guest rooms are at what Savannah calls the "garden level," meaning sunken basement-level rooms with what amounts to a worm's-eye view.

One of Savannah's favorite bed-and-breakfasts, **The Kehoe House** (123 Habersham St., 912/232-1020, www.kehoehouse.com, $225-300) is a great choice for its charm and attention to guests. Its historic location, on quiet little Columbia Square catty-corner to the Isaiah Davenport House, is within walking distance to all the downtown action, but far enough from the bustle to get some peace out on one of the rocking chairs on the veranda.

HISTORIC DISTRICT SOUTH

$150-300

One of Savannah's original historic B&Bs, the **Eliza Thompson House** (5 W. Jones St., 912/236-3620, www.elizathompsonhouse.com, $200-250) is a bit out of the bustle on serene, beautiful Jones Street, but still close enough for you to get involved whenever you feel the urge. You can enjoy the various culinary offerings—breakfast, wine and cheese, nighttime munchies—either in the parlor or on the patio overlooking the house's classic Savannah garden.

The circa-1896 ★ **Foley House Inn** (14 W. Hull St., 912/232-6622, www.foleyinn.com, $220-350) is a four-diamond B&B with some rooms available at a three-diamond price. Its 19 individualized Victorian-decor guest rooms, in two town houses, range from the smaller Newport overlooking the "grotto courtyard" to the four-poster, bay-windowed Essex room, complete with a fireplace and a whirlpool bath. The location on Chippewa Square is pretty much perfect: well off the busy east-west thoroughfares but in the heart of Savannah's active theater district and within walking distance of anywhere.

VICTORIAN DISTRICT

$150-300

★ **The Gastonian** (220 E. Gaston St., 912/232-2869, www.gastonian.com, $225-350), circa 1868, is a favorite choice for travelers to Savannah, mostly for its 17 sumptuously decorated guest rooms and suites, all with working fireplaces, and the always outstanding full breakfast. They pile on the epicurean delights with teatime, evening nightcaps, and complimentary wine. This is one of the six properties owned by the local firm HLC, which seems to have consistently higher standards than most out-of-town chains.

How ironic that a hotel built in a former mortuary would be one of the few Savannah hotels not to have a resident ghost story. But that's the case with **Mansion on Forsyth Park** (700 Drayton St., 912/238-5158, www.mansiononforsythpark.com, $200-350), which dominates an entire block alongside Forsyth Park, including partially within the high-Victorian former Fox & Weeks Mortuary building. Its sumptuous guest rooms, equipped with big beds, big baths, and big-screen TVs, scream "boutique hotel," as does the swank little bar and the alfresco patio area.

TYBEE ISLAND

Most of the hotels on Tybee Island are what we describe in the South as "rode hard and put away wet," meaning that they see a lot of wear and tear from eager vacationers. I encourage a B&B stay. Also be aware that places on Butler Avenue, even the substandard ones, charge a premium during the high season (Mar.-Oct.).

$150-300

For those looking for the offbeat, try the **Atlantis Inn** (20 Silver Ave., 912/786-8558, www.atlantisinntybee.com, $150-200). Its reasonably priced, whimsically themed rooms are a hoot, and you're a short walk from the ocean and a very easy jaunt around the corner from busy Tybrisa Street. The downside, however, is no dedicated parking.

The best B&B-style experience on Tybee can be found at **The Georgianne Inn** (1312 Butler Ave., 912/786-8710, www.georgianne-inn.com, $175-250), a short walk off the beach and close to most of the island's action, yet not so close that you can't get away when you want to. The complimentary bikes to use while you're there are a nice plus.

CAMPING

The best campground in town is at the well-managed and rarely crowded **Skidaway Island State Park** (52 Diamond Causeway, 912/598-2300, www.gastateparks.org, parking $5 per vehicle per day, tent and RV sites $26-40). There are 88 sites with 30-amp electric hookups. A two-night minimum stay is required on weekends, and there's a three-night minimum for Memorial Day, Labor Day, Independence Day, and Thanksgiving.

There's one campground on Tybee Island, the **River's End Campground and RV Park** (915 Polk St., 912/786-5518, www.cityoftybee.org, water-and-electric sites $34, 50-amp full-hookup sites $45, cabins $150) on the north side. River's End offers 100 full-service sites plus some primitive tent sites. The highlights, however, are the incredibly cute little cabins; book well in advance. During Tybee's sometimes-chilly off-season (Nov.-Mar.), you can relax and get warm inside the common River Room. River's End also offers a swimming pool and laundry facilities.

Transportation and Services

AIR

Savannah is served by the fairly efficient **Savannah/Hilton Head International Airport** (SAV, 400 Airways Ave., 912/964-0514, www.savannahairport.com), directly off I-95 at exit 104. The airport is about 20 minutes from downtown Savannah and 45 minutes from Hilton Head Island. Airlines with routes to SAV include American Airlines (www.aa.com), Allegiant (www.allegiant.com), Delta (www.delta.com), JetBlue (www.jetblue.com), Sun Country (www.suncountry.com), and United (www.ual.com).

Taxis and Uber provide transportation into Savannah. The maximum cab fare for destinations in the historic district is $28.

CAR

Savannah is the eastern terminus of I-16, and that interstate is the most common entrance to the city. However, most travelers get to I-16 via I-95, taking the exit for downtown Savannah (Historic District).

Paralleling I-95 is the old coastal highway, now U.S. 17, which goes through Savannah. U.S. 80 is Victory Drive for most of its length through town; after you pass through Thunderbolt on your way to the islands area, however, it reverts to U.S. 80, the only route to and from Tybee Island.

When you're driving downtown and come to a square, the law says traffic within the square *always* has the right of way. In other words, if you haven't yet entered the square, you must yield to any vehicles already in the square.

Car Rentals

The majority of rental car facilities are at the Savannah/Hilton Head International Airport, including **Avis** (800/831-2847), **Budget** (800/527-0700), **Dollar** (912/964-9001), **Enterprise** (800/736-8222), **Hertz** (800/654-3131), **National** (800/227-7368), and **Thrifty** (800/367-2277). Rental locations away from the airport are **Avis** (7810 Abercorn St., 912/354-4718), **Budget** (7070 Abercorn St., 912/355-0805), and **Enterprise** (3028 Skidaway Rd., 912/352-1424; 9505 Abercorn St., 912/925-0060; 11506-A Abercorn Expressway, 912/920-1093; 7510 White Bluff Rd., 912/355-6622).

TRAIN

Savannah is on the New York-Miami *Silver Service* of **Amtrak** (2611 Seaboard Coastline Dr., 912/234-2611, www.amtrak.com). To get to the station on the west side of town, take I-16 west and then I-516 north. Immediately take the Gwinnett Street-Railroad Station exit and follow the Amtrak signs.

BUS

Chatham Area Transit (www.catchacat.org, Mon.-Sat. 5:30am-11:30pm, Sun. 7am-9pm, $1.25, includes one transfer, free for children under 41 inches tall, exact change only), Savannah's publicly supported bus system, is quite thorough and efficient considering Savannah's relatively small size. Plenty of routes crisscross the entire area.

Of primary interest to visitors is the free **Dot Express Shuttle** (daily 7am-9pm), which travels a continuous circuit route through the historic district with 11 stops at hotels, historic sites, and the Savannah Visitors Center. The shuttle is wheelchair accessible.

TAXI

Taxi services in Georgia tend to be less regulated than in other states, but service is plentiful in Savannah and is generally reasonable. The chief local provider is **Yellow Cab** (866/319-9646, www.savannahyellowcab.com). For wheelchair accessibility, request cab number 14. Other providers include **Adam Cab** (912/927-7466), **Magikal Taxi Service** (912/897-8294), and **Sunshine Cab** (912/272-0971).

If you're not in a big hurry, it's always fun to take a **Savannah Pedicab** (912/232-7900, www.savannahpedicab.com) for quick trips around downtown, or with the competing company **Royal Bike Taxi** (912/341-3944, www.royalbiketaxi.com). In both cases your friendly driver will pedal one or two passengers anywhere within the historic district, and you essentially pay what you think is fair (I recommend $5 per person minimum).

PARKING

Parking is at a premium in downtown Savannah. Traditional coin-operated meter parking is available throughout the city, but more and more the city is going to self-pay kiosks, which accept debit/credit cards. Bottom line: Be sure to pay for all parking weekdays 8:30am-5pm.

As of this writing, one big plus is there is *no* enforcement of parking meters at all on weekends or any day after 5pm. However, there is a very unpopular political move afoot to expand paid parking to Saturdays and evenings, so check the meters on arrival.

The city operates several parking garages at various rates and hours: the **Bryan Street Garage** (100 E. Bryan St.), the **Robinson Garage** (132 Montgomery St.), the **State Street Garage** (100 E. State St.), the **Liberty Street Garage** (401 W. Liberty St.), and the new **Whitaker Street Garage** underneath revitalized Ellis Square.

Tybee Island has paid parking year-round daily 8am-8pm.

TOURIST INFORMATION

Visitors Centers

The main clearinghouse for visitor information is the downtown **Savannah Visitors Center** (301 MLK Jr. Blvd., 912/944-0455, Mon.-Fri. 8:30am-5pm, Sat.-Sun. and holidays 9am-5pm). The newly revitalized Ellis Square features a small visitors kiosk (Mon.-Fri. 8am-6pm) at the northwest corner of the square, with public restrooms and elevators to the underground parking garage beneath the square.

Other visitors centers in the area include the **River Street Hospitality Center** (1 River St., 912/651-6662, daily 10am-10pm), the **Tybee Island Visitor Center** (S. Campbell Ave. and U.S. 80, 912/786-5444, daily 9am-5:30pm), and the **Savannah Airport Visitor Center** (464 Airways Ave., 912/964-1109, daily 10am-6pm).

Visit Savannah (101 E. Bay St., 877/728-2662, www.savannahvisit.com), the local convention and visitors bureau, maintains a list of lodgings on its website.

Hospitals

Savannah has two very good hospital systems. Centrally located near midtown, **Memorial Health University Hospital** (4700 Waters Ave., 912/350-8000, www.memorialhealth.com) is the region's only Level 1 Trauma Center and is one of the best in the nation. The St. Joseph's-Candler Hospital System (www.sjchs.org) has two units, **St. Joseph's Hospital** (11705 Mercy Blvd., 912/819-4100) on the extreme south side and **Candler Hospital** (5401 Paulsen St., 912/819-6000), closer to midtown.

Police

The Savannah-Chatham County Metropolitan Police Department has jurisdiction throughout the city of Savannah and unincorporated Chatham County. For nonemergencies, call 912/651-6675; for emergencies, call 911.

Media

The daily newspaper of record is the ***Savannah Morning News*** (912/525-0796, www.savannahnow.com). It puts out an entertainment insert, called "Do," on Thursdays. The free weekly newspaper in town is ***Connect Savannah*** (912/721-4350, www.connectsavannah.com), hitting stands each Wednesday. Look to it for culture and music coverage as well as an alternative take on local politics and issues.

Two glossy magazines compete: the hipper ***The South*** magazine (912/236-5501, www.thesouthmag.com) and the more establishment ***Savannah*** magazine (912/652-0293, www.savannahmagazine.com).

The Golden Isles

Look for ★ to find recommended sights, activities, dining, and lodging.

Highlights

★ **Jekyll Island Historic District:** Relax and soak in the salty breeze at this onetime playground of the country's richest people (page 231).

★ **The Village:** The center of social life on St. Simons Island has shops, restaurants, a pier, and a beachside playground (page 236).

★ **Fort Frederica National Monument:** An excellently preserved tabby fortress dates from the first days of English settlement in Georgia (page 237).

★ **Harris Neck National Wildlife Refuge:** This former wartime airfield is now one of the East Coast's best birding locations (page 243).

★ **Cumberland Island National Seashore:** This undeveloped island paradise has wild horses, evocative abandoned ruins, and over 16 miles of gorgeous beach (page 248).

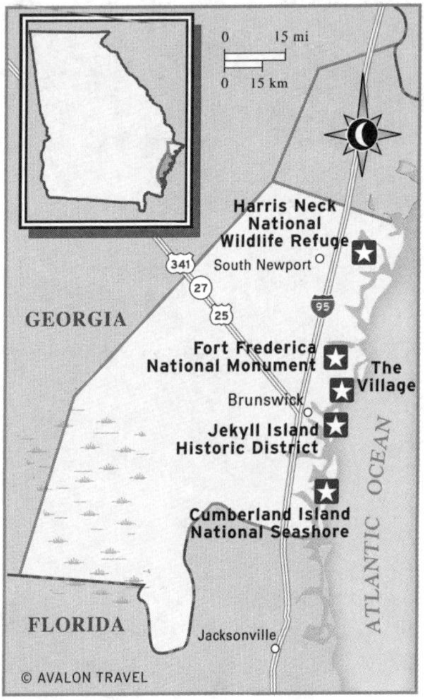

The Georgia coast retains a timeless mystique evocative of an era before the coming of Europeans, even before humankind itself.

Often called the Golden Isles because of the play of the afternoon sun on the vistas of marsh grass, its other nickname, "the Debatable Land," is a nod to its centuries-long role as a constantly shifting battleground of European powers.

On the map it looks relatively short, but Georgia's coastline is the longest contiguous salt marsh environment in the world—a third of the country's remaining salt marsh. Abundant with wildlife, vibrant with exotic, earthy aromas, constantly refreshed by a steady, salty sea breeze, it's a place with no real match anywhere else.

Ancient Native Americans held the area in special regard. Avaricious for gold as they were, the Spanish also admired the almost monastic enchantment of Georgia's coast, choosing it as the site of their first colony in North America. They built a subsequent chain of Roman Catholic missions, now long gone.

While the American tycoons who used these barrier islands as personal playgrounds had avarice of their own, we must give credit where it's due: Their self-interest kept these places largely untouched by the kind of development that has plagued many of South Carolina's barrier islands to the north.

PLANNING YOUR TIME

Many travelers take I-95 south from Savannah to the Golden Isles, but **U.S. 17** roughly parallels the interstate—in some cases so closely that drivers on the two roads can see each other—and is a far more scenic and enriching drive for those with a little extra time to spend. Indeed, U.S. 17 is an intrinsic part of the life and lore of the region, and you are likely to spend a fair amount of time on it regardless.

Geographically, Brunswick is similar to Charleston in that it lies on a peninsula laid out roughly north-south. And like Charleston, it's separated from the Atlantic by barrier islands, in Brunswick's case St. Simons Island and Jekyll Island. Once you get within city limits, however, Brunswick has more in common with Savannah due

Previous: Fort Frederica National Monument; a wild horse at Cumberland Island National Seashore.
Above: the legendary Jekyll Island Club.

The Golden Isles

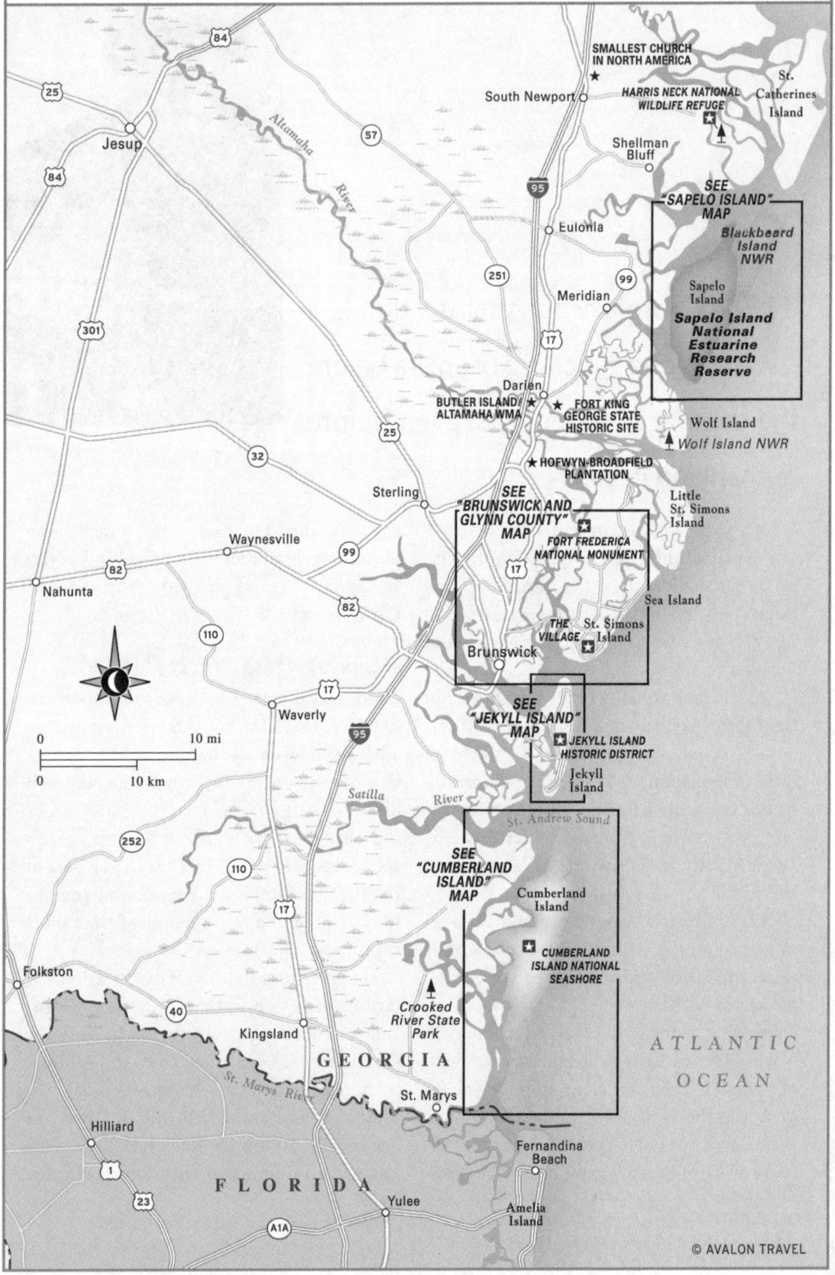
SMALLEST CHURCH IN NORTH AMERICA
South Newport
HARRIS NECK NATIONAL WILDLIFE REFUGE
St. Catherines Island
Jesup
Altamaha River
Shellman Bluff
SEE "SAPELO ISLAND" MAP
Blackbeard Island NWR
Eulonia
Meridian
Sapelo Island
Sapelo Island National Estuarine Research Reserve
Darien
BUTLER ISLAND/ ALTAMAHA WMA
FORT KING GEORGE STATE HISTORIC SITE
Wolf Island
Wolf Island NWR
HOFWYN-BROADFIELD PLANTATION
Sterling
SEE "BRUNSWICK AND GLYNN COUNTY" MAP
Little St. Simons Island
FORT FREDERICA NATIONAL MONUMENT
Waynesville
Nahunta
Sea Island
THE VILLAGE
St. Simons Island
Brunswick
Waverly
SEE "JEKYLL ISLAND" MAP
JEKYLL ISLAND HISTORIC DISTRICT
Jekyll Island
0 10 mi
0 10 km
Satilla River
St. Andrew Sound
SEE "CUMBERLAND ISLAND" MAP
Cumberland Island
CUMBERLAND ISLAND NATIONAL SEASHORE
Folkston
Crooked River State Park
Kingsland
GEORGIA
ATLANTIC OCEAN
St. Marys River
St. Marys
Hilliard
Fernandina Beach
FLORIDA
Yulee
Amelia Island
© AVALON TRAVEL

to its Oglethorpe-designed grid layout. **Brunswick** itself can easily be fully experienced in a **single afternoon.** But really—as its nickname "Gateway to the Golden Isles" indicates—Brunswick is an economic and governmental center for Glynn County, to which Jekyll Island and St. Simons Island, the real attractions in this area, belong.

Both Jekyll Island and St. Simons Island are well worth visiting, and have their own separate pleasures—Jekyll more contemplative, St. Simons more upscale. Give an **entire day to Jekyll** so you can take full advantage of its relaxing, open feel. A **half day** can suffice for **St. Simons** because most of its attractions are clustered in the Village area near the pier, and there's little beach recreation to speak of.

Getting to the undeveloped barrier islands, Sapelo and Cumberland, takes planning because there is no bridge to either. Both require a ferry booking and hence a more substantial commitment of time. There are no real stores and few facilities on these islands, so pack along whatever you think you'll need, including food, water, medicine, suntan lotion, insect repellent, and so on. **Sapelo Island** is limited to **day use** unless you have prior reservations, with the town of Darien in McIntosh County as the gateway. The same is true for Cumberland Island National Seashore, with the town of St. Marys in Camden County as the gateway.

Brunswick and Glynn County

Consider Brunswick sort of a junior Savannah, sharing with that larger city to the north a heavily English flavor, great manners, a city plan with squares courtesy of General James Oglethorpe, a thriving but environmentally intrusive seaport, and a busy shrimping fleet. Despite an admirable effort at downtown revitalization, most visitors to the area seem content to employ Brunswick, as its nickname implies, as a "Gateway to the Golden Isles" rather than as a destination in itself.

SIGHTS

Brunswick Historic District

Most of the visitor-friendly activity centers on **Newcastle Street,** where you'll find the bulk of the galleries, shops, and restored buildings. Adjacent in the historic areas are some nice residential homes.

The new pride of downtown is **Old City Hall** (1212 Newcastle St., 912/265-4032, www.brunswickgeorgia.net/och2.html), an amazing circa-1889 Richardsonian Romanesque edifice designed by noted regional architect Alfred Eichberg, who also planned many similarly imposing buildings in Savannah. Today it doubles as a rental event facility as well as a part-time courthouse; call ahead to take a gander inside.

Another active restored building is the charming **Ritz Theatre** (1530 Newcastle St., 912/262-6934, www.goldenislearts.org), built in 1898 to house the Grand Opera House and the offices of the Brunswick and Birmingham Railroad. This ornate three-story Victorian transitioned with the times, becoming a vaudeville venue, then a movie house.

Mary Ross Waterfront Park

Mary Ross Waterfront Park, a downtown gathering place at Bay and Gloucester Streets, also has economic importance as a center of local industry—it's here where Brunswick's shrimp fleet is moored and the town's large port facilities begin. In 1989 the park was dedicated to Mary Ross, member of a longtime Brunswick shrimping family and author of the popular Georgia history book *The Debatable Land.*

Lover's Oak

At the intersection of Prince and Albany Streets is the **Lover's Oak,** a nearly 1,000-year-old tree. Local lore tells us that it has been a secret

Brunswick and Glynn County

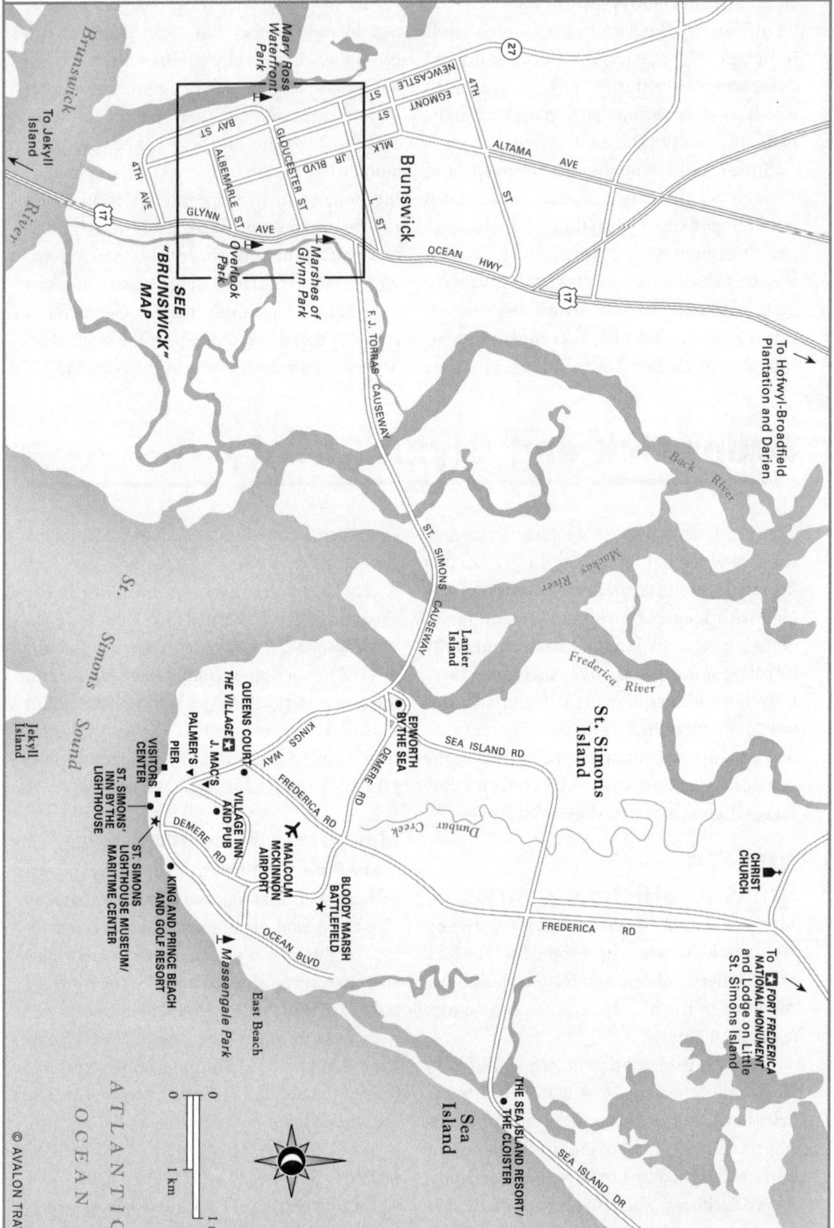

Brunswick

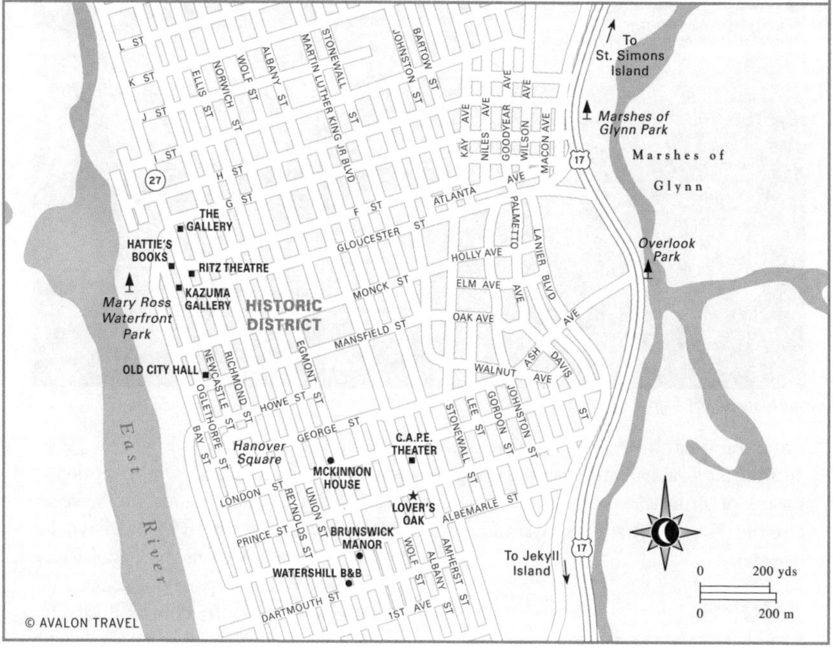

meeting place for young lovers for centuries (though one does wonder how much of a secret it actually could have been). It's about 13 feet in diameter and has 10 sprawling limbs.

Amid the light industrial sprawl of this area of the Golden Isles Parkway is the interesting little **Overlook Park,** just south of the visitors center on U.S. 17—a good, if loud, place for a picnic. From the park's picnic grounds or overlook you can see the fabled **Marshes of Glynn,** which inspired Georgia poet Sidney Lanier to write his famous poem of the same title under the **Lanier Oak,** located a little farther up the road in the median.

Hofwyl-Broadfield Plantation

South Carolina doesn't own the patent on well-preserved old rice plantations, as the **Hofwyl-Broadfield Plantation** (5556 U.S. 17, 912/264-7333, www.gastateparks.org, Wed.-Sun. 9am-5pm, last main house tour 4pm, $8 adults, $5 children), a short drive north of Brunswick, proves. With its old paddy fields along the gorgeous and relatively undeveloped Altamaha River estuary, the plantation's main home is an antebellum wonder, with an expansive porch and a nice house museum that includes silver, a model of a rice plantation, and a slide show. There's also a pleasant nature trail.

FESTIVALS AND EVENTS

Each Mother's Day at noon, parishioners of the local St. Francis Xavier Church hold the **Our Lady of Fatima Processional and Blessing of the Fleet** (www.brunswick.net), begun in 1938 by the local Portuguese fishing community. After the procession, at about 3pm at Mary Ross Waterfront Park, comes the actual blessing of the shrimping fleet.

Foodies will enjoy the **Brunswick Stewbilee** ($9 adults, $4 children), held on the second Saturday in October 11:30am-3pm.

the Marshes of Glynn at Overlook Park

Pro and amateur chefs showcase their skills in creating the local signature dish and vying for the title of "Brunswick Stewmaster." There are also car shows, contests, displays, and much live music.

SHOPS

Right in the heart of the bustle on Newcastle is a good indie bookstore, **Hattie's Books** (1531 Newcastle St., 912/554-8677, www.hattiesbooks.com, Mon.-Fri. 10am-5:30pm, Sat. 10am-4pm). Not only do they have a good selection of local and regional authors, you can also get a good cup of coffee.

Like Beaufort, South Carolina, Brunswick has made the art gallery a central component of its downtown revitalization, with nearly all of them on Newcastle Street. Near Hattie's you'll find the **Ritz Theatre** (1530 Newcastle St., 912/262-6934, Tues.-Fri. 9am-5pm, Sat. 10am-2pm), which has its own art gallery inside. Farther down is **The Gallery on Newcastle Street** (1626 Newcastle St., 912/554-0056, www.thegalleryonnewcastle.com, Thurs.-Sat. 11am-5pm), showcasing the original oils of owner Janet Powers.

FOOD

Brunswick isn't known for its breadth of cuisine options, and, frankly, most discriminating diners make the short drive over the causeway to St. Simons Island. One exception in Brunswick that really stands out, however, is **Indigo Coastal Shanty** (1402 Reynolds St., 912/265-2007, www.indigocoastalshanty.com, Tues.-Fri. 11am-3pm, Fri.-Sat. also open 5pm-10pm, $12). This friendly, smallish place specializes in creative coastal themes, with dishes like the Charleston Sauté (shrimp and ham with peppers), Fisherman's Bowl (shrimp and fish in a nice broth), and even that old Southern favorite, a pimento cheeseburger.

ACCOMMODATIONS

In addition to the usual variety of chain hotels—most of which you should stay far away from—there are some nice places to stay in Brunswick at very reasonable prices if you want to make the city a base of operations. In the heart of Old Town in a gorgeous Victorian is the ★ **McKinnon House** (1001 Egmont St., 912/261-9100, www.mckinnonhousebandb.com, $125), which had a cameo role in the 1974 film *Conrack*. Today, this bed-and-breakfast is Jo Miller's labor of love, a three-suite affair with some plush interiors and an exterior that is one of Brunswick's most photographed spots. Surprisingly affordable for its elegance, the **WatersHill Bed & Breakfast** (728 Union St., 912/264-4262,

Brunswick Stew

Virginians insist that the distinctive Southern dish known as Brunswick stew was named for Brunswick County, Virginia, in 1828, where a political rally featured stew made from squirrel meat. But all real Southern foodies know the dish is named for Brunswick, Georgia. Hey, there's a plaque to prove it in downtown Brunswick—although it says the first pot was cooked on July 2, 1898, on St. Simons Island, not in Brunswick at all. However, I think we can all agree that "Brunswick stew" rolls off the tongue much more easily than "St. Simons stew." You can find the famous pot in which the first batch was cooked on F Street near Mary Ross Waterfront Park.

The first Brunswick Stew was cooked in this pot.

It seems likely that what we now know as Brunswick stew is based on an old colonial recipe, adapted from Native Americans, that relied on the meat of small game—originally squirrel or rabbit but nowadays mostly chicken or pork—along with vegetables like corn, onions, and okra simmered over an open fire. Today, this tangy, thick, tomato-based delight is a typical accompaniment to barbecue throughout the Lowcountry and the Georgia coast, as well as a freestanding entrée on its own. Here's a typical recipe from Glynn County, home of the famous Brunswick Stewbilee festival held the second Saturday of October:

SAUCE

Melt ¼ cup butter over low heat, then add:
1¾ cups ketchup
¼ cup yellow mustard
¼ cup white vinegar

Blend until smooth, then add:
½ tablespoon chopped garlic
1 teaspoon ground black pepper
½ teaspoon crushed red pepper
½ ounce Liquid Smoke
1 ounce Worcestershire sauce
1 ounce hot sauce
½ tablespoon fresh lemon juice

Blend until smooth, then add:
¼ cup dark brown sugar
Stir constantly and simmer for 10 minutes, being careful not to boil. Set aside.

STEW

Melt ¼ pound butter in a two-gallon pot, then add:
3 cups diced small potatoes
1 cup diced small onion
2 14½-ounce cans chicken broth
1 pound baked chicken
8-10 ounces smoked pork

Bring to a boil, stirring until potatoes are nearly done, then add:
1 8½-ounce can early peas
2 14½-ounce cans stewed tomatoes
1 16-ounce can baby lima beans
¼ cup Liquid Smoke
1 14½-ounce can creamed corn

Stir in sauce. Simmer slowly for two hours. Makes one gallon of Brunswick stew.

www.watershill.com, $100) serves a full breakfast and offers a choice of five themed suites, such as the French country Elliot Wynell Room or the large Mariana Mahlaney Room way up in the restored attic. Another good B&B is the **Brunswick Manor** (825 Egmont St., 912/265-6889, www.brunswickmanor.com, $130), offering four suites in a classic Victorian and a tasty meal each day.

The most unique lodging in the area is the ★ **Hostel in the Forest** (Hwy. 82, 912/264-9738, www.foresthostel.com, $25, cash only). Formed more than 30 years ago as an International Youth Hostel, the place initially gives off a hippie vibe, with an evening communal meal (included in the rates) and a near-total ban on cell phones. But don't expect a wild time: No pets are allowed, the hostel discourages young children, and quiet time is strictly enforced beginning at 11pm. To reach the hostel, take I-95 exit 29 and go west for two miles. Make a U-turn at the intersection at mile marker 11. Continue east on Highway 82 for 0.5 mile. Look for a dirt road on the right with a gate and signage. This is now a "membership" organization so you'll need to join before booking.

TRANSPORTATION AND SERVICES

Brunswick is directly off I-95. Take exit 38 to the Golden Isles Parkway, and take a right on U.S. 17. The quickest way to the historic district is to make a right onto Gloucester Street. Plans and funding for a citywide public transit system are pending, but currently Brunswick has no public transportation.

A downtown **information station** is in the Ritz Theatre (1530 Newcastle St., 912/262-6934, Tues.-Fri. 9am-5pm, Sat. 10am-2pm).

The newspaper of record in town is the ***Brunswick News*** (www.thebrunswicknews.com). The main **post office** (805 Gloucester St., 912/280-1250) is downtown.

Jekyll Island

Few places in the United States have as paradoxical a story as Jekyll Island (www.jekyllisland.com). Once the playground of the world's richest people—whose indulgence allowed the island to escape the overdevelopment that plagues nearby St. Simons—Jekyll then became a dedicated vacation area for Georgians of modest means, by order of the state legislature. Today, it's somewhere in the middle—a great place for a relaxing nature-oriented vacation that retains some of the perks of luxury of its Gilded Age pedigree.

After securing safe access to the island from the Creeks in 1733, Georgia's founder, General James Oglethorpe, gave the island its modern name, after his friend Sir Joseph Jekyll. In 1858, Jekyll Island was the final port of entry for the infamous voyage of *The Wanderer*, the last American slave ship. After intercepting the ship and its contraband manifest of 409 African slaves—the importation of slaves having been banned in 1808—its owners and crew were put on trial and acquitted in Savannah.

As a home away from home for the country's richest industrialists—including J. P. Morgan, William Rockefeller, and William Vanderbilt—in the late 1800s and early 1900s, Jekyll Island was the unlikely seat of some of the most crucial events in modern American history. It was at the Jekyll Island Club in 1910 that the Federal Reserve banking system was set up, the result of a secret convocation of investors and tycoons. Five years later on the grounds of the club, AT&T president Theodore Vail would listen in on the first transcontinental phone call.

ORIENTATION

You'll have to stop at the entrance gate and pay a $6 "parking fee" to gain daily access to this state-owned island; a weeklong pass is $28. (Bicyclists and pedestrians don't need to pay.)

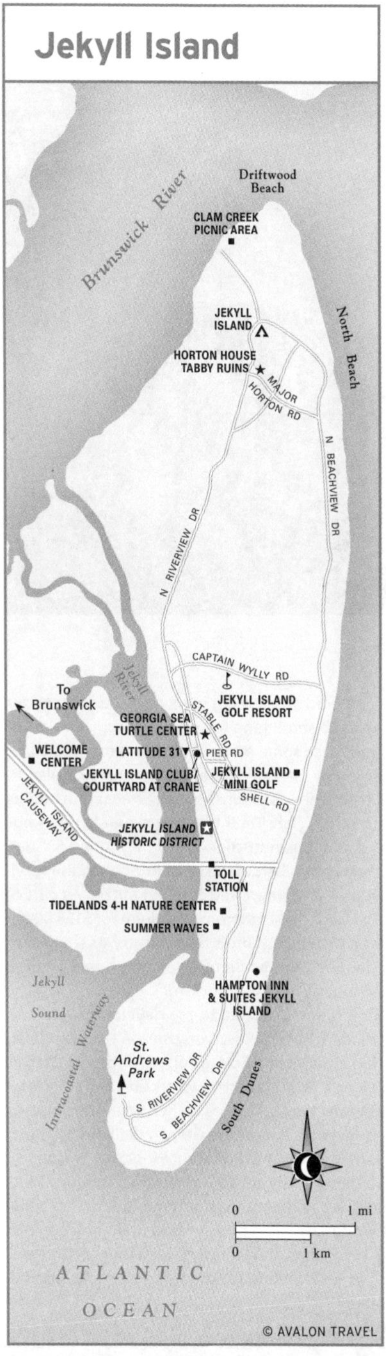

A friendly attendant will give you a map and a newsletter, and from there you're free to enjoy the whole island at your leisure.

SIGHTS

★ Jekyll Island Historic District

A living link to one of the most glamorous eras of American history, the **Jekyll Island Historic District** is also one of the largest ongoing restoration projects in the southeastern United States. A visit to this 240-acre riverfront area is like stepping back in time to the Gilded Age, with croquet grounds, manicured gardens, and even ferry boats with names like the *Rockefeller* and the *J. P. Morgan*. The historic district essentially comprises the buildings and grounds of the old **Jekyll Island Club,** not only a full-service resort complex—consisting of the main building and several amazing "cottages" that are mansions themselves—but a sort of living-history exhibit chronicling that time when Jekyll was a gathering place for the world's richest and most influential people.

The Queen Anne-style main clubhouse, with its iconic turret, dates from 1886. Within a couple of years the club had already outgrown it, and the millionaires began building the ornate cottages on the grounds surrounding it. In 2000 renovations were done on the most magnificent outbuilding, the 24-bedroom Crane Cottage, a Mediterranean villa that also hosts a fine restaurant.

The **Jekyll Island Museum** (100 Stable Rd., 912/635-4036, www.jekyllisland.com, daily 9am-5pm, free), in the historic district at the old club stables, houses some good history exhibits.

Georgia Sea Turtle Center

Within the historic district in a whimsically renovated 1903 building is the **Georgia Sea Turtle Center** (214 Stable Rd., 912/635-4444, www.georgiaseaturtlecenter.org, daily 9am-5pm, $7 adults, $5 children), which features interactive exhibits on these important marine creatures, for whom Jekyll Island is a major nesting ground. Don't miss the attached rehabilitation building, where you can see the center's

Jekyll Island's Millionaire's Club

the Jekyll Island Club

After the Civil War, as the Industrial Revolution gathered momentum seemingly everywhere but Georgia's Golden Isles, a couple of men decided to do something to break the foggy miasma of Reconstruction that had settled into the area and make some money in the process. In the late 1870s, John Eugene DuBignon and his brother-in-law Newton Finney came up with a plan to combine DuBignon's long family ties to Jekyll with Finney's extensive Wall Street connections in order to turn Jekyll into an exclusive winter hunting club. Their targeted clientele was a no-brainer: the newly minted American mega-tycoons of the Industrial Age. Finney found 53 such elite millionaires willing to pony up to become charter members of the venture, dubbed the Jekyll Island Club. Among them were William Vanderbilt, J. P. Morgan, and Joseph Pulitzer. As part of the original business model, in 1886 Finney purchased the island from DuBignon for $125,000.

With the formal opening two years later began Jekyll Island's half century as a premier playground for the country's richest citizens, centered on the Victorian winter homes, called "cottages," built by each member and preserved today in the historic district.

In 1910, secret meetings of the so-called "First Name Club" led to the development of the Aldrich Plan, which laid the groundwork for the modern Federal Reserve System. A few years later, AT&T president Theodore Vail, nursing a broken leg at his Mound Cottage on Jekyll, participated in the first transcontinental telephone call on January 25, 1915, among New York City, San Francisco, and the special line strung down the coast from New York and across Jekyll Sound to the club grounds. Also on the line were the telephone's inventor, Alexander Graham Bell, his assistant Thomas Watson, the mayors of New York and San Francisco, and President Woodrow Wilson.

The millionaires continued to frolic on Jekyll through the Great Depression, but worsening international economic conditions reduced the club's numbers, even though the cost of membership was lowered in 1933. The outbreak of World War II and the resulting drain of labor into the armed forces put a further cramp in the club's workings, and it finally closed for good in 1942. The state would acquire the island after the war in 1947, turning the once-exclusive playground of millionaires into a playground for all the people.

turtles in various states of treatment and rehabilitation before they are released into the wild. Children and adults alike will enjoy this unique opportunity to see these creatures up close and learn about the latest efforts to protect them.

In an effort to raise awareness about the need to protect the nesting areas of the big loggerheads that lay eggs on Jekyll each summer, the Sea Turtle Center also guides **nighttime tours** (early June-Aug. daily 8:30pm and 9:30pm) on the beach in order to explain about the animals and their habitat and hopefully to see some loggerheads in action. These tours fill up fast, so make reservations in advance.

Driftwood Beach

Barrier islands like Jekyll are in a constant state of southward flux as currents erode the north end and push sand down the beach to the south end. This phenomenon has created **Driftwood Beach,** as the soil has eroded from under the large trees, causing them to fall and settle into the sand. In addition to being a naturalist's wonderland, it's also a starkly beautiful and strangely romantic spot. Drive north on Beachview Drive until you see a pullover on your right immediately after the Villas by the Sea (there's no signage). Park and take the short trail through the maritime forest, and you'll find yourself right there among the fallen trees and sand.

Horton House Tabby Ruins

Round the curve and go south on Riverview Drive, and you'll see the large frame of a two-story house on the left (east) side of the road. That is the ruins of the old **Horton House,** built by Jekyll's original English-speaking settler, William Horton. The house has survived two wars, a couple of hurricanes, and a clumsy restoration in 1898. Its current state of preservation is thanks to the Jekyll Island Authority and various federal, state, and local partners.

Frenchman Christophe Poulain du Bignon would live in the Horton House for a while after purchasing the island in the 1790s. Across the street from the house is the poignant little **Du Bignon Cemetery,** around which winds a nicely done pedestrian and bike path overlooking one of the most beautiful areas of marsh you'll see in all the Golden Isles.

ENTERTAINMENT AND NIGHTLIFE

There's no real nightlife to speak of on Jekyll, it being intended for quiet, affordable daytime relaxation. The focus instead is on several annual events held at the **Jekyll Island Convention Center** (1 N. Beachview Dr., 912/635-3400), which has undergone a massive restoration to bring it in line with modern convention standards.

At the beginning of the New Year comes one of the area's most beloved and well-attended events, the **Jekyll Island Bluegrass Festival** (www.adamsbluegrass.com). Many of the genre's biggest traditional names come to play at this casual multiday gathering. The focus here is on the music, not the trappings, so come prepared to enjoy wall-to-wall bluegrass played by the best in the business.

In September as the harvest comes in off the boats, the **Wild Georgia Shrimp and Grits Festival** (www.jekyllisland.com, free admission) promotes the value of the Georgia shrimping industry by focusing on how good the little critters taste in various regional recipes.

SPORTS AND ACTIVITIES

Hiking and Biking

Quite simply, Jekyll Island is a paradise for bicyclists and walkers, with a well-developed and very safe system of paths totaling about 20 miles and running the circumference of the island. The paths go by all major sights, including the Jekyll Island Club in the historic district. In addition, walkers and bicyclists can enjoy much of the seven miles of beachfront at low tide.

Rent your bikes at **Jekyll Island Miniature Golf** (100 James Rd., 912/635-2648, daily 9am-8pm, $5.25 per hour, $11.50 per day). Take a left when you dead-end after the entrance gate, then another left.

Golf and Tennis

True to Jekyll Island's intended role as a playground for Georgians of low to medium income, its golf and tennis facilities—all centrally located at the middle of the island—are quite reasonably priced. The **Jekyll Island Golf Resort** (322 Captain Wylly Rd., 912/635-2368, www.jekyllisland.com, greens fees $40-60) comprises the largest public golf resort in Georgia. A total of 63 holes on four courses—Pine Lakes, Indian Mound, Oleander, and Ocean Dunes (nine holes)—await. Check the resort's website for "golf passport" packages that include local lodging.

The adjacent **Jekyll Island Tennis Center** (400 Captain Wylly Rd., 912/635-3154, www.gate.net/~jitc, $25 per hour) boasts 13 courts, 7 of them lighted, as well as a pro shop (daily 9am-6pm).

Water Parks

Summer Waves (210 S. Riverview Dr., 912/635-2074, www.jekyllisland.com, Memorial Day-Labor Day, $20 adults, $16 children under 48 inches tall) is just what the doctor ordered for kids with a surplus of energy. The 11-acre facility has a separate section for toddlers to splash around in, with the requisite more daring rides for hard-charging preteens. Hours vary, so call ahead.

Horseback Riding and Tours

Victoria's Carriages and Trail (100 Stable Rd., 912/635-9500, Mon.-Sat. 11am-4pm) offers numerous options, both on horseback as well as in a horse-drawn carriage, including carriage tours of the island (Mon.-Sat. every hour 11am-4pm, $15 adults, $7 children). There's a 6pm-8pm night ride ($38 per couple). Horseback rides include a one-hour beach ride ($55) that leaves at 11am, 1pm, and 3pm and a sunset ride (6:30pm, $65) that lasts a little over an hour. Victoria's is at the entrance to the Clam Creek Picnic Area on the north end of the island, directly across the street from the Jekyll Island Campground.

The **Tidelands 4-H Center** (912/635-5032) gives 1.5-2-hour Marsh Walks (Mon. 9am, $5 adults, $3 children) leaving from Clam Creek Picnic Area, and Beach Walks ($5 adults, $3 children) leaving Wednesdays at 9am from the St. Andrews Picnic Area and Fridays at 9am from South Dunes Picnic Area.

FOOD

Cuisine offerings are few and far between on Jekyll. I'd suggest you patronize one of the three dining facilities at the **Jekyll Island Club** (371 Riverview Dr.), which are all open to nonguests. They're not only delicious but pretty reasonable as well, considering the swank setting. My favorite is the ★ **Courtyard at Crane** (912/635-2400, lunch Sun.-Fri. 11am-4pm, Sat. 11am-2pm, dinner Sun.-Thurs. 5:30pm-9pm, $27-38). Located in the circa-1917 Crane Cottage, one of the beautifully restored tycoon villas, the Courtyard offers romantic evening dining (call for reservations) as well as tasty and stylish lunch dining in the alfresco courtyard area or inside.

For a real and figurative taste of history, make a reservation at the **Grand Dining Room** (912/635-2400, breakfast Mon.-Sat. 7am-11am, Sun. 7am-10am, lunch Mon.-Sat. 11:30am-2pm, brunch Sun. 10:45am-2pm, dinner daily 6pm-10pm, dinner $26-35), the club's full-service restaurant. Focusing on continental cuisine—ordered either à la carte or as a prix fixe "sunset dinner"—the Dining Room features a pianist each evening and for Sunday brunch. Jackets or collared shirts are required for men.

For a tasty breakfast, lunch, or dinner on the go or at odd hours, check out **Café Solterra** (912/635-2600, daily 7am-10pm), great for deli-type food and equipped with Starbucks coffee. There are two places for seaside dining and cocktails at the historic Jekyll Island Club Wharf: **Latitude 31** (1 Pier Rd., 912/635-3800, www.crossoverjekyll.com, Tues.-Sun. 5:30pm-10pm, $15-25, no reservations) is an upscale seafood-oriented fine-dining place, while the attached **Rah Bar** (Tues.-Sat. 11am-close, Sun. 1pm-close, depending on weather) serves up oysters and shellfish in a very casual setting; try the Lowcountry boil or the crab legs.

the Courtyard at Crane

ACCOMMODATIONS

Under $150

While most bargain lodging on Jekyll is sadly subpar, the old **Days Inn** (60 S. Beachview Dr., 912/635-9800, www.daysinnjekyll.com, $100) has undergone remodeling lately and is the best choice if budget is a concern (and you don't want to camp, that is). It has a good location on the south side of the island with nice ocean views.

$150-300

Any discussion of lodging on Jekyll Island begins with the legendary ★ **Jekyll Island Club** (371 Riverview Dr., 800/535-9547, www.jekyllclub.com, $199-490), which is reasonably priced considering its history, postcard-perfect setting, and delightful guest rooms. Some of its 157 guest rooms in the club and annex areas are available for under $200. There are 60 guest rooms in the main club building, and several outlying cottages, chief among them the Crane, Cherokee, and Sans Souci Cottages, are also available. All rates include use of the big outdoor pool overlooking the river, and a neat amenity is a choice of meal plans for an extra daily fee.

The first hotel built on the island in 35 years, the ★ **Hampton Inn & Suites Jekyll Island** (200 S. Beachview Dr., 912/635-3733, www.hamptoninn.com, $180-210) was constructed according to an exacting set of conservation guidelines, conserving much of the original tree canopy and employing various low-impact design and building techniques. It's one of the best eco-friendly hotel designs I've experienced.

Camping

One of the niftiest campgrounds in the area is the **Jekyll Island Campground** (197 Riverview Dr., 912/635-3021, tent sites $25, RV sites $32). It's a friendly place with an excellent location at the north end of the island. There are more than 200 sites, from tent to full-service pull-through RV sites. There's a two-night minimum on weekends and a three-night minimum on holiday and special-event weekends; reservations are recommended.

TRANSPORTATION AND SERVICES

Jekyll Island is immediately south of Brunswick. You'll have to pay a $6 per vehicle fee to get onto the island. Once on the island, most sites are on the north end (a left as you reach the dead-end at Beachview Dr.).

The main circuit route around the island is Beachview Drive, which suitably enough changes into Riverview Drive as it rounds the bend to landward at the north end.

Many visitors choose to bicycle around the island once they're here, which is certainly the best way to experience both the sights and the beach itself at low tide.

The **Jekyll Island Visitor Center** (901 Downing Musgrove Causeway, 912/635-3636, daily 9am-5pm) is on the long causeway along the marsh before you get to the island. Set in a charming little cottage it shares with the Georgia State Patrol, the center has a nice gift shop and loads of brochures on the entire Golden Isles region.

St. Simons Island

Despite a reputation for aloof affluence, the truth is that St. Simons Island is also very visitor friendly, and there's more to do here than meets the eye.

Fort Frederica, now a National Monument, was a key base of operations for the British struggle to evict the Spanish from Georgia—which culminated in 1742 in the decisive Battle of Bloody Marsh. In the years after American independence, St. Simons woke up from its slumber as acre after acre of virgin live oak was felled to make the massive timbers of new warships for the U.S. Navy, including the USS *Constitution.* In their place was planted a new crop—cotton. The island's antebellum plantations boomed to world-class heights of profit and prestige when the superior strain of the crop known as Sea Island cotton came in the 1820s.

The next landmark development for St. Simons didn't come until the building of the first causeway in 1924, which led directly to the island's resort development by the mega-rich industrialist Howard Coffin of Hudson Motors fame, who also owned nearby Sapelo Island to the north.

ORIENTATION

Because it's only a short drive from downtown Brunswick on the Torras Causeway, St. Simons has much less of a remote feel than most other Georgia barrier islands, and it's much more densely populated than any other Georgia island except for Tybee. Most visitor-oriented activity on this 12-mile-long, heavily residential island is clustered at the south end, where St. Simons Sound meets the Atlantic.

SIGHTS

★ The Village

Think of **"The Village"** at the extreme south end of St. Simons as a mix of Tybee's downscale accessibility and Hilton Head's upscale exclusivity. This compact, bustling area only a few blocks long offers not only boutique shops and stylish cafés, but also vintage stores and busking musicians.

St. Simons Lighthouse Museum

Unlike many East Coast lighthouses, which tend to be in hard-to-reach places, anyone can walk right up to the **St. Simons Lighthouse Museum** (101 12th St., 912/638-4666, www.saintsimonslighthouse.org, Mon.-Sat. 10am-5pm, Sun. 1:30pm-5pm, $12 adults, $5 children). Once inside, you can enjoy the museum's exhibit and take the 129 steps up to the top of the 104-foot beacon—which is, unusually, still active—for a gorgeous view of the island and the ocean beyond.

Maritime Center

A short walk from the lighthouse and also administered by the Coastal Georgia Historical Society, the **Maritime Center** (4201 1st St., 912/638-4666, www.saintsimonslighthouse.org, Mon.-Sat. 10am-5pm, Sun. 1:30pm-5pm, $12 adults, $5 children) is at the historic East Beach Coast Guard Station. Authorized by

Golden Isles on the Page

And now from the Vast of the Lord will the waters of sleep
Roll in on the souls of men,
But who will reveal to our waking ken
The forms that swim and the shapes that creep
Under the waters of sleep?
And I would I could know what swimmeth below when the tide comes in
On the length and the breadth of the marvelous marshes of Glynn.

Sidney Lanier

Many authors have been inspired by their time in the Golden Isles, whether to pen flights of poetic fancy, page-turning novels, or politically oriented chronicles. Here are a few of the most notable names:

- **Sidney Lanier:** Born in Macon, Georgia, Lanier was a renowned linguist, mathematician, and legal scholar. Fighting for the Confederacy during the Civil War, he was captured while commanding a blockade runner and taken to a POW camp in Maryland, where he came down with tuberculosis. After the war, he stayed at his brother-in-law's house in Brunswick to recuperate, and it was during that time that he took up poetry, writing the famous "Marshes of Glynn," quoted above.
- **Eugenia Price:** Although not originally from St. Simons, Price remains the best-known local cultural figure, setting her *St. Simons Trilogy* here. After relocating to the island in 1965, she stayed here until her death in 1996. She's buried in the Christ Church cemetery on Frederica Road.
- **Tina McElroy Ansa:** Probably the most notable literary figure currently living on St. Simons Island is award-winning African American author Tina McElroy Ansa. Few of her books are set in the Golden Isles region, but they all deal with life in the South, and Ansa is an ardent devotee of St. Simons and its relaxed, friendly ways.
- **Fanny Kemble:** In 1834, this renowned English actress married Georgia plantation heir Pierce Butler, who would become one of the largest slave owners in the United States. Horrified by the treatment of Butler's slaves at Butler Island, just south of Darien, Georgia, Kemble penned one of the earliest antislavery chronicles, *Journal of a Residence on a Georgian Plantation in 1838-1839.* Kemble's disagreement with her husband over slavery hastened their divorce in 1849.

President Franklin Roosevelt in 1933 and completed in 1937 by the Works Progress Administration, the East Beach Station took part in military action in World War II, an episode chronicled in exhibits at the Maritime Center.

★ Fort Frederica National Monument

The expansive and well-researched **Fort Frederica National Monument** (Frederica Rd., 912/638-3639, www.nps.gov/fofr, daily 9am-5pm, free) lies on the landward side of the island. Established by General James Oglethorpe in 1736 to protect Georgia's southern flank from the Spanish, the fort (as well as the village that sprang up around it, in which the Wesley brothers preached for a short time) was named for Frederick Louis, the Prince of Wales. The feminine suffix *-a* was added to distinguish it from the older Fort Frederick in South Carolina.

You don't just get to see a military fort here (actually the remains of the old powder magazine; most of the fort itself eroded into the river long ago); this is an entire colonial townsite a mile in circumference, originally modeled after a typical English village. A self-guided walking tour through the beautiful grounds shows foundations of building sites that have been uncovered, including taverns, shops, and the private homes of influential citizens. Closer to the river is the large tabby structure of the garrison barracks.

Bloody Marsh Battlefield

There's not a lot to see at the site of the **Battle of Bloody Marsh** (Frederica Rd., 912/638-3639, www.nps.gov/fofr, daily 8am-4pm, free). Essentially just a few interpretive signs overlooking a beautiful piece of salt marsh, the site is believed to be near the place where British soldiers from nearby Fort Frederica ambushed a force of Spanish regulars on their way to besiege the fort. The battle wasn't actually that bloody—some accounts say the Spanish lost only seven men—but the stout British presence convinced the Spanish to leave St. Simons a few days later, never again to project their once-potent military power that far north in the New World.

While the Battle of Bloody Marsh site is part of the National Park Service's Fort Frederica unit, it's not at the same location. Get to the battlefield from the fort by taking Frederica Road south, and then a left (east) on Demere Road. The site is on your left as Demere Road veers right, in the 1800 block.

Christ Church

Just down the road from Fort Frederica is historic **Christ Church** (6329 Frederica Rd., 912/638-8683, www.christchurchfrederica.org, daily 2pm-5pm). The first sanctuary dates from 1820, but the original congregation at the now-defunct town of Frederica held services under the oaks at the site as early as 1736. The founder of Methodism, John Wesley, and his brother Charles both ministered to island residents during 1736-1737.

Christ Church's claim to fame in modern culture is as the setting of local novelist Eugenia Price's *The Beloved Invader,* the first work in her Georgia trilogy. The late Price, who died in 1996, is buried in the church cemetery.

Tours

St. Simons Island Trolley Tours (912/638-8954, www.stsimonstours.com, daily 11am, $22 adults, $10 ages 4-12, free under age 4) offers just that, a ride around the island in comparative comfort, leaving from the pier.

Fort Frederica National Monument

ENTERTAINMENT AND NIGHTLIFE

Nightlife

Unlike some areas this far south on the Georgia coast, there's usually a sizable contingent of young people on St. Simons out looking for a good time. The island's premier club, **Rafters Blues and Raw Bar** (315½ Mallory St., 912/634-9755, www.raftersblues.com, Mon.-Sat. 4:30pm-2am), known simply as "Rafters," brings in live music most every Thursday-Saturday night, focusing on the best acts on the regional rock circuit.

My favorite spot on St. Simons for a drink or an espresso—or a panini, for that matter—is **Palm Coast Coffee, Cafe, and Pub** (316 Mallory St., 912/634-7517, www.palmcoastssi.com, daily 8am-10pm). This handy little spot, combining a hip, relaxing coffeehouse with a hearty menu of brunchy items, is in the heart of the Village. The kicker, though, is the cute little bar the size of a large walk-in closet right off the side of the main room—a little bit of Key West on St. Simons.

Inside the Village Inn is the popular nightspot the **Village Pub** (500 Mallory St., 912/634-6056, www.villageinnandpub.com, Mon.-Sat. 5pm-midnight, Sun. 5pm-10pm). Slightly more upscale than most watering holes on the island, this is the best place for a quality martini or other premium cocktail.

SHOPS

Most shopping on St. Simons is concentrated in the Village and is a typical beach town mix of hardware and tackle, casual clothing, and souvenir stores. A funky highlight is **Beachview Books** (215 Mallory St., 912/638-7282, Mon.-Sat. 10:30am-5:30pm, Sun. 11:30am-3pm), a rambling used bookstore with lots of regional and local goodies, including books by the late great local author Eugenia Price. Probably the best antiques shop in this part of town is **Village Mews** (504 Beachview Dr., 912/634-1235, Mon.-Sat. 10am-5pm).

SPORTS AND ACTIVITIES

Beaches

Keep going from the pier past the lighthouse to find **Massengale Park** (daily dawn-dusk), with a playground, picnic tables, and restrooms right off the beach on the Atlantic side. The beach itself on St. Simons is underwhelming compared to some in these parts, but it's easily accessible from the pier area and good for a romantic stroll if it's not high tide. There's a great playground, Neptune Park, right next to the pier overlooking the waterfront.

Kayaking and Boating

With its relatively sheltered landward side nestled in the marsh and an abundance of wildlife, St. Simons Island is an outstanding kayaking site, attracting connoisseurs from all over. A good spot to put in on the Frederica River is the **Golden Isles Marina** (206 Marina Dr., 912/634-1128, www.gimarina.com), which is actually on little Lanier Island on the Torras Causeway right before you enter St. Simons proper. For a real adventure, put in at the ramp at the end of South Harrington Street off Frederica Road, which will take you out Village Creek on the seaward side of the island.

Undoubtedly the best kayaking outfitter and tour operator in this part of the Golden Isles is **SouthEast Adventure Outfitters** (313 Mallory St., 912/638-6732, www.southeastadventure.com, daily 10am-6pm), which also has a location in nearby Brunswick.

Biking

The best place to rent bikes is **Monkey Wrench Bicycles** (1700 Frederica Rd., 912/634-5551). You can rent another kind of pedal-power at **Wheel Fun Rentals** (532 Ocean Blvd., 912/634-0606), which deals in four-seat pedaled carts with steering wheels.

Golf and Tennis

A popular place for both sports is the **Sea Palms Golf and Tennis Resort** (5445

Frederica Rd., 800/841-6268, www.seapalms.com, greens fees $70-80) in the middle of the island, with three 9-hole public courses and three clay courts. The **Sea Island Golf Club** (100 Retreat Rd., 800/732-4752, www.seaisland.com, greens fees $185-260) on the old Retreat Plantation as you first come onto the island has two award-winning 18-hole courses, the Seaside and the Plantation. Another public course is the 18-hole **Hampton Club** (100 Tabbystone Rd., 912/634-0255, www.hamptonclub.com, greens fees $95) on the north side of the island, part of the King and Prince Beach and Golf Resort.

FOOD

While the ambience at St. Simons has an upscale feel, don't feel like you have to dress up to get a bite to eat—the emphasis is on relaxation and having a good time.

Breakfast and Brunch

★ **Palmer's Village Cafe** (223 Mallory St., 912/634-5515, www.palmersvillagecafe.com, Tues.-Sun. 7:30am-2pm, $10-15), formerly called Dressner's, is right in the middle of the Village's bustle. It's one of the island's most popular places but still has enough seats that you usually don't have to wait. Sandwiches and burgers are great, but breakfast all day is the real attraction and includes lovingly crafted omelets, hearty pancakes, and a "build your own biscuit" menu.

Seafood

A popular seafood place right in the action in the Village is **Barbara Jean's** (214 Mallory St., 912/634-6500, www.barbarajeans.com, Sun.-Thurs. 11am-9pm, Fri.-Sat. 11am-10pm, $7-20), which also has a variety of imaginative veggie dishes to go along with its formidable seafood menu, including some excellent she-crab soup and crab cakes. They also have plenty of good landlubber treats.

Fine Dining

★ **Nancy** (26 Market St., 912/634-0885, www.nancyssi.com, lunch Tues.-Sat. 11:30am-2pm, dinner Thurs.-Sat. 6pm-10pm, $30) is an interesting concept: An upscale fine-dining spot with an affiliated boutique women's clothing shop. Nancy Herdlinger and chef Abney Harper run this enterprise in a newer area a short drive outside the Village. It's one of the premier fine-dining spots on the Georgia coast south of Savannah. Any seafood dish is great, but I suggest the short ribs if they're on the tightly curated menu.

Inside the King and Prince Resort, you'll find the old-school glory of the **Blue Dolphin** (201 Arnold Rd., 800/342-0212, lunch daily 11am-4pm, dinner daily 5pm-10pm, $15-30), redolent of the *Great Gatsby* era. The Blue Dolphin claims to be the only oceanfront dining on the island, and the views are certainly magnificent.

ACCOMMODATIONS

Under $150

A charming and reasonable place a stone's throw from the Village is ★ **Queens Court** (437 Kings Way, 912/638-8459, $85-135), a traditional roadside motel from the late 1940s, with modern upgrades that include a nice outdoor pool in the central courtyard area. Despite its convenient location, you'll feel fairly secluded.

You couldn't ask for a better location than that of the **St. Simons' Inn by the Lighthouse** (609 Beachview Dr., 912/638-1101, www.saintsimonsinn.com, $120-300), which is indeed in the shadow of the historic lighthouse and right next to the hopping Village area. A so-called "condo-hotel," each of the standard and deluxe suites at the inn are individually owned by off-site owners—however, each guest gets full maid service and a complimentary breakfast.

$150-300

The best-known lodging on St. Simons Island is the ★ **King and Prince Beach and Golf Resort** (201 Arnold Rd., 800/342-0212, $249-320). Originally opened as a dance club in

1935, the King and Prince brings a swank old-school glamour similar to the Jekyll Island Club (though less imposing). And like the Jekyll Island Club, the King and Prince is also designated as one of the Historic Hotels of America. Its nearly 200 guest rooms are spread over a complex that includes several buildings, including the historic main building, beach villas, and freestanding guesthouses. Some standard rooms can go for under $200 even in the spring high season. Winter rates for all guest rooms are appreciably lower and represent a great bargain. For a dining spot overlooking the sea, try the **Blue Dolphin** (lunch daily 11am-4pm, dinner daily 5pm-10pm, $15-30). The resort's Hampton Club provides golf for guests and the public.

An interesting B&B on the island that's also within walking distance of most of the action on the south end is the 28-room **Village Inn & Pub** (500 Mallory St., 912/634-6056, www.villageinnandpub.com, $160-245), nestled among shady palm trees and live oaks. The pub, a popular local hangout in a renovated 1930 cottage, is a nice plus.

Over $300

Affiliated with the Sea Island Resort, the **Lodge at Sea Island** (100 Retreat Ave., 912/638-3611, $650-2,500) is actually on the south end of St. Simons Island on the old Retreat Plantation. Its 40 grand guest rooms and suites all have great views of the Atlantic Ocean, the associated Plantation Course links, or both. Full butler service makes this an especially pampered and aristocratic stay.

TRANSPORTATION AND SERVICES

Get to St. Simons through the gateway city of Brunswick. Take I-95 exit 38 for Golden Isles, which will take you to the Golden Isles Parkway. Take a right onto U.S. 17 and look for the intersection with the Torras Causeway, a toll-free road that takes you the short distance onto St. Simons.

The **St. Simons Visitors Center** (530-B Beachview Dr., 912/638-9014, www.bgivb.com, daily 9am-5pm) is in the St. Simons Casino Building near Neptune Park and the Village. The main newspaper in St. Simons is the ***Brunswick News*** (www.thebrunswicknews.com). The **U.S. Postal Service** (800/275-8777) has an office at 620 Beachview Drive.

LITTLE ST. SIMONS ISLAND

This 10,000-acre privately owned island, accessible only by water, is almost totally undeveloped—thanks to its salt-stressed trees, which discouraged timbering—and boasts seven miles of beautiful beaches. All activity centers on the circa-1917 ★ **Lodge on Little St. Simons Island** (1000 Hampton Point Dr., 888/733-5774, www.littlestsimonsisland.com, from $625), named one of the top five U.S. resorts by *Condé Nast Traveler* in 2016. Within it lies the famed Hunting Lodge, where meals and cocktails are served. With 15 ultra-plush guest rooms and suites in an assortment of historic buildings, all set amid gorgeous natural beauty—there are five full-time naturalists on staff—the Lodge is a reminder of what St. Simons proper used to look like. The guest count is limited to 30 people.

Transportation

Unless you enlist the aid of a local kayaking charter company, you have to be a guest of the Lodge to have access to Little St. Simons. The ferry, a 15-minute ride, leaves from a landing at the northern end of St. Simons at the end of Lawrence Road. Guests have full use of bicycles once on the island and can also request shuttle transportation just about anywhere.

SEA ISLAND

The only way to enjoy Sea Island—basically a tiny appendage of St. Simons facing the Atlantic Ocean—is to be a guest at ★ **The Sea Island Resort** (888/732-4752, www.seaisland.com, from $700). The legendary facility, which underwent extensive renovations in 2008, is routinely ranked as one of the best resorts in the United States. The rooms at the resort's premier lodging institution, **The Cloister,** nearly defy description—enveloped in old-world luxury, they also boast 21st-century technology.

Transportation

Get to Sea Island by taking Torras Causeway onto the island and then making a left onto Sea Island Causeway, which takes you all the way to the gate marking the only land entrance to the island.

Darien and McIntosh County

The small fishing and shrimping village of Darien in McIntosh County has an interesting and historic pedigree of its own. It is centrally located near some of the best treasures the Georgia coast has to offer, including the Harris Neck National Wildlife Refuge, the beautiful Altamaha River, and the sea island of Sapelo, and it also boasts what many believe to be the best traditional seafood restaurants in the state.

Unlike Anglophilic Savannah to the north, the Darien area has had a distinctly Scottish flavor from the beginning. In 1736, Scottish Highlanders established a settlement at the mouth of the Altamaha River at the bequest of General James Oglethorpe, who wanted the tough Scots protecting his southern border from the Spanish.

Darien's heyday was in that antebellum period, when for a brief time the town was the world's largest exporter of cotton, floated down the Altamaha on barges and shipped out through the town's port. The Bank of Darien was the largest bank south of Philadelphia in the early 1800s. Almost nothing from this period remains, however, because on June 11, 1863, a force of mostly African American Union troops burned Darien to the ground, with all its homes and warehouses going up in smoke (the incident was portrayed in the movie *Glory*).

In the pre-interstate highway days, U.S. 17 was the main route south to booming Florida. McIntosh County got a bad reputation for "clip joints," which would fleece gullible travelers with a variety of illegal schemes. This

the Darien shrimping fleet

period is recounted in the best seller *Praying for Sheetrock* by Melissa Fay Greene.

SIGHTS

Smallest Church in North America

While several other churches claim that title, fans of the devout and of roadside kitsch alike will enjoy the tiny and charming little **Memory Park Christ Chapel** (U.S. 17, daily 24 hours). The original 12-seat chapel was built in 1949 by local grocer Agnes Harper, when the church was intended as a round-the-clock travelers' sanctuary on what was then the main coastal road, U.S. 17. Upon her death, Harper simply willed the church to Jesus Christ. Sadly, in late 2015 an arsonist burned Mrs. Harper's church to the ground. A community effort, however, rebuilt it as closely as possible. Get there by taking I-95 exit 67 and going south a short way on U.S. 17; the church is on the east side of the road.

★ Harris Neck National Wildlife Refuge

Literally a stone's throw away from the "Smallest Church" is the turnoff onto the seven-mile Harris Neck Road leading east to the **Harris Neck National Wildlife Refuge** (912/832-4608, www.fws.gov/harrisneck, daily dawn-dusk, free). In addition to being one of the single best sites in the South from which to view wading birds and waterfowl in their natural habitat, Harris Neck also has something of a poignant backstory. For generations after the Civil War, an African American community descended from the area's original slaves quietly struggled to eke out a living here by fishing and farming.

The settlers' land was taken by the federal government during World War II to build a U.S. Army Air Force base. Now a nearly 3,000-acre nationally protected refuge, Harris Neck gets about 50,000 visitors a year to experience its mix of marsh, woods, and grassland ecosystems and for its nearly matchless bird-watching. Most visitors use the four-mile "wildlife drive" to travel through the refuge, stopping occasionally for hiking or bird-watching.

Kayaks and canoes can put in at the public boat ramp on the Barbour River. Near the landing is the **Gould Cemetery**, an old African American cemetery that is publicly accessible. Charming handmade tombstones evoke the post-Civil War era of Harris Neck before the displacement of local citizens to build the airfield.

old cemetery at Harris Neck National Wildlife Refuge

To get here, take I-95 exit 67 and go south on U.S. 17 about one mile, then east on Harris Neck Road (Hwy. 131) for seven miles to the entrance gate on the left.

Shellman Bluff

Just northeast of Darien is the old oystering community of **Shellman Bluff.** It's notable not only for the stunning views from the high bluff, but also for fresh seafood. Go to **Shellman's Fish Camp** (1058 River Rd., 912/832-4331, call ahead) to put in for a kayak or canoe ride. Save room for a meal; there are some great seafood places here.

Fort King George State Historic Site

The oldest English settlement in what would become Georgia, **Fort King George State Historic Site** (1600 Wayne St., 912/437-4770, www.gastateparks.org/fortkinggeorge, Tues.-Sun. 9am-5pm, $7.50 adults, $4.50 children) for a short time protected the Carolinas from attack, from its establishment in 1721 to its abandonment in 1727. Walking onto the site, with its restored 40-foot-tall cypress blockhouse fort, instantly reveals why this place was so important: It guards a key bend in the wide Altamaha River, vital to any attempt to establish transportation and trade in the area.

Tours

Altamaha Coastal Tours (229 Ft. King George Rd., 912/437-6010, www.altamaha.com) is your best bet for taking a guided kayak tour (from $50) or renting a kayak (from $20 per day) to explore the beautiful Altamaha River.

FOOD

McIntosh County is a powerhouse in the food department, and as you might expect, fresh and delicious seafood in a casual atmosphere is the order of the day here.

The Old School Diner (1080 Jesse Grant Rd. NE, Townsend, 912/832-2136, http://oldschooldiner.com, Wed.-Fri. 5:30pm-9:30pm, Sat.-Sun. noon-9:30pm, $15-30, cash only) is located in a whimsical semirural compound seven miles off U.S. 17, just off Harris Neck Road on the way to the wildlife refuge. The draw here is succulent fresh seafood in the coastal Georgia tradition. Old School's prices aren't so old school, but keep in mind that the portions are huge, rich, and filling.

Even farther off the main roads than the Old School Diner, the community of Shellman Bluff is well worth the drive. Find ★ **Hunters Café** (Shellman Bluff, 912/832-5771, lunch Mon.-Fri. 11am-2pm, dinner Mon.-Fri. 5pm-10pm, Sat.-Sun. 7am-10pm, $10-20) and get anything that floats your boat—it's all fresh and local. Wild Georgia shrimp are a particular specialty, as is the hearty cream-based crab stew. Take a right off Shellman Bluff Road onto Sutherland Bluff Drive, then a left onto New Shellman Road. Take a right onto the unpaved River Road and you can't miss it.

Another Shellman Bluff favorite is ★ **Speed's Kitchen** (Shellman Bluff, 912/832-4763, Thurs.-Sat. 5pm-close, Sun. noon-close, $10-20), where people move anything but fast, and the fried fish and crab-stuffed flounder are out of this world. Take a right off Shellman Bluff Road onto Sutherland Bluff Drive. Take a right onto Speed's Kitchen Road.

ACCOMMODATIONS

If you want to stay in McIntosh County, I strongly recommend booking one of the five charming guest rooms at ★ **Open Gates Bed and Breakfast** (301 Franklin St., Darien, 912/437-6985, www.opengatesbnb.com, $125-140). This lovingly restored and reasonably priced inn is on historic and relaxing Vernon Square in downtown Darien.

SAPELO ISLAND

One of those amazing, undeveloped Georgia barrier islands that can only be reached by boat, Sapelo also shares with some of those islands a link to the Gilded Age.

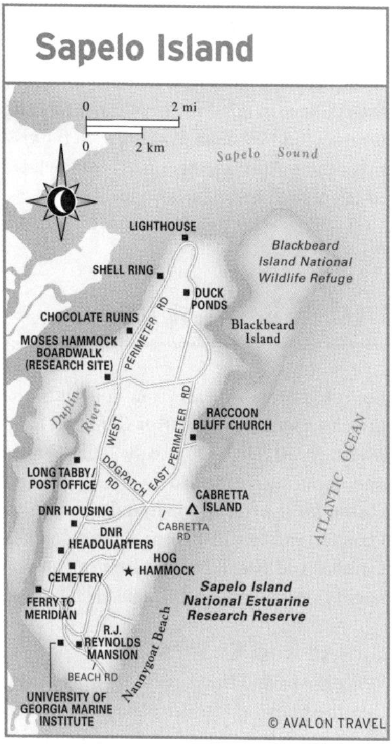

History

The Spanish established a Franciscan mission on the north end of the island in the 1500s. Sapelo didn't become fully integrated into the Lowcountry plantation culture until its purchase by Thomas Spalding in the early 1800s. After the Civil War, many of the nearly 500 former slaves on the island remained, with a partnership of freedmen buying land as early as 1871.

Hudson Motors mogul Howard Coffin bought all of Sapelo, except for the African American communities, in 1912, building a palatial home and introducing a modern infrastructure. Coffin hit hard times in the Great Depression and in 1934 sold Sapelo to tobacco heir R. J. Reynolds, who consolidated the island's African Americans into the single Hog Hammock community. By the mid-1970s the Reynolds family had sold the island to the state, again with the exception of the 430 acres of Hog Hammock, which at the time had slightly more than 100 residents. Today most of the island is administered for marine research purposes under the designation of **Sapelo Island National Estuarine Research Reserve** (www.sapelonerr.org).

Sights

Once on the island, you can take guided tours under the auspices of the Georgia Department of Natural Resources. Wednesday 8:30am-12:30pm is a tour of the island that includes the **R. J. Reynolds Mansion** (www.reynoldsonsapelo.com) on the south end as well as Hog Hammock and the Long Tabby ruins. Saturday 9am-1pm is a tour of the historic **Sapelo Lighthouse** on the north end along with the rest of the island. June-Labor Day there's an extra lighthouse and island tour Friday 8:30am-12:30pm. March-October on the last Tuesday of the month they do an extra-long day trip, 8:30am-3pm. Tours cost $10 adults, $6 children, free under age 6. Call 912/437-3224 for reservations. You can also arrange private tours.

Another key sight on Sapelo is a 4,500-year-old **Native American shell ring** on the north end, one of the oldest and best preserved anywhere. Beach lovers will especially enjoy the unspoiled strands on Sapelo, including the famous **Nannygoat Beach.**

Accommodations

While it's theoretically possible to stay overnight at the **R. J. Reynolds Mansion** (www.reynoldsonsapelo.com), it is limited to groups of at least 16 people. Realistically, to stay overnight on Sapelo you need a reservation with one of the locally owned guesthouses. One recommendation is Cornelia Bailey's six-room **The Wallow** (912/485-2206, call for rates) in historic Hog Hammock. The Baileys also run a small campground, **Comyam's Campground** (912/485-2206, $10 pp). Another option is **The Weekender** (912/485-2277, call for rates).

Transportation and Services

Visitors to Sapelo must embark on the ferry at the **Sapelo Island Visitors Center** (912/437-3224, www.sapelonerr.org, Tues.-Fri. 7:30am-5:30pm, Sat. 8am-5:30pm, Sun. 1:30pm-5pm, $10 adults, $6 ages 6-18) in little Meridian, Georgia, on Highway 99 north of Darien. The visitors center actually has a nice nature hike of its own as well as an auditorium where you can see an informative video. From here it's a half-hour trip to Sapelo over the Doboy Sound. Keep in mind you must call in advance for reservations before showing up at the visitors center. April-October it's recommended to call at least a week in advance.

Cumberland Island and St. Marys

Actually two islands—Great Cumberland and Little Cumberland—Cumberland Island National Seashore is the largest and one of the oldest of Georgia's barrier islands, and also one of its most remote and least developed. Currently administered by the National Park Service, it's accessible only by ferry or private boat. Most visitors to Cumberland get here from the gateway town of St. Marys, Georgia, a nifty little fishing village.

ST. MARYS

Much like Brunswick to the north, the fishing town of St. Marys plays mostly a gateway role, in this case to the Cumberland Island National Seashore. During the colonial period, St. Marys was the southernmost U.S. city. In 1812 a British force took over Cumberland Island and St. Marys, with a contingent embarking up the St. Marys River to track down the customs collector.

Unlike towns such as Darien, which was put to the torch by Union troops, St. Marys was saved from destruction in the Civil War. A hotel was built in 1916 (and hosted Marjorie Kinnan Rawlings, author of *The Yearling*), but tourists didn't discover the area until the 1970s. It was also then that the U.S. Navy built the huge nuclear submarine base at Kings Bay, currently the area's largest employer with almost 10,000 workers.

Orientation

Most activity in downtown St. Marys happens up and down Osborne Street, which perhaps not coincidentally is also how you get to the **Cumberland Island Visitor Center** (113 St. Marys St., 912/882-4335, daily 8am-4:30pm) and from there board the *Cumberland Queen* for the trip to the island. (Note: The Cumberland Island Visitor Center and the Cumberland Island Museum are in two different places, about a block apart.)

Sights and Events

Tying the past to the present, it's only fitting that the home of the Kings Bay Submarine Base (which is not open to the public) has a museum dedicated to the "Silent Service." The **St. Marys Submarine Museum** (102 St. Marys St., 912/882-2782, www.stmaryswelcome.com, Tues.-Sat. 10am-4pm, Sun. 1pm-5pm, $5 adults, $3 children) on the riverfront has a variety of exhibits honoring the contribution of American submariners, including a bunch of cool models. There's a neat interactive exhibit where you can look through the genuine sub periscope that sticks out of the roof of the museum.

A block down Osborne Street from the waterfront—and *not* at the actual Cumberland Island Visitor Center or the actual ferry dock—is the handsome little **Cumberland Island National Seashore Museum** (129 Osborne St., 912/882-4336, www.stmaryswelcome.com, Wed.-Sun. 1pm-4pm, free). It has several very informative exhibits on the natural and human history of Cumberland, as well as a room devoted to the short but fascinating role the island played in the War of 1812.

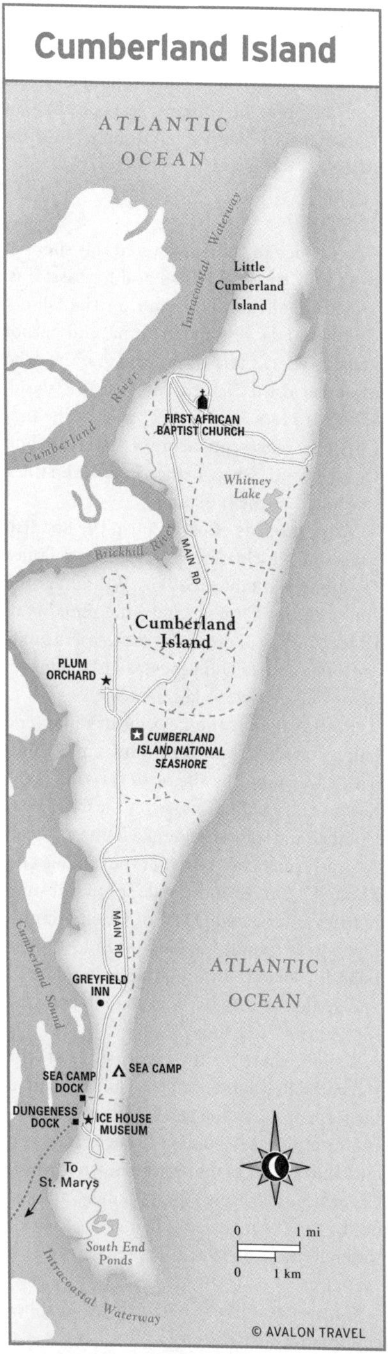

The most notable historic home in St. Marys is the **Orange Hall House Museum** (311 Osborne St., 912/576-3644, www.orangehall.org, Tues.-Sat. 9am-4pm, Sun. 1pm-4pm, $3 adults, $1 children). This beautiful Greek Revival home, circa 1830, survived the Civil War and was the center of town social life during the Roaring '20s.

Food

St. Marys cannot compete in culinary sophistication with Charleston or Savannah, but it does have some of the freshest seafood around. One of the best places to eat seafood on the waterfront in St. Marys is at **Lang's Marina Restaurant** (307 W. St. Marys St., 912/882-4432, lunch Tues.-Fri. 11am-2pm, dinner Wed.-Sat. 5pm-9pm, $15-20). Another pair of good waterfront spots, right next to each other, are **The Shark Bite** (104 W. St. Marys St., 912/576-6993, Tues.-Sat. 11am-9pm, $12-20), which has great burgers and live music, and **Riverside Café** (106 W. St. Marys St., 912/882-3466, Tues.-Sat. 11am-9pm, $15-20), which specializes in Greek favorites.

Accommodations

The most notable lodging for historical as well as economic value is the 18-room **Riverview Hotel** (105 Osborne St., 912/882-3242, www.riverviewhotelstmarys.com, under $100). It was built in the 1920s and has hosted such notables as author Marjorie Rawlings, John Rockefeller, poet Sidney Lanier, and Andrew Carnegie. ★ **Emma's Bed and Breakfast** (300 W. Conyers St., 912/882-4199, www.emmasbedandbreakfast.com, under $200) is situated on four beautiful acres in downtown St. Marys in a grand Southern-style mansion with all the trappings and hospitality you'd expect.

More outdoorsy visitors can stay at cottage, tent, or RV sites at **Crooked River State Park** (6222 Charlie Smith Sr. Hwy., 912/882-5256, www.gastateparks.org). There are 62 tent and RV sites (about $22) and 11 cottages ($85-110) as well as primitive camping ($25).

Transportation and Services

Take I-95 exit 3 for Kingsland-St. Marys Road (Hwy. 40). This becomes Osborne Road, the main drag of St. Marys, as it gets closer to town. The road by the waterfront is St. Marys Street.

The **St. Marys Convention and Visitors Bureau** (406 Osborne St., 912/882-4000, www.stmaryswelcome.com) is a good source of information not only for the town but for Cumberland Island, but keep in mind that this is not actually where you catch the ferry to the island.

★ CUMBERLAND ISLAND NATIONAL SEASHORE

Not only one of the richest estuarine and maritime forest environments in the world, **Cumberland Island National Seashore** (912/882-4335, reservations 877/860-6787, www.nps.gov/cuis) is one of the most beautiful places on the planet, as everyone learned when the "it" couple of their day, John F. Kennedy Jr. and Carolyn Bessette, were wed on the island in 1996. With more than 16 miles of gorgeous beach and an area of over 17,000 acres, there's no shortage of scenery.

Cumberland is far from pristine: It has been used for timbering and cotton, is dotted with evocative abandoned ruins, and hosts a band of beautiful but voracious wild horses. But it is still a remarkable island paradise in a world where those kinds of locations are getting harder and harder to find.

There are two ways to enjoy Cumberland: day trip or overnight stay. An early arrival and departure on the late ferry, combined with bike rental and a tour, still leaves plenty of time for day-trippers to relax. Camping overnight on Cumberland is quite enjoyable, but it's a bit rustic and probably isn't for novices.

Important note: Distances on the map can be deceiving. Cumberland is very narrow but also very long—about 18 miles tip to tip. You can walk the width of the island in minutes, but you will not be able to hike its length even in a day.

You can have a perfectly enjoyable time on Cumberland just hanging out on the more populated south end, but those who want to explore the island fully should consider renting a bike or booking seats on the new National Park Service van tour around the island.

History

The Timucuan Indians revered this site, visiting it often for shellfish and for sassafras, a medicinal herb common on the island. Cumberland's size and great natural harbor made it a perfect base for Spanish friars, who established the first mission on the island, San Pedro Mocama, in 1587. In fact, the first Christian martyr in Georgia was created on Cumberland, when Father Pedro Martinez was killed by the Indians.

As part of his effort to push the Spanish back into Florida for good, General James Oglethorpe established Fort William at the south end of Cumberland—the remains of which are now underwater—as well as a hunting lodge named Dungeness, an island placename that persists today.

But inevitably, the Lowcountry planters' culture made its way down to Cumberland, which was soon the site of 15 thriving plantations and small farms. After the Civil War, Cumberland was set aside as a home for freed African Americans—part of the famous and ill-fated "40 acres and a mule" proposal—but politics intervened: Most of Cumberland's slaves were rounded up and taken to Amelia Island, Florida, although some remained and settled at Cumberland's north end (the "Settlement" area today).

As elsewhere on the Georgia coast, the Industrial Revolution came to Cumberland in the form of a vacation getaway for a mega-tycoon, in this case Thomas Carnegie, industrialist and brother of the better-known Andrew Carnegie of Carnegie Library fame. Carnegie built a new, even grander Dungeness, which suffered the same fate as its predecessor in a 1959 fire.

Cumberland Island narrowly avoided becoming the next Hilton Head—literally—in

Wild Horses of Cumberland

the wild horses of Cumberland Island

Contrary to popular opinion, Cumberland Island's famous wild horses are not direct descendants of the first horses brought to the island by Spanish and English settlers, although feral horses have certainly ranged the island for most of recorded history. The current population of about 140 or so is actually descended from horses brought to the island by the Carnegie family in the 1920s. Responding to overwhelming public opinion, the National Park Service leaves the herd virtually untended and unsupervised. The horses eat, live, fight, grow up, give birth, and pass away largely without human influence, other than euthanizing animals who are clearly suffering and have no hope of recovery.

You're not guaranteed to see wild horses on Cumberland, but the odds are heavily in your favor. They often congregate to graze around the Dungeness ruins, and indeed any open space. Over the years they've made trails through the forest and sand dunes, and can often be seen cavorting on the windy beach in the late afternoon and early evening.

Each stallion usually acquires a "harem" of dependent mares, and occasionally you might even witness spirited competition between stallions for mares and/or territory.

Gorgeous and evocative though these magnificent animals are, they have a big appetite for vegetation and frankly are not the best thing for this sensitive barrier island ecosystem. But their beauty and visceral impact on the visitor is undeniable, which means the horses are likely to stay as long as nature will have them.

And yes, these really are *wild* horses, meaning you should never try to feed or pet them, and you certainly won't be riding them.

1969 when Hilton Head developer Charles Fraser bought the northern tip of the island and began bulldozing a runway. The dwindling but still influential Carnegies joined with the Georgia Conservancy to broker an agreement that resulted in dubbing Cumberland a National Seashore in 1972, saving it from further development. A $7.5 million gift from the Mellon Foundation enabled the purchase of Fraser's tract and the eventual incorporation of the island within the National Park Service.

To learn more about Cumberland's fascinating history, visit the **Cumberland Island National Seashore Museum** (129 Osborne St., 912/882-4336, www.stmaryswelcome.com,

Plum Orchard can be toured on the second and fourth Sunday of the month.

Wed.-Sun. 1pm-4pm, free) while you're in St. Marys, a block away from the actual ferry docks.

Sights

The ferry typically stops at two docks a short distance from each other, the Sea Camp dock and the Dungeness dock. At 4pm, rangers offer a "dockside" interpretive program at the Sea Camp. A short way farther north at the Dungeness Dock, rangers lead a highly recommended "Dungeness Footsteps Tour" at 10am and 12:45pm, concentrating on the historic sites at the southern end of the island. Also at the Dungeness dock is the little **Ice House Museum** (912/882-4336, daily 9am-5pm, free), containing a range of exhibits on the island's history from Native American times to the present day.

Down near the docks are also where you'll find the stirring, almost spooky **Dungeness Ruins** and the nearby grave marker of Light-Horse Harry Lee. (You're very likely to see some wild horses around this area too.) The cause of the 1866 fire that destroyed the old Dungeness home is still unknown. Another even grander home was built on the same site during the Victorian era, but also fell victim to fire in the 1950s. It's these Victorian ruins you see today.

A very nice addition to the National Park Service offerings is a daily "Lands and Legacies" van tour (reservations 877/860-6787, $15 adults, $12 seniors and children) that takes you all around the island, eliminating the need for lengthy hikes. It's ideal for day-trippers—if a bit long at six hours—but anyone can take the ride. It leaves from the Sea Camp Ranger Station soon after the first morning ferry arrives. Reservations are strongly recommended.

Moving north on the Main Road (Grand Ave.)—a dirt path and the only route for motor vehicles—you come to the **Greyfield Inn** (904/261-6408, www.greyfieldinn.com). Because it is a privately owned hotel, don't trespass through the grounds. A good way farther north, just off the main road, you'll find the restored, rambling 20-room mansion **Plum Orchard,** another Carnegie legacy. Guided tours of Plum Orchard are available on the second and fourth Sunday of the month ($6 plus ferry fare); reserve a space at 912/882-4335.

At the very north end of the island, accessible only by foot or by bicycle, is the former freedmen's community simply known as **The Settlement,** featuring a small cemetery and the now-famous **First African Baptist Church** (daily dawn-dusk)—a 1937 version of the 1893 original—a humble and rustic one-room church made of whitewashed logs and in which the 1996 Kennedy-Bessette wedding took place.

Sports and Activities

There are more than 50 miles of hiking trails all over Cumberland, about 15 miles of nearly isolated beach to comb, and acres of maritime forest to explore—the latter an artifact of Cumberland's unusually old age for a barrier island. Upon arrival, you might want to rent a bicycle at the **Sea Camp dock** (no reservations, arrange rentals on the ferry, adult bikes $16 per day, youth bikes $10, $20 overnight). The only catch with the bikes is that you shouldn't plan on taking them to the up-country campsites.

Shell-and-sharks-teeth collectors might want to explore south of Dungeness Beach as well as between the docks. Unlike some parks, you are allowed to take shells and fossils off the island.

Wildlife enthusiasts will be in heaven. More than 300 species of birds have been recorded on the island, which is also a favorite nesting ground for female loggerhead turtles in the late summer. Of course, the most iconic image of Cumberland Island is its famous **wild horses,** a free-roaming band of feral equines who traverse the island year-round, grazing as they please.

Cumberland Island is home to some creepy-crawlies, including mosquitoes, gnats, and, yes, ticks, the latter of which are especially prevalent throughout the maritime forest as you work your way north. Bring high-strength insect repellent with you, or buy some at the camp store. Rangers recommend you do a frequent "tick check" on yourself and your companions.

Accommodations

The only "civilized" lodging on Cumberland is the 13-room ★ **Greyfield Inn** (Grand Ave., 904/261-6408, www.greyfieldinn.com, $475), ranked by the American Inn Association as one of the country's "Ten Most Romantic Inns." Opened in 1962 as a hotel, the Greyfield was built in 1900 as the home of the Carnegies. The room rates include meals, transportation, tours, and bicycle usage.

Many visitors opt to camp on Cumberland (reservations 877/860-6787, limit of seven nights, $4) in one of three basic ways: at the **Sea Camp,** which has restrooms and shower facilities and allows fires; the remote but pleasant **Stafford Beach,** a vigorous three-mile hike from the docks and with a basic restroom and shower; and pure wilderness camping farther north at **Hickory Hill, Yankee Paradise,** and **Brickman Bluff,** all of which are a several-mile hike away, do not permit fires, and have no facilities of any kind. Reservations are required for camping. All trash must be packed out on departure, as there are no refuse facilities on the island. Responsible alcohol consumption is limited to those 21 and over.

Insect life is abundant. Bring heavy-duty repellent or purchase some at the camp store.

Transportation and Services

The most vital information about Cumberland is how to get ashore in the first place. Most visitors do this by purchasing a ticket on the *Cumberland Queen* at the **Cumberland Island Visitor Center** (113 St. Marys St., St. Marys, 877/860-6787, daily 8am-4:30pm, $20 adults, $18 seniors, $12 under age 13) on the waterfront in St. Marys. I strongly suggest calling or faxing ahead. Be aware that there are often very long hold times by phone.

The ferry ride is 45 minutes each way. You can call for reservations Monday-Friday 10am-4pm. The ferry does not transport pets, bicycles, kayaks, or cars. However, you can rent bicycles at the Sea Camp dock once you're there. Every visitor to Cumberland over age 16 must pay a $4 entry fee, including campers.

March 1-November 30, the ferry leaves St. Marys daily at 9am and 11:45am, returning from Cumberland at 10:15am and 4:45pm. March 1-September 30 Wednesday-Saturday, there's an additional 2:45pm departure from Cumberland back to St. Marys. December 1-February 28 the ferry operates only Thursday-Monday. Make sure you arrive and check in at least 30 minutes before your ferry leaves.

One of the quirks of Cumberland, resulting from the unusual way in which it passed into federal hands, is the existence of some private property on which you mustn't trespass, except where trails specifically allow it. Also, unlike the general public, these private landowners are allowed to use vehicles. For these reasons, it's best to make sure you have a map of the island, which you can get before you board the ferry at St. Marys or at the ranger station at the Sea Camp dock.

There are no real stores and very few facilities on Cumberland. *Bring whatever you think you'll need,* whether it be food, water, medicine, suntan lotion, insect repellent, toilet paper, or otherwise.

Background

REV. MARTIN LUTHER KING, JR.
1929 ~ 1968
"Free at last, Free at last,
Thank God Almighty
I'm Free at last."
CORETTA SCOTT KING
1927 ~ 2006
"And now abide Faith, Hope,
Love, These Three; but the
greatest of these is Love."
1 Cor. 13:13

The Landscape

From its highest point at Brasstown Bald overlooking the Tennessee border, to the sandy barrier islands of the coast, Georgia's geography and geology work together. Though it's hundreds of miles away, the Blue Ridge mountains of North Georgia have a major influence on the coast, and it's there that your overview of Georgia's natural landscape should begin.

GEOGRAPHY AND GEOLOGY

Regions

The **Blue Ridge,** southernmost part of the Appalachian Mountains and named for its distinctive haze, pushes 100 miles into the central and northeast section of North Georgia. Formed from a collision about 300 million years ago between the North American and African continents, the Appalachians were originally at least as tall as the Himalayas are today. But erosion has taken its toll, and they are mere shadows of their former selves. The erosion has had the side effect of making the mountains' rich bounty of gold, copper, marble, and other minerals particularly accessible, the extraction of which has molded the economic and cultural character of all of North Georgia. The mountainous topography has also contributed to a more benign economic sector, with hikers, rafters, and other outdoor adventurers coming to see the hundreds of waterfalls all through the Blue Ridge region and its foothills.

Along the border with the Carolinas, the Blue Ridge crest in places is part of the **Eastern Continental Divide.** The Blue Ridge doesn't extend into the northwest portion of Georgia however, which is often called the **"Ridge and Valley"** country. There you will find smaller ranges like the Cohuttas, and the Cumberland Plateau. They are separated from the Blue Ridge by several geologic formations and faults, along the general route marked by Highway 5. The Blue Ridge's southern boundary and the beginning of the Piedmont region are generally considered to be along the Brevard Fault.

Georgia's most populous geological region, the **Piedmont** is a rocky, hilly area. This is where you will find stone outcroppings, such as the great granite features of Stone Mountain and Arabia Mountain, both outside Atlanta. The Piedmont is bordered on the east by the **fall line,** an ancient Mesozoic shoreline about 20 miles wide, so named because it's there where rivers make a drop toward the sea, generally becoming navigable. Georgia's key cities on the fall line are, from east to west, Augusta on the Savannah River, Milledgeville on the Oconee River, Macon on the Ocmulgee River, and Columbus on the Chattahoochee River.

The **Upper Coastal Plain** begins adjacent to the fall line zone. There you can sometimes spot sand hills, usually only a few feet in elevation, generally thought to be the vestigial remains of primordial sand dunes and offshore sandbars. The Ohoopee Natural Dunes area near Swainsboro is the most notable example. Well beyond the fall line is the **Lower Coastal Plain,** gradually built up over 150 million years by sedimentary runoff from the Appalachian Mountains. The entire Coastal Plain was sea bottom for much of the earth's history, and in some eroded areas you can see dramatic proof of this in prehistoric shells, sharks' teeth, and fossilized whalebones and oyster beds, often many miles inland.

Sea level has fluctuated wildly with climate and geological changes through the eons. At

Previous: beach swing on Tybee Island; the tomb of Martin Luther King Jr. and his wife Coretta Scott King in Atlanta.

various times over the last 50 million years, the Coastal Plain has submerged, surfaced, and submerged again. Its particular soil types nurtured the enormous primordial Longleaf Pine forests of pre-European contact. A fire-activated habitat, the longleaf forests were perpetuated by the Native American habit of setting huge controlled burns.

Rivers

We know that it's in Appalachia where so much of the coast's freshwater (in the form of rain) comes together and flows southeast, in the form of alluvial, or sediment-bearing, rivers, to the Atlantic Ocean. But the specific origins of many of Georgia's mighty rivers are not always so obvious.

The headwaters of the great Savannah River, for example, are near deep Tallulah Gorge in extreme North Georgia. The Flint River, one of the South's most scenic, essentially begins as runoff drainage near Atlanta (the creek that eventually becomes the Flint actually runs through a culvert under a runway at the Atlanta airport). Some rivers form out of the confluence of smaller rivers, such as Georgia's mighty Altamaha, actually the child of the Ocmulgee and Oconee Rivers in the middle of the state.

While most Georgia rivers begin as mere trickles down from the Blue Ridge, visitors from drier climates are sometimes shocked to see how huge the rivers can get farther towards the coast of Georgia, how wide and voluminous as they saunter to the sea, their seemingly slow speed belying the massive power they contain. To be sure, damming and dredging have enlarged the sheer quantity of water in many of them.

The **blackwater river** is a particularly interesting Southern phenomenon, duplicated elsewhere only in South America and one example each in New York and Michigan. While alluvial rivers generally originate in highlands and carry with them a large amount of sediment, blackwater rivers originate in low-lying areas and move slowly toward the sea, carrying with them very little sediment.

Rather, their dark tea color comes from the tannic acid of decaying vegetation all along their banks, washed out by the slow, inexorable movement of the river toward the sea. While I don't necessarily recommend drinking it, "blackwater" is for the most part remarkably clean and hygienic despite its dirty color.

Blackwater courses featured prominently in this guide are Ebenezer Creek near Savannah and the Suwannee River, which originates in the Okefenokee Swamp and empties in the Gulf of Mexico. Georgia's Altamaha River is a hybrid of sorts because it is partially fed by the blackwater Ohoopee River.

With very few exceptions, Georgia's rivers have been heavily dammed, mostly for hydroelectric power. The Altamaha is the only major undammed river. The Flint River, while heavily impounded downstream, has a nearly 200-mile-long stretch of undammed course.

Where there are dams there are lakes, and Georgia has plenty of artificially-constructed reservoirs, most converted into recreational and fishing areas. During the big push for hydropower in the early 20th century, no beautiful natural feature was immune; even portions of scenic Tallulah Gorge were submerged in the craze to electrify metro areas, primarily Atlanta. Chief examples of manufactured, heavily-trafficked lakes today include Lake Lanier, Lake Seminole, Lake Burton, Lake Chatuge, Lake Rabun, Lake Sinclair, Lake Oconee, and the multiple Savannah River lakes: Hartwell, Russell, and Clark's Hill (Strom Thurmond).

FLINT RIVER FACTS

It's not the biggest or the most undeveloped river in Georgia, but the Flint takes its place among the most scenic and naturally vital in the state. It begins humbly, as ground seepage in a culvert south of Atlanta, its headwaters trickling under a runway at Hartsfield-Jackson International Airport.

Over the course of the next 220 miles, the Flint River runs free and undammed, a remarkable resource for wildlife and recreation alike. The large wetlands the Flint helps feed are the farthest inland swamps in the United States.

Though the Flint is eventually impounded near Albany and several points south, this long unfettered run is prized as prime habitat for shoal bass, the Halloween darter, freshwater mussels, crayfish, and the endangered shoals spider lily, first discovered by William Bartram in the 1770s.

Many of these species, some found only in this area, faced imminent threat in 1974, when a hydroelectric dam was proposed in the Sprewell Bluff area on the east side of Pine Mountain, one of the richest habitats on the Flint River. Then-Governor Jimmy Carter vetoed the project, a courageous move that helped establish the modern conservation movement. Sprewell Bluff Wildlife Management Area today is a popular spot for anglers, rafters, hunters, birders, and hikers.

Estuaries

The place where a river interfaces with the ocean is called an estuary, and it's perhaps the most interesting place of all. Estuaries are heavily tidal in nature (indeed, the word derives from *aestus,* Latin for tide) and feature brackish water and heavy silt content. The Georgia portion of the U.S. coast typically has about a 6-8-foot tidal range, and the coastal ecosystem depends on this steady ebb and flow for life itself. At high tide, shellfish open and feed. At low tide, they literally clam up, keeping saltwater inside their shells until the next tide comes. Waterbirds and small mammals feed on shellfish and other animals at low tide, when their prey is exposed. High tide brings an influx of fish and nutrients from the sea, in turn drawing predators like dolphins, who often come into tidal creeks to feed.

Salt Marsh

All this water action in both directions—freshwater coming from inland, saltwater encroaching from the Atlantic—results in the phenomenon of the salt marsh, the single most recognizable feature of the Georgia coast. (Freshwater marshes are more rare, Florida's Everglades being perhaps the premier example.)

Far more than just a transitional zone between land and water, marsh is also nature's nursery. Plant and animal life in marshes tends to be not only diverse, but encompassing multitudes. Though you may not see its denizens easily, on close inspection you'll find the marsh absolutely teeming with creatures. Visually, the main identifying feature of a salt marsh is its distinctive, reed-like marsh grasses, adapted to survive in brackish water. Like estuaries, marshes and all life in them are heavily influenced by the tides, which bring in nutrients.

Beaches and Barrier Islands

The often stunningly beautiful, broad beaches of Georgia are almost all situated on barrier islands, long islands parallel to the shoreline and separated from the mainland by a sheltered body of water. Because they are formed by the deposit of sediment by offshore currents, they change shape over the years, with the general pattern of deposit going from north to south (that is, the northern end will begin eroding first).

Most of the barrier islands are geologically quite young, only being formed within the last 25,000 years or so. Natural erosion, by current and by storm, combined with the accelerating effects of dredging for local port activity has quickened the decline of many barrier islands. As the name indicates, barrier islands are another of nature's safeguards against hurricane damage. Though ephemeral by nature, barrier islands have played an important role in the area's settlement. In fact, nearly every major settlement on the Georgia coast today, including Savannah, Darien, and Brunswick, is built on the vestiges of massive barrier islands that once guarded a primordial shoreline many miles inland from the present one.

By far the largest of these ancient barrier islands, now on dry land, is the Trail Ridge, which runs from Jesup, Georgia, alongside the Okefenokee Swamp down to Starke, Florida. The Trail Ridge's height along its distance made it a favorite route first for Native Americans and then for railroads, which still run along its crest today. The Trail Ridge is actually responsible for the formation of the Okefenokee Swamp. The Ridge effectively acts as a levee on the swamp's eastern side, preventing its drainage to the sea.

CLIMATE

One word comes to mind when one thinks about Southern climate: hot. That's the first word that occurs to Southerners as well, but virtually every survey of why residents are attracted to the area puts the climate at the top of the list. Go figure.

How hot is hot? The average July high in Savannah is about 92°F. In Dalton on the other end of the state near the mountains, it's only a couple of degrees less during the same month. The wettest months do vary. Inland, the wettest months are often January and July. But on the coast, August and September are the wettest months. Despite what you might think, the coast doesn't get the highest precipitation in the state; the Blue Ridge sees significantly higher rainfall on average and is indeed one of the rainiest areas in the U.S.; something to keep in mind when camping.

In North Georgia things can get pretty frigid during the winter, as you might expect. The average January low in Hiawassee in the Blue Ridge is about 28°F. Most North Georgia towns will see maybe a week's worth of snow in a normal year; elsewhere in the state snow is largely absent, and on the coast almost entirely unheard of. Winters on the coast are quite mild, but can seem much colder than they actually are because of the dampness in the air. The average January low in Savannah is a balmy 39°F.

Hurricanes

The major weather phenomenon for residents and visitors alike is the mighty hurricane. These massive storms, with counterclockwise-rotating bands of clouds and winds pushing 200 miles per hour, are an ever-present danger to the coast in June-November of each year.

Historically the Georgia coast has been relatively safe, if not immune, from major hurricane activity. In fact, as of this writing the last really major storm to directly hit the Georgia coast was in 1898. Meteorologists chalk this up to the Georgia coast's relatively sheltered, concave position relative to the rest of the Southeastern coastline, as well as prevailing pressure and wind patterns that tend to deflect the oncoming storms.

Local TV, websites, and print media can be counted on to give more than ample warning in the event a hurricane is approaching the area during your visit. Whatever you do, do not discount the warnings. It's not worth it. If the locals are preparing to leave, you should too.

ENVIRONMENTAL ISSUES

The Piedmont area of Georgia, primarily around the Atlanta area, continues to experience rampant development, both in the form of residential areas as well as the highway system that serves them. As Atlanta spreads outward, it pushes more and more environmental issues on the surrounding area, particularly air pollution caused by auto traffic and stress on drinking water resources.

The coast of Georgia is experiencing a double whammy: Not only is it also under enormous development pressure, its distinctive wetlands are extraordinarily sensitive to human interference. New and often-poorly planned subdivisions and resort communities continue to pop up, though the recent economic downturn slowed that trend somewhat. Vastly increased port activity, particularly in Savannah, is taking a devastating toll on the salt marsh and surrounding barrier islands.

Logging

Logging and the timber industry have had an enormous effect on Georgia from top to bottom. The sturdy live oaks of the Sea Islands served to defend a young country, forming the basis for the hulls of mighty warships for the fledgling American Navy, such as the U.S.S. *Constitution*. By the middle of the 19th century, Georgia was the country's leading lumber producer and the leading manufacturer of naval stores such as turpentine and rosin. Naval stores were mostly derived from the vast and ancient longleaf pine forests of the Upper Coastal Plain, a species virtually logged to extinction as a result.

By 1890, Georgia sawmills were cutting more than 1.6 million board feet per day. The "pristine" Okefenokee Swamp was by no means immune; most of its old-growth cypresses were logged extensively during that period.

The mountains of North Georgia weren't immune either, and huge environmental damage was caused there as a direct result of logging. The copper industry caused extensive clear-cutting, the timber being needed for the smelters. Gold mining caused entire mountainsides to be hosed or detonated away. Shipment methods for felled timber involved makeshift dams, which were then blown up to intentionally cause the cut trees to flood downstream so they could go to market.

The cumulative effect of this devastation and overharvesting caused the number of lumber mills in North Georgia to decline dramatically in the early 20th century, accompanied by a decline in population. Indeed, this calamity directly brought about the national forest movement in the United States.

One of the first acquisitions was a 30,000-acre tract bought by the federal government in 1911, which would form the basis for the later, and much more enormous, Chattahoochee National Forest, now comprising over 700,000 acres, including 30,000-acre Cohutta Wilderness Area, largest in the eastern United States. To be sure, the National Forests also serve the logging industry as well, and their tracts are culled extensively to this day.

A new way forward came in the 1930s when Charles Herty, a chemist at the University of Georgia, and incidentally their first football coach, came up with a process to make white paper out of young pines. Thus began the great conversion of much old agricultural land to truly vast pine farms, which you're almost certain to see driving anywhere around Georgia's Coastal Plain. Those sulfurous paper mills you often see, and mostly smell, are where those pines eventually end up.

Mining

You don't often hear about it, but Georgia is actually one of the most heavily mined states in the country, and has been for much of its history. The most obvious example is the great gold rush of the 1830s and 1840s, the first in the country. Centered on the large and easily accessed vein of high-quality gold in the Dahlonega area, the gold rush not only brought an enormous financial boon to the state, it encouraged speedy settlement in the form of "Land Lotteries." Sadly, in order to make room for the settlers and eliminate competing claims to the gold, it was decided that North Georgia's original inhabitants, the Cherokee Indians, would have to go. Thus began the tragic Trail of Tears, in which the Cherokee were removed at gunpoint to march in desolation to new homes in the Oklahoma Territory far away.

The gold mining brought environmental destruction, especially after the more easily obtained nuggets were panned from creeks and streams. Eventually huge hoses were used to literally wash away entire mountainsides, the ore then crushed and sifted for gold. Then came the dynamite and even more destruction.

Iron ore was the preferred mining industry in the northwest portion of the state in the Ridge and Valley country, but the techniques were similarly invasive. Stone is also extensively quarried throughout Georgia, including "Elberton granite" in the northeast portion of the state and marble from Pickens County in North Georgia.

However, the leading mineral export of Georgia is kaolin, or clay, harvested in huge quantities from cities in the Upper Coastal Plain, chiefly around Sandersville.

Air Pollution

Despite growing awareness of the issue, air pollution is still a big problem in Georgia. Automobile traffic around metro Atlanta contributes to poor air quality and appreciable amounts of smog. Paper mills on the coast still operate, putting out their distinctive rotten-eggs odor, and auto emissions standards are notoriously lax in Georgia. The biggest culprits, though, are coal-powered electric plants, which are the norm throughout the region and which continue to pour large amounts of toxins into the atmosphere.

Plants and Animals

PLANTS

The most iconic plant life of the region is the **Southern live oak,** the official state tree of Georgia. Named because of its evergreen nature, a live oak is technically any one of a number of evergreens in the *Quercus* genus, many of which reside on the Georgia coast; but in local practice, it almost always refers to the Southern live oak. Capable of living over 1,000 years and possessing wood of legendary resilience, the Southern live oak is one of nature's most magnificent creations.

Fittingly, the iconic plant of the coast grows on the branches of the live oak. Contrary to popular opinion, **Spanish moss** is neither Spanish nor moss. It's an air plant, a wholly indigenous cousin to the pineapple. Also contrary to folklore, Spanish moss is not a parasite nor does it harbor parasites while living on an oak tree, though it can after it has already fallen to the ground. Also growing on the bark of a live oak, especially right after a rain shower, is the **resurrection fern,** which can stay dormant for amazingly long periods of time, only to spring back to life with the introduction of a little water.

Other types of oaks are common throughout Georgia, including white, scarlet, and red oaks. The live oak may be Georgia's state tree, but far and away its most important commercial tree is the pine, used for paper, lumber, and turpentine. Rarely seen in the wild today due to tree farming, which has covered most of southern Georgia, the dominant species is now the **slash pine,** often seen in long rows on either side of rural highways. Before the introduction of large-scale monoculture tree farming, however, a rich variety of native pines flourished in the upland forest inland from the maritime forest, including **longleaf** and **loblolly** pines.

Right up there with live oaks and Spanish moss in terms of instant recognition would have to be the colorful, ubiquitous **azalea,** a flowering shrub of the *Rhododendron* genus. Over 10,000 varieties have been cultivated through the centuries, with quite a wide range of them on display during blooming season: March-April. The Masters golf tournament in Augusta, in particular, has been closely associated with the azalea from its inception due to the masterful groundskeeping at Augusta National Golf Club.

Another great floral display comes from the **camellia,** a cold-hardy evergreen with flowers that generally bloom in late winter (January-March). Other colorful ornamentals of the area include the ancient **Southern magnolia,** a native evergreen with distinctive large white flowers (evolved before the advent of bees in North America); and the **flowering dogwood,** which for its very hard wood—great for daggers, hence its original name "dagwood"—is actually quite fragile.

Up in the mountains, throngs of leaf-watchers come every autumn to enjoy the shifting colors of the Eastern cottonwood, the black walnut, the chalk maple, the white ash, and all kinds of hickory trees. Purely indigenous trees also on colorful display include the black tupelo, the red maple, the sycamore, and the sassafras. The evergreen Fraser fir of Christmas tree fame grows naturally only in Fannin County.

Moving into watery areas, you'll find the remarkable **bald cypress,** a flood-resistant conifer recognizable by its tufted top, its great height (up to 130 feet), and its distinctive "knees," parts of the root that project above the waterline and which are believed to help stabilize the tree in lowland areas. Much prized for its beautiful, pest-resistant wood, great stands of cypress once dominated the coast; sadly, overharvesting and destruction of wetlands has made the magnificent sight of this ancient, dignified species much less common. The acres of **smooth cordgrass** for which the Golden Isles are named are plants of the *Spartina alternaflora* species.

ANIMALS

On the Land

Perhaps the most iconic land animal, or semi-land animal, anyway, of Georgia is the legendary **American alligator,** the only species of crocodile native to the area. Contrary to their fierce reputation, locals know these massive reptiles, 6-12 feet long as adults, to be quite shy. If you come in the colder months you won't see one at all, since alligators require warm temperatures to become active and feed. Often all you'll see is a couple of eyebrow ridges sticking out of the water, and a gator lying still in a shallow creek can easily be mistaken for a floating log. But should you see one or more gators basking in the sun—a favorite activity on warm days for these cold-blooded creatures—it's best to admire them from afar. A mother alligator, in particular, will destroy anything that comes near her nest. Despite the alligator's short, stubby legs, they run amazingly fast on land, faster than you, in fact.

If you're driving on a country road at night, be on the lookout for **white-tailed deer,** which, besides being quite beautiful, also pose a serious road hazard. Because development has dramatically reduced the habitat and therefore the numbers of their natural predators, deer are very plentiful throughout the area.

The coast hosts fairly large populations of playful **river otters.** Not to be confused with the larger sea otters off the West Coast, these fast-swimming members of the weasel family inhabit inland waterways and marshy areas, with dominant males sometimes ranging as much as 50 miles within a single waterway.

While you're unlikely to encounter an otter, if you're camping you might easily run into the **raccoon,** an exceedingly intelligent and crafty relative of the bear, sharing that larger animal's resourcefulness in stealing your food. Though nocturnal, raccoons will feed whenever food is available. Rabies is prevalent in the raccoon population and you should always, always keep your distance.

Another common campsite nuisance, the **opossum** is a shy, primitive creature that is much more easily discouraged. North America's only marsupial, an opossum's usual "defense" against predators is to play dead. That said, however, they have an immunity to snake venom and often feed on the reptiles, even the most poisonous ones.

Once fairly common in Georgia, the **black bear** has suffered from hunting and habitat destruction. There are about 5,000 left in the wild in Georgia, in three areas: The North Georgia mountains, the Ocmulgee River watershed in Middle Georgia, and the Okefenokee Swamp.

In the Water

Without a doubt the most magnificent denizen, if only part-time, of the Southeastern coast is the **North American right whale,** which can approach 60 feet in length. Each year from December to March the mothers give birth to their calves and nurse them in the warm waters off the Georgia coast in an eons-old ritual. (In the summers they like to hang around the rich fishing grounds off the New England coast, though biologists still can't account for their whereabouts at other times of the year.) Whaling and encounters with ship propellers have taken their toll, and numbers of this endangered species are dwindling fast now, with less than 500 estimated left in the world.

Another of humankind's aquatic cousins, the **Atlantic bottle-nosed dolphin**, is a frequent visitor to the coast, coming far upstream into creeks and rivers to feed. Don't be fooled by their cuteness, however. Dolphins live life with gusto and aren't scared of much. They're voracious eaters of fish, amorous and energetic lovers, and will take on an encroaching shark in a heartbeat.

Another beloved part-time marine creature of the barrier islands of the coast is the **loggerhead turtle**. Though the species prefers to stay well offshore the rest of the year, females weighing up to 300 pounds come out of the sea each May-July to dig a shallow hole in the dunes and lay over 100 leathery eggs, returning to the ocean and leaving the eggs to hatch on their own after two months.

The most abundant and sought-after recreational species in the coastal area is the **spotted sea trout** followed by **red drum**. Local anglers also pursue many varieties of **bass**, **bream**, **sheepshead**, and **crappie**. It may sound strange to some accustomed to considering it a "trash" fish, but many types of **catfish** are not only plentiful here all throughout Georgia but are a common and well-regarded food source.

Recreational lakes, almost all constructed by people, are found throughout the state, and the chief fish on them is the largemouth bass. The biggest are typically caught on the western lakes such as Walter F. George and Seminole on the Alabama border (you can also catch shoal bass there as well). But the Savannah River lakes of Hartwell and Clark's Hill are great bass grounds as well, as are the adjacent lakes Sinclair and Oconee. Lake Lanier outside Atlanta is known for its striped and spotted bass.

Trout fishing, for three main species (rainbow, brown, and brook), is done on 4,000 miles of rivers and streams, though quirky soils in Georgia mean they aren't as productive as some states. There are extensive regulations on trout fishing in Georgia; go to www.georgiawildlife.com for full info. Popular spots include the Conasauga River, the Chattahoochee River, Hoods Creek, Jones Creek, Amicalola Creek, and Dukes Creek. Interestingly, trout fishing on Moccasin Creek off Lake Burton is limited to those 12 and under and senior citizens.

Crustaceans and shellfish have been a key food staple in the area for thousands of years, with the massive shell middens of the coast being testament to Native Americans' healthy appetite for them. The beds of the local variant, the **eastern oyster**, aren't what they used to be, due to over-harvesting, water pollution, and disruption of habitat. Oysters spawn May-August, hence the old folk wisdom about eating oysters only in months with the letter "r," so as not to disrupt the breeding cycle.

Each year in April-January, shrimp boats trawl for **shrimp**, the most popular seafood item in the United States. Another important commercial crop is the **blue crab**, the species used in such Lowcountry delicacies as crab cakes. You'll often see floating markers bobbing up and down in rivers throughout the region. These signal the presence directly below of a crab trap, often of an amateur crabber.

A true living link to primordial times, the alien-looking **horseshoe crab** is frequently found on coastal beaches during the spring mating season (it lives in deeper water the rest of the year). More closely related to scorpions and spiders than crabs, the horseshoe has evolved hardly a lick in hundreds of millions of years.

In the Air

Birds in Georgia come in four types: permanent residents like the **northern cardinal**; summer breeders like the **indigo bunting**; winter residents that return north to nest in the spring; and spring and fall migrants flying between summer nesting grounds in Northern states and Canada.

Up in the mountains at significant elevation is the only place you'll see **Canada** warblers, winter wrens, veerys, yellow-bellied sapsuckers, and dark-eyed juncos. Georgia is visited by 11 hummingbird species during the year, but only the tiny ruby-throated hummingbird is known to nest here.

Down in wiregrass country of Middle and South Georgia among the pines you'll find the most common area woodpecker, the huge pileated woodpecker with its huge crest. Less common is the smaller, more subtly marked red-cockaded woodpecker. Once common in the primordial inland longleaf pine forests, the species is now endangered, its last sanctuaries being the big tracts of relatively undisturbed land on military bases and on wildlife refuges.

When on the coast, consider yourself fortunate to see an endangered wood stork, though their numbers are on the increase. The only storks to breed in North America, they're usually seen on a low flight path across the marsh. Often confused with the wood stork is the gorgeous white ibis, distinguishable by its orange bill and black wingtips. Like the wood stork, the ibis is a communal bird that roosts in colonies.

Other similar-looking coastal denizens are the white-feathered great egret and snowy egret, the former distinguishable by its yellow bill and the latter by its black bill and the tuft of plumes on the back of its head. Egrets are in the same family as herons. The most magnificent is the great blue heron. Despite their imposing height, up to four feet tall, these waders are shy. So how to tell the difference between all these wading birds at a glance? It's actually easiest when they're in flight. Egrets and herons fly with their necks tucked in, while storks and ibises fly with their necks extended.

Dozens of species of shorebirds comb the beaches, including sandpipers, plovers, and the wonderful and rare American oystercatcher, instantly recognizable for its prancing walk, dark brown back, stark white underside, and long, bright-orange bill. And don't forget the delightful, water-loving painted bunting, particularly drawn to the barrier islands of the coast and riverine areas near the marsh.

The bald eagle, which had no recorded nests anywhere in the state as recently as the late 1970s, has made quite a comeback thanks to aggressive conservation policies. The chief raptor of the salt marsh is the fish-eating osprey.

And of course don't forget the Georgia state bird, the oddly charming brown thrasher, typically found churning up dirt and leaves close to the ground in residential areas.

Insects

Down here they say that God invented bugs to keep the Yankees from completely taking over the South. And insects are probably the most unpleasant fact of life in the Southeastern coastal region.

The list of annoying indigenous insects must begin with the infamous sand gnat. This tiny and persistent nuisance, a member of the midge family, lacks the precision of the mosquito with its long proboscis. No, the sand gnat is more torture-master than surgeon, brutally gouging and digging away its victim's skin until it hits a source of blood. Most prevalent in the spring and fall, the sand gnat is drawn to its prey by the carbon dioxide trail of its breath.

While long sleeves and long pants are one way to keep gnats at bay, the only real antidote to the sand gnat's assault (other than never breathing) is the Avon skin care product Skin So Soft, which has taken on a new and wholly unplanned life as the South's favorite anti-gnat lotion. In calmer moments grow to appreciate the great contribution sand gnats make to the salt marsh ecosystem as food for birds and bats.

Running a close second to the sand gnat are the over three dozen species of highly aggressive mosquito, which breed anywhere a few drops of water lie stagnant. Not surprisingly, massive populations blossom in the rainiest months, in late spring and late summer, feeding in the morning and late afternoon. Like the gnat, the mosquito homes in on its victim by trailing the plume of carbon dioxide exhaled in the breath; the biters are always female.

But undoubtedly the most viscerally loathed of all pests on the Lowcountry and Georgia coasts is the so-called "palmetto bug," or **American cockroach.** These black, shiny, and sometimes grotesquely massive insects, up to two inches long, are living fossils, virtually unchanged over hundreds of millions of years. And perfectly adapted as they are to life in and among wet, decaying vegetation, they're unlikely to change a bit in 100 million more years.

Popular regional use of the term "palmetto bug" undoubtedly has its roots in a desire for polite Southern society to avoid using the ugly word "roach" and its connotations of filth and unclean environments. But the colloquialism actually has a basis in reality. Contrary to what anyone tells you, the natural habitat of the American cockroach—unlike its kitchen-dwelling, much-smaller cousin, the German cockroach—is outdoors, often up in trees. They only come inside human dwellings when it's especially hot, especially cold, or especially dry outside. Like you, the palmetto bug is easily driven indoors by extreme temperatures and by thirst.

Other than visiting the Southeast during the winter, when the roaches go dormant, there's no convenient antidote for their presence. The best way to keep them out of your life is to stay away from decaying vegetation and keep doors and windows closed on especially hot nights.

History

BEFORE THE EUROPEANS

Based on studies of artifacts found throughout the state, anthropologists know that the first humans arrived in Georgia at least 13,000 years ago, at the tail end of the Ice Age. During this **Paleoindian Period,** sea levels were over 200 feet lower than present levels, and large mammals such as wooly mammoths, horses, and camels were hunted for food and skins. However, rapidly increasing temperatures, rising sea levels, and efficient hunting techniques combined to quickly kill off these large mammals, relics of the Pleistocene Era, ushering in the **Archaic Period.** Still hunter-gatherers, Archaic Period Indians began turning to small game such as deer, bear, and turkey, supplemented with fruit and nuts.

The latter part of the Archaic era saw more habitation on the coasts, with an increasing reliance on fish and shellfish for sustenance. It's during this time that the great **shell middens** of the Georgia coast trace their origins. Basically serving as trash heaps for discarded oyster shells, the middens grew in size and as they did they took on a ceremonial status, often being used as sites for important rituals and meetings. Such sites are often called **shell rings,** and the largest yet found was over 9 feet high and 300 feet in diameter.

The introduction of agriculture and improved pottery techniques about 3,000 years ago led to the **Woodland Period** of Native American settlement. Extended clan groups were much less migratory, establishing year-round communities of up to 50 people, who began the practice of clearing land to grow crops. The ancient shell middens of their forefathers were not abandoned, however, and were continually added onto.

Native Americans had been cremating or burying their dead for years, a practice which eventually gave rise to the construction of the first **mounds** during the Woodland Period. Essentially built-up earthworks sometimes marked with spiritual symbols, often in the form of animal shapes, mounds not only contained the remains of the deceased, but items like pottery to accompany the deceased into the afterlife. The most notable Woodland sites in Georgia are the **Rock Eagle Effigy** outside Eatonton and the amazing **Kolomoki Mounds** site near Blakely, which at its peak was the most populous settlement north of Mexico.

Increased agriculture led to increased population, and with that population growth came competition over resources and a more formal notion of warfare. This period, from about 800AD-1600AD, is termed the **Mississippian Period** and is the apex of Native American culture north of Mexico.

It was the Mississippians who would be the first Native Americans in what's now the continental United States to encounter European explorers and settlers after Columbus. The Native Americans who would later be called **Creek Indians** were the direct descendants of the Mississippians in lineage, language, and lifestyle.

The Mississippians were not only prodigious mound builders, they also constructed elaborate wooden villages and evolved a top-down class system. Their cities, generally positioned along key trails and rivers, formed a sophisticated network of trade and interrelationships that spanned Florida up to Ohio.

Along with Kolomoki, which was begun a bit earlier and also was a Mississippian site, there are two notable Mississippian mound sites in Georgia: **Etowah Mounds** outside Cartersville and **Ocmulgee Mounds** in Macon, which also features the newer **Lamar Mound.**

By about 1400AD, however, change came to the Mississippian culture for reasons that are still not completely understood. In some areas, large chiefdoms began splintering into smaller subgroups, in an intriguing echo of the medieval feudal system going on concurrently in Europe. In either case, the result was the same: The landscape of the Southeast became less peopled, as many of the old villages, built around huge central mounds, were abandoned. As tensions and paranoia between the chiefdoms increased, the contested land between them became more and more dangerous for the poorly armed or poorly connected. Indeed, at the time of the Europeans' arrival much of the coastal area was more thinly inhabited than it had been for many decades, a situation only exacerbated by the diseases introduced by the explorers.

THE SPANISH ARRIVE

The first serious exploration of the coast came in 1526, when Spanish adventurer Lucas Vazquez de Ayllon and about 600 colonists made landfall at Winyah Bay in South Carolina, near present-day Georgetown. They didn't stay long, however, immediately moving down the coast and trying to set down roots in the St. Catherine's Sound area of modern-day Liberty County, Georgia.

That colony, called San Miguel de Gualdape, was the first European colony in America. (The continent's oldest continuously occupied settlement, St. Augustine, Florida, wasn't founded until 1565.) The colony also brought with it the seed of a future nation's dissolution: slaves from Africa. While San Miguel de Gualdape lasted only six weeks due to political tension and a slave uprising, conclusive artifacts from its brief life have been discovered in the area.

Of far greater impact was Hernando de Soto's infamous, ill-fated trek of 1539-1543 from Florida through southwest Georgia to Alabama, where the Spanish explorer died of a fever after four years of depredations against the indigenous population. Setting ashore near modern Tampa Bay, de Soto and his men crossed the Florida Panhandle into Georgia near modern Bainbridge on the Flint River. Traveling up the Flint, they passed near present-day Montezuma, then crossed to the east side of the river to the chiefdom of Toa.

They progressed until they came to the Ocmulgee River, where they found an island where meat had been abandoned still roasting on a wooden barbacoa frame over a wood fire—the first recorded instance of barbecue in Georgia. Shortly after they came to the Ichisi chiefdom near the Lamar mound site at Macon, where after a peaceful greeting with the chief de Soto ordered a cross set atop a mound. North from Macon they encountered several more chiefdoms, crossing the Savannah River a bit north of modern Augusta, beginning the portion of their trek through the Carolinas and east Tennessee before turning back into Georgia at the Indian town of Coosa, where Carters Lake now lies.

It was now August 1540. De Soto left Coosa and headed back south, crossing the Etowah River near the Etowah Mound site at present-day Cartersville, stopping at a chiefdom near modern Rome, Georgia. By September they had passed into Alabama, never to see Georgia again. He did not find the gold he anticipated, but de Soto's legacy was soon felt throughout the Southeast in the form of various diseases for which the Mississippian tribes had no immunity whatsoever: smallpox, typhus, influenza, measles, yellow fever, whooping cough, diphtheria, tuberculosis, and bubonic plague.

While the cruelties of the Spanish certainly took their toll, far more damaging were these deadly diseases to a population totally unprepared for them. Within a few years, the Mississippian people, already in a state of internal decline, were losing huge percentages of their population to disease, echoing what had already happened on a massive scale to the indigenous tribes of the Caribbean after Christopher Columbus's expeditions.

As the viruses they introduced ran rampant, the Europeans themselves stayed away for a couple of decades after the ignominious end of de Soto's fruitless quest. During that quarter-century, the once-proud Mississippian culture continued to disintegrate, dwindling into a shadow of its former greatness. In all, disease would claim the lives of at least 80 percent of all indigenous inhabitants of the western hemisphere.

The Mission Era

It's rarely mentioned as a key part of U.S. history, but the Spanish missionary presence on the Georgia coast was longer and more comprehensive than its much more widely known counterpart in California.

St. Augustine governor Pedro Menendez de Aviles, over "biscuits with honey" on the beach at St. Catherine's Island in Georgia with a local chief, negotiated for the right to establish a system of Jesuit missions in two coastal chiefdoms: the Mocama on and around Cumberland Island, and the Guale (pronounced "wallie") to the north. Those early missions, the first north of Mexico, were largely unsuccessful. But a renewed, organized effort by the Franciscan Order came to fruition during the 1580s. Missions were established all along the Georgia coast, from the mainland near St. Simons and Sapelo Islands, on the Altamaha.

Spanish power waned under the English threat, however. A devastating Indian raid in 1661 on a mission at the mouth of the Altamaha River, possibly aided by the English, persuaded the Spanish to pull the mission effort to the barrier islands. But even as late as 1667, right before the founding of Charleston, South Carolina, there were 70 missions still on the Georgia coast. Pirate raids and slave uprisings finished off the Georgia missions for good by 1684. In an interesting postscript, 89 Native Americans—the sole surviving descendants of Spain's Georgia missions—evacuated to Cuba with the final Spanish exodus from Florida in 1763.

OGLETHORPE'S VISION

In 1729, the colony of Carolina was divided into north and south. In 1731, a colony to be known as Georgia, after the new English king, was carved out of the southern part of the Carolina land grant. A young general, aristocrat, and humanitarian named James Edward Oglethorpe gathered together a group of trustees to take advantage of that grant.

While Oglethorpe would go on to found Georgia, his wasn't the first English presence. A garrison built Fort King George in modern-day Darien, Georgia, in 1721. A cypress blockhouse surrounded by palisaded earthworks, the fort defended the southern reaches of

England's claim for seven years before being abandoned in 1728.

On February 12, 1733, after stops in Beaufort and Charleston, the ship *Anne* with its 114 passengers made its way to the highest bluff on the Savannah River. The area was controlled by the peaceful Yamacraw tribe, who had been encouraged by the powers-that-be in Charleston to settle on this vacant land 12 miles up the river to serve as a buffer for the Spanish. Led by an elderly chief, or *mico,* named Tomochichi, the Yamacraw enjoyed the area's natural bounty of shellfish, fruit, nuts, and small game.

Ever the deft politician, Oglethorpe struck up a treaty and eventually a genuine friendship with Tomochichi. To the Yamacraw Oglethorpe was a rare bird, a white man who behaved with honor and was true to his word. The tribe reciprocated by helping the settlers and pledging fealty to the crown. Oglethorpe reported to the trustees that Tomochichi personally requested "that we would Love and Protect their little Families."

In negotiations with local tribes the persuasive Oglethorpe convinced the coastal Creek to cede to the crown all Georgia land to the Altamaha River "which our Nation hath not occasion for to use" in exchange for goods. The tribes also reserved the Georgia Sea Islands of Sapelo, Ossabaw, and St. Catherine's. Oglethorpe's impact was felt farther down the Georgia coast, as St. Simons Island, Jekyll Island, Darien, and Brunswick were settled in rapid succession, and with them the entrenchment of the plantation system and slave labor.

While the trustees' utopian vision was largely economic in nature, like Carolina the Georgia colony also emphasized religious freedom. While to modern ears Oglethorpe's original ban of Roman Catholics from Georgia might seem incompatible with this goal, the reason was a coldly pragmatic one for the time: England's two main global rivals, France and Spain, were both staunchly Catholic countries.

Spain Vanquished

Things heated up on the coast in 1739 with the so-called War of Jenkins' Ear, which despite its seemingly trivial beginnings over the humiliation of a British captain by Spanish privateers was actually a proxy struggle emblematic of changes in the European balance of power. A year later Oglethorpe cobbled together a force of settlers, Indian allies, and Carolinians to reduce the Spanish fortress at St. Augustine, Florida.

The siege failed, and Oglethorpe retreated to St. Simons Island to await the inevitable counterattack. In 1742, a massive Spanish force invaded the island but was eventually turned back for good with heavy casualties at the **Battle of Bloody Marsh.** That clash marked the end of Spanish overtures on England's colonies in America.

Though Oglethorpe returned to England a national hero, things fell apart in Savannah. The settlers became envious of the success of Charleston's slave-based rice economy and began wondering aloud why they couldn't also make use of free labor.

With Oglethorpe otherwise occupied in England, the Trustees of Georgia—distant in more ways than just geographically from the new colony—bowed to public pressure and relaxed the restrictions on slavery and rum. By 1753 the trustees voted to return their charter to the crown, officially making Georgia the 13th and final colony of England in America.

With first the French and then the Spanish effectively shut off from the American East Coast, the stage was set for an internal battle between England and its burgeoning colonies across the Atlantic.

REVOLUTION AND INDEPENDENCE

It's a persistent but inaccurate myth that Georgia was reluctant to break ties with England. While the Lowcountry's cultural and economic ties to England were certainly strong, the **Stamp Act** and the **Townshend Acts** combined to turn public sentiment against the mother country there as elsewhere in the colonies. Planters in what would be called Liberty County, Georgia, also strongly agitated for the cause. War broke out between the colonists and the British in New England, and soon made its way southward. Three Georgians—Button Gwinnett, Lyman Hall, and George Walton—signed the Declaration of Independence on July 4, 1776.

The British took Savannah in 1778. Royal Governor Sir James Wright returned from exile to Georgia to reclaim it for the crown, the only one of the colonies to be subsumed again into the British Empire. A polyglot force of colonists, Haitians, and Hessians attacked the British fortifications on the west side of Savannah in 1779, but were repulsed with heavy losses.

Such a pitched battle was rare in Georgia; the bulk of the Revolutionary War in the Southern theater was a guerrilla war of colonists versus the British as well as a civil war between patriots and loyalists, or **Tories.** The main such engagement in Georgia was the Battle of Kettle Creek in February 1779. In which a Loyalist force specifically intended to gather support in the backcountry for the royal cause was defeated by a combined militia force under Colonel Andrew Pickens of South Carolina and Colonel John Dooly and Lieutenant Colonel Elijah Clarke of Georgia.

After independence, two Georgians, Abraham Baldwin and William Few Jr., signed the new U.S. Constitution in 1787. Georgia became the fourth state to enter the Union when it ratified the Constitution on January 2, 1788. It was during that decade that the University of Georgia, first university in the nation established by a state government, was granted its charter, opening its doors in Athens in 1801.

THE ANTEBELLUM ERA

In 1786, a new crop was introduced that would only enhance the financial clout of the coastal region: cotton. A former loyalist colonel, Roger Kelsal, sent some seed from the West Indies to his friend James Spaulding, owner of a plantation on St. Simons Island, Georgia. This crop, soon to be known as **Sea Island cotton** and considered the best in the world, would supplant rice as the crop of choice for coastal plantations. At the height of the Southern cotton boom in the early 1800s, a single Sea Island cotton harvest on a single plantation might go for $100,000 in 1820 money!

While Charleston was still by far the largest, most powerful, and most influential city on the Southeastern coast of the United States, at the peak of the cotton craze Savannah was actually doing more business. It's during this time that most of the grand homes of downtown Savannah's Historic District were built. This boom period, fueled largely by cotton exports, was perhaps most iconically represented by the historic sailing of the SS *Savannah* from Savannah to Liverpool in 29 days, the first transatlantic voyage by a steamship.

Another crucial agricultural breakthrough happened in Georgia: Eli Whitney's invention of the cotton gin while visiting the Mulberry Grove plantation of Catharine Greene, widow of General Nathanael Greene. The dramatic efficiencies introduced by the cotton gin not only increased the South's dependence on that staple crop, it also further reinforced the slave economy, already well established through the rice trade.

The Gold Rush

Cotton wasn't the only moneymaker in Georgia in the antebellum era. The North Georgia mountains were the site of America's first gold rush. By 1830 4,000 miners were panning for gold on one creek alone. The amount and quality of gold was so extravagant that the U.S. Mint opened a branch office in Dahlonega in 1838. Before closing at the outbreak of the Civil War it had produced 1.5 million gold coins.

Of course the original inhabitants of the Gold Rush land were Cherokee Indians. Writing in a tribal newspaper, one said of the rush, "Our neighbors who regard no law and pay no respects to the laws of humanity are now reaping a plentiful harvest.... We are an abused people." Those words were prophetic, and decades of government activity oriented toward removing Creek and Cherokee from Georgia came to a head when gold was used as an excuse to take final action.

The Trail of Tears

Even before the Gold Rush, the state of Georgia had held "Land Lotteries" to distribute land seized from Cherokees and Creeks through various treaties often of dubious provenance; the land seized totaled about three quarters of the state's land area. Around the time of the Gold Rush, a series of court decisions led to a potential Constitutional crisis involving the state of Georgia and the federal government under President Andrew Jackson, who, while fully supporting Indian removal, was also concerned with asserting federal power over the states.

As the extent of the gold deposits were realized and with the signing of the pivotal Treaty of New Echota in 1835, the U.S. Army found the legal justification to forcibly remove remaining Cherokees from Georgia into "Indian Territory" in present-day Oklahoma. Events came to a head during the unusually frigid winter of 1838-39, when thousands of Cherokee were forced onto what became known as the "Trail of Tears," about 4,000 dying on the miserable journey without proper food and clothes.

The Railroad

During the pivotal antebellum era of the 1830s to the 1850s, the construction of rail lines connecting Georgia's major cities of the time—Athens, Augusta, Macon, and Savannah—was another huge development in Georgia. Atlanta, originally named Terminus, was founded in 1837 as the end of the rail system's line. By the outbreak of Civil War, Georgia had more miles of rail lines than any other Southern state, a fact that at the end of that conflict would haunt the state.

Secession

Long-simmering tensions between Southern states, primarily South Carolina, and the federal government over the issue of the expansion of slavery reached a tipping point with the election of the nominally abolitionist president Abraham Lincoln in November 1860.

During the subsequent "Secession Winter" before Lincoln took office in January, seven states seceded from the union, first among them South Carolina, followed by Mississippi, Florida, Alabama, Georgia, Louisiana, and Texas. Georgia's Secession Convention in the state capital of Milledgeville was among the most divided of all, given that large portions of the state, particularly the north and the southeast, had little economic interest in slavery.

However, Georgians played key roles in the nascent Confederate government, with Alexander H. Stephens of Crawfordville acting as vice president, Robert Toombs of Washington its secretary of state, and Thomas R.R. Cobb of Athens as the author of the Confederate Constitution. Meanwhile, pugnacious Georgia Governor Joseph E. Brown frequently butted heads with Confederate President Jefferson Davis over issues of, ironically enough, state's rights.

CIVIL WAR

War finally began with the firing on Ft. Sumter in Charleston harbor by secessionist forces. Almost immediately the South Carolina and Georgia coasts were blockaded by the much-larger Union Navy. Union forces used newly developed rifled cannons in 1862 to quickly reduce Fort Pulaski at the mouth of the Savannah River—previously thought impregnable and the world's most secure fortress—garrisoning it and leaving Savannah itself in Confederate hands.

White Southerners evacuated the coastal cities and plantations for the hinterland, leaving slaves behind to fend for themselves. In some coastal areas, African Americans and Union garrison troops settled into an awkward coexistence. Many islands under Union control, such as Cockspur Island where Fort Pulaski sat, became endpoints in the Underground Railroad.

Georgian troops served the Confederacy in every theater of the war, but large-scale fighting didn't hit the state until the Union pushed down into North Georgia from Chattanooga, Tennessee, which along with Atlanta was a major rail hub for the Confederacy. The last major Confederate victory of the war came at Chickamauga in September 1863, when Confederate General Braxton Bragg, with considerable assistance from General James Longstreet, a Georgia native, pushed Union troops under General William Rosecrans back into Tennessee after three days of brutal fighting. However, the Union Army still held Chattanooga and continued to consolidate their forces for General William Sherman's eventual push to capture the real prize, Atlanta, and deal a dual blow to the Confederacy by seizing a major transportation and commercial hub as well as likely guaranteeing Lincoln's reelection later in 1864.

The spring was a fateful one for the South, as Sherman's initial forays into the area north of Atlanta were successful. Unrest in the top Confederate ranks led to Jefferson Davis firing General Joseph Johnston and replacing him with General John B. Hood, even as Sherman's army was gathering for the final assault only five miles from the city. Hood's attacks against the Union lines were too little, too late, and by the end of the summer of 1864 Hood had evacuated Atlanta and left it to its fate. Sherman telegraphed Lincoln, "Atlanta is ours and fairly won."

It was during roughly the same period that the notorious Camp Sumter POW camp operated near Andersonville, the name by which it's mostly known today. At its height of prisoner population, so many captured Union troops roasted in the sun within its unsheltered, stockaded space that it would have been the Confederacy's fifth largest city.

After three months of occupying Atlanta, Sherman was set to begin his fabled "March to the Sea" in an attempt to break the Southern will to fight for good, by destroying the means of supporting an army. On his way out of Atlanta in November, he gave the order to burn everything in the city that might be useful to the Southern war effort. The arson extended to private residences, and the entire downtown area burned in a massive and controversial conflagration.

The March to the Sea was made easier by Hood's removal of his forces to the west in an effort to draw Sherman towards Tennessee again. Sherman didn't take the bait, and with the way clear to the coast, he broke standard protocol not only by splitting his forces, but by operating without a supply line, instead wanting his army to forage off the land and whatever supplies they could take from the populace.

He divided his 60,000-man army into two equal wings: one would head towards Augusta and the other towards Macon. They both met at the state capital of Milledgeville, where the statehouse was ransacked and anything of remote military value was put to the torch. A Confederate cavalry force under General Joseph Wheeler harried Union forces the whole way, but to little effect. Union "bummers" took what they wanted from local farms, and railroad-wrecking crews heated railroad tracks into twisted messes called "Sherman's neckties."

Newly-freed former slaves followed in the Union Army's wake virtually the entire way to the sea, their numbers growing each week. On December 9 at Ebenezer Creek outside Savannah, a Union commander, ironically named Jefferson Davis, ordered a pontoon bridge taken away before the entourage of the emancipated could cross. Many drowned in the attempt to cross the creek on their own. Scathing headlines in the North resulted, but Sherman backed Davis's decision as militarily sound. In Savannah, Sherman concluded his March to the Sea in December 1864, famously giving the city to Lincoln as a Christmas present, along with 25,000 bales of cotton.

But Georgia wasn't quite out of the war's

headlines yet. Fleeing the disintegrating war zone in Virginia, Jefferson Davis met with his cabinet for the last time on May 5, 1865, in Washington, Georgia, essentially dissolving the Confederate government. Five days later, still on the run, he was captured by Union cavalry near Irwinville in the center of the state.

RECONSTRUCTION

For a brief time, Sherman's benevolent dictatorship on the coast held promise for an orderly postwar future. In 1865, he issued his sweeping "40 acres and a mule" order seeking dramatic economic restitution for coastal Georgia's free blacks. However, politics reared its ugly head in the wake of Lincoln's assassination and the order was rescinded, ushering in the chaotic Reconstruction era, echoes of which linger to this day.

Even as the trade in cotton and naval stores resumed to even greater heights than before, urban life and racial tension became more and more problematic. It was at this time that the foundation for Jim Crow and its false promise of "separate but equal" was laid. Racial in origin, the Jim Crow laws also displayed a clear socioeconomic bias as well; it was during Reconstruction that in some areas the practice evolved of wealthy whites walking on one side of the streets and poor whites and all blacks walking on the other side.

Atlanta was gradually rebuilt and quickly regained its dominant transportation status. In an acknowledgement of the city's overriding importance to the state, the state capital was moved there from Milledgeville in 1868, a scant four years after it was burned to the ground. By 1880, Atlanta had surpassed Savannah as Georgia's largest city. The "New South" movement, spearheaded by *Atlanta Journal-Constitution* editor Henry W. Grady, posited a region less about agriculture than about industry and progressive thought.

Despite the upheaval of Reconstruction, the Victorian era in Georgia was remarkably robust, with fortunes being made and glittering downtowns and residential areas rebuilt all over the state. A number of newly-minted African American millionaires gained prominence during this time as well, most notably in Atlanta and Macon. The exclusive Jekyll Island Club opened in 1886, bringing the world's wealthiest people to the Georgia coast to play.

RECONCILIATION AND DEPRESSION

The Spanish-American War of 1898 was a major turning point for the South, the first time since the Civil War that Americans were joined in patriotic unity. President McKinley himself addressed troops bivouacked in Savannah's Daffin Park before being sent on to fight in Cuba.

For all that, agriculture remained a vital part of Georgia's economy. Cotton remained crucial, as did logging. Throughout the late 1800s Georgia was the world's leading producer of naval stores, derived from vast tracts of pine trees.

FDR

Beginning in 1915 the old cotton-growing states of the South saw the arrival of the tiny but devastating boll weevil, which all but wiped out the cotton trade. Sharecroppers, a large percentage of the population and never far from economic disaster in the best of times, were especially hit hard. Old-tensions flared as the Ku Klux Klan was revived on Stone Mountain.

During the 1920s, then-New York Governor Franklin D. Roosevelt began visiting the Warm Springs area of Georgia to seek relief from his worsening polio symptoms. He saw firsthand the struggle of rural Southerners, and these experiences would influence many domestic initiatives, such as the Rural Electrification program, after he was elected president in 1932.

The coming of the Great Depression in the early 1930s was for most Georgians just a worsening of an already bad economic situation. While FDR's New Deal programs had some positive effect, they were later in coming to the South and were less effective because of resistance on the part of state politicians such as Governor Eugene Talmadge of Georgia, who was a staunch segregationist to boot and sought to limit any benefits of Roosevelt's largesse to white citizens only.

The cities fared a good bit better due to their transportation and manufacturing importance. Atlanta in particular weathered the Depression well, at the same time seeing a robust growth in the black middle class, a background that nurtured a young Martin Luther King Jr. in the then-prosperous black neighborhood called "Sweet Auburn." The auto bug bit Atlanta hard (it's still felt there today) and the first car suburbs were built.

The chief legacy today of the Depression era in Georgia, other than FDR's Little White House at Warm Springs, is the work of the Civilian Conservation Corps (CCC), a 10-year jobs program which resulted in the construction of most of Georgia's state parks, many of which feature original structures built by "Roosevelt's Tree Army" that are still very much in use today. Parts of the great Appalachian Trail were also cleared by the CCC, with many of the shelters used by through-hikers today still in steady use.

Gone with the Wind

Another development in the 1930s, which would have far-reaching ramifications for Georgia, was the writing of *Gone with the Wind* by Margaret Mitchell over a 10-year span in Atlanta. Shortly after her dramatic tale of the waning days of the Confederacy was published in 1936, it became a global sensation. A short three years later, Atlanta became the toast of a nation as Hollywood's elite gathered there for the world premiere of the film version. The book and film remain some of America's most popular and enduring cultural motifs, and probably resulted in untold billions of dollars in ancillary benefits for Georgia tourism.

WORLD WAR II AND THE POSTWAR BOOM

With the attack on Pearl Harbor and the coming of World War II, military facilities of all kinds swarmed into Georgia, making the state absolutely indispensable to the war effort. Populations and long-depressed living standards rose as a result. In many outlying areas, such as the Sea Islands, electricity came for the first time.

The enormous Bell Bomber plant was built in Marietta near Atlanta, producing thousands of B-29 bombers for the final air offensive against the empire of Japan. Robins Air Force Base near Macon became one of America's largest and most important domestic air bases. Fort Benning in Columbus became the U.S. Army's main infantry, paratrooper, and Ranger training base. The "Mighty Eighth" Air Force was founded in Savannah, and enormous Fort Stewart was built in nearby Hinesville. In shipyards in Savannah and Brunswick, hundreds of Liberty ships were built to transport cargo to the citizens and allied armies of Europe.

America's postwar infatuation with the automobile—and its troublesome child, the suburb—brought exponential expansion of metro areas, especially Atlanta, along with a callous disregard for much of the historic fabric of the past. It was in response to the car-craze that several society matrons in Savannah got together and founded the Historic Savannah Foundation, which helped preserve many of the priceless structures that today form the basis of Savannah's thriving tourist economy.

CIVIL RIGHTS

Contrary to popular opinion, the civil rights era wasn't just a blip in the late 1960s. The gains of that decade were the fruits of efforts begun decades prior. Many of the efforts involved efforts to expand black suffrage. Though African Americans secured the nominal right to vote years before, primary contests in Georgia were not under the jurisdiction of federal law. As a result, Democratic Party primary elections, de facto general elections because of that party's total dominance in the South at the time, were effectively closed to African American voters.

Other efforts, such as the groundbreaking "Albany Movement" of the early 1960s, sought to equalize and integrate public facilities and common areas. The efforts in Albany were at first unsuccessful, but their methods of peaceful resistance to segregationist policies were deeply influential on civil rights leaders such as Martin Luther King Jr., who took part in them.

Atlanta public schools began integrating in 1961. In 1965 the city would elect its first black alderman, and 11 African Americans were elected to the state legislature. Julian Bond, Georgia's first black congressman, was sent to Washington in 1967. Atlanta's first African American mayor, Maynard Jackson, was elected in 1969.

The civil rights era would spawn another political career, when a peanut farmer in tiny Plains, Georgia, was inspired to fight for social justice and equality by running for the Georgia State Senate. Jimmy Carter would go on to be governor in 1971 and then U.S. president in 1976. In an intriguing and somewhat prophetic blend of the forces that would shape American politics into the Obama era, Carter was both the first statewide Southern officeholder to publicly embrace full civil rights as well as the first evangelical Christian president.

GEORGIA TODAY

Throughout the 1980s, Georgia, and especially Atlanta, underwent an enormous boom driven by many of the same factors contributing to similar success stories throughout the U.S. Sun Belt. When the economic boom of the 1990s came, Atlanta was firmly cemented as a major convention and corporate business center.

Down in Savannah, their big tourism boom, still going on today, began with the publication of John Berendt's *Midnight in the Garden of Good and Evil* in 1995. A year later, Atlanta would host the 1996 Summer Olympics, which though marred by a bombing in Centennial Olympic Park, was pulled off quite successfully and signaled Atlanta's emergence as a truly global city, not that there was ever really any doubt.

More recently, Georgia's generous tax incentives have made the Peach State the largest center of TV and film industry outside Hollywood itself, with credits including *The Walking Dead* and *The Hunger Games*, with most of the action shot in metro Atlanta.

Government and Economy

GOVERNMENT

The capital of Georgia is Atlanta. The state legislature (technically called the General Assembly) meets 40 days a year "under the Gold Dome," or statehouse downtown. The upper house is the State Senate, which has 56 seats. The lower house is the House of Representatives, currently with 180 seats. The governor of Georgia serves a four-year term and lives in the Governor's Mansion in Buckhead.

Georgia is unique among all states in the union for the extraordinary number of counties it has: 159. This is not just a product of the state's sheer physical size; Montana is a good bit larger physically and only has 56 counties. Georgia's huge number of fairly small-sized counties is a direct result of the old **county unit system,** a method of political organization begun in 1917 whereby votes in party primary elections were awarded by county: urban counties six votes each, town counties four votes, and rural counties two votes each. What the county unit system meant in practice was that Georgia's rural counties could exert political control far outstripping their actual share of the population.

The county unit system wasn't removed until 1962 after a landmark court case which

President Jimmy Carter would later call "one of the most momentous political decisions of the century in Georgia."

Political Parties

For many decades, the South was dominated by the Democratic Party. Originally the party of slavery, segregation, and Jim Crow, the Democratic Party began attracting Southern African American voters in the 1930s with the election of Franklin D. Roosevelt. The allegiance of black voters was further cemented in the Truman, Kennedy, and Johnson administrations.

The region would remain solidly Democratic until a backlash against the civil rights movement of the 1960s drove many white Southerners, ironically enough, into the party of Lincoln. This added racial element, so confounding to Americans from other parts of the country, remains just as potent today.

The default mode in the South today is that white voters are massively Republican, and black voters massively Democratic. Since Georgia is 63 percent white, doing the math translates to an overwhelming Republican dominance. The GOP currently controls the governor's mansion and the state legislature. However, plenty of progressive enclaves exist, particularly in Atlanta, Athens, and Savannah.

ECONOMY

Thanks largely to Atlanta's economic importance, Georgia hosts over 25 Fortune 1,000 company headquarters, including those of Home Depot, UPS, Coca-Cola, Delta Airlines, Gulfstream Aerospace (in Savannah), and Aflac (in Columbus). Kia Motors opened its first U.S. assembly plant in West Point, near Atlanta. **Tourism** is also crucial.

While the Peach State isn't actually the nation's largest producer of peaches anymore (that would be South Carolina), its agricultural output is truly impressive. Chicken processing and export are extremely important, with Gainesville claiming the title of "Poultry Capital of the World." Albany is the center of world pecan production. Georgia is also the biggest grower of peanuts in the country. Other major agricultural products are apples, soybeans, corn, and of course sweet Vidalia onions.

The extractive industries are also well represented. Georgia is the national leader in clay and kaolin production and export, and other mined products include granite, marble, and limestone. The military is a huge economic driver in Georgia. The state hosts some of America's biggest and most vital bases. Cargo shipping at the port of Savannah has also increased dramatically.

However, the **textile** industry, an industrial giant from the late 19th century until the late 20th century, and the **furniture** businesses of the Piedmont have fallen off to nearly nothing as manufacturers move their operations overseas. The once-thriving **fishing** industry is also in steep decline due to globalization and pollution.

People and Culture

Contrary to how the region is portrayed in the media, Georgia is hardly exclusive to natives with thick accents who still obsess over the Civil War and eat grits three meals a day. As you will quickly discover, in some areas, such as Atlanta, Savannah, and St. Simons Island, there are plenty of transplants from other parts of the country. You can spend a whole day in Atlanta and not hear a single drawl or twang.

In any case, don't make the common mistake of assuming you're coming to a place where footwear is optional and electricity is a recent development (though it's true that a few islands didn't get electricity until the 1950s and 1960s). Because so much new construction has gone on in the South in the last quarter-century or so, you might find some aspects of the infrastructure, specifically the roads and the electrical utilities, actually superior to where you came from.

As part of the much-maligned Appalachian region, North Georgia has perhaps faced the steepest climb to respectability. The popular and critically acclaimed film *Deliverance,* based on the James Dickey novel, did little to dispel traditional notions of North Georgia as an uneducated, dangerous backwater. However, beginning in the 1960s, a project of Rabun County High School led to the groundbreaking *Foxfire* magazine and series of books, chronicling the vanishing folkways and culture of the Blue Ridge mountains for future generations to appreciate.

POPULATION

Georgia is the ninth most populous state in the union, with nearly 10 million people. Atlanta is by far its biggest city, its metro area accounting for half that total. Whites make up 63 percent of Georgia's population and African Americans 31 percent. While the Latino population is under 10 percent, it is the most rapidly growing demographic.

RELIGION

Of religious Georgians, the leading denomination by far is Baptist, followed by Methodist, Roman Catholic, and various other lesser-known denominations. Less than 1 percent of Georgia's population is Jewish and Islamic.

MANNERS

The prevalence and importance of good manners is the main thing to keep in mind about the South. While it's tempting for folks from more outwardly assertive parts of the world to take this as a sign of weakness, that would be a major mistake. Bottom line: Good manners will take you a long way here. Southerners use manners, courtesy, and chivalry as a system of social interaction with one goal above all: to maintain the established order during times of stress. A relic from a time of extreme class stratification, etiquette and chivalry are ways to make sure that the elites are never threatened—and, on the other hand, that even those on the lowest rungs of society are afforded at least a basic amount of dignity. But as a practical matter, it's also true that Southerners of all classes, races, and backgrounds rely on the observation of manners as a way to sum up people quickly. To any Southerner, regardless of class or race, your use or neglect of basic manners and proper respect indicates how seriously they should take you—not in a socioeconomic sense, but in the big picture.

The typical Southern sense of humor—equal parts irony, self-deprecation, and good-natured teasing—is part of the code. Southerners are loath to criticize another individual directly, so often they'll instead take the opportunity to make an ironic joke. Self-deprecating humor is also much more common in the South than in other areas of the country. Because of this, you're also expected to be able to take a joke yourself without being too sensitive.

Etiquette

It's rude here to inquire about personal finances, along with the usual no-go areas of religion and politics. Here are some other specific etiquette tips:

- **Basics:** Be liberal with "please" and "thank you," or conversely, "no, thank you" if you want to decline a request or offering.
- **Eye contact:** With the exception of very elderly African Americans, eye contact is not only accepted in the South, it's encouraged. In fact, to avoid eye contact in the South means you're likely a shady character with something to hide.
- **Handshake:** Men should always shake hands with a *very* firm, confident grip and appropriate eye contact. It's OK for women to offer a handshake in professional circles, but is otherwise not required.
- **Chivalry:** When men open doors for women here—and they will—it is not

thought of as a patronizing gesture but as a sign of respect. Also, if a female of any age or appearance drops an object on the floor, don't be surprised if several nearby males jump to pick it up. This is considered appropriate behavior and not at all unusual.

- **The elderly:** Senior citizens—or really anyone obviously older than you—should be called "sir" or "ma'am." Again, this is not a patronizing gesture in the South but is considered a sign of respect. Also, in any situation where you're dealing with someone in the service industry, addressing them as "sir" or "ma'am" regardless of their age will get you far.
- **Bodily contact:** Interestingly, though public displays of affection by romantic couples are generally frowned upon here, Southerners are otherwise pretty touchy-feely once they get to know you. Full-on body hugs are rare, but Southerners who are well acquainted often say hello or good-bye with a small hug.
- **Driving:** With the exception of the interstate perimeter highways around the larger cities, drivers in the South are generally less aggressive than in other regions. Cutting sharply in front of someone in traffic is taken as a personal offense. If you need to cut in front of someone, poke the nose of your car a little bit in that direction and wait for a car to slow down and wave you in front. Don't forget to wave back as a thank-you. Similarly, using a car horn can also be taken as a personal affront, so use your horn sparingly, if at all. In rural areas, don't be surprised to see the driver of an oncoming car offer a little wave. This is an old custom, sadly dying out. Just give a little wave back; they're trying to be friendly.

Essentials

Transportation

AIR

While some may be tempted to fly into Atlanta's Hartsfield-Jackson International Airport because of the sheer number of flights into that facility, unless your destination is Atlanta, I strongly advise against it because of the massive congestion in the area. **Hartsfield-Jackson Atlanta International Airport** (ATL, 6000 North Terminal Pkwy., 404/530-6600, www.atl.com) is the world's busiest, serving nearly 100 million passengers a year. Its flagship airline is Delta, with 60 percent of the airport's traffic. In all, about two dozen airlines fly in and out to domestic destinations as well as Europe, Asia, and South America.

The state's second-most comprehensive airport is **Savannah/Hilton Head International Airport** (SAV, 400 Airways Ave., 912/964-0514, www.savannahairport.com), directly off I-95 at exit 104, about 20 minutes from downtown Savannah.

The only other major airport in Georgia is **Augusta Regional Airport** (AGS, 1501 Aviation Way, 706/798-3236, www.flyags.com). Another option for coastal and southeast Georgia is **Jacksonville International Airport** (JAX, 2400 Yankee Clipper Dr., 904/741-4902, www.jia.com), about 20 miles north of Jacksonville, Florida. While it's a two-hour drive from Savannah, this airport's proximity to the attractions south of Savannah makes it attractive for visitors to the region.

CAR

Unless you're only staying in public transit-rich Atlanta or walkable Savannah, a vehicle is mandatory to enjoy your stay in Georgia.

The road-building lobby is politically very powerful in Georgia, and as a result the state and county highways are appreciably better funded and maintained than in many other states. When possible I always choose the local highways over the interstates because they are comparatively less crowded and in many cases are of equal or better quality.

But if you prefer traveling on the interstate highway system, Georgia is very well served; it includes north-south I-95, north-south I-75 and I-85 (which combine through Atlanta), the east-west I-20 across the northern half of the state, and the least-traveled example, east-west I-16 between Savannah and Macon. Shorter connecting interstate highways include the notorious I-285 around Atlanta, I-575 through North Georgia, I-185 from Columbus to I-85 proper, the small loop of I-516 in Savannah, and two "shortcut" segments, I-675 south of Atlanta and I-475 around Macon.

A common landmark road throughout the coastal region is U.S. 17, which used to be known as the Coastal Highway and which currently goes by a number of local incarnations as it winds its way down the coast, roughly paralleling I-95.

Car Rentals

Renting a car is easy and fairly inexpensive as long as you play by the rules, which are simple. You need either a valid driver's license from any U.S. state or a valid International Driving Permit from your home country, and you must be at least 25 years old.

If you do not either purchase insurance coverage from the rental company or already have insurance coverage through the credit card you rent the car with, you will be 100 percent responsible for any damage caused to

Previous: the fishing pier on Jekyll Island; an alligator in Okefenokee Swamp.

the car during your rental period. While purchasing insurance at the time of rental is by no means mandatory, it might be worth the extra expense just to have that peace of mind.

Key rental car companies in the state include **Hertz** (www.hertz.com), **Avis** (www.avis.com), **Thrifty** (www.thrifty.com), **Enterprise** (www.enterprise.com), and **Budget** (www.budget.com). Some rental car locations are in the cities, but the vast majority of outlets are at airports, so plan accordingly. The airport locations have the bonus of generally being open for longer hours than their in-town counterparts.

TRAIN

Passenger rail service in the car-dominated United States is far behind that in other developed nations, both in quantity and quality. The southeast coastal portion and the northern portion of the state are served by two lines of **Amtrak** (www.amtrak.com), the national rail system. Amtrak stations on the northern route are in Atlanta, Gainesville, and Toccoa. Stations on the southeast route are in Savannah and Jesup.

BUS

There are several **Greyhound** (800/229-9424, www.greyhound.com) stations in the Atlanta metro area, including at the airport, Marietta, Norcross, and LaGrange. Other stations are in Albany, Macon, Savannah, Columbus, Valdosta, and Hinesville (Fort Stewart).

While rates are reasonable and the vehicles are high-quality, this is by far the slowest possible way to travel, as buses stop frequently and sometimes for lengthy periods of time.

Recreation

CAMPING

Many state parks offer fully equipped rental cabins with modern amenities that rival a hotel's. Generally speaking, such facilities tend to book early, so make reservations as soon as you can. Keep in mind that during the high season (Mar.-Nov.) there are often minimum rental requirements. Be aware that the closer you are to the Appalachian Mountains, the higher the rainfall. Be prepared to camp wet. Dogs are allowed in state parks, but they must be leashed at all times.

Georgia State Parks (www.gastateparks.org) charge a $5 per vehicle parking fee per day on top of whatever the camping fees are, generally around $25. However, if you plan on visiting multiple parks in one day—entirely possible in some areas with a high volume of parks, such as North Georgia—that one-day $5 pass gets you into all parks for that day. There are plenty of private campgrounds as well, but if at all possible utilize the state parks system, not only because it's great, but because increased use will help ensure adequate future funding.

Camping is also possible at several Forest Service campgrounds within the massive **Chattahoochee National Forest** (www.fs.usda.gov). These sites are more geared to tent camping and are less expensive, around $15 a night, but with a lower level of amenities compared to the fairly deluxe standards of many Georgia state parks.

Unlike in the Western states, bears are a much less prevalent hazard in Georgia campgrounds. However, raccoons and opossums can and will get into your foodstuff; take precautions. In the lower portions of Georgia during the warmer months, gnats and mosquitoes are persistent pests, especially at dusk feeding time. Bring repellent.

HIKING, BIKING, CLIMBING, AND CAVING

Georgia offers many hundreds of miles of excellent, multi-habitat hiking, and that's not even counting the nearly 100 miles of the Appalachian Trail. Nearly every state park offers its own trail system, from short-ish to quite extensive, and there are voluminous wilderness areas, mostly managed by the U.S. Forest Service.

North Georgia is far and away the hiking capital of the state, particularly the stretch from the Cohutta Wilderness east to Brasstown Bald, the Appalachian Trail, and the Raven Cliffs Wilderness. But the Pine Mountain area around FDR State Park north of Columbus offers a particularly gratifying trail system as well.

Several areas of Georgia offer extensive climbing opportunities. The chief examples of environments conducive to good rock climbing and bouldering are Cloudland Canyon State Park and the entire Lookout-Pigeon Mountain area in northwest Georgia; Tallulah Gorge State Park in northeast Georgia; Mt. Yonah in north-central Georgia; Currahee Mountain at Toccoa; and Providence Canyon in southwest Georgia.

Spelunking is particularly popular in the northwest corner of the state, or "TAG Corner" (signifying the borders of Tennessee, Alabama, and Georgia). Cloudland Canyon is the premier starting place for your experience, which typically is done under the auspices of a guided tour unless you're already an experienced spelunker.

Plenty of Georgia municipalities are offering extensive greenway networks for urban walking and biking. Chief examples include Atlanta's BeltLine, the Columbus Riverwalk, the Augusta Riverwalk, the Ocmulgee Greenway in Macon, and the North Oconee River Greenway in Athens.

Mountain biking is popular everywhere in the Piedmont and North Georgia areas, but is particularly impressive on the Bear Creek Trail near Ellijay, the Bull Mountain run around Dahlonega, the Pinhoti North Trail near Dalton, the Pinhoti South Trail near Summerville, and the very popular trail network around Helen. Unicoi State Park has its own mountain bike trail network.

FISHING AND BOATING

In Georgia, a regular fishing license is $9, a one-day license $3.50. A separate license is required for trout fishing. Go to http://georgiawildlife.com for more information or to purchase a license online.

Georgia is full of recreational lakes with full boat access. Chief among them are Clarks Hill, Lake Hartwell, and Lake Russell on the Savannah River; Lake Lanier, Lake George, and Lake Seminole on the Chattahoochee River; Lake Oconee and Lake Sinclair on the Oconee River; and Lake Rabun, Lake Burton, Lake Tallulah Falls, and Lake Tugalo on the Tallulah River.

Georgia's rivers also provide extensive trout and flyfishing opportunities, with the best examples being Dukes Creek near Helen, the Conasauga River in the Cohutta Wilderness, the Chattooga River in northeast Georgia, Dicks Creek near Cleveland, and the upper Flint River.

One of the coolest things about the Georgia coastal area is the prevalence of the Intracoastal Waterway, a combined artificially-constructed and natural sheltered seaway going from Miami to Maine. Many boaters enjoy touring the coast by simply meandering up or down the Intracoastal, putting in at marinas along the way. Dozier's operates a Waterway Cruising Guide to the Intracoastal Waterway at www.waterwayguide.com.

KAYAKING, CANOEING, AND RAFTING

Whitewater rafters will particularly enjoy Georgia, with excellent runs on the **Chattooga and Chattahoochee Rivers.** The Chattahoochee near Atlanta is already known for its various "Shooting the Hootch" activities, but the Hootch near Columbus is getting a boost from a city project to demolish some obsolete earthwork dams and construct a whitewater course there to encourage tourism. The **Flint River** also contains some whitewater sections near Thomaston.

Most every state park in Georgia, it seems, has some kind of lake on which you can do some canoeing. Most of them offer canoe rental for very reasonable rates.

The best pure kayaking areas are found

on the Coastal Plain, especially in the vast Altamaha River basin. The **Altamaha River Canoe Trail** extends 140 miles from Lumber City to the Altamaha estuary near Darien.

The **Okefenokee Swamp** offers many miles of kayaking within its vast interior, with multiple canoe trails. Because it is federally run, however, there are some guidelines. Go to www.fws.gov/okefenokee/WildernessCanoeing.html for more info.

The Savannah area has rich kayaking and canoeing at **Tybee Island, Skidaway Island,** and the blackwater **Ebenezer Creek** west of town.

BEACHES

By law, beaches in the United States are fully accessible to the public up to the high-tide mark during daylight hours, even if the beach fronts private property and even if the only means of public access is by boat. While certain seaside resorts have over the years attempted to make the dunes in front of their property exclusive to guests, this is actually illegal, though it can be hard to enforce.

On federally run National Wildlife Refuges, access is limited to daytime hours, from sunrise to sunset.

It is a misdemeanor to disturb the **sea oats,** those wispy, waving, wheat-like plants among the dunes. Their root system is vital to keeping the beach intact. Also never disturb a turtle nesting area, whether it is marked or not.

The main beach in Georgia is outside Savannah at **Tybee Island,** with full accessibility from end to end. The beach on the north end is smaller and quieter, while the south end is wider, windier, and more populated. There are public parking lots, but you can park at metered spots near the beach as well.

Farther south, a very good beach is at **Jekyll Island,** a largely undeveloped barrier island owned by the state. There are three picnic areas with parking: **Clam Creek, South Dunes,** and **St. Andrew.**

Nearby **St. Simons Island** does have a beach area, but it is comparatively narrow and small. Adjacent **Sea Island** is accessible only if you're a guest of the Sea Island Club.

The rest of Georgia's barrier islands are only accessible by ferry, charter, or private boat. Many outfitters will take you on a tour to barrier islands such as Wassaw or Sapelo; don't be shy about inquiring. The most gorgeous beach of all is at **Cumberland Island National Seashore.**

NATIONAL WILDLIFE REFUGES

There are eight National Wildlife Refuges in Georgia:

- **Banks Lake NWR** (www.fws.gov/bankslake)
- **Blackbeard Island NWR** (www.fws.gov/blackbeard)
- **Bond Swamp NWR** (www.fws.gov/bondswamp)
- **Harris Neck NWR** (www.fws.gov/harrisneck)
- **Okefenokee NWR** (www.fws.gov/okefenokee)
- **Piedmont NWR** (www.fws.gov/piedmont)
- **Wassaw NWR** (www.fws.gov/wassaw)
- **Wolf Island NWR** (www.fws.gov/wolfisland)

Admission is generally free. Access is limited to daytime hours (sunrise-sunset). Keep in mind that some hunting is allowed on some refuges.

Travel Tips

WOMEN TRAVELING ALONE

Women should take the same precautions they would take anywhere else in the United States. Many women traveling to this region have to adjust to the prevalence of traditional chivalry. In the South, if a man opens a door for you, it's considered a sign of respect, not condescension.

Another adjustment is the possible assumption that two or three women who go to a bar or tavern together might be there to invite male companionship. This misunderstanding can happen anywhere, but in some parts of the South it might be more prevalent.

While small towns in the Carolinas and Georgia are generally very friendly and law-abiding, some are more economically depressed than others and hence prone to more crime. Always take commonsense precautions no matter how bucolic the setting may be.

TRAVELERS WITH DISABILITIES

While the vast majority of attractions and accommodations make every effort to comply with federal law regarding those with disabilities, as they're obligated to do, the historic nature of much of this region means that some structures simply cannot be retrofitted for maximum accessibility. This is something you'll need to find out on a case-by-case basis, so call ahead.

GAY AND LESBIAN TRAVELERS

Despite Georgia's essential conservatism, many places in the state can be considered quite gay friendly, especially in larger cities like Atlanta, Athens, and Savannah. Visit **QNotes** (www.q-notes.com) for info on LGBTQ community resources and activities. Atlanta in particular has a large and thriving LGBT community. The "official" guide is ***GA Voice*** (www.gay-atlanta.com).

SENIOR TRAVELERS

Both because of the large proportion of retirees in the state and because of the South's traditional respect for the elderly, the area is quite friendly to senior citizens. Many accommodations and attractions offer a seniors discount, which can add up over the course of a trip. Always inquire before making a reservation, however, as check-in time is sometimes too late.

TRAVELING WITH PETS

While the United States is very pet friendly, that friendliness rarely extends to restaurants and other indoor locations. More and more accommodations are allowing pet owners to bring pets, often for an added fee, but inquire before you arrive. In any case, keep your dog on a leash at all times. Some beaches in the area permit dog-walking at certain times of the year, but as a general rule, keep dogs off beaches unless you see signs saying otherwise.

Health and Safety

CRIME

While crime rates are generally above national averages in much of this region, especially in inner-city areas, incidents of crime in the more heavily touristed areas are no more common than elsewhere. In fact, these areas might be safer because of the amount of foot traffic and police attention.

By far the most common crime against visitors is simple theft, primarily from cars. (Pickpocketing, thankfully, is quite rare in the United States). Always lock your car doors. Conversely, only leave them unlocked if you're absolutely comfortable living without whatever's inside at the time. As a general rule, I try to lock valuables—such as CDs, a recent purchase, or my wife's purse—in the trunk. (Just make sure the "valet" button, allowing the trunk to be opened from the driver's area, is disabled.)

Should someone corner you and demand your wallet or purse, just give it to them. Unfortunately, the old advice to scream as loud as you can is no longer the deterrent it once was, and in fact may hasten aggressive action by the robber.

A very important general rule to remember is not to pull over for cars you do not recognize as law enforcement, no matter how urgently you might be asked to do so. This is not a common occurrence, but a possibility you should be aware of. A real police officer will know the correct steps to take to identify him or herself. If you find yourself having to guess, then do the safe thing and refuse to stop.

If you are the victim of a crime, *always call the police.* Law enforcement wants more information, not less, and at the very least you'll have an incident report in case you need to make an insurance claim for lost or stolen property.

Remember that in the United States as elsewhere, no good can come from a heated argument with a police officer. The place to prove a police officer wrong is in a court of law, perhaps with an attorney by your side, not at the scene.

For emergencies, always call 911.

AUTO ACCIDENTS

If you're in an auto accident, you're bound by law to wait for police to respond. Failure to do so can result in a "leaving the scene of an accident" charge or worse. In the old days, cars in accidents had to be left exactly where they came to rest until police gave permission to move or tow them. However, the states in this guide have recently loosened regulations so that if a car is blocking traffic as a result of an accident, the driver is allowed to move it enough to allow traffic to flow again. That is, if the car can be moved safely; if not, you're not required to move it out of the way.

Since it's illegal to drive without auto insurance, I'll assume you have some. And because you're insured, the best course of action in a minor accident, where injuries are unlikely, is to patiently wait for the police and give them your side of the story. In my experience, police react negatively to people who are too quick to start making accusations against other people. After that, let the insurance companies deal with it; that's what they're paid for.

If you suspect any injuries, call 911 immediately.

ILLEGAL DRUGS

Marijuana, heroin, methamphetamine, and cocaine and all its derivatives are illegal in the United States with only a few exceptions, none of which apply to Georgia. The use of ecstasy and similar mood-elevators is also illegal.

ALCOHOL

The drinking age in all of the United States is 21. Most restaurants that serve alcoholic beverages allow those under 21 inside. Generally speaking, if only those over 21 are allowed inside, you will be greeted at the door by someone asking to see identification. These people are often poorly trained, and anything other than a state driver's license may confuse them, so be forewarned.

Drunk driving is a problem on U.S. roads. Always drive defensively, especially late at night, and obey all posted speed limits and road signs—and never assume the other driver will do the same. You may never drive with an open alcoholic beverage in the car, even if it belongs to a passenger.

GETTING SICK

Unlike most developed nations, the United States has no comprehensive national health care system. Visitors from other countries who need nonemergency medical attention are best served by going to freestanding medical clinics. The level of care is typically very good, but unfortunately you'll be paying out of pocket for the service.

For emergencies, however, do not hesitate to go to the closest hospital emergency room, where the level of care is generally also quite good, especially for trauma. Worry about payment later; emergency rooms in the United States are required to take true emergency cases whether or not the patient can pay for services.

Pharmaceuticals

Unlike in many other countries, antibiotics are available in the United States only on a prescription basis and are not available over the counter. Most cold, flu, and allergy remedies are available over the counter. While homeopathic remedies are gaining popularity in the United States, they are nowhere near as prevalent as in Europe.

Medications with the active ingredient ephedrine are available in the United States without a prescription, but their purchase is now tightly regulated to cut down on the use of these products to make the illegal drug methamphetamine.

NOT GETTING SICK

Vaccinations

As of this writing, there are no vaccination requirements to enter the United States. Contact your embassy before coming to confirm this before arrival, however.

In the autumn, at the beginning of flu season, preventive influenza vaccinations, simply called "flu shots," often become available at easily accessible locations like clinics, health departments, and even supermarkets.

Humidity, Heat, and Sun

There is only one way to fight the South's high heat and humidity, and that's to drink lots of fluids. A surprising number of people each year refuse to take this advice and find themselves in various states of dehydration, some of which can land you in a hospital. Remember: If you're thirsty, you're already suffering from dehydration. The thing to do is keep drinking fluids before you're thirsty, as a preventative action rather than a reaction.

Always use sunscreen, even on a cloudy day. If you do get a sunburn, get a pain relief product with aloe vera as an active ingredient. On extraordinarily sunny and hot summer days, don't even go outside between the hours of 10am and 2pm.

HAZARDS

Insects

Because of the recent increase in the mosquito-borne West Nile virus, the most important step to take in staying healthy in the Lowcountry and Southeast coast—especially if you have small children—is to keep mosquito bites to a minimum. Do this with a combination of mosquito repellent and long sleeves and long pants, if possible. Not every mosquito bite will give you the virus; in fact, chances are quite slim that one will. But don't take the chance if you don't have to.

The second major step in avoiding insect nastiness is to steer clear of **fire ants,** whose large gray or brown dirt nests are quite common in this area. They attack instantly and in great numbers, with little or no provocation.

They don't just bite; they inject you with poison from their stingers. In short, fire ants are not to be trifled with. While the only real remedy is the preventative one of never coming in contact with them, should you find yourself being bitten by fire ants, the first thing to do is to stay calm. Take off your shoes and socks and get as many of the ants off you as you can. Unless you've had a truly large number of bites—in which case you should seek medical help immediately—the best thing to do next is wash the area to get any venom off, and then disinfect it with alcohol if you have any handy. Then a topical treatment such as calamine lotion or hydrocortisone is advised. A fire ant bite will leave a red pustule that lasts about a week. Try your best not to scratch it so that it won't get infected.

Outdoor activity, especially in woodsy, undeveloped areas, may bring you in contact with another unpleasant indigenous creature, the tiny but obnoxious **chigger,** sometimes called the redbug. The bite of a chigger can't be felt, but the enzymes it leaves behind can lead to a very itchy little red spot. Contrary to folklore, putting fingernail polish on the itchy bite will not "suffocate" the chigger, because by this point the chigger itself is long gone. All you can do is get some topical itch or pain relief and go on with your life. The itching will eventually subside.

For **bee stings,** the best approach for those who aren't allergic to them is to immediately pull the stinger out, perhaps by scraping a credit card over the bite, and apply ice if possible. A topical treatment such as hydrocortisone or calamine lotion is advised. In my experience, the old folk remedy of tearing apart a cigarette and putting the tobacco leaves directly on the sting does indeed cut the pain. But that's not a medical opinion, so do with it what you will. A minor allergic reaction can be quelled by using an over-the-counter antihistamine. If the victim is severely allergic to bee stings, go to a hospital or call 911 for an ambulance.

Threats in the Water

While enjoying area beaches, a lot of visitors become inordinately worried about **shark attacks.** Every couple of summers there's a lot of hysteria about this, but the truth is that you're much more likely to slip and fall in a bathroom than you are even to come close to being bitten by a shark in these shallow Atlantic waters.

A far more common fate for area swimmers is to get stung by a **jellyfish,** or sea nettle. They can sting you in the water, but most often beachcombers are stung by stepping on beached jellyfish stranded on the sand by the tide. If you get stung, don't panic; wash the area with saltwater, not freshwater, and apply vinegar or baking soda.

Lightning

The southeastern United States is home to vicious, fast-moving thunderstorms, often with an amazing amount of electrical activity. Death by lightning strike occurs often in this region and is something that should be taken quite seriously. The general rule of thumb is that if you're in the water, whether at the beach or in a swimming pool, and hear thunder, get out of the water immediately until the storm passes. If you're on dry land and see lightning flash a distance away, that's your cue to seek safety indoors. Whatever you do, do not play sports outside when lightning threatens.

Information and Services

MONEY

Automated teller machines (ATMs) are available in all the urban areas covered in this guide. Be aware that if the ATM is not owned by your bank, not only will that ATM likely charge you a service fee, but your bank may charge you one as well. While ATMs have made traveler's checks less essential, traveler's checks do have the important advantage of accessibility, as some rural and less-developed areas have few or no ATMs. You can purchase traveler's checks at just about any bank.

Establishments in the United States only accept the national currency, the U.S. dollar. To exchange foreign money, go to any bank.

Generally, establishments that accept credit cards will feature stickers on the front entrance with the logo of the particular cards they accept, although this is not a legal requirement. The use of debit cards has dramatically increased in the United States. Most retail establishments and many fast-food chains are now accepting them. Make sure you get a receipt whenever you use a credit card or a debit card.

Tipping

Unlike many other countries, service workers in the United States depend on tips for the bulk of their income. In restaurants and bars, the usual tip is 15 percent of the pretax portion of the bill for acceptable service, 20 percent (or more) for excellent service. For large parties, usually six or more, a 15-18 percent gratuity is sometimes automatically added to the bill.

It's also customary to tip hotel bell staff about $2 per bag when they assist you at check-in and checkout of your hotel; some sources recommend a minimum of $5.

For taxi drivers, 15 percent is customary as long as the cab is clean, smoke-free, and you were treated with respect and taken to your destination with a minimum of fuss.

INTERNET ACCESS

Visitors from Europe and Asia are likely to be disappointed at the quality of Internet access in the United States, particularly the area covered in this guide. Fiber-optic lines are still a rarity, and while many hotels and B&Bs now offer in-room Internet access—some charge, some don't, so make sure to ask ahead—the quality and speed of the connection might prove poor.

Wireless (Wi-Fi) networks also are less than impressive, although that situation continues to improve on a daily basis in coffeehouses, hotels, and airports. Unfortunately, many Wi-Fi access points in private establishments are for rental only.

PHONES

Generally speaking, the United States is behind Europe and much of Asia in terms of cell phone technology. Unlike Europe, where "pay-as-you-go" refills are easy to find, most American cell phone users pay for monthly plans through a handful of providers. Still, you should have no problem with cell phone coverage in urban areas. Where it gets much less dependable is in rural areas and on beaches. Bottom line: Don't depend on having cell service everywhere you go. As with a regular landline, any time you face an emergency, call 911 on your cell phone.

All phone numbers in the United States are seven digits preceded by a three-digit area code. You may have to dial a 1 before a phone number if it's a long-distance call, even within the same area code.

Resources

Suggested Reading

NONFICTION

Bryson, Bill. *A Walk in the Woods: Rediscovering America on the Appalachian Trail.* New York: Anchor, 2006. Entertaining and affecting tales from the length of the Appalachian Trail.

Carter, Jimmy. *Keeping Faith: Memoirs of a President.* Fayetteville: University of Arkansas Press, 1995. The 39th president's own account of his time in the White House from Plains, Georgia.

Gray, Marcus. *It Crawled from the South: An R.E.M. Companion.* Cambridge, MA: Da Capo Press, 1997. The complete guide to the band R.E.M., from personal histories to lyrics.

Greene, Melissa Fay. *Praying for Sheetrock.* New York: Ballantine, 1992. Greene explores the racism and corruption endemic in McIntosh County, Georgia, during the civil rights movement.

Hannon, Lauretta. *The Cracker Queen: A Memoir of a Jagged, Joyful Life.* New York: Gotham, 2010. A humorous recounting of the more dysfunctional aspects of the author's life in middle Georgia and Savannah.

Jones, Bobby. *Down the Fairway.* Latham, NY: British American Publishing, 1995. Golf history, lore, and lessons from the great Atlantan who founded Augusta National Golf Club.

Kemble, Fanny. *Journal of a Residence on a Georgian Plantation in 1838-1839.* Athens: University of Georgia Press, 1984. English actress's groundbreaking account of her stay on a rice plantation in McIntosh County, Georgia.

Ray, Janisse. *Ecology of a Cracker Childhood.* Minneapolis: Milkweed Editions, 2000. Heartfelt memoir of growing up amid the last stands of the longleaf pine ecosystem in southeast Georgia.

Washington, James Melvin, ed. *A Testament of Hope: The Essential Writings and Speeches of Martin Luther King, Jr.* New York: HarperOne, 1990. A collection of works by the Atlanta native and civil rights icon.

FICTION

Berendt, John. *Midnight in the Garden of Good and Evil.* New York: Vintage, 1994. Not exactly fiction but far from completely true, this modern crime classic reads like a novel while remaining one of the unique travelogues of recent times.

Caldwell, Erskine. *God's Little Acre.* Athens: University of Georgia Press, 1995. Scandalous in its time for its graphic sexuality, Caldwell's best-selling 1933 novel chronicles socioeconomic decay in the mill towns of South Carolina and Georgia during the Great Depression.

Caldwell, Erskine. *Tobacco Road.* Athens: University of Georgia Press, 1932. Lurid and sensationalist, this portrayal of a shockingly dysfunctional rural Georgia family during the Depression paved the way for *Deliverance.*

Dickey, James. *Deliverance.* New York: Delta, 1970. Gripping and socially important tale of a North Georgia rafting expedition gone horribly awry.

Harris, Joel Chandler. *The Complete Tales of Uncle Remus.* New York: Houghton Mifflin, 2002. The Atlanta author broke new ground in oral history by compiling these African American folk stories.

Mitchell, Margaret. *Gone with the Wind.* New York: MacMillan, 1936. The Atlanta author's immortal tale of Scarlett O'Hara and Rhett Butler. One of the most popular books of all time.

O'Connor, Flannery. *Flannery O'Connor: Collected Works.* New York: Library of America, 1988. A must-read volume for anyone wanting to understand the South and the Southern Gothic genre of literature.

Internet Resources

TOURISM AND RECREATION

Explore Georgia
www.exploregeorgia.org
The state's official tourism website.

Georgia State Parks
http://gastateparks.org
Historical and visitor information for Georgia's underrated network of state parks and historic sites, including camping reservations.

NATURE

Georgia Department of Natural Resources Wildlife Resources Division
www.georgiawildlife.com
Lots of specific information on hunting, fishing, and outdoor recreation in Georgia's various regions.

Paddle Georgia
www.garivers.org
Georgia River Network site that clues you in on guided trips and tours of the state's rivers, creeks, and marshes.

HISTORY AND CULTURE

Foxfire
www.foxfire.org
Website of the long-standing nonprofit cultural organization based in Rabun County, Georgia, that seeks to preserve Appalachian folkways.

Lost Worlds
www.lostworlds.org
Well-researched and readable exploration of Georgia's extensive pre-Columbian Native American history.

New Georgia Encyclopedia
www.georgiaencyclopedia.org
A mother lode of concise, neutral, and well-written information on the natural and human history of Georgia from prehistory to the present.

Index

A

B

C

D

E

F

G

H

IJ

KL

M

N

O

P

QR

S

T

UV

WXYZ

List of Maps

Photo Credits

Title page photo: Gracie statue in Savannah's Bonaventure Cemetery © James Pintar | Dreamstime; page 4 © Williamwise1 | Dreamstime.com; page 5 © Revgeo | Dreamstime.com; page 6 (top left) © Kellyvandellen | Dreamstime.com, (top right) © Masterlu | Dreamstime.com, (bottom) © F11photo | Dreamstime.com; page 7 (top) © Gonepaddling | Dreamstime.com, (bottom left) © Drverner | Dreamstime.com, (bottom right) © Gnagel | Dreamstime.com; page 8 © Sepavo | Dreamstime.com; page 9 (top) © Jim Morekis, (bottom left) © Fallondoyle | Dreamstime.com, (bottom right) © Pivariz | Dreamstime.com; pages 10-11 © F11photo | Dreamstime.com; page 12 © F11photo | Dreamstime.com; page 13 (top) © Jim Morekis, (center) © Jason B. James/Sandfly BBQ, (bottom) © Wickedgood | Dreamstime.com; page 14 © Wizreist | Dreamstime.com; page 15 © Americanspirit | Dreamstime.com; page 17 © Jim Morekis; page 18 © Mikephotos | Dreamstime.com; page 19 © Sayran | Dreamstime.com; page 20 © Jim Morekis; page 22 © Sepavo | Dreamstime.com; page 23 © F11photo | Dreamstime.com; page 24 © Sepavo | Dreamstime.com; page 25 (top) © Sepavo | Dreamstime.com, (bottom) © Jim Morekis; page 27 © Jim Morekis; page 29 © Jim Morekis; page 34 © Jim Morekis; page 35 © Jim Morekis; page 36 © Jim Morekis; page 37 © Adam Jones, Ph.D./Global Photo Archive/Flickr; page 38 © Jim Morekis; page 39 © Jim Morekis; page 40 © Jim Morekis; page 42 © Jim Morekis; page 44 (both) © Jim Morekis; page 46 © Jim Morekis; page 52 © Jim Morekis; page 57 © Jim Morekis; page 83 © Americanspirit | Dreamstime.com; page 89 (top) © Jim Morekis, (bottom) © Noonie | Dreamstime.com; page 91 © Jim Morekis; page 94 © Jim Morekis; page 95 © Jim Morekis; page 97 © Mishella | Dreamstime.com; page 98 © Jim Morekis; page 99 © Erastef | Dreamstime.com; page 101 © Jack Anthony / www.jackanthonyphotography.com; page 102 © Bbsimpson | Dreamstime.com; page 105 © Jim Morekis; page 106 © Jim Morekis; page 108 © Jim Morekis; page 109 © Jim Morekis; page 113 © Jim Morekis; page 114 © Jim Morekis; page 117 © Jim Morekis; page 122 © Jim Morekis; page 128 (both) © Jim Morekis; page 109 © Jim Morekis; page 113 © Jim Morekis; page 135 © Jim Morekis; page 137 © Jim Morekis; page 138 © Jim Morekis; page 142 © Jim Morekis; page 145 © Jim Morekis; page 146 © Jim Morekis; page 148 © Jim Morekis; page 151 © Jim Morekis; page 155 © Gnagel | Dreamstime.com; page 157 © Jim Morekis; page 158 NPS photo by E. Leonard; page 164 © Jim Morekis; page 167 (both) © Jim Morekis; page 169 © Christi | Dreamstime.com; page 177 © Jim Morekis; page 178 public domain/ Wikimedia Commons; page 182 © Jim Morekis; page 186 © Bingoye1 | Dreamstime.com; page 188 © Jim Morekis; page 189 (top) © Jim Morekis, (bottom) © Dndavis | Dreamstime.com; page 192 © Jim Morekis; page 193 © Jim Morekis; page 198 © Jim Morekis; page 199 © Jim Morekis; page 204 © Jim Morekis; page 209 © Jim Morekis; page 221 (top) © Jim Morekis, (bottom) © Brianwelker | Dreamstime.com; page 223 © Jim Morekis; page 428 © Jim Morekis; page 229 © Jim Morekis; page 232 © Jim Morekis; page 235 © Jim Morekis; page 238 © Jim Morekis; page 242 © Jim Morekis; page 243 © Jim Morekis; page 249 © Jim Morekis; page 250 © Stockage | Dreamstime.com; page 253 (top) © Digidreamgrafix | Dreamstime.com, (bottom) © Lpkb | Dreamstime.com; page 276 (top) © Bratty1206 | Dreamstime.com, (bottom) © Williamwise1 | Dreamstime.com

Also Available